TWIN MYTHCONCEPTIONS

TWIN MYTHCONCEPTIONS
False Beliefs, Fables, and Facts about Twins

NANCY L. SEGAL, Ph.D.
Professor of Psychology and Director, Twin Studies Center
California State University
Psychology Department
Fullerton, CA, United States

ACADEMIC PRESS
An imprint of Elsevier

Academic Press is an imprint of Elsevier
125 London Wall, London EC2Y 5AS, United Kingdom
525 B Street, Suite 1800, San Diego, CA 92101-4495, United States
50 Hampshire Street, 5th Floor, Cambridge, MA 02139, United States
The Boulevard, Langford Lane, Kidlington, Oxford OX5 1GB, United Kingdom

Notices
Knowledge and best practice in this field are constantly changing. As new research and experience
broaden our understanding, changes in research methods, professional practices, or medical treatment
may become necessary.

Practitioners and researchers must always rely on their own experience and knowledge in evaluating and
using any information, methods, compounds, or experiments described herein. In using such information or methods they should be mindful of their own safety and the safety of others, including parties
for whom they have a professional responsibility.

To the fullest extent of the law, neither the Publisher nor the authors, contributors, or editors, assume
any liability for any injury and/or damage to persons or property as a matter of products liability,
negligence or otherwise, or from any use or operation of any methods, products, instructions, or ideas
contained in the material herein.

Library of Congress Cataloging-in-Publication Data
A catalog record for this book is available from the Library of Congress

British Library Cataloguing-in-Publication Data
A catalogue record for this book is available from the British Library

ISBN: 978-0-12-803994-6

For information on all Academic Press publications
visit our website at https://www.elsevier.com/books-and-journals

Publisher: Nikki Levy
Acquisition Editor: Nikki Levy
Editorial Project Manager: Barbara Makinster
Production Project Manager: Nicky Carter
Designer: Matthew Limbert

Typeset by Thomson Digital

Identical female twins. Photo credit: Chana Liba Garelick; Photo courtesy: Miriam Cohen

Male-female twin babies: Reprinted by permission. Image source: shutterstock.com/ Veronica Galkina
http://www.shutterstock.com/gallery-107404p1.html

Mixed-Race Twins: Reprinted by permission. Image source: Barcroftmedia.com

For twins, triplets, and more who do so much for science
just by being themselves

and

To my late parents, Esther and Al Segal, who raised
my twin sister and me with fair-mindedness and foresight

CONTENTS

ABOUT THE AUTHOR

Dr. Nancy L. Segal received a BA degree in psychology and literature from Boston University (1973), and MA (1974) and Ph.D. (1982) degrees in the Social Sciences and Behavioral Sciences from the University of Chicago. She is currently a Professor of Psychology at California State University, Fullerton and Director of the Twin Studies Center. She has authored over 200 scientific articles and book chapters, as well as several books on twins.

Dr. Segal has received several international awards, including the *James Shields Award for Lifetime Contributions to Twin Research* (International Society for Twin Studies) and the *International Making a Difference Award* (Multiple Births Canada). She is also the 2016 recipient of the *Wang Family Excellence Award* from California State University. Dr. Segal has contributed to national and international media, including the *New York Times* and the *Washington Post*. She has been a frequent guest on national and international television and radio programs, such as the *Today Show, Good Morning America*, the *Martha Stewart Show*, the *Oprah Winfrey Show*, and *The Forum (BBC)*.

FOREWORD

Francis Galton, Charles Darwin's half-cousin, launched the modern study of twins in the late 19th century, but it was not until the late 20th century that geneticists and psychologists developed the tools to analyze the relative influences of nature and nurture (genes and environment) and tease apart the variables that matter most in making us who we are. These sciences are behavior genetics and evolutionary psychology and there is today perhaps no one more knowledgeable on twins and what they can tell us about human nature than Nancy Segal, whose many books on the subject—*Indivisible by Two, Born Together—Reared Apart, Entwined Lives*—present her own research and that of other scientists on everything we know about this most revealing natural experiment.

In *Twin Mythconceptions*, Segal reviews (and where appropriate debunks) the many false beliefs and fables about twins, including the differences between identical and fraternal twins, virtual twins, unrelated look-alikes, twins switched at birth, identical twins raised in separate environments, the genetics and biology of the twinning process, how modern reproductive technologies are changing our perspectives on the twinning process, and such misnomers as twins are alike in every way, that all young twins should be separated on their first day of school (to cement their individual identity), and that twinning does not skip generations, nor is it caused by "ingesting the honey from the guira, the green fruit of the Siguaraya tree that is linked to both fertility and multiple births" in Cuba! And twins cannot read each other's minds through ESP or other psychical powers better than anyone else, which is to say they can't do it at all because no one can.

As an example of what twins can tell us about human nature, consider the question of why people are religious. Is it in our nature to believe in God, join religions, and engage in spiritual practices, or is this something we learn from our parents, peers, and religious leaders?

In one study of 53 pairs of identical twins reared apart and 31 pairs of fraternal twins reared apart, scientists with the Minnesota Study of Twins Reared Apart (where Segal cut her scientific teeth) looked at five different measures of religiosity and found that the correlations between identical twins were typically double those for fraternal twins, and subsequent analysis led them to conclude that genetic factors account for 41–47% of the observed variance in their measures of religious beliefs. That's close to half! And for a trait most of us would think is surely almost entirely learned from our environment.

Or consider two much larger twin studies, one of which examined 3810 pairs of twins in Australia and another 825 pairs of twins in England. The twin researchers found similar percentages of genetic influence on religious beliefs, comparing identical and fraternal twins on numerous measures of beliefs and social attitudes, initially concluding that approximately 40% of the variance in religious attitudes was genetic. But here is where it gets interesting. These scientists also documented substantial correlations between the social attitudes of spouses. Why? Because of something called "assortative mating," better known as "like seeks like." That is, most of us are more likely to marry someone with whom we share many foundational beliefs, such as religious faith. When these researchers included a variable for assortative mating in their behavioral genetics models on these twins, they found that approximately 55% of the variance in religious attitudes is genetic, around 39% is attributed to the nonshared environment, about 5% is unassigned, and only about 3% is attributable to the shared family environment (and, hence, to cultural transmission via parents). This is an important finding because it implies that people who grow up in religious families who themselves later become religious do so mostly because they have inherited a disposition, from one or both parents, to resonate positively with religious sentiments, not because they were taught, or learned, to become religious.

Segal shows that such similarities among twins across the cognitive and behavioral spectrum are common, but this unfortunately leads to more mythconceptions, such as that twins are more likely to have autism, or that if one identical twin is homosexual then so too must be the other (the probability of an identical twin being gay if he or she has a gay twin ranges from .18 to .65, Segal notes). Nor do twins come in Good–Evil pairs, they are not more likely to get divorced than nontwins, and when they marry another twin pair they are not socially (or, apparently, personally!) interchangeable. And twins enable us to think through knotty ethical questions, such as: Would cloning a human detract from individuality? Of course not, any more than it does in twins, since each member of a twin pair is an autonomous individual no less than nontwins.

These and many other matters related to the nature of human nature are illuminated by twins and their many permutations, which makes Nancy

Segal one of the preeminent commentators of our time on this most vexing question, to which I will give the last word to the Bard of Avon:

> *Haste still pays haste, and leisure answers leisure;*
> *Like doth quit like, and Measure still for Measure.*

Michael Shermer
Publisher *Skeptic Magazine*,
Columnist *Scientific American*,
Presidential Fellow Chapman University

ACKNOWLEDGMENTS

Writing acknowledgments for completed work is a task I truly savor. The work is now finished (except for some editorial changes and photo permissions), letting me lean back and remember the many people who so generously supported me along the way. While only one name can grace the cover of this book, there are multitudes of colleagues, friends, and twins whose fingerprints I see on every page.

I am so happy that my publisher at Elsevier, Nikki Levy, found me. In early 2015, Nikki read my profile in the January issue of the *American Psychological Association Monitor* and invited me to put together a handbook on twin research. With sabbatical time approaching I was eager to work on another book, but I had a different idea in mind—a book that would identify and dispel the many myths and misconceptions surrounding twins and twin research. The idea for this book actually came from my boyfriend, Professor of Philosophy Dr. Craig K. Ihara, during our discussion of projects I could undertake during the 2015–16 academic year while on leave. I loved the idea and Nikki was enthusiastic. We met for lunch the following June at the *Blind Burro* on J Street in San Diego, and the deal was done. Elsevier's other staff members, especially Barbara Makinster (Senior Editorial Project Manager), Nicky Carter (Senior Project Manager), and Narmatha Mohan (Copyrights Coordinator), were lovely to work with.

Two near and dear people read different versions of the manuscript in its early and final stages. Lauren Gonzalez, writer, journalist, and psychotherapist, has been my friend since the summer 2000 when we took creative nonfiction writing together at Columbia University. Lauren offered her usual excellent editorial comments and suggestions that I could not resist. My boyfriend (Craig) added dash and polish to the text, as well as moments of dancing pleasure during much needed breaks in my work schedule.

My colleague, Dr. Jeffrey M. Craig, Honorary Principal Research Fellow in the University of Melbourne's Paediatrics Department and Deputy Director of the Australian Twin Registry, read the penultimate version of the text for accuracy and precision. Other colleagues, friends, and acquaintances forwarded a steady stream of articles, news clips, and research findings that helped keep me updated. Too numerous to name, I will mention those colleagues I heard from most often: J. Bruce Beckwith, Thomas J. Bouchard Jr., Wei-Min Chen, Kaare Christensen, the late Irving I. Gottesman, Leonard

L. Heston, Jaakko Kaprio, Alec Roy, Amanda Killian, Frederick Naftolin, Stephen Rich, Mark Umstad, and Ann Weinstein. My twin sister Anne and brother-in-law Mark, both avid readers of the *New York Times* and other news sources, did likewise. As I have emphasized in this book and in many of my other publications, having a twin sister is what opened my eyes to this exciting field.

Kelly Donovan, identical twin and graphic artist par excellence, prepared several figures that appear in this book. Levent Efe, medical illustrator extraordinaire, did likewise. I am grateful to several behind-the-scenes people who helped me secure rights for cartoon permissions, namely Christy Higgins and Allison Ingram.

California State University, Fullerton, my academic home for the last quarter of a century, has been consistently supportive of my varied research and writing projects. Many of my students assisted during various phases of the project, especially Vanessa Sanchez who never failed to produce the stacks of research articles I requested regularly. Britteny Hernandez and Hannah Bojorquez also worked long hours to finish last-minute tasks.

I have reserved my final thanks for the countless twins and their families who have made my job so informative and fun. Sometimes I feel guilty because most researchers work hard to find subjects and to secure their consent for participation. However, like the 1870s investigator Sir Francis Galton whose work drew twins to his laboratory, I have been fortunate that twins seek me out to offer their time in research, and to share their compelling stories. Each twin pair is a unique take on human development, filling in a bit more of our complex life story.

Nancy L. Segal

INTRODUCTION

MYTHCONCEPTIONS AND PERSONAL PERSPECTIVES

I wrote this book partly because friends, families, twins, colleagues—and I—find twin-related scientific facts and figures intriguing, informative, and sometimes hard to believe. Assorted twin-related trivia are also engaging, not just for their entertainment value, but because each nugget holds a small bit of truth. Mostly, I wrote *Twin Mythconceptions* because of the abundance of misinformation and misunderstandings regarding twins. This book is for anyone who has ever wondered why identical twins show similarities and differences, which couples are likely to have twins, if separating twins at school is a good idea, or if females with twin brothers are different from females with twin sisters. Twins, families, researchers, physicians, and anyone with a taste for multiple birth facts and figures should find interesting and meaningful material.

The first two chapters are more technical than the others. Chapter 1 summarizes the biological differences between identical and fraternal (nonidentical) twins and the many variations there are of each type. Chapter 2 explains the different research designs that use twins to study the origins of behavior and disease. It is perfectly fine to skip these two chapters and head immediately to the myths and misunderstandings that begin in Chapter 3.

THE POWER OF TWO

Twins are eye-catching. The sight of two individuals who look and act so much alike challenges our beliefs about individuality and human uniqueness. The idea that physical and behavioral traits can be closely replicated in two infants, children, or adults runs counter to our expectation that no other person in the world could be like us. Specific talents and skill sets can also be replicated in genetic duplicates. Bernard and Harold Shapiro ascended tough academic ladders to become presidents of leading universities. The Kacynski twins were childhood actors who became Poland's Prime Minister (Jaroslaw) and President (Lech) in 2005 and 2006, respectively. Janet Murgía became President of the National Council of La Raza, while her twin sister Mary was appointed Judge of the United States Court of Appeals' ninth district. And a set of identical Estonian triplets, Leila, Lily, and Llina Luik—the "Trio to Rio"—ran an Olympic marathon in 2016 [1].

Some relatives and friends, even researchers, believe that identical twins think alike and act alike because they are treated alike. However, the behaviorist notion that certain experiences always produce predictable outcomes was abandoned long ago. Instead, numerous twin studies show that our behaviors come from interactions between our genetic predispositions and environmental events. Identical twins raised in different environments by different families may both be either excited by the latest technological gadgets or totally uninterested. In contrast, fraternal twins raised together in the same home may vary greatly in their level of enthusiasm. The home environment is just not the same for each child in a family. And the idea that identical twins' personalities are shaped almost exclusively by how they are treated by others is another of many mythconceptions I will address and put to rest with this book.

Nonidentical or fraternal twins come in many forms—same-sex male, same-sex female, opposite-sex—and more when we examine their actual biological origins. Fraternal twins occur naturally about twice as often as identical twins in western populations, but they are the "hidden pairs." That is because fraternal twins generally do not look as much alike, so are easy to miss. And they are often overlooked by the media because they lack the intense visual interest and remarkably matched behaviors of identical twins. However, fraternal twins are crucial to the world of science and many mythconceptions surround these pairs, as well. Some people think that twin research rests solely on identical pairs, a serious misunderstanding that I will put to rest.

False beliefs surround male–female twins as well. When I conducted my first twin study as a University of Chicago graduate student, a parent of a participating pair asked me if opposite-sex twins could be genetically identical. I was shocked by this question, but have heard it in various forms from audiences and letter writers on repeated occasions: "I have a set of identical twins in my family (one boy, one girl—same face)." The idea that ordinary opposite-sex twins could be genetically identical is another mythconception I will tackle in the hope of removing it from common belief.

There are many provocative notions surrounding twins [2]. The Yorùbá tribe of western Nigeria, holding the world's second highest twinning rate next to Benin, regards twin births as signs of either great fortune or misfortune. This ambivalence is explained by their double vision of twins as posing threats to the family and society while recognizing their great ability to bring about happiness, wealth, and prosperity [3]. Deceased twins are highly venerated in Yorùbán culture and artists are commissioned to craft statues in their honor [4]. In contrast, until recently residents of the Calabar region of southeastern Nigeria believed that one twin was the child of the devil, but because it was uncertain as to which twin was which, both twins were killed. Mothers of twins were also severely ostracized and banished from their community [5].

The origins of twinning have also been the subjects of speculation and story telling. In 2014, I visited a two-block section of Havana, Cuba called "The Street of Twins" because out of only 224 residents, 12 twin pairs live in that neighborhood, exceeding the 2010 national multiple birth rate of 1% by quite a factor of 5 [6, 7]. Some people living on that street attribute twin births to ingesting the honey from the guira, the green fruit of the Siguaraya tree that is linked to both fertility and multiple births [7]. Twins also easily lend themselves to explorations of duality—good and evil, rich and poor, moral and amoral—two halves of the same whole. I believe that twins' rarity, identity, complementarity, and mystery make them especially vulnerable to folk tales and half-truths.

MYTHCONCEPTIONS

What are mythconceptions? I use this term to cover the common misunderstandings, mistakes, and miscommunications that have permeated beliefs about twins ever since Sir Francis Galton first recognized the power of twin studies in 1875 [8]. I prided myself on inventing this marvelous term until I learned that it formed part of the title of Gregory Leland's 2007 book, *Stupid History: Tales of Stupidity, Strangeness and Mythconceptions Throughout the Ages.*

Mythconceptions are evident in scientific circles, as well as in the popular media and in public conversation. Some arise and spread because they make sense, even though they lack hard scientific backing. A good example concerns the link between the time that a fertilized egg divides to create identical twins and the resulting arrangement of fetal membranes. The common wisdom is that early splitting results in two placentae, as well as two sets of fetal membranes (two chorions and two amnions), whereas later splitting results in shared structures, but this has never been proven. Other mythconceptions, such as the belief that twinning skips generations, or that twins can read each other's minds, come about because certain events are observed in some families, appear to have a real basis in fact and are circulated in scientific journals or by word of mouth.

These untruths are not helpful to anyone, and may foster frustration and concern among families and physicians facing situations that do not meet these expectations. Parents with family histories of twinning may be perplexed, or even disappointed, to have produced only nontwin children. Identical twins who experience tension in their relationship may wonder if there is something inherently wrong about their twinship because they do not feel the intimate twin bond that everyone expects them to feel. Other mythconceptions are also harmful to twins, either physically or psychologically, such as the belief that all twins (both identical and fraternal) are alike in every way, or that all young twins should be routinely separated on their first day of school. The mandatory classroom separation of young twins for the purpose of fostering their identities is one of the most damaging mythconceptions of all. Every September as the new school term begins I receive scores of emails from concerned parents whose twins feel extremely anxious and distressed over being apart from their twin brother or sister. This is a subject to which I will return and for which I will show that every twin pair is different and that there should be no single policy.

PERSONAL PERSPECTIVES

I sometimes joke that my interest in twins started at birth, the day I entered the world 7 minutes ahead of my fraternal twin sister, Anne (Fig. 1.1). But, of course, my understanding of twinship as a concept and as a family relationship category did not take root until I was about 4. (Some people would disagree with me, claiming intrauterine knowledge of twinship. That is an idea for which there is no scientific merit and to which I will return later in this book.) But from a very young age I recall having a constant companion by my side and correcting people when they called me by the wrong name. (People did not actually confuse Anne and me as individuals, but they

Figure 1.1 *The author (right) and her fraternal twin sister, Anne (left). (Photo credit: Michael Keel).*

sometimes forgot which name went with which twin.) I also remember arguing with my sister over who was "fra" and who was "ternal" (I vaguely recall that we both wanted to be "fra" since that syllable came first, but that is a situation we have yet to resolve). I also remember begging our mother to tell us who was born first. Our mother wisely guarded our birth-order status in order to avoid within-pair hostilities, insisting that we were born at exactly the same time. She maintained this fiction until we turned 7, at which time our older fraternal twin friend, Susan (who was two minutes younger than her brother Barry), insisted that we could not be born at exactly the same time. Our mother had no choice but to admit that I was the firstborn twin, a revelation I will discuss more fully later in the book. It turns out that birth order matters, but not necessarily in the way many people think it does. Being first or second born has different biological and psychological significance in natural deliveries and cesarean sections.

My interest in twins deepened when I was closer to 5 or 6 and became acutely aware of the physical and behavioral differences that divided Anne and me. I was then (and still am) 4 inches shorter with dark straight hair, while she was, and is, taller with lighter brown curly hair. We were both athletic as children, but she has always been faster and stronger than I in most sports. Our interests also diverged. I studied ballet for several years, beginning at the age of 8, at about the time she asked our parents for act-ing lessons. As a child I thought these differences were astonishing because we were raised in the same family and had so many shared experiences. I have no idea if Anne was as surprised by our differences as I was because we never discussed it, as is typical of some fraternal twin pairs. She has never shown as much attentiveness to twins and twinning as I have.

There were other differences between us that did not seem linked to any obvious learning experiences or social events. My parents carefully of-fered the same opportunities to both of us, but we reacted differently. For example, Anne was an avid reader of many books from an early age—I can still hear her yelling out, "Dad what spells -----?" In contrast, whereas Anne liked variety and read widely, I enjoyed reading several books over and over again. My favorites were the first volume in the *Bobbsey Twins* collection and selected biographies in the Landmark series for children, especially those of Wolfgang Amadeus Mozart and Eleanor Roosevelt. I read each of those volumes about 8 times when I was 10 or 11.

Over the years I figured out that the family environment my sister and I shared was not the same for the two of us. Like most children, we both created our own environments out of the opportunities available to us.

When I entered college as a psychology major I learned that the concept of crafting one's environment out of what's available had a name—*active-gene environment correlation*. The same family environment is *not* the same for all the children in a family because each child's genetically influenced tendencies lead him or her in certain directions. Treating children the same way does not guarantee identical outcomes. And given any siblings' different interests and talents, which are partly genetically based, similar treatment may not be possible or even fair.

SCIENCE AND SOCIETY

Twins are rich living laboratories, telling us so much about the nuances and vagaries of human behavior just by being themselves. There are many ways to study twins, each of which falls into one of two main categories: What I call the comparative approach (Track One) and what I call the "twins for twins" approach (Track Two). Most researchers are situated exclusively in one camp or the other, but I am one of the few who enjoys the freedom to move back and forth between them.

Track One studies capitalize on the difference in genetic relatedness between monozygotic (MZ or identical) and dizygotic (DZ or fraternal twins). I will say much more about twin types and research methods in the next few chapters, but for now it is enough to say that MZ or identical twins share virtually all their genes, whereas DZ or fraternal twins share half their genes, on average. Greater resemblance between MZ than DZ twins in mathematical reasoning, running speed, or diabetes susceptibility shows that genes play a role in fashioning these traits. This is information that can and should be used by the general nontwin population when considering medical treatment, family counseling, or related services. For example, a number of twin studies tell us that anxiety is partly affected by our genes; [9] therefore, children with one or two anxious parents may wish to avoid stressful situations as much as possible. One identical twin may be more anxious than his or her cotwin (twin partner) and the reasons behind this may help others control their own anxious tendencies.

Some twin research critics think that twin research findings do not apply to the general population, a mythconception I hope to set right [10]. However, twin studies provide important information about behavioral development, disease predisposition, and physical growth that can help everyone make better decisions about emotional well-being, medical care, and dietary practices.

A second way of studying twins is the "twins for twins" approach. These Track Two studies focus on behavioral, physical, and social characteristics, situations, and dilemmas that are generally exclusive to twins. A good example is twins' average delayed language development, relative to singletons. Parents often direct less individual speech to each twin in attempts to give each child equal attention. Consequently, twins receive less language experience overall than nontwins. In addition, due to spending a lot of time together, many twins develop private expressions and gestures that are not understood by others. Another area of concern is twins' increased frequency of congenital anomalies. This is especially true for identical twins who result from splitting of the fertilized egg (zygote). Zygotic division is sometimes linked to midline malformations, such as spina bifida and cleft palate. Lastly, some twins undergo individuation-separation concerns, possibly because people have difficulty telling them apart or because they are constantly being compared with one another. Not all twins experience all of these problems and some pairs experience none whatsoever. It is just that twins, on average, are more likely to experience some of them than are singletons or nontwins.

The families of twins are also of great interest to researchers from both the scientific and "twins for twins" perspectives. Scientific issues might include the genetic bases of twinning, cross-cultural differences in twinning rates, or prenatal detection of twin-to-twin transfusion syndrome (TTTS). "Twins for twins" researchers would be more interested in exploring the frequency and complexity of parents' speech directed toward each twin, the financial burdens of raising two or more near-in-age children, and the extent to which multiple birth children threaten the status of their older nontwin siblings. Given the rising twin birth rates from 1980 to the present, findings from both types of researchers are becoming more and more important. In the past, researchers pursuing the scientific approach have had little to do with researchers pursuing the twins for twins approach. This is unfortunate because the two types of researchers have complementary interests and many common goals. Based on a number of recent conferences I have attended it now appears that the two are starting to come together.

Both approaches to twin research have their share of mythconceptions. Exposing these myths from all sides, and providing evidence that invites clear thinking and reasoned judgment about what is true, what is not true, and what might be true is my mission. When I was a new PhD investigator I was advised by some colleagues to keep my own twinship hidden for fear that I would be perceived as less than objective in my work. But as a seasoned scientist, a twins for twins specialist, and a twin myself I can provide a three-dimensional view of this vital landscape—dispelling yet another myth that twins should not study twins.

REFERENCES

[1] N.L. Segal, Entwined Lives: Twins and What They Tell us About Human Behavior, Plume, New York, 2000; J. Longman, The Trio to Rio, New York Times, June 3, 2016, p. SP1.

[2] A. Piontelli, Twins in the World: The Legends They Inspire and the Lives They Lead, Palgrave MacMillan, New York, (2008).

[3] A. White, The trouble with twins: Image and ritual of the Yorùbá ère ìbejì, 2010.

[4] N.L. Segal, Art for twins: Yorùbá artists and their statues, Twin Res. Hum. Genet. 17(3) (2014) 215–221; F. Leroy, T. Olaleye-Oruene, G. Koeppen-Schomerus, E. Bryan, Yorùbá customs and beliefs pertaining to twins, Twin Res. 5(2) (2002) 132–136.

[5] A.J. Bueltmann, White Queen of the Cannibals: The Story of Mary Slessor of Calabar, Literary Licensing, LLC, Whitefish, MT, 2011; Mary Slessor Foundation, Twins and Adopted Family, Available from: http://maryslessor.org/2014/04/her-adopted-family/

[6] B. Marcheco-Teruel, M. Cobas-Ruiz, N. Cabrera-Cruz, et al., The Cuban Twin Registry: initial findings and perspectives, Twin Res. Hum. Genet. 16 (1) (2012) 98–103.

[7] N.L. Segal, B. Marcheco-Teruel, I. "Street of Twins:" multiple births in Cuba II, The Cuban Twin Registry: an update, Twin Res. Hum. Genet. 17(4) (2014) 347–353; A. Rodriguez, 12 Sets of Cuban Twins Live on Consecutive Havana Blocks, World, Huffington Post, October 4, 2013. Available from: http://www.huffingtonpost.com/2013/10/04/havana-twins_n_4044696.html

[8] F. Galton, The history of twins as a criterion of the relative powers of nature and nurture, J. Anthropol. Inst. 5 (1875) 391–406.

[9] K. Tambs, N. Czajkowsky, E. Roysamb, M.C. Neale, T. Reichborn-Kjennerud, S.H. Aggen, et al., Structure of genetic and environmental risk factors for dimensional representations of DSM-IV anxiety disorders, Br. J. Psychiatry 195(4) (2009) 301–307.

[10] K. Christensen, J.W. Vaupel, N.V. Holm, A.I. Yashin, Mortality among twins after age 6: fetal origins hypothesis versus twin method, Br. Med. J. 310 (6977) (1995) 432–436.

CHAPTER 1

Twin Types: More Than Just Two

Just by acting naturally, twins provide a myriad of explanations and ideas as to why people are the way that they are. This initial chapter surveys the different types of pairs that inhabit the world of twins. Contrary to common belief, there are more than just two types of twins and distinguishing among them is a scientific endeavor all its own. I will also address the question: why are twins so interesting? It seems that everyone I encounter—colleagues, acquaintances, people I befriend on airplanes—wants to hear more about my area of study. Everyone is also eager to share their own personal twin stories. Yet no one has credibly solved the simple question: what makes twins so interesting? I have some answers.

While this chapter does not address mythconceptions just yet, some inevitably surface for they are unavoidable in any discussion of this field. Rather, the foregoing provides a good backdrop for appreciating the myths and misunderstandings surrounding differences between identical and fraternal twins and what these differences tell us about human behavior and development. I identify terms and abbreviations as they appear, but those that are most important or used most frequently are included in Appendix 5 for convenience.

TWIN TYPES: NOT JUST TWO

The classic twin study design and its variants are simple and elegant. The simplicity comes from the natural occurrence of twins that vary in their genetic relatedness and social contact. The elegance comes from researchers' ability to arrange particular comparisons between twin pairs to tease apart the genetic and environmental influences on human behavioral, physical, and medical traits.

It is important to understand the biological differences between monozygotic (identical or MZ) and dizygotic (fraternal or DZ) twins to appreciate how twins are used in research. Most people think that there are just two types of twins, but there are actually many more. Both MZ and DZ pairs include fascinating variations that add to what we currently know, and can potentially know, about factors affecting who we are and who we might become. In this chapter I discuss the importance of classifying twins as iden-

Twin Mythconceptions
http://dx.doi.org/10.1016/B978-0-12-803994-6.00001-9

tical or fraternal, a process known as zygosity determination. The methods used for determining zygosity are now highly sophisticated, but there are exceptional cases that can make classification challenging. Note: I will use both the scientific terms (MZ and DZ) and familiar labels (identical and fraternal) for the different types of twins throughout the book.

MZ (Identical) Twins

As I mentioned earlier, a basic understanding of zygosity determination, or how twins are classified as identical (MZ) or fraternal (DZ) is essential before moving on to mythconceptions about them. MZ twins result when a single fertilized egg (zygote) divides very soon after conception. (Controversies surrounding the timing and consequences of this event are discussed in another chapter.) MZ twins (presumably) share 100% of their genes and are of the same sex, two males or two females. (I will address this issue later, as well.) Identical triplets, quadruplets, and quintuplets (the higher-order multiples) originate from additional splitting of one or more zygotes that originate from the same single fertilized egg. What causes zygotes to divide is an unanswered question in reproductive biology; however, several intriguing theories pointing to delayed implantation or genetic factors have been proposed [1,2]. Conventional scientific wisdom states that MZ twinning occurs randomly, which would mean that all mothers everywhere are equally likely to conceive them. This is a fascinating subject that is drawing attention to twinning "hotspots"—areas that seem to teem with multiples.

Table 1.1 summarizes the numbers and birth rates of twins, triplets, and more born in the United States in 2014, the latest year for which such information is available. The birth rate for twins increased by 79% since 1980, but dropped by 41% for triplets and other higher-order multiples since 1998 after a four-fold increase in the 1980s and 1990s. Note that these

Table 1.1 Multiple births in the United States (2014)

Numbers	135,336
Number of triplet births	4,233
Number of quadruplet births	246
Number of quintuplet births and higher	47
Birth rates	
Twin birth rate	33.9/1,000
Triplet or higher-order birth rate	113.5/1,000

Source: Centers for Disease Control (www.cdc.gov/nchs/fastats/multiple.htm).

figures do not distinguish between identical and fraternal sets. These data can be difficult to come by because twin-type testing of same-sex pairs (an important topic I will address) is not routinely practiced in hospital settings unless twins are part of an ongoing study.

The *Hellin-Zeleny law (HZL)*, developed in 1895, would estimate the rates of naturally conceived identical twins, triplets, and quadruplets as approximately 1/250, 1/71,289, and 1/19,034,163, respectively [3,4]. (Please refer to Appendix 1 for an explanation of the calculations behind these figures and for more of the story.) However, modern analyses of the accuracy of the *HZL* show that, despite its central role in twinning statistics over the years, it does not hold as a general rule. Many factors, such as improved prenatal detection of multiple births, better management of multiple pregnancies and deliveries, and the use of assisted reproductive technologies (ARTs) have altered twinning rates considerably since the *HZL* was put forth. Some improvements to this law have been proposed [5].

As mentioned in the introduction, in 2014 I visited the "Street of Twins" in Havana, Cuba, a tree-lined neighborhood that includes 12 sets of twins (10 MZs and 2 DZs) [6]. All of these twins, who ranged in age from 6–65 years, were conceived naturally. In 2013, I was part of an NBC twins special, filmed at Castle Heights Elementary School in Lebanon, Tennessee. The school was famous for having 15 sets of twins, both MZ and DZ, conceived either naturally or by way of ART. Large pockets of twins have also been identified in other parts of the United States. Three schools, Valley Southwoods Freshman High School in West Des Moines, Iowa; Staples High School in Westport, Connecticut; and Maine South High School in Park Ridge, Illinois share the current record of having 16 twin pairs in a single grade level. Highcrest Middle School in Wilmette, Illinois earned the *Guinness Book* world record for its 24-twin pair student roster in the 2012–13 academic year [7]. Explanations for these occurrences are plentiful, but their accuracy varies.

Identical twins represent approximately one-third of all naturally conceived twins, which occur in 1 in 80 births in western nations. The natural identical twinning rate of about 1/250 births does not generally differ across countries or cultures, although there are geographical exceptions as I indicated earlier. The advent of assisted reproduction over the last 30–40 years has dramatically increased the overall twinning rate (both identical and fraternal), from nearly 1 in 60 births (18.9/1000) in 1980 to over 1 in 30 births (33.7/1000) in 2013 [8].

However, while the twinning rate is the highest it has ever been, the highest number of twins born in the United States was 138,961 in 2007.

In contrast, the United States' triplet rate declined by over 40% in 2014 since peaking in 1998 because successful ART pregnancies are now possible with fewer transferred embryos [9]. Interestingly, the "twinning boom" seems to be ending in one out of four developed countries, also due to reduction in the number of embryos transferred during in vitro fertilization (IVF) procedures (the simultaneous implantation of two or more eggs that were fertilized by separate sperm) [10]. However, assisted reproduction with a single embryo increases the chance of producing identical twins, a topic to which I will return. In 2013, in the United States, multiples accounted for 43.6% of ART-conceived infants in states with mandated health coverage for ART treatment, and 46.2% of ART-conceived infants in states without mandated coverage. However, the *number* of ART-conceived multiples was larger in states with mandated coverage because more people were seeking ART treatment [11].

For more on estimating the relative frequencies of identical and fraternal twins, please see "Does Weinberg Rule?" in Appendix 1.

MZ Twin Variations

There are several different types of MZ or identical twins. Most MZ twin pairs include two right-handed pair members (cotwins), but about 25% are either opposite-handed and/or show other evidence of reversed physical features. These MZ twin pairs can variously show opposite birthmarks, moles, dental patterns, eye dominance, fingerprints, handprints, or hair whorls (circular or spiral hair patterns where the hair root meets the scalp). For example, one twin may have a mole on the right arm, while the cotwin has a mole on the left arm. MZ twins' fingerprints are not exactly alike, but a particular image on one twin's right index finger might be mirrored on the cotwin's left index finger—in fact, I just found a pair of reared-apart male twins who showed exactly that. Over the years I have seen reversals in cleft lip in a young female pair and opposite nondescended testicles in a young male pair (which corresponded to their writing hands!). Some identical twins have even shown reversals in internal organs, like the abdomen or heart [12]. The biological mechanisms that give rise to these differences, possibly delayed zygotic splitting, have been debated for some time [13].

We also know that about one-third of MZ twins have separate placentae and fetal membranes (chorions and amnions), as do all DZ twins with rare exception. Placentae are temporary structures enabling transmission of oxygen and nutrients from mother to fetus, as well as the release of carbon dioxide and waste materials from the fetus. The amnion and chorion are, respectively, the inner and outer membranes that surround the developing zygote. The amnion develops at about 7–9 days after conception, differentiating out of the trophoblast or outer ring of dividing cells. The amnion encloses the zygote in amniotic fluid, maintaining constant temperature and providing protective cushioning. The chorion forms by the end of the second week, emerging out of the trophoblast. Small projections known as chorionic villi develop and attach to the intrauterine wall, and the placenta starts to develop [14].

If a third of MZ twins have separate fetal structures then most of the remaining two-thirds share their placenta and chorion, but have separate amnions. A very small percentage of MZ twins (1–2%) share all three structures [15], but each fetus has a separate umbilical cord. Sharing fetal membranes places 10–15% of single-chorion MZ twins at risk for twin-to-twin transfusion syndrome (TTTS) in which the placental tissue of one twin is drained by a vein from the other twin, characterized by unequal blood flow to one twin [16]. This situation can cause marked cotwin discrepancies in body size and hemoglobin level because of the one-way circulation, and if not checked can cause the demise of one or both twins. Fortunately, advanced prenatal technologies, such as laser surgery and reduction of amniotic fluid, can correct many such cases [17,18]. Chorionicity is determined by sonographic scanning at about 11–12 weeks; after that, visualization during the second trimester is very difficult. Twin pregnancies show a triangle (lambda) where the membranes meet the two placentae. Monochorionic twins show a thin amnion between each fetus, and a T shape where the membranes meet the single shared placenta, as seen in Fig. 1.1 [19,20].

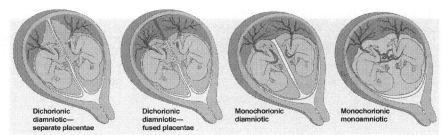

Dichorionic diamniotic— separate placentae

Dichorionic diamniotic— fused placentae

Monochorionic diamniotic

Monochorionic monoamniotic

Figure 1.1 *Traditional models of identical twinning.* Pictured are four types of identical twins with different arrangements of the placentae and fetal membranes. Note that the cords of monochorionic–monoamniotic twins are typically entangled. The first two illustrations also apply to fraternal twins, showing why twin type can be misdiagnosed from inspection of the placentae and membranes. *(Illustration by Levent Efe).*

Current knowledge as to why MZ twins differ with respect to the number of placentae and fetal membranes focuses on the timing of the zygotic split. However, this explanation has been challenged and debated, as I explain later.

Conjoined Twins

Conjoined twins are the rare identical pairs that are not fully separate from one another. It is generally thought that the two embryos fail to separate fully within the first 2 weeks after conception, once zygotic division is initiated. However, another possible explanation is that conjoined twins result from the fusion of two separate embryos. What causes this type of twinning, which occurs in approximately 1/200 identical twin births, is a controversial topic that I will revisit in another chapter.

Twins who are physically connected were once labeled "Siamese" after the famous pair, Chang and Eng, born in Siam (now Thailand) in 1811. The label Siamese twins, which is inappropriate and even derogatory, has been replaced by the more descriptive and biologically accurate term of *conjoined twins*. Most surviving conjoined twins are female, probably because female fetuses and neonates are more physically mature than their male counterparts, so are better able to withstand adverse prenatal conditions. In fact, a newborn female has the physical maturity of a 4–6-week-old male [21]. This sex difference in hardiness is also evident if we compare primary and secondary sex ratios, meaning the relative proportions of males to females that are conceived and delivered, respectively. The largest analysis to date shows a primary sex ratio of .50, indicating that males and females are conceived at the same rate. However, week-specific estimates based on fetal deaths and live births in the United States (1995–2004) show a slight decline in males between 18 weeks (gestation time since conception) and 45 weeks [22]. Thus, we may partly understand why most conjoined twin pairs are female rather than male, although further research on this difference is needed.

There are many variations of conjoined twins, classified according to their shared organs. For example, the most frequent form of conjoined twins is fused from the anterior thorax (upper chest) to the umbilicus (navel) and known as thoracopagus [23]. The rarest type is craniopagus twins which occur at a rate of .6 per million births and share various brain structures and functions [24]. A full description of the many types and subtypes of conjoined twins is beyond the scope of this book, but the different types have been well documented, underlining their wide variety. It is important to refer to a particular type of conjoined twinning when considering issues of delivery and management [25].

The Mütter Museum in Philadelphia displays the livers and plaster cast of the torsos of Chang and Eng. And Vienna's National Natural History Museum (Naturhistoriches Museum Wien) houses an extraordinary collection of conjoined twins with fused heads, known as Janiceps. Janiceps conjoined twins were named after Janus, the Roman god of beginnings and transitions with two faces (one at the front and one at the back of the head), looking in opposite directions [26,27]. Fig. 1.2 shows a sculpture of Old Janus from Italy (A), a set of spontaneously delivered Janiceps twins from Australia (B), and a skeletal Janiceps specimen from a rare collection in Vienna (C).

Mosaicism and X-Inactivation

Before turning to the different types of fraternal twins, I want to briefly mention two other curious biological events. These events can actually cause genetic differences between identical twins, adding to the curiosity and variation among them. The first event is *mosaicism* in which DNA may change spontaneously in some cells after conception. Replication of both the original and the altered cells then occurs in the developing organism, making the affected individual a kind of patchwork of cells. Mosaicism in one identical twin, but not the other, can lead to behavioral and physical differences between these cotwins. For example, one twin in a pair of 23-year-old identical female twins showed minor physical abnormalities and mental delay, while her twin sister did not. This was explained by an unusual chromosomal change that occurred in the affected twin after the zygote divided. Interestingly, the unaffected sister showed the same alteration in the same proportion of her blood cells, but the alteration did not originate with her—instead, it was apparently transmitted to her prenatally from her sister as a result of the transfusion syndrome, discussed earlier [28]. When a person's cells originate from different sources we call this *chimerism*, an event I discuss later in the section on fraternal twins [29].

The second biological event to note is *X chromosome inactivation* (also called lyonization after Mary Lyon who first described this process in 1961 [30]). Lyonization affects only females (twins and singletons), not males. Females have two X chromosomes in each of their cells. Soon after conception, one X chromosome in each pair becomes inactive or simply "shuts down"; therefore, only one X chromosome in each female cell is expressed. Which of the X chromosomes in each cell undergoes silencing is a matter of chance—a 50–50 split, just like a coin toss. But like a coin toss, the active–inactive splits

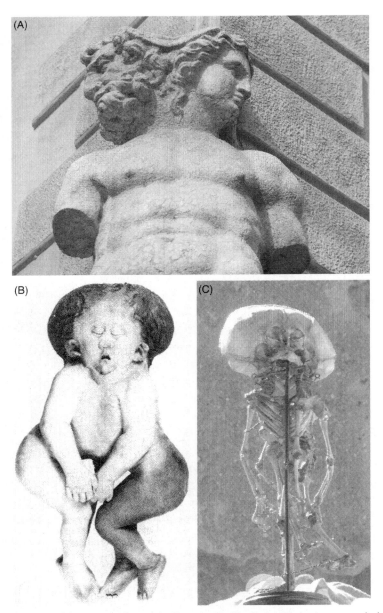

Figure 1.2 (A) Old Janus sculpture in Reggio, Emilia, Italy. (B) Janiceps–cephalotho-racopagus conjoined twins, right lateral view. In this pair, the upper bodies are fused, while the lower bodies are separate. The stillborn twins were delivered vaginally at 32 weeks' gestation. (C) Actual skeleton of Janiceps conjoined twins showing hydrocepha-lus or build-up of fluid in the brain. *(Part A, Reprinted with permission. Image source: Shut-terstock.com/photo by Kisel Cotiw-an; Part B, photo source: D.G. Greening, Vaginal delivery of conjoined twins, Med. J. Aust. 2 (7) (1981) 356–359. Reprinted with permission: © Copy-right 1981, The Medical Journal of Australia; Part C, Source: Pathologic-anatomical collec-tion: National Natural History Museum (NHM)—Vienna (Naturhistoriches Museum Wien). Photo credit: Dr. Wolfgang M. Schleidt).*

are sometimes 20–80% or 10-90%, an effect called skewing. If the inactivation happens *after* the zygote splits then one twin may have a 50–50 split, whereas her cotwin may have a 20–80 split. When this happens there can be marked behavioral or physical differences between these female identical twins—*but only for recessive (nondominant) traits influenced by genes on the X chromosome*, such as color blindness and X-linked mental retardation. In other words, both MZ twins might inherit a gene for color blindness, located on one of their X chromosomes. However, only the twin with 80% of those particular X chromosomes active would be color blind.

Several years ago I came across the first case of identical female twins in which only one twin expressed the very debilitating condition known as Lesch–Nyhan disease (LND). LND is caused by a mutation on the X chromosome, resulting in learning disabilities, postural problems (dystonia), speech impairments, and compulsive self-injurious behaviors, such as biting of the lips and fingers [31,32]. Skewed X-inactivation in fibroblasts (cells found in connective tissue) was found in the affected twin (99.5% of her normal genes were inactive) but her cotwin showed the *reverse* pattern (86% of her mutant genes were inactive). These analyses explain why one sister was healthy and the other was not. These events have changed the way we think about identical female twins, replacing old beliefs with new truths [33]. Genetic identity does not mean behavioral identity because environmental events, both before and after birth, can intervene [34].

DZ (Fraternal) Twins

Most DZ twins result when a woman releases two eggs simultaneously, or relatively close in time, followed by fertilization by two separate sperm. These twins share 50% of their genes, on average, by descent, just like regular full siblings who are born apart. DZ twins can be same-sex or opposite-sex, events that occur with about equal frequency. The release and fertilization of more than two eggs at a time can result in nonidentical triplets, quadruplets, or quintuplets. However, more complex multiples may arise. For example, it is possible that one of two separately fertilized eggs divides yielding triplets composed of an identical twin pair with a fraternal cotriplet.

Fraternal twinning is more likely with advanced maternal age (at or after the mid-thirties), relatively greater maternal height and weight, family history of twinning, African ancestry, greater coital frequency, and/or resumption of sexual relations after periods of abstinence [35]. Specific genes linked to fraternal twinning in humans and nonhumans have been reported

[35–37]. A 2016 study, based on data from mothers in the United States, Iceland and the Netherlands, found 2 genes that raised the DZ twinning risk from 10.7/1000 (the frequency in the Dutch population) to 12.71/1000 if all females had 2 copies of both genes [38–39].

A genetic basis for DZ twinning is also strengthened by the presence of small, relatively isolated communities with high DZ twinning rates and elevated inbreeding (marriages between genetic relatives). Examples are Candido Godói in southern Brazil and the Åland Islands on a Finnish archipelago [40,41].

The natural DZ twinning rate is about 8/1000 births in western nations, but the frequencies vary dramatically across different populations. DZ twins are less common in Asian nations (4/1000) and more common in African nations (16/1000) [42]. I will examine the reasons for these differences later on.

The recent dramatic increase in western twinning frequencies due to ARTs has involved mostly DZ twins. That is because IVF, fertility drugs, and other reproductive technologies create separate zygotes. IVF was introduced into the United States in 1981, after the first such successful birth in England in 1978 [43]. Physicians wishing to improve the odds that an infertile couple would have at least one child implanted multiple embryos in women's wombs. (Recall the famous 2009 case of Octomom, the California woman whose six implanted embryos yielded eight babies—two of her embryos divided to produce identical twins.) Now that the technology has been refined, successful pregnancies and deliveries are likely with just one embryo [44].

The vast majority of DZ twins have two separate chorions, amnions, and placentae. There are some exceptions to this rule, namely DZ twin pairs with a single chorion. These presumably rare twins have led to lively discussions about the twinning events giving rise to these unusual pairs [45]. More on this is coming.

DZ Twin Variations

Besides the standard same-sex or opposite-sex pairs, DZ twins come packaged in several curious forms. Some DZ twins have different fathers because of superfecundation. Once an egg is released there is a window of opportunity for fertilization to occur, lasting between 12 and 48 h [46–48]. Furthermore, sperm are viable for 7–10 days. Consequently, if a woman releases two eggs and has sexual relations with different partners during that brief period, it is possible for her to conceive superfecundated twins.

These children share the same genetic relationship as half-siblings—an average of 25%—because they have one parent in common. Still, they are recognized as a naturally occurring variant of DZ twinning. A woman having sexual relations on multiple occasions with the same partner can also conceive superfecundated twins. However, in this case the twins' genetic relationship is 50%, on average, just like typical DZ twins and full siblings. Superfecundation involving different fathers is presumed to be rare, but it is likely that cases go undiscovered.

Superfecundation would be detected if a father sought paternity testing because he suspected his partner had been unfaithful—and she had been. A male might request testing if he perceived little physical resemblance between himself and one or both twins. Under somewhat different circumstances, in May 2015, a New Jersey mother sought child support for her fraternal twin children. When she revealed that she had had an extramarital affair, a court-ordered paternity test found that two fathers were involved; the alleged father's DNA was compatible with one twin, but not with the other twin [49]. And in March 2016, 2-year-old superfecundated twins were identified in Vietnam's capital city of Hanoi, after a relative noticed the twins' dramatically different physical characteristics (one twin had curly hair, while the other twin had straight hair) [50]. DNA testing revealed that the twins did, indeed, have different fathers, but the same mother. This was the first report of superfecundation in that country and, according to Professor Li Dinh Luong, President of the Vietnam Genetic Association, it was one of less than 10 known occurrences worldwide. As I indicated earlier, there may be more since some remain hidden.

Interestingly, and unrelated to these cases, more frequent sexual activity in young women seems to raise the chance of fraternal twinning, based partly on the elevated frequency of fraternal twins conceived outside versus inside wedlock [51]. A related study did not find differences in sexual activity frequency among parents of MZ twins, DZ twins, and singletons, but those researchers did not consider extramarital affairs [52].

Superfetation, another presumably rare process, can also give rise to atypical DZ twins. These twins would occur if a woman released a second egg 3–4 weeks after one that had already been fertilized, and this second egg was fertilized, as well. If just one partner were involved, superfetated twins would share the same genetic relationship as typical DZ twins, but would most likely show developmental discrepancies at birth since one twin would have undergone a longer gestational period. (Most cases that I have reviewed show that superfetated twins are born on the same day. However, twins do not always share their date of birth, a curious situation I will discuss later.) But superfetated twins can also be fathered by *different* individuals, turning them into "half-siblings" genetically speaking. The medical literature includes case studies and short reviews of superfetated twin pairs, so their true frequency is hard to determine [53,54]. In search of an explanation to the rule that conception prevents further ovulation, researchers have focused on the later phase of the menstrual cycle. It may be that high levels of the female hormone estradiol allow a second ovulation and a second conception to occur even after fertilization has taken place.

The varieties of DZ twinning do not stop here. Polar body twinning has been called the "third twin type," a label reserved by family members to describe twins who look and act less alike than MZ twins, but more alike than DZ twins. Seventy-year-old identical twin, John C. Garrett, told me that he and his twin brother considered themselves to be "2/3 alike and 1/3 different" until they treated themselves to a DNA test last year—and were shocked to discover that they were MZ twins. However, polar body twins do exist and have been documented in the scientific literature, but they appear to be rare [55]. Polar bodies, which form as the early egg cell develops into a mature egg, contain the same genetic information as the mature egg, but are generally not fertilized and eventually die. There is a lot to the polar body twinning story that I have included in Appendix 3.

Uncommon Connections

Based on their extremely dissimilar physical features, some DZ twins appear to come from different families, even different countries. These otherwise ordinary fraternal twins most likely have mothers and fathers from mixed-race marriages. Given the unpredictability of gene transmission, an African-American mother and a Caucasian-European father can produce children who resemble a United Nations delegation writ small. Physical contrasts between children are heightened when they are twins, rather than siblings, because twins are of the same age. A British couple, Alison Spooner and Dean Durrant, gave birth to two sets of DZ twin girls, one pair in 2001, and the other in 2008. In each pair one twin resembled her light-skinned mother and one her dark-skinned father. In the eldest pair, daughter Lauren is fair and daughter Hayleigh is dark, while the twins in the younger pair, Leah and Miya, are respective matches for their older sisters. The twins' mother Alison is Caucasian in background, while their father Dean is of West Indian origin, exciting the medical world because of what it reveals about the genetic transmission of skin tone and other physical traits [56]. The twins, Lauren and Hayleigh, appear on the cover of this book.

Skin tone is influenced by a host of genetic factors, in conjunction with environmental influences and gene–gene interactions (epistatic effects) [57]. It is suspected that the Spooner–Durrant cotwins inherited different genes linked to light and dark skin colors. No one has formally studied these unusual pairs, but my interviews with some "ethnically divergent" DZ twins show that they can have very different life experiences based on their appearance. My former student, Dawn Perez and her DZ cotwin Robin, born to a Hispanic father and Caucasian mother, display the contrasting skin tones and facial features of their father and mother, respectively. Dawn, the Hispanic looking cotwin admitted that, in accordance with stereotypes, people tend to regard her as less intelligent and less capable than Robin, her Caucasian-looking twin sister.

Daniel and James Kelly are also fraternal twins divided along skin color lines. Born to a Caucasian mother, Alyson, and a Jamaican father, Errol, Daniel is blonde and light-skinned and James is dark-haired and dark-skinned. Their contrasting looks have been traced to Errol's genetic mix—people of Caribbean descent may carry both genes coding for dark skin tones and genes coding for light skin tones. That is because in the late 1700s–1800s, plantation owners introduced European DNA into Caribbean populations through the rape of female slaves. Apparently Errol passed on more African DNA to James and more European DNA to Daniel. The twins' mother worried because the lighter-skinned Daniel experienced more race-based discrimination than his brother when his fellow students saw him as black, while he identified as white [58].

I wish that someone would conduct a formal study of the psychological effects of membership in an "ethnically different" looking twin pair. Such twins are probably more common than we know because of the rising rates of marriage across national, racial, and ethnic lines. Such studies would have important messages for mixed-race couples raising nontwin children who are becoming more plentiful in the population, and for the wider issue of how people from different races are perceived.

Chimeras and More

Some DZ twins are chimeras. Chimeras are individuals with genetically different tissues or different cell lines that originated from different zygotes. This phenomenon is well known in cattle twins, due to their two-way prenatal blood exchanges. In about 90% of the cases the chorions connect, allowing passage of male hormones to the female twin. This event has no consequence if the cattle twins are same-sex—but if the cattle twins are opposite-sex the female twin usually becomes infertile, a consequence called the freemartin effect. This happens because the placental membranes fuse early in cattle gestation, and the earlier they fuse the more profound is the masculinization effect. The freemartin effect, first described by the Scottish surgeon John Hunter in 1779, generated considerable interest [59–61]. A special 1916 article in the journal *Science* by Frank R. Lillie stated that, "This presents an uncomfortable case in twinning and sex-determination, and it has consequently been the cause of much speculation (p. 611) [62]." That comment is as timely today as it was then.

Other nonhuman animals, such as marmosets and mice, have also shown evidence of chimerism. The marmoset has one of the most interesting chimeric stories to tell [63]. A case study showed fusion of marmoset twins' placentae, allowing the sharing of cells and DNA. Consequently, marmoset twins can "give birth" to their cotwin's children! One twin inherits one set of DNA, while the other twin inherits two sets. If the twin with two DNA sets mates, then the offspring could carry either his/her original DNA or his/her cotwin's DNA. Genetically speaking, the one newborn would be a child and the other newborn would be a niece or nephew, even though both the child and the niece/nephew were conceived sexually by the same individual marmoset.

In view of the forgoing, it seems reasonable to expect that human male and female cotwins from opposite-sex pairs would show behavioral and physical effects from exposure to cross-sex hormones while in the womb. In support of this view, nontwin females exposed to excess androgen levels before birth [a condition called congenital adrenal hyperplasia (CAH)], are sometimes born with ambiguous genitals and tend to prefer boy-typical toys, although these girls usually identify as females [64]. Nontwin males whose bodies do not respond to the male hormone androgen [a condition known as androgen insensitivity syndrome (AIS)] are born appearing like females, are raised as females, and identify as females; AIS is usually detected when these women fail to have a menstrual period [65]. Of course, these conditions involve more extreme hormonal effects than opposite-sex DZ twins would experience prenatally, but they suggest that some effects might be apparent. However, what seems reasonable is not always true, and what is true may surprise.

Human chimerism was first reported in 1953 in a female twin when her blood sample showed a mixture of A and O cells. When asked if she had a twin she answered in the affirmative, noting that her twin brother had passed away 25 years earlier in infancy. But his cells still survived [66]. After that, chimerism was thought to be rare in humans until a 1996 study from the Netherlands detected blood chimerism in approximately 8% of DZ twin pairs and 21% of DZ triplet sets. Subsequent to that study, other reports of chimerism in DZ twins have appeared [61]. In fact, chimerism in an unusual DZ twin pair with a single chorion has been reported. What makes this case especially noteworthy is that the chimerism was detected in buccal cells (cells from the inner lining of the cheeks and lips), rather than in blood [67].

Evidence of chimerism in opposite-sex DZ twin pairs raises questions about the possible masculinization of female cotwins and feminization of male cotwins. Both science and speculation have weighed in on this topic, which I address more closely in subsequent chapters.

Zygosity Diagnosis: MZ or DZ?

Zygosity is the scientific term for twin type. Classifying twins as MZ (identical) or DZ (fraternal) is an essential first step in conducting research that will yield valid and replicable findings. Identical twins (theoretically) share 100% of their genes, while fraternal twins share, on average, 50% of their genes. Therefore, fraternal twins as a group would be expected to be less alike than identical twins for traits that are genetically influenced.

The classic twin method (described in detail in Chapter 2) can compare the similarity of samples of MZ and DZ twin pairs in virtually all human traits. As I explained earlier, greater resemblance between MZ twins is consistent with genetic influence (heritable effects) on the trait under study. If some MZ twins are mislabeled as DZ then the pairs in the DZ sample will be more similar overall than typical DZ twins. Conversely, if DZ twins are mislabeled as MZ, the pairs in the MZ group will be more dissimilar overall than typical MZ twins. Either way, the degree to which genes underlie individual differences in a trait (heritability) would be *underestimated* because the resemblance between cotwins in the two twin samples would be accidentally equalized.

Beyond the value to science, knowledge of twin type is important for twins and for the parents who raise them. A debate published in the *British Journal of Obstetrics and Gynaecology* highlighted many of the reasons for twin-type diagnosis to be important [68]. Included among them are better understanding of twins' developmental milestones and more insightful evaluation of twins' medical life histories. For example, some newborn MZ cotwins show marked weight differences due to their unequal nutritional supply during gestation. Newborn DZ cotwins can also show weight differences, partly due to their differing genetic backgrounds. If parents believe their twins are DZ when in fact they are MZ, they may assume the twins' size difference is due to their different genes, and overlook necessary dietary supplements for their lighter weight MZ twin child. Additionally, if one twin develops a food allergy or a serious psychiatric condition, it would be prudent to know if the cotwin were also at risk—if one twin was diagnosed with bipolar disorder, an MZ cotwin would have a 55% chance of developing this condition, whereas a DZ cotwin would have just a 7% chance [69].

Psychologically, twins need to know their zygosity with certainty for reasons of identity, self-esteem, and peace of mind [70]. Close family members and friends of twins often mistake identical for fraternal twins because of their exquisite sensitivity to subtle differences between the twins. MZ twins themselves may experience confusing mismatches if they are labeled DZ twins when their experiences resonate as those of MZ twins. My colleague, Barbara McDowell, the former director of the Women's Studies Center at California State University, and her sister Betsy never felt like fraternal twins despite what their mother had told them. Their behavioral similarities and social closeness with one another made them feel like identical twins. Last year, I arranged for Barbara and Betsy to have the DNA test that finally proved them right. They were thrilled to celebrate the news of their newly discovered identical twinship with their family and friends.

It often works the other way with fraternal twins who relish the differences they have experienced all their lives. High school seniors, Jerry and Pete, were fairly certain that they were fraternal twins because that is what their parents had always told them. They had been gestated in separate placentae, consistent with their being fraternal twins, but *not* ruling out the possibility of their being identical. Jerry and Pete looked just similar enough to cause their parents (and me) to question their belief about their sons' zygosity—so when the family contacted me to discuss a different twin issue, I encouraged them to have the twins' DNA tested. Here is what their mother wrote upon learning that her twins were fraternal: "The boys are relieved that they are not identical... They were hesitant to participate in the testing and really did not want to learn they were identical. Pete in particular (the older one) seemed especially elated to be fraternal. We are grateful that you suggested completing the test so that we finally know for sure."

The routine/universal DNA testing of same-sex newborn twins is supported by virtually every twin researcher and clinician I know. Ways of advising families about how to obtain such testing were discussed among researchers, physicians, and parents at "Healthier Kids: Insights From Twin Research," a conference I attended at the Royal Childrens Hospital, in Melbourne, Australia in December 2014. Given their sex difference, male–female pairs are typically classified as DZ, although some exceptional mixed-sex MZ twin cases have been reported, as I will explain later.

There are a number of methods for assessing zygosity, including:

• Physical resemblance questionnaires. A variety of questionnaires and inventories can classify twins with a high degree of certainty [71,72]. The first such questionnaire was not designed or implemented until 1961 in Sweden [35,73]. This study posed several questions to a final sample of 200 twin pairs concerning similarity in physical features and confusion by others. Just one question—Were you and your twin as alike as two peas in a pod?—yielded a 98% accuracy rate, as assessed against blood-typing results (for five independent blood group systems), when twin pair members provided the same answer. And a 1979 study in Norway correctly classified 94%, or 203 out of 215 twin pairs, based on answers to a similarly phrased question: When growing up, were you as alike as two peas in a pod, of unusual sib-similarity, or quite different? [74]

A favorite zygosity questionnaire of mine is the Nichols & Bilbro protocol that allows classification ordered across different levels of certainty [71]. These forms (completed by parents or by the twins themselves) ask questions about similarities and differences in highly heritable features, such as hair color and eye color, as well as confusion by parents, teachers, and close friends. Results from these studies have been validated against results from more objective, scientific methods, such as extensive blood group testing and DNA analysis. Physical resemblance questionnaires can be used in studies for which the molecular genetic methods described next are not feasible. However, there are limitations to questionnaires because some populations, such as the Japanese, show reduced variability in some traits. Most Japanese people have straight dark hair and dark eyes; therefore, questionnaire items about twins' similarities in hair color and eye color are uninformative since fraternal twins would match to the same degree as identical twins. Furthermore, some twins are separated in school, making responses to items about confusion by teachers and friends questionable.

- DNA analysis. The most accurate, easily performed measure of twin type involves within-pair comparison of (usually) 15 short tandem repeat (STR) markers. STRs are uniquely repeating patterns in specified DNA regions. Complete concordance (resemblance) for all markers identifies MZ twins with virtual certainty. That is because there is a very high degree of individuality in STRs, making it very unlikely for two nonidentical twins to match across all 15 markers [75]. This is a noninvasive procedure that extracts DNA from buccal smears (cells obtained by gently rubbing the inner cheek with a special swab). DNA testing is offered by genetics laboratories around the world for personal twin testing, and is the same type of test used in forensic analysis, that is, "DNA fingerprinting." It is also done as part of the twin-based molecular genetic studies that I will describe in the chapter that follows.

- Serological studies (analysis of about eight blood group systems), dermatoglyphic analysis (total fingerprint ridge count), and placental examination (one or two placentae) were used in pre-1980s studies to classify twins as MZ or DZ. These measures remain of interest, but their substitution for DNA analysis, molecular genetic studies, or even questionnaires would not be done today because of possible errors in diagnosis. Occasionally, DZ twins inherit matching blood groups, especially those that occur commonly. For example, type O positive occurs among 37% of Caucasians in the United States [76] and the M gene in the MNS blood group system is present in 78% [77]. Even though blood-typing typically involves comparing twins across multiple blood group factors, it is possible (but rare) for DZ twins to match on all of them because they share the same parents, yielding inaccurate results.

- Other twin-type indices include fingerprints and placentae, but they are best used in combination with other measures. MZ twins' fingerprints are not exactly the same due to various prenatal influences and insults, and can differ considerably in some cases. And, as indicated previously, both MZ and DZ twins can have one or two placentae, making classification on that basis problematic. My colleague, the late University of Minnesota professor, David Lykken, showed that combining blood groups, fingerprints, ponderal index (a measure of leanness, calculated as weight in kilograms/height in cubic centimeters), and cephalic index (a measure of head size, calculated as head width in centimeters × 100/ head length in centimeters) classifies twins with 99.9% accuracy [78]. But regardless of zygosity, each individual twin pair is a unique take on human nature and a fascinating study all its own.

Why Twins Intrigue?

There are lingering questions about twins that lack good answers. One of them is: Why do people enjoy twins as much as they do?

Whenever I pose this question the most "insightful" answer I get is, "Because they are amazing!" "Why are they amazing?" I ask. "Because they just are!" These are unsatisfactory responses to a deeply intriguing question.

I believe that the sight of two individuals who look and act so much alike challenges our beliefs and expectations about individual differences and human uniqueness. The idea that physical and behavioral traits can be faithfully replicated in two infants, children, or adults runs counter to our expectations about human beings' individuality. This is especially true when we hear about the identical singers and songwriters, Tegan and Sara Quin, who won Juno Awards for the best single and best musical group of 2014 [79], or the identical tennis double, Bob and Mike Bryan, who are number one in world rankings [80]. The college presidents, Harold and Bernard Shapiro, who presided over top-ranked universities (Princeton in Princeton, New Jersey and McGill in Montreal, Canada) at the same time also defy the odds [81]. This great exception to our belief system forces us to rethink our take on what shapes human intelligence, personality, and talent. The conversations we conduct with others and with ourselves over these issues goes to the heart of what interests us most [82].

In the next chapter, my brief review of the twin-based approach to individual differences research describes many informative twin designs. Some of these designs (i.e., the ways of using twins and their relatives in research) will be familiar to mothers and fathers raising twins. That is because parents see these designs replayed at home, at school, and in playgrounds. When identical twins achieve identical test scores, or a bossy fraternal female twin tells her twin brother how to behave, families are witnessing twin research in small scale. In fact, parents of twins are among the best observers of behavior I know and I often grill them for new ideas when I speak to their organizations.

REFERENCES

[1] G. Steinman, The mechanism initiating and controlling monozygotic twinning in humans remains to be elucidated, Twin Res. Hum. Genet. 3 (2000) 337.
[2] D. Cyranoski, Developmental biology: two by two, Nature 458 (7240) (2009) 826–829.
[3] Mosby's Medical Dictionary, ninth ed., Elsevier, 2009. Available from: http://medical-dictionary.thefreedictionary.com/Hellin's+law
[4] A. Scheinfeld, Twins and Supertwins, J.B. Lippincott, New York, NY, (1967).

[5] J. Fellman, A.W. Eriksson, Statistical analyses of Hellin's law, Twin Res. Hum. Genet. 12 (2) (2009) 191–200.

[6] N.L. Segal, B. Marcheco-Teruel, I. "Street of twins: the Cuban twin registry: an update, Twin Res. Hum. Genet. 17 (4) (2014) 347–353.

[7] USA Today. Seeing Double: Illinois School Boasts 24 Sets of Twins, 10 June, 2013. Available from: http://www.usatoday.com/story/news/nation/2013/06/10/twins-record/2408099/

[8] M.A. Joyce, B.E. Hamilton, M.J.K. Osterman, S.C. Curtin, T.J. Matthews, Births: Final Data for 2013, National Vital Statistics Reports 64 (1) (2015) 1–68.

[9] B.E. Hamilton, M.A. Joyce, M.J.K. Osterman, S.C. Curtin, T.J. Matthews, Births: Final Data for 2014, National Vital Statistics Reports 64 (12) (2015) 1–64.

[10] G. Pison, C. Monden, J. Smits, Is the Twin-Boom in Developed Countries Coming to an End? Working Paper, No. 216, Institut National d'Études Démographiques, 2014.

[11] D.M. Kissin, S.L. Boulet, D.J. Jamieson, Fertility treatments in the United States, Obstet. Gynecol. 128 (2) (2016) 387–390.

[12] J. Song, A. Song, A. Shim, E. Kim, M. Song, Mirror-image identical twins presenting in mirror-image hip cysts: a case report and review of the literature, Rheumatology S(17) (2) (2013) 161–1149.

[13] M. Bulmer, Francis Galton: Pioneer of Heredity and Biometry, Johns Hopkins University Press, Baltimore, MD, (2003).

[14] L.E. Berk, Child Development, ninth ed., Allyn & Bacon, Boston, MA, (2012).

[15] A. Post, K. Heyborne, Managing monoamniotc twin pregnancies, Clin. Obstet. Gynecol. 58 (3) (2015) 643–653.

[16] R.W. Redline, Nonidentical twins with a single placenta—disproving dogma in perinatal pathology, N. Engl. J. Med. 349 (2) (2003) 111–114.

[17] M.V. Senat, J. Deprest, M. Boulvain, A. Paupe, N. Winer, Y. Ville, Endoscopic laser surgery versus serial amnioreduction for severe twin-to-twin transfusion syndrome, N. Engl. J. Med. 351 (2) (2004) 136–144. Laser surgery has a higher success rate (76%) than amnioreduction (56%).

[18] A. Johnson, Diagnosis and management of twin–twin transfusion syndrome, Clin. Obstet. Gynecol. 58 (3) (2015) 611–631 Laser surgery can currently correct 70-80+ of the cases.

[19] S.A. Durbin, A sonographer's perspective: Quintero staging system for twin-to-twin transfusion syndrome in monochorionic twins, J. Diagn. Med. Sonogr. 27 (3) (2011) 122–125.

[20] T. Dias, T. Arcangeli, A. Bhide, R. Napolitano, S. Mahsud-Dornan, B. Thilaganathan, First-trimester ultrasound determination of chorionicity in twin pregnancy, Ultrasound Obstet. Gynecol. 38 (5) (2011) 530–532.

[21] C. Hutt, Males and Females, Penguin, Ontario, Canada, (1975).

[22] S.H. Orzack, J.W. Stubblefield, V.R. Akmaev, P. Colls, S. Munné, T. Scholl, J.E. Zuckerman, The human sex ratio from conception to birth, Proc. Natl. Acad. Sci. 112 (16) (2015) E2102–E2111.

[23] R.T. Collins, T. Bhatti, D.S. Huff, P.M. Weinberg, Images in cardiovascular medicine: thoracopagus conjoined twins, Circulation 118 (14) (2008) 1496.

[24] D.J. Harvey, A. Totonchi, A.E. Gosain, Separation of craniopagus twins over the past 20 years: a systematic review of the variables that lead to successful separation, Plast. Reconstr. Surg. 138 (1) (2016) 190–200.

[25] C. Quigley, Conjoined Twins: An Historical, Biological and Ethical Issues Encyclopedia, McFarland, Jefferson, NC, (2006).

[26] "Janus." Available from: http://www.crystalinks.com/janus.html

[27] "jani-, Janus." Available from: http://wordinfo.info/unit/2523

[28] S. Bourthoumieu, C. Yardin, F. Terro, B. Gilbert, C. Laroche, R. Saura, et al. Mono-zygotic twins concordant for blood karyotype, but phenotypically discordant: a case of "mosaic chimerism", Am. J. Med. Genet. A 135 (2) (2005) 190–194.

[29] A mosaic non-twin individual can have different colored eyes (heterochromia) if the DNA difference involves an eye color gene. This can also happen to a chimera due to the different genes in each cell. A. Johnson, Eye Color, 2012. Available from: http://genetics.thetech.org/ask-a-geneticist/inheritance-heterochromia

[30] P.S. Harper, Mary Lyon and the hypothesis of random X chromosome inactivation, Hum. Genet. 130 (2) (2011) 169–174.

[31] L. De Gregorio, H.A. Jinnah, J.C. Harris, W.L. Nyhan, D.J. Schretlen, L.M. Trom-bley, J.P. O'Neill, Lesch–Nyhan disease in a female with a clinically normal monozy-gotic twin, Mol. Genet. Metab. 85 (1) (2005) 70–77.

[32] R. Plomin, J.C. DeFries, V.S. Knopik, J.M. Neiderhiser, Behavioral Genetics, ninth ed., Worth Publishers, New York, NY, (2013).

[33] A.L. Burgemeister, B. Zirn, F. Oeffner, S.G. Kaler, G. Lemm, E. Rossier, H.M. Büt-tel, Menkes disease with discordant phenotype in female monozygotic twins, Am. J. Med. Genet. A 167A (2015) 2826–2829.

[34] N. Martin, D. Boomsma, G. Machin, Twin-pronged attack on complex traits, Nat. Genet. 17 (14) (1997) 387–392.

[35] N.L. Segal, Entwined Lives: Twins and What They Tell Us About Human Behavior, Plume, New York, NY, (2000).

[36] J.S. Palmer, Z.Z. Zhao, C. Hoekstra, N.K. Hayward, P.M. Webb, D.C. Whiteman, et al. Novel variants in growth differentiation factor 9 in mothers of dizygotic twins, J. Clin. Endocrinol. Metab. 91 (11) (2006) 4713–4716.

[37] G. Sirugo, D.R. Edwards, K.K. Ryckman, C. Bisseye, M.J. White, B. Kebbeh, et al. PTX3 genetic variation and dizygotic twinning in The Gambia: could pleiotropy with innate immunity explain common dizygotic twinning in Africa? Ann. Hum. Genet. 76 (6) (2012) 454–463.

[38] H. Mbarek, S. Steinberg, D.R. Nyholt, S.D. Gordon, M.B. Miller, A.F. McRae, et al. Identification of common genetic variants influencing spontaneous dizygotic twinning and female fertility, Am. J. Hum. Genet. 98 (5) (2016) 898–908.

[39] H. Mbarek, C.V. Dolan, D.I. Boomsma, Two SNPs associated with spontaneous DZ twinning: effect sizes and how we communicate them, Twin Res. Hum. Genet. 19 (5) (2016) 418–421.

[40] A. Tagliani-Ribeiro, M. Oliveira, A.K. Sassi, M.R. Rodrigues, M. Zagonel-Oliveira, G. Steinman, et al. Twin Town in South Brazil: a Nazi's experiment or a genetic founder effect? PLoS One 6 (2011) e20328.

[41] A.W. Eriksson, Human twinning in and around the Aland Islands, Commentationes Biologicae 64 (1973) 1–159.

[42] Y. Imaizumi, K. Nonaka, The twinning rates by zygosity in Japan, 1975-1994, Acta Genet. Med. Gemellol. 46 (1) (1997) 9–22 Australian Twin Registry. "Facts and Figures." Available from: https://www.twins.org.au/twins-and-twin-families/about-twins/facts-and-figures.

[43] E. Comeau, First Test-tube Baby in U.S. Reflects on the Death of an IVF Pioneer, April 10, 2013. Available from: http://www.boston.com/lifestyle/health/fitness/get-movingblog/2013/04/when_there_are.html

[44] S. Guy, One Embryo as Good as Two for IVF Success, November 4, 2009. Available from: http://ivf.net/ivf/one-embryo-as-good-as-two-for-ivf-success-o4568.html.

[45] Souter, et al. A report of dizygous monochorionic twins, N. Engl. J. Med. 349 (2) (2003) 154–158.

[46] N.L. Segal, Zygosity diagnosis: when physicians and DNA disagree, Twin Res. Hum. Genet. 18 (2015) 613–618.

[47] H. Asseta, New Jersey Judge Rules Twin Girls Have Different Fathers, May 8, 2015. Available from: http://www.cnn.com/2015/05/08/us/new-jersey-twins-two-fathers/index.html

[48] C.C. Luu, P.D. Tran, Twins With Different Fathers Found in Vietnam, March 8, 2016. Available from: http://edition.cnn.com/2016/03/07/health/twins-with-different-fathers-vietnam/index.html

[49] B. Mueller, Paternity Case for a New Jersey Mother of Twins Bears Unexpected Results: Two Fathers, May 7, 2015. Available from: http://www.nytimes.com/2015/05/08/nyregion/paternity-case-for-a-new-jersey-mother-of-twins-bears-unexpected-results-two-fathers.html?_r=0.

[50] C.C. Luu, P.D. Tran, March 8, 2016, BBC News, March 9, 2016, Vietnam Twins Found to Have Different Fathers in Rare Case. Available from: http://www.bbc.com/news/world-asia-35761281

[51] W.H. James, Coital frequency and twinning—a comment, J. Biosoc. Sci. 24 (1) (1992) 135–136.

[52] B. Bonnelyke, J. Olsen, J. Nielsen, Coital frequency and twinning, J. Biosoc. Sci. 22 (2) (1990) 191–196.

[53] P. Bourgoin, J. Marc, C. Merger, J.N. Delatte, A case of a dizygotic twin pregnancy where superfetation seems indisputable, J. Gynecol. Obstet. Biol. Reprod. 24 (4) (1994) 440–443.

[54] J.J. Tarín, M.A. García-Pérez, C. Hermenegildo, A. Cano, Unpredicted ovulations and conceptions during early pregnancy: an explanatory mechanism of human superfetation, Reprod. Fertil. Dev. 25 (7) (2013) 1012–1019.

[55] F.R. Bieber, W.E. Nance, C.C. Morton, J.A. Brown, F.O. Redwine, R.L. Jordan, T. Mohanakumar, Genetic studies of an acardiac monster: evidence of polar body twinning in man, Science 213 (4509) (1981) 775–777.

[56] Amazing Couple to Have Set No. 2. Available from: http://www.thesun.co.uk/sol/homepage/news/article1295476.ece

[57] O. Maronas, et al. Development of a forensic skin colour predictive test, FSI Genet. 13 (2014) 34–44.

[58] J. Moorhead. Different But the Same: A Story of Black and White Twins. Guardian, September 23, 2011. Available from: http://www.theguardian.com/lifeandstyle/2011/sep/24/twins-black-white

[59] J.S. Hunter, Account of the freemartin, Philos. Trans. R. Soc. Lond. 69 (1779) 279–293.

[60] What is a Freemartin?. Available from: http://www.thecattlesite.com/articles/975/what-is-a-freemartin/

[61] K. Chen, R.H. Chmait, D. Vanderbilt, S. Wu, L. Randolph, Chimerism in monochorionic dizygotic twins: case study and review, Am. J. Med. Genet. 161 (7) (2013) 1817–1824.

[62] F.R. Lillie, The theory of the free-martin, Science 43 (1916) 611–613.

[63] Chimerism. Available from: http://zochimerism.weebly.com/humans-and-animals.html

[64] V. Pasterski, et al. Prenatal hormones and childhood sex-segregation: playmate and play style preferences in girls with congenital adrenal hyperplasia, Horm. Behav. 59 (4) (2011) 549–555.

[65] I.A. Hughes, J.D. Davies, T.I. Bunch, V. Pasterski, K. Mastroyannopoulou, J. MacDougall, Androgen insensitivity syndrome, Lancet 380 (9851) (2012) 1149–1428.

[66] I. Dunsford, C.C. Bowley, A.M. Hutchison, J.S. Thompson, R. Sanger, R.R. Race, Human blood-group chimera, Br. Med. J. 2 (4827) (1953) 81.

[67] S. Fumoto, K. Hosoi, H. Ohnishi, K. Hoshina, K. Yan, H. Saji, A. Oka, Chimerism of buccal membrane cells in a monochorionic dizygotic twin, Pediatrics 133 (4) (2014) e1097–e1100.

[68] Craig, et al. BJOG Debate. Zygosity testing should not be recommended for all same sex twins: AGAINST, Br. J. Obstet. Gynecol. 122 (12) (2015) 1641.

[69] R. Plomin, J.C. DeFries, V.S. Knopki, J.M. Neiderhiser, Behavioral Genetics, sixth ed., Worth Publishers, New York, NY, (2013).

[70] T.L. Cutler, K. Murphy, J.L. Hopper, L.A. Keogh, Y. Dai, J.M. Craig, Why accurate knowledge of zygosity is important to twins, Twin Res. Hum. Genet. 18 (3) (2015) 298–305.

[71] R.C. Nichols, W.C. Bilbro Jr., The diagnosis of twin zygosity, Acta Genet. Stat. Med. 16 (3) (1966) 265–275.

[72] H.H. Goldsmith, A zygosity questionnaire for young twins: a research note, Behav. Genet. 21 (3) (1991) 257–269.

[73] R. Cederlöf, L. Friberg, E. Jonsson, L. Kaij, Studies on similarity diagnosis in twins with the aid of mailed questionnaires, Acta Genet. Stat. Med. 11 (4) (1961) 338–362.

[74] S. Torgersen, The determination of twin zygosity by means of a mailed questionnaire, Acta Genet. Med. Gemellol. 28 (3) (1979) 225–236.

[75] National Forensic Science Technology Center, A Simplified Guide to DNA Evidence, 2013. Available from: http://www.forensicsciencesimplified.org/dna/principles.html

[76] American Red Cross, Blood Types, 2015. Available from: http://www.redcrossblood.org/learn-about-blood/blood-types

[77] National Center for Biotechnology Information, Blood Groups and Red Cell Antigens. Available from: http://www.ncbi.nlm.nih.gov/books/NBK2274/.

[78] D.T. Lykken, The diagnosis of zygosity in twins, Behav. Genet. 8 (5) (1978) 437–463.

[79] S. Sperounes, Junos 2014 Tegan and Sara, Serena Ryder, Bieber Win Top Awards, Postmedia News, March 30, 2014. Available from: http://o.canada.com/entertainment/music/junos-2014-tegan-and-sara-serena-ryder-win-top-awards

[80] N.M. de Crinis, Bryan Brothers Bring No. 1 World Doubles Ranking to BNP Paribas Open. Palm Springs Life, March 2015. Available from: http://www.palmspringslife.com/Palm-Springs-Life/Desert-Guide/March-2015/Bryan-Brothers-Bring-No-1-World-Doubles-Ranking-to-BNP-Paribas-Open/.

[81] N.L. Segal, Indivisible by Two: Lives of Extraordinary Twins, Plume, New York, NY, (2005).

[82] An essay worth reading on the topic of why twins fascinate is by Nick Ripatrazone, "On Our Fascination With Twins", July 14, 2015. Available from: http://lithub.com/on-our-fascination-with-twins/.

CHAPTER 2

Living Laboratories: Double Designs and Multiple Methods

There are many ways that MZ and DZ twins can be "arranged" in research to tease apart the genetic and environmental influences on various traits. Some of these designs involve just the twins, but others also include the twins' children and/or their parents and nontwin siblings. Some will seem familiar because these "arrangements" occur naturally in households everywhere. A look at how twin data are gathered is my next question.

TWINS AND TWIN METHODS

Most studies compare the degree of similarity between identical and fraternal twins with respect to a trait of interest. A recent summary of findings from 2,748 publications, based on 17,804 traits and 14,558,903 twin pairs, found that the degree of genetic influence on how much traits vary from person to person within a population (heritability) is, on average, 49% [1]. This figure leaves the remaining 51% to nongenetic (environmental plus random) effects. There is a lot of misunderstanding about what heritability does and does not mean. The expressions "a gene for this" or "a gene for that," are also largely suspect; please stay tuned.

Researchers today use all the methods that I have outlined next. These methods or designs can be either experimental or naturalistic in nature, while some capture elements of both. Experimental studies are those in which researchers choose the participants and arrange the conditions. Naturalistic studies are those in which researchers examine informative situations that simply arise. The rapid development of molecular genetic methods during the last several decades has also given researchers new ways of studying the origins of behavioral, physical, and medical traits. These approaches have been described in considerable detail in other sources so only brief sketches are provided next to clarify their basic differences.

- Classic twin method. The British investigator Sir Frances Galton (1875/1876) is widely credited with inventing and applying the classic twin method. (But see the final chapter for the continuing controversy over the real pioneer.) The classic twin design compares the degree of

Twin Mythconceptions
http://dx.doi.org/10.1016/B978-0-12-803994-6.00002-0

25

resemblance between samples of MZ and DZ twin pairs [2,3]. Twin resemblance can be based on cotwin similarity of test scores, height and weight, or speech patterns among other things. Greater resemblance between MZ than DZ twins demonstrates, but does not prove, genetic influence on the trait under study. As an example, myopia (near-sightedness) is genetically influenced, but MZ cotwins might be more alike than DZ cotwins because of their shared prematurity, rather than their shared genes.

It is also possible that DZ cotwins (like my sister and me) might both be near-sighted due to their early birth. Some DZ cotwins might even be as alike as MZ cotwins when it comes to eyesight. Studies of vision using twins should consider gestational length when interpreting their findings.

Galton obtained his twin data by sending "circulars of inquiry" to twins he knew and to the relatives of twins. He received replies from 80 pairs who indicated "close similarity." Galton did not specify the questions he posed to the twins, but appears to have asked for descriptive, narrative material since a number of the twins provided considerable detail about their lives, personalities, and medical histories. He closely examined the twins' statements for evidence of behavioral and physical similarities and differences. The biology of twinning was unknown in Galton's time, but he reasoned that there were two types of twins: those who looked alike and those who did not. This distinction corresponds, respectively (but very approximately), to the two types we recognize today: identical and fraternal. The biological differences between twin types were not worked out until the years 1919–25 [4].

Underlying the classic twin design and other twin research methods is the equal environments assumption (EEA). The EEA asserts that environmental factors affecting a particular trait are the same for MZ and DZ twins. If the EEA is not upheld then the results from that study are questionable.

Consider the following example: It is reasonable to assume that dressing alike affects MZ and DZ twins' personality similarity to the same degree. However, if MZ twins, but not DZ twins, are purposefully dressed alike *and* this treatment does make MZ twins' personalities more similar, then the EEA would be violated. However, if MZ twins themselves *chose* the same outfits more often than DZ twins and were more alike in personality, then the EEA would not be compromised. This example shows that researchers need to carefully consider the nature *and* the source of environmental influences on twins. The EEA, while challenged by some twin research critics, has been widely supported [5]. By the way, it was shown long ago that MZ twins who play together as children, spend time together as adolescents, have the same teachers, sleep in the same bedroom, and/or have parents who dress them alike and purposefully treat them alike are not more similar in personality than those who do not [6]. Additional discussion of this issue awaits Chapter 10.

- Cotwin control (the experimental version). The experimental version of cotwin control utilizes MZ twins to assess the effects of different teaching methods, physical routines, and medical treatments on various outcomes. This strategy can be applied either at the single case level or with many twin pairs in a large-scale study [7]. A classic 1942 paper set forth both the logic and the limitations of this approach for studying individual twin pairs [8]. In this study, one identical twin was trained for several weeks in stair climbing and block manipulation, and was later compared to her identical twin who had not been trained in those tasks. The twins displayed comparable abilities, showing that the natural process of physical maturation was the primary influence on these skills.

    For the sake of data integrity, care must be taken by researchers and participants to insure that the untreated cotwins do not acquire study-relevant information or skills (either from their cotwin or anyone else) that might affect their performance. If the untrained or untreated twin in the 1942 stair climbing study secretly watched her twin climb stairs and practiced on her own, the conclusion that maturation explained the twins' matched abilities would have been wrong.

    Another example of experimental cotwin control is that of the identical twin astronauts, Scott and Mark Kelly. Scott inhabited the International Space Station for an entire year (March 2015–March 2016), while Mark remained on earth. This NASA-sponsored project was done to compare the twins' cognitive skills, reaction times, and health status to better understand how space travel affects human behavioral and physical functioning [9].

- Cotwin control (the naturalistic version). The naturalistic version of cotwin control uses MZ cotwins with existing differences in order to find the nongenetic or environmental causes of discordance (difference) between them. The identical female Genain Quadruplets, studied at the National Institute of Mental Health (NIMH) in the 1960s, were each diagnosed with schizophrenia by the age of 24, albeit to differing degrees of severity. The greater frequency and severity of symptoms shown by some of the quadruplets over others was variously associated with their life history events (e.g., the organization of the quads into "favored" and "unfavored" pairs), biochemical factors, and cerebral pathology [10,11].

In order to protect the identity of the quads their names were changed in a way that followed the four letters of the institute (NIMH) where they were studied: Nora, Iris, Myra, and Hester. And Genain, a Greek word that means "dreadful birth" or "dire gene," is not their real family name. I was very privileged to have served as a research assistant for this study during my first summer as a graduate student. My task was to read through the quads' correspondence sent to the principal investigator, Dr. David Rosenthal, to identify different concepts and themes—consequently, I know their real names.

The case of the Genain Quadruplets is a classic study in twin research, due to its unique subjects and subject matter. This study's support for both genetic and environmental contributions to schizophrenia (diathesis–stress theory) came at a time when environmental explanations of mental disorder were enthusiastically embraced by the scientific community, with little acknowledgment of inherited effects. We now know that some environmental effects can be passed down from parent to child, as I will explain in the section on epigenetics.

Cotwin control studies of twins discordant for schizophrenia, conducted since the 1960s, have implicated various nongenetic factors (e.g., obstetric complications and structural brain anomalies) in the disease. Why only one of two genetically identical twins exposed to prolonged labor should become schizophrenic has not been resolved [12]. Other studies have examined MZ cotwins discordant for the diagnoses and/or the severity of other genetically influenced conditions, such as autism and diabetes, in the search for culpable nongenetic factors. Differences in gene expression (epigenetics) have been found for twins who differ in their severity of autistic symptoms and in diagnoses of diabetes-1 [13,14].

- Twin-family designs. Methods combining twins and their families are the malleable Gumbys of twin research because you can twist around their parts to create novel configurations. The children-of-twins (COT) design includes research involving adult twin parents, their partners, and children. MZ twin families revise ordinary family relations because twin aunts and uncles become genetic "mothers" and "fathers" to their cotwin's children. The same genetic reasoning transform cousins into genetic "half-siblings." In contrast, DZ twin families preserve the ordinary

Figure 2.1 *Identical twin "half-sibling" family.* The identical female twins are the aunts and genetic "mothers" of their nieces and nephews. The nieces and nephews from the two families are first cousins, as well as genetic "half-siblings." *(Photo credit: Dr. Nancy L. Segal).*

aunt/uncle–niece/nephew and first cousin relationships. An identical twin family is shown in Fig. 2.1.

I love this very relevant quote from *Littlewood's Miscellaney*, which gives readers a glimpse into academic life at Cambridge's Trinity College, in England.

One of the most eminent of biologists was asked whether two sons, one from each of two marriages, of identical twin brothers to identical twin sisters, would be identical; he replied 'yes', and was corrected by a philosopher whose pigeon holes are always in unusually good working order (p. 186) [15].

Of course, the biologist was wrong! In the relatively unusual cases in which MZ twins marry MZ twins, aunts and uncles turn into genetic "parents," and cousins morph into *genetic "full siblings"* [16]. Which genes get transmitted from parents to children is a matter of chance. It would, therefore, be practically impossible for the two identical couples to create genetically identical sons and daughters—just as it would be for any ordinary couple who had two or more children.

These twin-family designs allow endless informative comparisons, such as the degree of resemblance between parents and children who share genes and environments versus aunts and nieces who share only genes. This design also allows assessment of spouse similarity (assortative mating), both within and between MZ twin couples. The twin-family design has been used to study numerous behaviors, including age at menarche [17] and bipolar disorder [18]. A photograph of identical Israeli twins Niv and Ran, who married identical twins Leah and Rebecca, shows the two fathers proudly displaying their infant daughters born just 20 min apart. In fact, the two newborns (cousins) are genetically equivalent to fraternal twins because their mothers' most likely provided similar intrauterine environments [19]. DZ twin families can be studied as an informative comparison group for these studies.

A close "relative" of the COT design is the parents-of-twins (POT) design that includes twin children or adolescents, their parents, and possibly their full siblings. This approach offers a look at how parental treatment and twins' perceptions of parental treatment affect twin resemblance in behavior. This method has been used to study behaviors, such as expressions and perceptions of parental warmth [20], the nature of family relationships, and the appearance of depressive symptoms [21]. For example, developmental research has found that identical twins receiving more maternal negativity and less warmth than their cotwins show more antisocial behavioral problems [22]. This design has also been used to study risk factors for cardiac disease.

- Twins-as-couples. I coined the term *twins-as-couples* to denote a systematic design for studying the quality of twins' social relationships with one another. This approach compares the social-interactional features characterizing MZ and DZ cotwins as they complete activities together. Past studies have observed twins working on letter substitution and addition problems [23], jigsaw puzzles [24], and other games eliciting either cooperative or competitive behavior [25,26]. Some of these joint activities involved having twins work on the same tasks in close proximity to one another or had them interact with unrelated partners. I have also observed young MZ and DZ twins' playmate preferences in free play situations—the MZ twins stayed closer together and showed more meaningful social exchange than the DZ twins [24].

  Given the methods and goals of the twins-as-couples design, the participants in such studies are the *pairs* and the variables of interest are the *MZ versus DZ twin pairs' social-interactional processes and outcomes*. Whereas most twin methods compare the similarity in traits between MZ cotwins and DZ cotwins, the twins-as-couples approach compares the *quality of the relationships* shown by MZ twin pairs and DZ twin pairs as these cotwins interact with one another. Most studies find greater within-pair cooperation within MZ than DZ twinships, although there is overlap [26].

- Higher-order multiples. Triplets, quadruplets, quintuplets, and beyond belong to the special class of higher-order multiples. The members of these sets may be all MZ and female (like the famous Dionne quintuplets, born in 1937) [27], all DZ and mixed-sex (like the well-known McCaughey septuplets, born in 1997) [28], or an MZ–DZ combination (like the rare Scarr-Crosmas quadruplet boys, born in 2000, that I wrote about in 2005) [16]. What makes the Scarr-Crosmas quads special is that they entered the world as two sets of MZ twins that could be organized into four sets of DZ twins. Comparing the similarities and differences among selected pairs from this foursome can be enlightening since each boy's age and family background are the same. Consequently, similarities between the identical pairs and differences between the fraternal pairs can be associated with their shared and nonshared genes, respectively. I determined that the only surviving octuplets, a mixed-sex MZ–DZ set born in 2009, yielded 28 unique twin pairings [29].

- Twins and siblings. Some twin designs extend beyond the twins themselves to include the biological siblings with whom the twins were raised. Despite their age differences, these full sibling pairs (nontwin sibling and twin) share the same genetic relatedness as DZ twins, so they comprise an informative control group for both MZ and DZ twin pairs. Full siblings, especially if they are close in age to the twins, can provide an alternative approach to studying DZ twins—these nontwin–twin pairs can be contrasted with MZ twins as a convenient check on what MZ–DZ comparisons reveal. Full siblings also tell us how much age similarity matters for behavioral resemblance when full siblings are compared to their DZ twin counterparts. Twin-sibling designs have been used to study general intelligence [30], personality traits [31], and adult men's sexual interest in under age youth [32].

- Twins reared apart and together. A four-group twin design consisting of MZ and DZ twins reared apart (MZA and DZA, the "A" signifying "apart") and together (MZT and DZT, the "T" signifying "together") is multilayered and instructive. MZA twins provide direct estimates of genetic effects because they share genes, but not environments, while DZA twins constitute an informative comparison group. If, for example, MZA twins are more alike in intelligence than DZA twins (which they

Figure 2.2 *Two sets of identical reared-apart twins.* The female twins (Debbie on the left and Sharon on the right) met for the first time at the age of 45 years. The male twins met for the first time at the age of 24 years. Sadly, the male twin on the right (Tony) passed away in August 2016 at the age of 78 years, a difficult loss for his twin brother Roger. *(Photo credits: Dr. Nancy L. Segal).*

are), this tells us that genes affect intellectual development. Comparing MZA and MZT twin pairs tells how much sharing an environment affects behavioral and physical development. If MZT twins are more alike than MZA twins in age at menarche (which they are), this shows that living together affects the timing of the first menstrual period [33]. Adding the contrast between DZA and DZT twins tells us if shared and nonshared environments work the same way for MZ and DZ twins. Two reared-apart identical twin pairs are shown in Fig. 2.2.

It turns out that a rarely reported comparison contrasts MZA twins with DZT twins. However, I highlight this particular pairing when addressing people who are skeptical of genetic influences on behavior. I reason that if shared environments are a crucial contributor to behavior, then DZT twins (DZ twins reared together) should be more alike than MZA twins (MZ twins reared apart). They rarely are, underlining the importance of genetic factors.

A total of four reared-apart twin studies have been conducted, two in the United States (1937, 2012), one in the United Kingdom (1962), and one in Denmark (1965/1980) [4,34–36]. Reared-apart twin studies are ongoing in Sweden, China, and Japan [37–39]. The different twin samples are comprised mostly of adult twins, but I am tracking the development of young Chinese twins adopted by different families in the United States and elsewhere [40]. This study is the only one to compare the actual unfolding of the separated twins' behavioral and physical events. In contrast, the other reared-apart twin studies obtained retrospective (recalled) background information from twins reunited as adults. I hope to obtain fresh perspectives on the environmental factors that affect the behaviors of separated twins. I would also like to gain understanding of the unique experience of getting to know a cotwin being raised in a different family.

NOVEL TWIN AND TWIN-LIKE DESIGNS

- Virtual twins (VTs). I am studying VTs, who are same-age nonbiological siblings raised together from very early in life. I discovered my first VT pair, Jonathan and Carlton, in 1991, never imagining that my 2016 sample would approach 170 such sets. I believe this number reflects delayed childbearing leading to fertility difficulties, rising numbers of homeless youngsters, greater humanitarian concerns for children, and greater acceptance of nontypical family structures, such as same-sex parenting, community parenting, and blended families with children that include "mine, yours, and ours."

  Most of the VT pairs I have studied (75%) consist of two adoptees, while the remaining are comprised of one adoptee and one biological child (25%). Some other exceptional pairs were created by same-sex parents raising their own biological child and their partner's child, and couples raising an adoptee and a child conceived and carried via embryo donation. These novel sibships replay twinship, but without the genetic link, providing direct estimates of environmental influences on behavior. VTs are a better comparison with twins than are ordinary adopted siblings who differ in age and time of entry into their family [41].

- Switched-at-birth twins. Most reared-apart twins are separated because families lack the financial resources and/or emotional support for their proper care. In the past, single motherhood was another reason for relinquishing twins, although the stigma of single motherhood has faded significantly. Currently, there is greater appreciation for twins' unique bonds; so deliberate efforts by adoption personnel are made to place adopted away twins together. However, because assisted reproductive technology (ART) often produces twins, triplets, and more, some multiple birth infants are separated because families cannot cope with rearing two or more children at once. I will say more about this important topic later.

There also exists a special subset of reared-apart twins whose separation was caused by inadvertent switching by hospital personnel. There are now seven documented cases of switched-at-birth twins worldwide involving nine twin pairs. (The total number jumps from seven to nine because exchanges between one twin in each of two pairs— in Colombia and in Puerto Rico—created two unrelated sets on two occasions.) Just to be clear:

• Before the Switch
Original Pair A: Twin A1, Twin A2 (born together)
Original Pair B: Twin B1, Twin B2 (born together)

• After the Switch
Twin A1, Twin B1 (raised together)
Twin A2, Twin B2 (raised together)

and

Twin A1, Twin A2 (raised apart)
Twin B1, Twin B2 (raised apart)

Switched twins, presumed to be rare, create unusual VT pairs. These VTs intrigue me because they and their families *believe* they are DZ twins and they are raised as such. The truth about their relationship is typically revealed when one twin is confused for the other by a third party. I also know several cases that have not been publically recorded, as well as several twins who suspect that they were switched. It is a myth to assume that "everyone has a double" or a "look-alike" because sometimes being mistaken for someone else means something more—that there is a reared-apart twin or sibling out there.

Two sets of switched-at-birth twin brothers from Bogotá, Colombia are the latest and, in my opinion, the most remarkable case of all, explaining my spring 2015 and summer 2016 travel to South America to study them [42]. (My book about these twins with collaborator Yesika Montoya is currently in progress.) This foursome includes doubly switched MZ twins, Jorge and William, and Carlos and Wilber who discovered the truth about their birth when they were 25 years old. The parents of the other doubly exchanged sets in Puerto Rico became aware of the switch when the twins were under 2 years old and reclaimed their toddlers. In that case, the twins' cousin told her mother that a little girl in the medical clinic waiting room looked just like Marie Tairí who was at home. The twins' aunt agreed that the child looked exactly like her young niece, made some inquiries, and discovered the truth [43].

I recently heard from a young fraternal male twin (Tom) who suspected he was switched at birth when a stranger claimed to know him. The stranger even referred to Tom's "identical twin" (Mike) living in the same state in which Tom had been born. I helped arrange the mitochondrial (mtDNA) test that would reveal if Tom and his fraternal twin brother (Tim) had the same mother. (mtDNA resides outside the nucleus of the cell and is passed down intact from mother to children. Consequently, all children in a family share the same mtDNA.) After weeks of waiting, Tom and Tim's mtDNA matched, confirming their fraternal twin relationship. Tom wrote:

Yes, I was relieved to know we are brothers biologically. After rereading [your book] Someone Else's Twin, I came to understand better the angst and sadness caused by a switch, especially to the parents. I myself have twin daughters, and am very fond of them as most parents are, and such a mistake would be heartbreaking. I am glad my parents do not have to go through that. To find out you missed out on knowing your biological child, even if you had an experience with another one who you knew as your own, would be a wound that I don't think would ever fully heal.

My research experience tells me that Tom is right.

- Unrelated look-alikes. Unrelated look-alike (U-LAs) are people who look physically alike, but are genetically unrelated. They are well suited for assessing associations between appearance and personality. I have used U-LAs to examine criticisms directed against twin research, a topic to which I will return later. One of my former graduate students, Deborah Wilson-Ozima, alerted me to a rich source of these sensational subjects, maintained by the French Canadian photographer François Brunelle. Brunelle maintains a website ("I'm Not a Look-Alike") in which he invites participation from people who strongly resemble one another. I have also been creating a small U-LA registry of my own. I have discovered several pairs of look-alikes at school, at conferences, at airports, and in the media.

GENETIC STUDIES

Findings from the vast accumulation of twin and adoption studies that had been completed by the year 2000 led researcher Eric Turkheimer to delineate the first three laws of behavior genetics as follows: (1) all human traits are heritable, (2) genetic effects on behavior are greater than within-family environmental effects, and (3) factors other than genes and families explain a large proportion of behavioral variability [44]. However, since Turkheimer's summation of prior research at the turn of the millennium, rapid advances in molecular genetic techniques and analysis have moved twin research into exciting new domains—and the proposal of a fourth law of behavioral genetics. The fourth law states that, "a very typical human behavioral trait is associated with many genetic variants, each of which accounts for a very small percentage of the behavioral variability [45]." This fourth law evolved naturally from what is known, and what could be known, about how genes work.

Now that genetic influence on most traits has been established, many researchers have shifted their focus toward identifying specific genes underlying intelligence, personality, and illness. Genomics, a branch of biotechnology, has become the discipline du jour of behavioral and medical geneticists everywhere. Genomics involves applying genetic and molecular genetic techniques to gene mapping (finding the precise location of genes on chromosomes) and DNA sequencing (finding the order of base pairs in a stretch of DNA). These procedures assist our understanding of the structure and functioning of the human genome (the full complement of a person's genes). The different types of genomic studies are summarized next. Twins are playing key roles in many of these efforts.

- Genome-wide association studies (GWAS). GWAS investigations are dedicated to locating genes linked to human diseases. They do so by purifying twins' DNA, placing it on tiny chips and scanning the genome for DNA variations [known as single nucleotide polymorphisms (SNPs)], found more often in people with a particular disease than without it [46]. Identical twins are valued subjects in this quest, especially discordant pairs, because a tiny DNA variant in one twin may explain why one twin gets a disease and the other twin stays healthy [47]. Hypotheses about which genes may be involved are not specified, so any number of associations can be identified. Most complex traits like intellectual ability, extroverted personality, and body weight reflect the work of many genes; hence, the fourth behavioral genetics law.

  GWAS studies gained popularity in 2005 due to reduced laboratory costs and the methodological problems of the candidate-gene approach [48]. (The candidate-gene approach, also aimed at finding associations between different DNA sequences and different traits, was criticized for using smaller samples and preselected associations.) Information about disease risk obtained from GWAS studies can be used by everyone. This type of analysis is typically done for research purposes only because thousands of twin pairs (or nontwins) are involved, but twin zygosity is routinely assessed. This procedure involves purifying twins' DNA by scanning it for selected markers [49].

The GenomEU Twin Project, established in 2002, was the uniting of European twin registries to advance research with large twin samples. The different projects capitalize on the relative genetic relatedness of MZ and DZ twins to find genetic factors linked to complex human diseases. European collaborators include scientists from Denmark, Sweden, Norway, the Netherlands, Italy, and the United Kingdom. Other collaborators include scientists from Australia, Canada, and Estonia. Targeted health concerns are stature, obesity, migraine headache, coronary heart disease, stroke, and longevity. The databases include hundreds of thousands of twin pairs [4,50].

- Genome-wide complex trait analysis (GCTA). GCTA was developed to address the "missing heritability" problem posed by GWAS studies. Missing heritability refers to the fact that the genes that have been linked to certain traits cannot account for the full genetic effect. For example, twin studies show that the genetic influence on height is about 80–90%, but a DNA change associated with height explains less than 5%. The source of the remaining 75–85% of the genetic influence is unknown, but could come from rare gene variants or interactions between certain genes and certain environments among other things [4,51].

  GCTA estimates the variance explained by all the SNPs on a given chromosome or in the whole genome (a person's full set of genes) for a particular complex trait, such as intelligence. In this way it differs from GWAS studies that test associations of particular SNPs to the trait [52]. This approach can be used with nontwin participants, such as full siblings.

- Copy number variations (CNVs). GWAS studies have detected CNVs (duplications of long sections of DNA) in the course of their analyses. CNV differences between MZ cotwins, possibly linked to observed differences between them, have defined another direction for twin researchers. Studies of MZ twins discordant for Parkinson's disease [53], schizophrenia [54], and Alzheimer's disease [55] have applied this approach. A Parkinson's disease study reported CNV differences in 19 discordant pairs, but also in 10 unaffected pairs, urging cautious interpretation of the data. In other words, some copy number variations between twins may not be relevant to a particular disease (such as Parkinson's) or to anything else. In fact, everyone, including twins and nontwins, have CNVs that appear inconsequential. And CNVs in MZ twins are generally rare [56].

• Epigenetics is another popular selection from the current genetics research menu. Epigenetics is concerned with nongenetic factors that cause changes in gene expression, but do not cause changes in the DNA sequence. For example, the addition of a methyl group to a gene silences that gene, meaning that it will not be expressed even though it is still present. Why methylation occurs in some individuals and in some contexts is due to both genetic and nongenetic factors. Histone acetylation (the addition of a DNA-packaging acetyl group to a histone protein) activates the genes.

A study in Spain showed that MZ cotwins can differ more in their epigenetic profiles as they get older, and that identical twins who see each other often show fewer epigenetic differences than those who see each other less frequently. These findings, while in need of replication, could generate new insights into behavioral and physical development [57]. In fact, attempts to reproduce these results have been unsuccessful (J. Craig, Personal communication, July 10, 2016). In addition, MZ twins' epigenetic differences must also be reconciled with the finding that MZ twins reared apart and together are equally similar on many traits [58].

Epigenetic analyses do not investigate the full genome or a person's full set of genes. Instead, they focus on epigenetic effects on particular genes that are thought to affect a trait of interest. Identical twins start to diverge in some ways even before birth because of differences in how their genes get expressed. Still, their epigenetic similarity is greater than that of fraternal twins, suggesting a genetic influence on the methylation of certain genes. Interestingly, relationships between birth weight and the expression of genes involved with metabolism and heart functioning have been found. A study of 18-month-old twins showed that infants breastfed for 4–6 months were at less risk for obesity than infants who were breastfed for less than 4 months while receiving nonbreast milk supplements. This suggests that early interactions between nutrition and the epigenome have implications for development later in life [59,60]. At the other end of the lifespan, twin research has also shown that age-related changes in a person's DNA methylation profile (DNAm—addition of a methyl group to DNA) correlate highly with chronological age. Thus, DNAm is a reliable index of the aging process [61].

Some environmental experiences affecting one generation can also leave lingering (but reversible) legacies for the next generation, via the epigenome. Women in their early stages of pregnancy who survived the 1944–45 Dutch hunger famine delivered babies with elevated diabetes-2 and obesity rates, relative to individuals not exposed to the famine [62]. Factors, such as smoking, diet, and stress have also been implicated in epigenetic changes. Maternal posttraumatic stress disorder (PTSD) has been linked to risk for PTSD in the children of Holocaust survivors, consistent with epigenetic perspectives [63]. More recently, abnormal DNA methylation was identified in the muscle samples of MZ twins with diabetes-2, but not in their unaffected cotwins [64]. Epigenetic differences between MZ male twins may also explain their differences in sexual orientation [65].

Two types of what have been termed "epimutations" have been recognized. Primary epimutations result from direct disruption of DNA methylation or histone modification, while those that are secondary are due to a genetic defect that disrupts epigenetic programming [66]. Some epigenetic effects may be reversible in current or in subsequent generations. For example, many diseases, such as cancer are linked to epigenetic changes. Treatments that alter DNA methylation or histone acetylation are an exciting medical avenue because epigenetic changes are, by nature, reversible [67].

Despite advances in molecular genetic analysis and related fields, traditional twin studies remain informative and challenging approaches to understanding human nature. Some behaviors, such as creativity, humor, and love styles, have received far less research attention than intelligence, personality, and body weight. Other traits, such as genetic links between intensity ratings of sugars and high-potency sweeteners, are being investigated for the first time [68]. Unresolved issues surrounding school separation and the effects of in vitro fertilization on the development of multiple children linger. Identical twins are also uniquely suited to addressing the psychological consequences of human reproductive cloning for individuals and families, as I will describe in Chapter 11.

Above all, I believe that observing MZ and DZ twins' behaviors up close is the best way to understand what "genetic influence on behavior" really means. Just by acting naturally, twins are superb teachers of profound nature–nurture lessons. Witnessing differences between twins always leaves me with fresh ideas about the way the environment works. Spending time with twins and their families is the best way to disprove, challenge, or avoid the mythconceptions that surround them.

CROSS-CULTURAL CONSIDERATIONS

I often turn to Martin Bulmer's classic work, *The Biology of Twinning in Man*, for facts and figures on twinning [69]. While written in 1970, this book remains an authoritative source of a lot of twin-related information. Bulmer noted the marked differences in the rate of DZ twinning across populations: 1/330 in Asian nations, 1/125 in western nations, and 1/63 in African nations. Of course, these general figures did not anticipate the natural and artificial changes in twinning rates that have occurred in western nations since the 1980s.

Natural and artificially elevated twinning rates can be tracked by comparing data from low- to middle-income and high-income nations [70]. That is because assisted reproductive technology (ART) is readily available and relatively affordable to people earning comfortable incomes. The natural MZ twinning rate of 1/250 births is constant worldwide, as I explained earlier. However, there are cross-cultural differences in DZ twinning that affect overall national rates. Among low- to middle-income countries, the African nation of Benin claims the world's highest natural twinning rate at 27.9/1000 births. However, the frequent twinning of the Yorùbá population of southwestern Nigeria is better known, not just because Yorùbán twins are venerated with rituals, statues, and status [71], but because Yorùbán twinning has been famously associated with adding large quantities of yams to their diet [72]. A recent estimate is that twins (mostly DZ) occur in 45/1000 of Yorùbán deliveries [73]. However, Nigeria lags behind Benin overall, producing twins in 19/1000 births, still a high frequency.

Twinning rates in the United States and other high-income developed nations surpassed the rates of both Benin and Nigeria at 33.7/1000 births in 2013. This figure is actually up by 2% from 2012 [74]. Fertility treatments and delayed childbearing (which increases women's chances of bearing DZ twins) explain why US twin births have doubled since 1980.

At the low end of the distribution is Vietnam with the world's lowest natural twinning rate of 6.2/1000, followed by Bolivia at 6.7/1000 [70]. Interestingly, from 1975 to 1994 the Asian nation of Japan had both very low MZ (3.74 to 4.23/1000) and DZ twinning rates (1.86 to 2.27/1000) [75]. However, the introduction of fertility treatments raised Japan's overall twinning rate to 10.37/1000 in 2008 [76].

Honoring twinship is more common in cultures where twinning rates are high than where they are relatively low. The Yoùbá people are an excellent example of how frequent twinning and celebratory events related to twinning cooccur [77]. Alessandra Piontelli, who has researched twinning attitudes around the world, noted the multitude of objects symbolizing twins found throughout Benin's central markets [78]. In contrast Japan, once a very low-twinning nation, regarded twin births as shameful and akin to nonhuman animal litters. In ancient Japan, the birth of twins was concealed and one twin was secretly given away. Views in modern-day Japan are quite different and, in fact, Japan was the second country in the world after the United States (1960) to establish a national mothers of twins club (1968) [78–79] (Some people perceive a residual aversion to twins in modern-day Japan.)

I believe the advent of ART, developed in England in 1978 and introduced in Japan in 1980, has improved current Japanese contemporary attitudes toward twinning. It turns out that since 1981, ART and advancing maternal age conspired to raise Japanese twinning rates from 5.7/1000 to 9.9/1000 deliveries in 2003. MZ twinning stabilized at 4/1000 after 1990 and while DZ twinning declined, it recovered to 4/1000 in 2007. Japan also maintains active membership in ICOMBO (International Council of Multiple Birth Organizations). Furthermore, Japanese researchers established a Center for Twin Research in Osaka in the 1980s that is currently comprised of 47 researchers. Twin study projects are also ongoing in Tokyo at Keio University, Ochanomizu University, and a special school established in 1946 to attract twins. And Japan hosted the *International Congress of Twin Studies* in Tokyo (1992) and the 4th *International Network of Twin Registries (INTR) Consortium Meeting* in Osaka (2015), both of which I was thrilled to attend. In conjunction with the 1992 congress, I visited the twins' school, met mothers of twins, learned how to put on a kimono and prepare norimake (a delicious and attractively served seaweed and rice delicacy). At the more recent 2015 consortium, I was impressed by Japan's progress in establishing twin registries and twin research projects since 1992—besides savoring sushi and sake with my new colleagues.

The dynamic twin scene in Japan is happening in lots of places as more and more researchers are using twins to test new ideas about psychology, parenting, and politics. At the same time, there is a lot of misinformation and uncertainty about some basic aspects of twins. I will begin the next chapter with one of the greatest twin mysteries of all time.

REFERENCES

[1] T.J. Polderman, B. Benyamin, C.A. de Leeuw, P.F. Sullivan, A. van Bochoven, P.M. Visscher, D. Posthuma, Meta-analysis of the heritability of human traits based on fifty years of twin studies, Nat. Genet. 47 (7) (2015) 702–709 The number of twin pairs on which the 49% value is based is actually lower because some studies used the same sets.

[2] F. Galton, The history of twins as a criterion of the relative powers of nature and nurture, J. Anthropol. Inst. 5 (1875) 391–406 Reprinted with slight revision from: Fraser's Magazine, November 1875.

[3] F. Galton, Royal Anthropological Institute of Great Britain and Ireland 6 (1876) 391-406. Reprinted with slight revision.

[4] N.L. Segal, Born together-reared apart: the landmark Minnesota twin study, Harvard University Press, Cambridge, MA, (2012).

[5] R. See Plomin, J.C. DeFries, V.S. Knopik, J.M. Neiderhiser, Behavioral Genetics, sixth ed., Worth Publishers, New York, NY, (2013).

[6] J.C. Loehlin, R.C. Nichols, Heredity, Environment, and Personality: A Study of 850 Sets of Twins, University of Texas Press, Austin, TX, (1976).

[7] J. Goldberg, M. Fischer, Co-twin control methods, in: B. Everitt (Ed.), Encyclopedia of Statistics in Behavioral Science, John Wiley & Sons, New York, NY, 2005.

[8] A. Gesell, The method of co-twin control, Science 95 (2470) (1942) 446–448.

[9] J. Orwig, These Twin Brothers Are About to Help NASA Make History, March 24, 2015. Available from: http://www.businessinsider.com/nasa-twin-study-on-scott-and-mark-kelly-2015-3

[10] D. Rosenthal, Genain Quadruplets: A Case Study and Theoretical Analysis of Heredity and Environment in Schizophrenia, Basic Books, New York, NY, (1963).

[11] A.F. Mirsky, L.E. DeLisi, M.S. Buchsbaum, O.W. Quinn, P. Schwerdt, L.J. Siever, L. Mann, H. Weingartner, R. Zec, A. Sostek, et al. The Genain quaruplets: psychological studies, Psychiatry Res. 13 (1) (1984) 77–93.

[12] T.F. McNeil, E. Cantor-Graae, D.R. Weinberger, Relationship of obstetric complications and differences in size of brain structures in monozygotic twin pairs discordant for schizophrenia, Am. J. Psychiatry 157 (2) (2014) 203–212.

[13] V.W. Hu, B.C. Frank, S. Heine, N.H. Lee, J. Quackenbush, Gene expression profiling of lymphoblastoid cell lines from monozygotic twins discordant in severity of autism reveals differential regulation of neurologically relevant genes, BMC Genom 7 (1) (2006) 118.

[14] M. Stefan, W. Zhang, E. Concepcion, Z. Yi, Y. Tomer, DNA methylation profiles in type 1 diabetes twins point to strong epigenetic effects on etiology, J. Autoimmun 50 ((May) 2014) 33–37.

[15] J.E. Littlewood, in: B. Bollobás (Ed.), Littlewood's Miscellany, Cambridge University Press, Cambridge, 1986.

[16] N.L. Segal, Indivisible by Two: Lives of Extraordinary Twins, Harvard University Press, Cambridge, MA, (2007).

[17] J. Mendle, E. Turkheimer, B.M. D'Onofrio, S.K. Lynch, R.E. Emery, W.S. Slutske, N.G. Martin, Family structure and age at menarche: a children-of-twins approach, Dev. Psychol. 42 (3) (2006) 533.

[18] I.I. Gottesman, A. Bertelsen, Confirming unexpressed genotypes for schizophrenia: risks in the offspring of Fischer's Danish identical and fraternal discordant twins, Arch. Gen. Psychiatry 46 (10) (1989) 867–872.

[19] Virtual Jerusalem, Twins Married to Twins Have Babies 20 Minutes Apart, 2015. Available from: http://virtualjerusalem.com/news.php?Itemid=17476

[20] S.A. McGuire, N.L. Segal, S.L. Hershberger, Parenting as phenotype: a behavior genetic approach to understanding parenting, Parenting 12 (2-3) (2012) 192–201.

[21] D. Reiss, J.M. Neiderhiser, E.M. Hetherington, R. Plomin, The Relationship Code: Deciphering Genetic and Social Influences on Adolescent Development, Harvard University Press, Cambridge, MA, (2000).

[22] A. Caspi, T.E. Moffitt, J. Morgan, M. Rutter, A. Taylor, L. Arseneault, et al. Maternal expressed emotion predicts children's antisocial behavior problems: using monozygotic-twin differences to identify environmental effects on behavioral development, Dev. Psychol. 40 (2) (2004) 149.

[23] H. Von Bracken, Mutual intimacy in twins, Character Pers. 2 (4) (1934) 293–309.

[24] N.L. Segal, Twin research perspective on human development, in: N.L. Segal, G.E. Weisfeld, C.C. Weisfeld (Eds.), Uniting Psychology and Biology: Integrative Perspectives on Human Development, APA Press, Washington, DC, 1997, pp. 145–173.

[25] D. Cesarini, C.T. Dawes, M. Johannesson, P. Lichtenstein, B. Wallace, Genetic variation in preferences for giving and risk taking, Q. J. Econ. 124 (2) (2009) 809–842.

[26] N.L. Segal, J.E. Munson, W.D. Marelich, A.T. Goetz, S.A. McGuire, Meeting of minds: tacit coordination in monozygotic and dizygotic adolescent and adult twins, Pers. Individ. Dif. 58 (1) (2014) 31–36.

[27] W.E. Blatz, et al. Collected Studies on the Dionne Quintuplets, University of Toronto Press, Toronto, (1937).

[28] M.D. Lemonick, It's a Miracle, Time Magazine, December 1, 1997. Available from: http://content.time.com/time/magazine/article/0,9171,987455,00.html

[29] N.L. Segal, A. Altowaiji, C.K. Ihara, The birth of octuplets: a research puzzle, Twin Res. Hum. Genet. 12 (3) (2009) 328–331.

[30] R.S. Wilson, Twins and siblings: concordance for school-age mental development, Child Dev. 48 (1) (1977) 211–216.

[31] M.C. Keller, W.L. Coventry, A.C. Heath, N.G. Martin, Widespread evidence for non-additive genetic variation in Cloninger's and Eysenck's personality dimensions using a twin plus sibling design, Behav. Genet. 35 (6) (2005) 707–721.

[32] K. Alanko, B. Salo, A. Mokros, P. Santtila, Evidence for heritability of adult men's sexual interest in youth under age 16 from a population-based extended twin design, J. Sex. Med. 10 (4) (2013) 1090–1099.

[33] N.L. Segal, J.H. Stohs, Resemblance for age at menarche in female twins reared apart and together, Hum. Biol. 79 (6) (2007) 623–635.

[34] H.N. Newman, F.N. Freeman, K.J. Holzinger, Twins: A Study of Heredity and Environment, University of Chicago Press, Chicago, IL, (1937).

[35] J. Shields, Monozygotic Twins: Brought Up Apart and Together, Oxford University Press, London, UK, (1962).

[36] N. Juel-Nielsen, Individual and Environment: Monozygotic Twins Reared Apart, 1965/1980, International Universities Press, New York, NY.

[37] N.L. Pedersen, P. Lichenstein, P. Svdberg, The Swedish Twin Registry in the third millenium, Twin Res. Hum. Genet. 5 (5) (2002) 427–432.

[38] W. Gao, B. Zhou, W. Weihua Cao, et al. Utilizing the resource of twins reared apart: their distribution across nine provinces or cities of China, Twin Res. Hum. Genet. 18 (2) (2015) 210–216.

[39] K. Hayakawa, K. Kato, M. Onoi, et al. The Japanese study of twins reared apart and growing old separately, Twin Res. Hum. Genet. 9 (6) (2006) 806–807.

[40] N.L. Segal, J.H. Stohs, K. Evans, Chinese twin children reared apart and reunited: first prospective study of co-twin reunions, Adopt. Q. 14 (1) (2011) 61–78.

[41] N.L. Segal, T.X. Tan, J.L. Graham, Twins and virtual twins: do genetic (as well as experiential) factors affect developmental risks?, J. Exp. Child Psychol. 136 (2015) 55–69.

[42] S. Dominus, The Mixed-Up Brothers of Bogotá, New York Times Magazine, July 12, 2015, pp. 34-41, 48-52, 55.

[43] N.L. Segal, Someone Else's Twin: The True Story of Babies Switched at Birth, Prometheus Books, Amherst, NY, (2011).

[44] E. Turkheimer, Three laws of behavior genetics and what they mean, Curr. Dir. Psychol. Sci. 9 (5) (2000) 160–164.

[45] C.F. Chabris, J.J. Lee, D. Cesarini, D.J. Benjamin, D.I. Laibson, The fourth law of behavior genetics, Curr. Dir. Psychol. Sci. 24 (4) (2015) 304–312.

[46] National Human Genome Research Institute, Genome-Wide Association Studies. NIH, 2015. Available from: http://www.genome.gov/20019523

[47] NIH, What Are Genome-Wide Association Studies?, 2015. Available from: http://ghr. nlm.nih.gov/handbook/genomicresearch/gwastudies

[48] C.A. Rietveld, D. Conley, N. Eriksson, T. Esko, S.E. Medland, A.A. Vinkhuyzen, B.W. Domingue, Replicability and robustness of genome-wide-association studies for behavioral traits, Psychol. Sci. 25 (11) (2014) 1975–1986.

[49] National Forensic Science Technology Center, A Simplified Guide to DNA Evidence, 2013. Available from: http://www.forensicsciencesimplified.org/dna/principles.html

[50] Department of Public Health, University of Southern Denmark, GenomEuTwin, 2013. Available from: www.sdu.dk/en/om_sdu/institutter_centre/ist_sundhedstjenesteforsk/ centre/dtr/forskningsprojekter/genomeu

[51] O. Zuk, E. Hechter, S.R. Sunyaev, E.S. Lander, The mystery of missing heritability: genetic interactions create phantom heritability, Proc. Natl. Acad. Sci. USA 109 (4) (2012) 1193–1198.

[52] J. Yang, S.H. Lee, M.E. Goddard, P. Visscher, GCTA: a tool for genome-wide complex trait analysis, Am. J. Hum. Genet. 88 (1) (2011) 76–82.

[53] C.E.G. Bruder, A. Piotrowski, A.A.C.J. Gijsbers, et al. Phenotypically concordant and discordant monozygotic twins display different DNA copy-number-variation profiles, Am. J. Med. Genet. 82 (3) (2008) 763–771.

[54] S. Maiti, K.H. Kumar, C.A. Castellani, R. O'Reilly, S.M. Singh, Ontogenetic de novo copy number variations (CNVs) as a source of genetic individuality: studies on two families with MZD twins for schizophrenia, PLoS One 6 (3) (2011) e17125.

[55] K. Szigeti, New genome-wide methods for elucidation of candidate copy number variations (CNVs) contributing to Alzheimer's disease heritability, in: S.G. Oliver, J.I. Castrillo (Eds.), Systems Biology of Alzheimer's Disease, Springer, New York, NY, 2015, pp. 315–326.

[56] A.F. McRae, P.M. Visscher, G.W. Montgomery, N.G. Martin, Large autosomal copy-number differences within unselected monozygotic twin pairs are rare, Twin Res. Hum. Genet. 18 (1) (2015) 13–18.

[57] M.F. Fraga, E. Ballestar, M.F. Paz, S. Ropero, F. Setien, M.L. Ballestar, et al. Epigenetic differences arise during the lifetime of monozygotic twins, Proc. Natl. Acad. Sci. USA 102 (30) (2005) 10604–10609.

[58] A. Petronis, I.I. Gottesman, P. Kan, et al. Monozygotic twins exhibit numerous epigenetic differences: clues to discordance?, Schizophr. Bull. 29 (2) (2003) 169–178.

[59] R. Saffery, R. Morley, J.B. Carlin, J.H.E. Joo, M. Ollikainen, B. Novakovic, et al. Cohort profile: the Peri/Post-Natal Epigenetic Twins Study, Int. J. Epidemiol. 41 (1) (2012) 55–61.

[60] H.S. Temples, D. Willoughby, B. Holaday, C.R. Rogers, D. Wueste, W. Bridges, et al. Breastfeeding and growth of children in the Peri/Postnatal Epigenetic Twin Study (PETS): theoretical epigenetic mechanisms, J. Hum. Lact. 32 (3) (2016) 481–488.

[61] L. Christiansen, A. Lenart, Q. Tan, J.W. Vaupel, A. Aviv, M. McGue, K. Christensen, DNA methylation age is associated with mortality in a longitudinal Danish twin study, Aging Cell 15 (1) (2016) 149–154.

[62] Joslin Communications, Above DNA: Epigenetics and Diabetes, July 6, 2013. Available from: http://blog.joslin.org/2013/07/above-dna-epigenetics-and-diabetes/

[63] R. Yehuda, A. Bell, L.M. Bierer, J. Schmeidler, Maternal, not paternal, PTSD is related to increased risk for PTSD in offspring of Holocaust survivors, J. Psychiatr. Res. 42 (13) (2008) 1104–1111.

[64] F. Liu, Q. Sun, L. Wang, S. Nie, J. Li, Bioinformatics analysis of abnormal DNA methylation in muscle samples from monozygotic twins discordant for type 2 diabetes, Mol. Med. Rep. 12 (1) (2015) 351–356.

[65] M. Balter, Can epigenetics explain homosexuality puzzle?, Science 350 (6257) (2015) 148.

[66] J. McCarrey, The epigenome—a family affair, Science 350 (6261) (2015) 634–635.

[67] D. Simmons, Epigenetic influences and disease, Nat. Educ. 1 (1) (2008) 6.

[68] L.D. Hwang, G. Zhu, P.A. Breslin, D.R. Reed, N.G. Martin, M.J. Wright, A common genetic influence on human intensity ratings of sugars and high-potency sweeteners, Twin Res. Hum. Genet. 19 (4) (2015) 1–7.

[69] M.G. Bulmer, The Biology of Twinning in Man, Clarendon Press, Oxford, (1970).

[70] J. Smits, C. Monden, Twinning across the developing world, PLoS One 6 (9) (2011) e25239.

[71] N.L. Segal, Art for twins: Yorùbá artists and their statues, Twin Res. Hum. Genet. 17 (3) (2014) 215–221.

[72] N.L. Segal, Entwined Lives: Twins, What They Tell Us About Human Behavior, Plume, New York, NY, (2000).

[73] B.O. Olusanya, Perinatal outcomes of multiple births in southwest Nigeria, J. Health Popul. Nutr. 29 (6) (2011) 639.

[74] J.A. Martin, B.E. Hamilton, M.J. Osterman, S.C. Curtin, T.J. Matthews, Births: final data for 2013, Natl. Vital. Stat. Rep. 64 (1) (2015) 1–65.

[75] Y. Imaizumi, K. Ninaka, The twinning rates by zygosity in Japan, 1974-1994, Acta Genet. Med. Gemellol. 48 (1) (1997) 9–22.

[76] Y. Imaizumi, K. Hayakawa, Annual trend in zygotic twinning rates and their association with maternal age in Japan, 1999–2008, Gynecol. Obstet. 3 (6) (2013) 189.

[77] A causal connection between twinning rates and cultural attitudes, while plausible, cannot be assumed. Without documentation it is prudent to assume a feedback process; see D.G. Freedman, A biological view of man's social behavior, in: W. Etkin (Ed.), Social Behavior From Fish to Man, University of Chicago Press, Chicago, 1967, pp. 152–188.

[78] A. Piontelli, Twins in the Word: The Legends They Inspire and the Lives They Lead, Palgrave MacMillan, New York, NY, (2008) Despite their widespread veneration, twins in Benin also had a mysterious "shadier" side.

[79] E.M. Bryan, The Nature and Nurture of Twins, Baillière Tindall, East Sussex, England, 1983. Available from: http://www.nomotc.org/index.php?option=com_content&task =view&id=42&Itemid=37

CHAPTER 3

Mythconceptions About Twin Conceptions—I

Consultant Gerald M. Weinberg, while riding a bus in New York City, saw a mother with six small children get on. She asked the driver the amount of the fare; he told her that the cost was one dollar, but that children under the age of five could ride for free. When the woman deposited only one dollar [for herself] into the payment slot, the driver was incredulous. "Do you mean to tell me that all your children are under five years old?" The woman explained that she had three sets of twins. The driver replied, "Do you always have twins?" "No," said the woman, "most of the time nothing happens at all." [1]

Many beliefs about the biology of twinning are plausible, but unproven. And what may appear to characterize some twins and their families does not generalize across all twin pairs or populations. I am continually stunned by the vast amount of misinformation about who has twins and why, whether or not boy–girl twins can be identical, and if it is advisable to separate twins at school. Insufficient knowledge and illogical reasoning by some professionals and the public exacerbate the problem. My purpose is practical—not to trace the source(s) of these misunderstandings, but to expose them for what they are and replace them with scientifically trusted truths, although in so doing, the origins of some mythconceptions will come to light.

I have identified all mythconceptions, misunderstandings, and beliefs with a number and a Reality Check (True, Likely, Possible, Unlikely, False). A short answer (Short Answer) is provided for readers who prefer a brief, quick take on a particular topic. However, in all cases more detailed information about each mythconception or belief will follow (More of the Story). Sometimes seemingly unrelated topics appear together in the same chapter—I did this on purpose to encourage readers to discover ideas, notions, and beliefs that they might not otherwise seek.

Twin research has exploded in the last several decades. Therefore, I have highlighted what I believe are the most significant, interesting, or surprising issues and findings. In this chapter and in Chapter 4, the focus is on issues surrounding "mythconceptions" about twin conceptions, such as the events responsible for identical twins, factors affecting twinning rates, and whether or not twins run in families. This topic is so large that I needed another chapter to cover it all (Chapter 4). Subsequent chapters explore, but are not limited to, topics, such as telling twins apart (Chapter 5), twins' complex biology (Chapter 6), twins' intellectual and language skills—and assumed telepathic connections (Chapter 7), decisions surrounding same or separate classrooms for multiple birth children (Chapter 8), what twins tell us about sex and sex differences (Chapter 9), twin research on atypical behaviors (Chapter 10), twins, clones, and unusual twin-like siblings (Chapter 11), twin spouses and extraordinary look-alikes (Chapter 12), and continuing controversies and new directions in twin research (Chapter 13). Complete citations are provided for every chapter and are available in most professional libraries and on the Internet.

1. *Scientists know what causes the fertilized egg (zygote) to divide, resulting in identical (monozygotic or MZ) twins.*
   Reality Check: False
   Short Answer: Consider the following exchange between *USA Today* science correspondent April Holladay (AH) and a concerned questioner (CQ) [2]:

   > CQ: In the case of identical twins, what triggers a single fertilized egg to result in two embryos?
   > AH: Your first question has me stumped. I've asked medical experts from various universities and hospitals. The general consensus is: we don't know.

   That conversation, which occurred in 2001, could have taken place in 1915 or in 2015. It is extraordinary that in the 100+ years since that question was posed [3], and given our ability to send humans to the moon, unravel the human genome, and transmit tweets around the world, the biological events giving rise to identical twinning remain elusive. Despite sophisticated laboratory techniques, increased twinning rates, and advances in embryology and genetics, there is no proven explanation for why a fertilized egg divides, or why some families are more likely to have identical twins than others. Virtually all the research I reviewed, and I have reviewed just about every available source, indicated as much [4,5]. However, everyone—researchers, parents, twins, and those with curious minds—are intensely interested in finding the answer to this question, so the lack of one is not for the want of trying.
   More of the Story: Many explanations for why identical twinning occurs have been proposed over the years. Several scientific reasons borrow from what we know about twinning in some nonhuman species. For

example, delaying implantation has experimentally induced MZ twinning in rabbits, and reducing intrauterine oxygen has produced MZ twins in minnows and mice, so this might also occur naturally in humans [6]. The nine-banded armadillo *(Dasypus novemcinctus)*, a New World mammal with a tough skin, only conceives *identical quadruplets*, a naturally occurring event that is associated with its characteristically delayed implantation [7]. The mulita, a small mammal common in Uruguay and Argentina and closely related to the armadillo, can produce 7–12 genetically identical offspring [8].

Other explanations for identical twinning draw upon the legends and folklore of different cultures around the world. Some Madagascans believe that twins are caused by vengeful spirits, and evoke disastrous consequences. Some Sri Lankans think that twin births are signs of female infidelity [9]. And everywhere boastful fathers argue (half-jokingly) that twins reflect male virility—I know some of these proud, if mis-informed fathers!

In the end these myths lead back to deeper scientific questions. I suspect that the increased twinning rates reported by demographers and statisticians since 1980 have prompted researchers to redouble their efforts to understand the origins of identical twins. We now have an array of explanations, all with the caveat that each requires further refinement and better evidence. Please look at the section that immediately follows.

2. *Embryologists and twin researchers are inching closer to knowing the biological events behind identical twinning, but they are not there yet* [10].
Reality Check: True
Short Answer: Biologically minded scientists have developed a plausible explanation for identical twinning, based on the early developmental arrest (temporary pause in development) of the fertilized egg. This pause could be caused by various events, including delayed implantation, possibly due to low calcium concentration in the blastocyst (again, an early structure with cells that will become the embryo). Low calcium concentration in the blastocyst may be partly linked to breastfeeding during conception, ovulation induction, and in vitro fertilization (IVF).
More of the Story: Adequate calcium concentrations in the blastocyst are needed for normal cell adhesion (attachment of cells to one another) and implantation at about day 6 or 7 after fertilization [11]. Reduced calcium concentration can reverse cell adhesion, possibly delaying implantation. This would leave the bonds between the cells weak and subject to separation—hence, identical twinning. Lactation at the time

of conception may promote calcium deficiency because women who are nursing lose approximately 210 mg of calcium each day through expressing milk.

Interestingly, there are more female than male identical twins in most populations. Female zygotes (fertilized eggs) are biologically prepared for implantation later than male zygotes, so further implantation delays would favor female twins [12]. This model would also apply to conjoined twinning, the incomplete separation or physical connection of identical cotwins, that also includes a higher proportion of females than males.

Some studies, but not all, have linked identical twinning to pregnancies occurring within 6 months of a woman stopping her oral contraception regimen [13,14]. In addition, underweight women are more susceptible to ovulatory dysfunction than average weight women when discontinuing such medication, and both delayed ovulation and ovulatory dysfunction have been associated with identical twinning [15]. However, reduced estrogen levels could also be implicated in delayed implantation, irrespective of ending oral contraceptives. This might be especially true of women approaching the premenopausal years who turn to IVF to conceive.

Assisted reproductive technologies (ARTs), such as IVF and intracytoplasmic sperm injection (ICSI—injection of a single sperm directly into an egg), have also been linked to identical twinning. A Belgian study reported a higher rate of zygotic splitting (1.88%), among women who conceived through assisted reproduction, as compared with the expected rate (0.45%). Why was that? The researchers who conducted the study suggested that disruption of the zona pellucida (the membrane surrounding the ovum prior to implantation) is one of several mechanisms that could connect assisted reproduction to increased identical twinning. Sperm must penetrate the zona pellucida for fertilization to happen, after which this membrane disappears (a process called hatching) and implantation occurs [16]. Perhaps before its disappearance, the zona pellucida splits open at its weakest point (the site of sperm penetration), embryonic material protrudes, is pinched off and doubling occurs [17]. In fact, assisted hatching (making a small hole in the zona pellucida prior to implantation) increases the risk of identical twinning after the transfer of a single 2- to 3-day-old embryo. However, identical twinning is more common among embryos transferred at 5–6 days than at 2–3 days (in the absence of assisted hatching) among women who have had prior pregnancies [18,19].

The Belgian researchers reported an even higher percentage of identical twins when ovulation induction was examined separately (7%). This study also showed that the drug clomiphene citrate (clomid) was more effective in inducing twinning than other ovulatory agents, but the researchers could not figure out why [20,21]. Interestingly, a higher proportion of the rare identical twin pairs with single amnions (inner fetal membrane) was found among twin conceptions induced by drugs or by embryo transfer, as compared with spontaneously conceived pairs. The possibility that delayed implantation allows the chorion (outer fetal membrane) and amnion to fuse has been raised, but this has not been confirmed.

The "fact" that all conjoined twins are monoamniotic (have just one shared amnion) has been cited in support of this view [15]. However, *not all conjoined twins are monoamniotic*, a mythconception I will address later in this book.

Also as discussed later in this chapter, various theories of identical twinning look at genetic factors to explain why single fertilized eggs sometimes divide into two. Perhaps a gene or system of genes explains why identical twins are plentiful in some families and absent from others. Also along genetic lines, it may be that an "inherited defect" in a protein of the zona pellucida or the process of X chromosome inactivation in females causes the cells to separate. Another idea is that an older egg from a more mature woman might lack some nutritional and energy sources, leading to developmental delay and programming errors in the developing cells. Perhaps the cells do not recognize each other due to a mutation in one twin, causing the cells to move apart, yielding identical twins [6,22].

The foregoing explanations underline an important point: there are probably many reasons why women who conceive identical twins do so [23]. I believe that each explanation proposed so far has some truth to it. I also believe that further research scrutiny of parents who conceive identical twins may hold the answers we are searching for.

3. *Identical twinning runs in some families.*
   Reality Check: Likely
   Short Answer: It is commonly believed that identical twins *do not run in families*. However, several studies conducted since the 1990s have challenged this conventional wisdom—results from these studies even challenged me. For many years I read, taught, and believed that identical twinning is a random event and that every woman is equally likely to have them. After all, the identical twinning rate is fairly uniform across countries and cultures. But new data have made me think otherwise.

Due to the new evidence, I now believe that there are subsets of families that have a genetic potential for producing identical twins. At the same time, identical twins can appear randomly in many families for reasons we cannot fully explain.

More of the Story: Swedish investigators in the late 1990s were the first to use systematically gathered population data to determine if identical twinning runs in families [24]. Their data came from two sources: the Swedish Twin Registry that recorded all twin births from 1926 to 1991, and a medical registry that covered 99% of all births since 1973. Mothers who were MZ or identical twins themselves showed a significant increase in same-sex twin births. Applying the Weinberg Differential Rule (WDR, described in Appendix 1) for estimating the proportion of identical (MZ) and same-sex fraternal (DZ) twins yielded a higher number of MZ twin births in these data than expected, based on national figures. This result suggested that MZ twinning is genetically transmitted in some, but not all, families. A possible caveat in the study's procedure is that DNA testing of the MZ twin mothers' twin children was *not* performed. In other words, we cannot say with certainty that these mothers who were studied actually delivered MZ twins—they might have conceived and delivered DZ twins—we can only say that it seems likely. If the researchers had been able to scientifically establish that the twin children were MZ, I would have found the results more compelling.

A more recent 2009 study examined twinning in seven families, each of which had produced two or more identical twin pairs. Twins in one family appeared in three consecutive generations, and twins in several other families appeared more than once in the same generation. The presence of a dominant allele (form of a gene that is expressed regardless of the other allele with which it is paired) was considered a likely explanation for this high degree of MZ twinning [25]. However, a larger number of subjects would be needed to determine the real cause of MZ twinning—and good science seeks answers to the same question from many sources. One such source includes communities with unusually high rates of identical twins where the twins, their parents, and other relatives can be studied directly. I will get to this.

4. *The MZ twinning rate is 3-4/1000 or .3-.4% worldwide.*
   Reality Check: True, but…
   Short Answer: Authoritative texts on twins tell us that MZ twinning rates are consistent worldwide. The widely quoted figure of .3-.4% (3-4 twins/1000

births) refers to broad geographical locations, rather than smaller but potentially very informative population clusters. Group photos of some of these
communities are remarkable, giving the impression that a kind of Noah's
Ark is about to set sail. Fig. 3.1 shows identical female twins, each of whom
conceived and delivered a pair of identical twins.

More of the Story: A very high incidence of MZ twinning has been
observed in some relatively isolated communities in Pakistan and Jordan.
Mohammadpur Umri, an Indian farming village surrounded by mud
walls, has an MZ twinning rate of 1/10 births or 10% [26], compared
with the worldwide MZ twinning rate of .03–.04/10 or .3–.4%. Common genes, possibly linked to MZ twinning, have been found in the
members of some of these communities.

Jordan is another country with a rich pocket of identical twins. In
2004, a report of 13 sets of MZ twins (6 male and 7 female) from a
5-generation family captured the attention of Hanan Hamamy, head of
the National Center for Diabetes, Endocrinology and Genetics in Jordan's
capital city of Amman [27]. Hamamy's study suggested a hypothetical
dominant gene that could be traced through all five generations to a
common grandfather. This hypothetical gene may have been discovered.

Figure 3.1 Identical female twins who each conceived and delivered an identical twin
pair. *(Photo courtesy: Christian Fernandes).*

In 2012, I met Dr. Bruno Reversade at the biennial meeting of the *International Society for Twin Studies*, in Florence, Italy. Reversade, from the Institute of Medical Biology in Singapore, travels around the world to meet families with multiple identical twin sets. He has now studied 17 MZ twin sets spanning the five generations of this same Jordanian family. Based on his testing of these families, it seems that the genes belonging to the *ELA* (equine lymphocyte antigen) gene system may tell us something about how identical twins can run in families. One allele (form of a gene), found among 13 of the MZ twin pairs, is active only at the blastocyst stage (when the fertilized egg becomes a hollow structure containing the inner cell mass). This raises the question: how does this gene trigger MZ twinning? Reversade could only speculate that this gene may promote growth of the inner cell mass (cells that give rise to the embryo), causing it to divide, producing identical twins. The discovery of this gene brings us closer to the answer, but also deepens the mystery of what causes MZ twinning. The fact that the gene is present in so many of the twins across generations within families is compelling evidence that MZ twinning does not always happen randomly. Perhaps other families with MZ twins share other relevant genes that are worth finding. Families that claim only one MZ twin pair in their lineage are also worth studying for the biological and/or experiential clues that might explain their multiples.

5. *China has one of the lowest twinning rates among developed nations.*
   Reality Check: True
   Short Answer: China's MZ twinning rate is lower than that of most countries for which data are available. The 1990 MZ twinning rates in urban and rural areas were 2.36/1000 and 2.11/1000, respectively [28]. The overall twinning rates (MZ and DZ twins combined) in China's urban and rural areas were 9.04/1000 and 7.06/1000, respectively. Recall that the United States' twinning rate is 33.7/1000 births. Genetic factors affecting DZ twinning most likely explain why China and other Asian nations have the lowest twinning rates worldwide; the rate of MZ twinning is fairly constant across countries worldwide.
   More of the Story: A survey of twinning in Southeastern China showed that the twinning rate remained stable between 1993 and 2005, but increased somewhat among certain subgroups, a probable reflection of fertility treatments and ARTs [29].
   Examination of 1990 data showed that DZ twinning was higher among mothers in China's urban areas than in its rural ones, with the exception of mothers between 24 and 26 years of age. This observed

DZ twinning difference was explained by the differences in economic opportunities, second marriages, and family planning in urban versus rural families. Older women, especially city dwellers, were probably more likely to benefit from assisted reproduction than women from rural areas. Women living in cities also reached menarche (first menstruation) earlier (13.5 vs. 14.4 years) and menopause later (49.5 vs. 47.5 years), on average, compared with women living outside the city, giving the city women longer periods for reproduction [29]. However, while DZ twinning has increased somewhat in China, it has been explained mostly by advanced maternal age, rather than reproductive technologies. The slight increase in DZ twinning did not alter China's overall twinning rate between 1993 and 2005. It will be fascinating to track future twinning trends in China with respect to maternal age and reproductive practices.

Note that assisted reproductive methods were first introduced in China in 1988 and their use spread quickly. Since 2008, women in both urban and rural areas have sought fertility drugs to override China's One-Child Policy, enacted in 1979, that limits urban families to one child and rural families to two [30]. However, as indicated earlier, maternal age had a greater impact on Chinese twinning rates.

China does not have the lowest overall natural twinning rate in the world. This distinction belongs to Vietnam (6.2/1000), followed closely by Bolivia (6.7/1000) [31].

6. *Women in their mid-thirties and beyond are more likely to conceive fraternal twins than younger women.*
   Reality Check: True, but…
   Short Answer: My mother conceived my twin sister and me when she was 31 years old. We were conceived naturally, before assisted reproduction was available. My parents had planned on having two children, but not at the same time. Therefore, the prospect of having twins was quite daunting to my mother and father who learned about their multiples when my mother was 5 months pregnant. And there was little family history to go by—my mother's family included only one fraternal twin pair related by marriage, not by genes, while my father's family included a biological uncle whose cotwin had died at birth and a distantly related identical female twin pair. I've always wondered if I would have had younger twin siblings had my parents wanted more children—like the woman on the bus in the scenario that opened this chapter…

   Some prospective mothers may wonder (or presume) that conceiving later in life also increases the chances of having MZ twins. It is possible that older maternal age (generally thought to affect only DZ twinning) may be implicated in some cases of MZ twinning. That is because increased MZ twinning has been associated with in vitro fertilization, possibly due to hardening of the zona pellucida (the membrane surrounding the developing egg), which is characteristic of older oocytes (primitive eggs) [23]. There does not appear to be a very strong link between older maternal age and naturally conceived MZ twins. It is, however, an established scientific fact that most women who conceive fraternal twins naturally are older, on average, than women who conceive MZ twins and singletons.

Some researchers report that the peak time for having fraternal twins is when a woman is 37 years of age [32]. Other researchers find that the average age of fraternal twin mothers is 29.3 years [33] and the average age of singleton mothers is 27.9 years. The relationship between maternal age and fraternal twinning has been explained mostly by naturally increased levels of follicle-stimulating hormone (FSH) among older women, leading to double ovulation.

Having previously given birth to other children also improves a woman's chance of bearing fraternal twins, although the older-age effect is stronger. These factors are actually confounded because older mothers have more time to bear children than younger mothers [34]. Note that fraternal twin births, as well as births in general, tend to decline after about the age of 37, possibly due to more spontaneous abortions, aging eggs, and other fertility-related events [33]. Women cannot bear children indefinitely.

More of the Story: Fraternal twinning is more frequent among older than younger mothers, as indicated previously. However, national twinning rates are sometimes presented without distinguishing between the two twin types. The peak period for twinning (MZ and DZ combined) in developed countries (based on data from England, Wales, the United States, France, and Japan) is 35–39 years; of course, the relatively older maternal age range is mostly due to DZ twin births, which occur more often. Twins occur in 6/1000 births at maternal ages under 20 years; 15/1000 births at maternal ages 35–39 years; and 7/1000 births at ages 45 years and above [35]. The decline in twinning among women at age 45+ shows that twinning is more common among women who are "older," *not* the "oldest"—the association between older maternal age and fraternal twinning eventually drops off.

There is another reason why DZ twins may be more frequent among older mothers. In what I consider to be a brilliant evolutionary-inspired theory, it may be that older moms undergo an "adaptive trade-off" [36]. We know that older women are more likely to conceive a child with a genetic defect (e.g., Down syndrome), to experience a miscarriage, or to not conceive at all, relative to younger women. Therefore, the increased tendency of older women to conceive two children at once may be nature's response to offset these disadvantages—perhaps the body does a kind of "cost-benefit analysis" in this regard. That is to say, multiple pregnancies are riskier than singleton pregnancies, but they are a way of transmitting one's genes into future generations when chances for conception are starting to dim. Women do not consciously think about such things, but their bodies might act as if these issues matter.

A study using natural fertility data from the Utah Population Database found that women bearing twins enjoy reproductive advantages relative to mothers of singletons, namely shorter average inter-birth intervals, later ages at last birth, higher lifetime fertility and lower postmenopausal mortality. That study did not distinguish between mothers of identical twins and mothers of fraternal twins, but (based on natural twinning rates) it is likely that about two-thirds of the mothers had had fraternal twins [37].

7. *DZ twinning skips generations.*
Reality Check: False
Short Answer: It is not always necessary to understand the origins of myths; still, I would love to know how this particular one got started. In my many years of twin research that include interviews with hundreds (maybe thousands) of parents and twins, I have known only one or two families in which fraternal twins appeared in one generation, then disappeared in the next, only to reappear in the generation that followed. Perhaps the problem is that families do not historically record all twin births, or simply do not recall which of their relatives had twins and what type of twins (identical or fraternal) were delivered. Failure by modern families to track twin births more closely surprises me because increased twinning rates have expanded society's twinning consciousness to a great degree. However, not knowing if your aunt's twin children or your cousin's twin uncles are identical or fraternal does *not* surprise me because twin-type testing is not routinely performed—that is another story for another chapter.
More of the Story: A 2014 *Mothers' of Twins Club Newsletter* claimed, "fraternal twin girls have twice the chance of giving birth to twins as singletons" [38]. The source of this statistic was not cited—that's how myths propagate. The truth is that it is not possible to precisely predict the twin bearers in one's family. DZ twinning *does* run in families, but the pattern of transmission across generations is unknown. Furthermore, more than one gene may be responsible for DZ twinning, making it harder to trace within families than traits linked to single genes, such as those coding for blood type and color blindness. Many factors beyond genetics, such as maternal age, ethnicity,

and coital frequency, can also affect the probability of DZ twinning [39]. Therefore, knowing who will have DZ twins within a particular family is hard to determine. If DZ twinning seems to skip generations, this could reflect genetic factors *in those families,* chance events, and/or faulty recall.

Families with more than one naturally conceived DZ twin pair are, understandably, eager for explanations about their frequency of multiple births. They often ask me if the generational-skipping hypothesis applies to them, even if the birth of twins in their family does not consistently follow that pattern. I believe the popularity of this explanation comes from its simplicity, and its ease of application to one's own family by merely observing what might occur by chance. And the idea that DZ twins in a few families jump ship in one generation and reemerge in the next shows how individual events create a universal dogma that is hard to undo.

8. *Older fathers are more likely to have twins than younger fathers.*
Reality Check: True

Short Answer: As I write, I can imagine hearing hundreds of 40+ fathers beating their chests in pride… Plenty of anecdotes indicate that twinning tendencies can be transmitted down the paternal line, and some scientific studies agree. However, the effect of older fathers on twinning is much *less* than that of older mothers.

More of the Story: Research based on more than eight million United States births showed that fathers in their 40s are more likely to have twins than younger fathers. (This study included all twins, both MZ and DZ.) However, the increase in twinning rates for fathers was less than it was for mothers—it changed by just under 1% (from 2.1% to 3.0%) for males between the ages of less than 20 and 40 or more. In contrast, the twinning rate doubled for women older than 40 years, as compared to women under 20 years, especially among Caucasian non-Hispanic females. Paternal age also had the greatest effect on twinning among Caucasian non-Hispanic males.

A study conducted in Jerusalem, Israel corroborated the older father effect on twinning, but the effect was slight and limited to opposite-sex and male-male twin pairs. No definitive reasons for these findings were offered [40]. In fact, an explanation as to why older paternal age affects twinning is unknown [41]. There are clues as to how males may affect twinning, although they are not limited to older men. An elevated level of insulin growth factor-2 (*IGF-2*) is associated with cell growth and division, and a person's *IGF-2* level is partly genetically influenced. The *IGF-2* gene inherited from one's father is active, whereas the same gene inherited from one's mother is not active. Thus, it is possible that MZ twinning is enhanced in some families by the paternally transmitted level of *IGF-2* [23].

9. *ART increases the chances of MZ twinning, as well as DZ twinning.*
   Reality Check: True
   Short Answer: The link between ART and increased twinning rates in western nations has been well documented, but the greater increase in DZ than MZ twinning has attracted much more attention. Therefore, many couples conceiving twins via ART are surprised to learn that their twins are identical. In fact, MZ twinning rates following ART are between 2 and 12 times higher than the MZ twinning rate of .3–.4% from natural conceptions [42].
   More of the Story: The two biggest factors responsible for the rise in twin births since 1980 are (1) the use of ART, and (2) delayed childbearing. Methods for assisting infertile couples are more plentiful and effective than ever before. At the same time, women are spending longer periods of time in school earning advanced degrees, and participating in the workforce before beginning their families. Of course, delaying child-bearing raises the natural DZ twinning rate because double ovulation is more common among older women. However, the interesting twist is that older women risk having fertility problems by waiting to have children, so are more likely than younger women to seek reproductive assistance. It has been estimated that the influence of ART on twinning is 2–3 times greater than the influence of delaying childbirth, although this varies across countries—the effect of ART compared with delayed childbirth is 3 times greater in Japan, equal in Hungary and New Zealand, and 50% higher in Poland [43].
   Many factors associated with ART might make the difference between bearing twins and singletons [44]. These factors include (1) the age of the egg (oocyte), (2) the specific year of treatment, and (3) the embryo's developmental stage at the time of transfer. Specifically, younger eggs are more likely to result in MZ twins. However, over the course of a 10-year study (2000–09) the MZ twinning rate declined, probably due to the implanting of fewer embryos and the use of less mature blastocysts (hollow ball of cells whose inner cell mass becomes the embryo). The selection of more mature blastocysts was associated with elevated MZ twinning.

10. *"Mirror-image" twins are physical reversals of one another.*
    Reality Check: False
    Short Answer: "Mirror-image twin" is a commonly used phrase within the twin world or "twindom" as it is sometimes called. This term is unfortunate and misleading because there is no such thing as "mirror-image twins," that is, no twins that mirror each other in every respect.

According to the 2015 *Merriam-Webster Dictionary,* a mirror image is "something that has its parts reversely arranged in comparison with another similar thing or that is reversed with reference to an intervening axis or plane" [45]. It is true, however, that about 25% of identical twins show some *form* of mirror-imaging, such as left—right handedness, opposite birthmarks or moles, clockwise–counterclockwise direction of the hair whorls, opposite fingerprint patterns, dental structures, and/or facial asymmetries. I have also seen other, even more unusual examples of mirroring in MZ twin pairs, such as cleft lip and palate. A provocative case study showing that opposite-handed identical twins sometimes solve language and spatial rotation tasks using the opposite side of the brain has been reported [46]. The members of different identical twin pairs may show some or a combination of these features, but each individual twin in a particular pair is unlikely to be a complete mirror image or physical reversal of the other twin.

Twins with opposite facial contours (e.g., the left side of one twin's face is fuller and the right side of the other twins' face is fuller) may look more like their twin when standing before a mirror than when standing next to that person. Such twins may have trouble identifying themselves in pictures because what the mirror sees is not what the camera captures.

More of the Story: The question of what causes MZ twins to show mirror-imaging effects is an unsettled one. If we accept the conventional view that *timing is everything,* then the explanation centers on zygotic splitting that occurs relatively late, after the cells have become differentiated from one another. Consequently, exact duplication of the original fertilized egg would be unlikely, leaving physical reversals in the two resulting embryos [47]. In 1996 the East Flanders Twin Study found an expected higher frequency of left-handedness (17%) among 808 twin pairs (1616 individuals twins), compared with nontwins (8–10%), but handedness was unrelated to twin type or chorion type (a presumed indicator of when the fertilized egg divides). Given these findings, the researchers concluded that, "the belief that discordant handedness in monozygotic twins represents mirror-imaging is mythical" (p. 408) [48].

Perhaps timing is *not always* everything when it comes to identical twins' development. For example, there is some evidence that identical twins with a shared (single) chorion show greater personality similarity than twins with individual (two) chorions, but chorion type appears unrelated to intellectual resemblance [49,50]. I will revisit the topic of timing in Chapter 4.

Few studies have examined postnatal environmental factors that might explain identical twins' facial asymmetries. However, a 2015 twin study found that sleeping in a prone position, having tooth extractions, wearing dentures, and smoking cigarettes were associated with identical twins' facial reversals [51]. Body asymmetries have also been linked to developmental disturbance, providing another possible or additional explanation for twins' reversed features [52]. These findings, while intriguing, require further investigation because associations are not necessarily causal in nature—perhaps existing asymmetries caused some twins to sleep in certain positions or to require dental work, rather than the other way around.

Twins and nontwins can show reversals in some internal organs (a condition called *situs inversus partialis*) or reversals in all internal organs (a condition called *situs inversus totalis*). For example, in the case of *situs inversus*, the heart (which is typically located on the left side of the body) would be located on the right side. Twins are not more prone to *situs inversus* nontwins, with the possible exception of conjoined twins who actually share some physical structures—but even conjoined twins would not be complete mirror images due to the complex developmental events that give rise to them. *Situs inversus totalis* occurs in about 6,000–8,000 births; situs anomalies are present in about 1 in 10,000 people in the United States. These conditions are usually the result of random developmental events, although a genetic effect has been found in some families [53,54].

11. *Sharing a womb makes identical twins alike.*
     Reality Check: False
     Short Answer: To speak of myths among the general public who do not always have access to the latest studies is one thing. But I am constantly surprised by how many academics mistakenly assume that MZ twins are alike because they share a womb [55]. It makes intuitive sense to suppose that sharing a womb enhances resemblance between identical twins, but the opposite is true. In fact, there are many factors working *against* MZ twin similarity, and many occur *before* or *at* the time of birth. As indicated earlier, most importantly, about two-thirds of identical twins share a placenta, which poses the dangerous risk of fetal transfusion syndrome (one-way blood circulation) and consequent differences between identical cotwins in size and health. Identical twin

differences can also be related to other features of their intrauterine environment (e.g., fetal positioning) and their mother's physical health (e.g., HIV status; see later in the chapter).

More of the Story: Partial detachment of the umbilical cord is another prenatal event that can cause identical cotwins to differ. One of the first identical twin pairs I studied as part of my doctoral research, Kelli and Missi, showed marked height discrepancies—a 5-in. difference at age 8 and a 7-in. difference as adults. The shorter twin also suffered from cardiac difficulties and a borderline seizure disorder that her twin sister did not have. Their physical differences resulted largely from the fact that the smaller twin had a marginally attached placenta (velamentous cord insertion, in which the umbilical cord inserts on the chorionic membranes, rather than the placenta [56]), depriving her of sufficient prenatal nutrition. Delivery of this twin was induced because labor had either stopped or slowed down.

It is well known that identical twins generally have similar, but not identical personalities. Along these lines, I find it both curious and surprising that MZ twins with single chorions are *more alike* in personality than those with two [57]. That is because dichorionic MZ twins are not exposed to the same prenatal stresses and strains as their single-chorion counterparts; recall that single-chorion twins are those at risk for the twin-to-twin transfusion syndrome. No one has identified the actual mechanisms behind this puzzling finding of greater personality resemblance in twins whose prenatal environments are more stressful, and to different degrees, making this an important topic for further study. However, to the contrary, monochorionic twins do *not* appear to be more alike in mental ability than dichorionic twins, complicating the story even further.

Some studies (but not all) have shown that twins born to HIV-infected mothers are not equally likely to contract the infection—the twin positioned lower in the birth canal is more highly exposed to vaginal mucosa and, therefore, at greater risk [58]. How identical twins fare regarding outcomes from HIV exposure might also come from epigenetic factors (events that affect gene expression) and unknown twin–virus interactions that could affect how the disease progresses [59]. Chorioamnionitis (inflammation of the amnion and chorion due to bacterial infection) also affects the twin located lower in the uterus, usually the firstborn [60]. And six pairs of newborn twins that include one Zika-infected cotwin and one who was spared the infection have been found in Brazil. Physicians suspect that genetic factors may explain the (presumably fraternal) cotwins' different susceptibilities. A pair featured in a recent article were fraternal (Lucas and Laura) based on their sex difference, but the twin type of the other pairs was not given [61].

There are other mythconceptions, misunderstandings, misbeliefs, and distortions regarding twins, both inside and outside the womb. When I began writing this book I knew there were many, but I did not realize that there were *so* many. This discussion continues in Chapter 4 where I focus on more mythconceptions surrounding twin conceptions.

REFERENCES

[1] G.M. Weinberg, The Secrets of Consulting: A Guide to Giving and Getting Advice Successfully (Consulting Secrets Book 1) Amazon Digital Services LLC. Copyright by Gerald M. Weinberg, 2011.

[2] A. Holladay, Wonderquest: How Eggs Split to Form Identical Twins, 2001. Available from: http://usatoday30.usatoday.com/news/science/wonderquest/2001-05-09-why-twins-form.htm

[3] A. Scheinfeld, Twins and Supertwins, J.B. Lippincott Co, Philadelphia, PA, (1967).

[4] H. McNamara, S.C. Kane, J.M. Craig, R.V. Short, M.P. Umstad, A review of the mechanisms and evidence for typical and atypical twinning, Am. J. Obstet. Gynecol. 214 (2) (2016) 172–191.

[5] M.A. Weber, N.J. Sebire, Genetics and developmental pathology of twinning, Semin. Fetal Neonatal Med. 15 (6) (2010) 313–318.

[6] J. Hall, Twinning, Lancet 362 (9385) (2003) 735–743.

[7] G. Steinman, Letter: the mechanism initiating and controlling monozygotic twinning in humans remains to be elucidated, Twin Res. 3 (4) (2000) 337.

[8] K. Benirschke, P. Kaufman, Pathology of the Human Placenta, third ed., Springer, New York, (2013).

[9] A. Piontelli, Twins in the World: The Legends They Inspire and the Lives They Lead, Palgrave MacMillan, New York, NY, (2008).

[10] K. Benirschke, Monozygotic twinning, Surg. Pathol. Clin. 6 (1) (2013) 27–32.

[11] G. Steinman, E. Valderrama, Mechanisms of twinning. III. Placentation, calcium reduction and modified compaction, J. Reprod. Med. 46 (11) (2001) 995–1002.

[12] G. Steinman, Mechanisms of twinning. IV. Sex preference and lactation, J. Reprod. Med. 46 (11) (2001) 1003–1007.

[13] D.C. Macourt, P. Stewart, M. Zaki, Multiple pregnancy and fetal abnormalities in association with oral contraceptive usage, Aust. N Z J. Obstet. Gynaecol. 22 (1) (1982) 25–28.

[14] C. Hoekstra, Z.Z. Zhao, C.B. Lambalk, G. Willemsen, N.G. Martin, D.I. Boomsma, G.W. Montgomery, Dizygotic twinning, Hum. Reprod. Update 14 (1) (2008) 37–47.

[15] G. Steinman, Mechanisms of twinning. V. Conjoined twins, stem cells and calcium model, J. Reprod. Med. 47 (4) (2002) 313–321.

[16] Zona Pellucida. Available from: http://www.medicinenet.com/script/main/art.asp?articlekey=11822

[17] M.H. Kaufman, The embryology of conjoined twins, Childs Nerv. Syst. 20 (8-9) (2004) 508–525.

[18] J.R. Kanter, S.L. Boulet, J.F. Kawwass, D.J. Jamieson, D.M. Kissin, Trends and correlates of monozygotic twinning after single embryo transfer, Obstet. Gynecol. 125 (1) (2015) 111.

[19] Fertility Authority, Assisted Hatching IVF. Available from: https://www.fertilityauthority.com/fertility-treatment/vitro-fertilization-ivf-explained/assisted-hatching-ivf

[20] M. Alikani, N.A. Cekleniak, E. Walters, J. Cohen, Monozygotic twinning following assisted conception: an analysis of 81 consecutive cases, Hum. Reprod. 18 (9) (2003) 1937–1943.

[21] C. Derom, F. Leroy, R. Vlietinck, J.-P. Fryns, R. Derom, High frequency of iatrogenic monozygotic twins with administration of clomiphene citrate and a change in chorionicity, Fertil. Steril. 85 (3) (2006) 755–757.

[22] L. De Gregorio, H.A. Jinnah, J.C. Harris, W.L. Nyhan, D.J. Schretlen, L.M. Trombley, J.P. O'Neill, Lesch–Nyhan disease in a female with a clinically normal monozygotic twin, Mol. Genet. Metabol. 85 (1) (2005) 70–77.

[23] G. Steinman, Mechanisms of twinning. VI. Genetics and the etiology of monozygotic twinning in in vitro fertilization, J. Reprod. Med. 48 (8) (2003) 583–590.

[24] P. Lichtenstein, P.O. Olaussen, A.B. Källén, Twin births to mothers who are twins: a registry based study, Br. Med. J. 312 (7035) (1996) 879–881.

[25] G. Machin, Familial monozygotic twinning: a report of seven pedigrees, Am. J. Med. Genet. Semin. Med. Genet. 151c (2) (2009) 152–154.

[26] D. Cyranoski, Developmental biology: two by two, Nature 458 (7240) (2009) 826–829.

[27] H.A. Hamamy, H.K. Ajlouni, K.M. Ajlouni, Familial monozygotic twinning: report of an extended multi-generation family, Twin Res. 7 (3) (2004) 219–222.

[28] J.P. Gan, Z.H. Wu, Z.M. Tu, J. Zheng, The comparison of twinning rates between urban and rural areas in China, Twin Res. Hum. Genet. 10 (4) (2007) 633–637.

[29] X. Lu, J. Zhang, Y. Liu, T. Wang, Y. Lu, Z. Li, Epidemiology of twin births in southeast China: 1993–2005, Twin Res. Hum. Genet. 16 (2) (2013) 608–613.

[30] K. Evans, The Lost Daughters of China, Jeremy P. Tarcher/Putnam, New York, (2000).

[31] J. Smits, C. Monden, Twinning across the developing world, PLoS One 6 (9) (2011) e25239.

[32] N.G. Martin, G. Montgomery, Do Genes Influences Whether Someone Has Twins, Either Identical or Fraternal?, March 18, 2002. Available from: http://www.scientificamerican.com/article/do-genes-influence-whethe/

[33] O. Bomsel-Helmreich, W.A. Mufti, The mechanism of monozygosity and double ovulation, in: L.G. Keith, D.M. Keith (Eds.), Multiple Pregnancy: Epidemiology, Gestation and Perinatal Outcome, Parthenon Publishing Group, New York, 1995, pp. 25–40.

[34] I. MacGillivray, M. Samphier, J. Little, Factors affecting twinning, in: D.M. MacGillivray, B. Campbell, Thompson (Eds.), Twinning and Twins, John Wiley Sons, Chichester, England, 1988, pp. 67–97.

[35] G. Pison, C. Monden, J. Smits, Twinning rates in developed countries: trends and explanations, Popul. Dev. Rev. 41 (4) (2015) 629–649.

[36] L.S. Forbes, The evolutionary biology of spontaneous abortion in humans, Trends Ecol. Evol. 12 (11) (1997) 446–450.

[37] D.L. Robson, K.R. Smith, Twinning in humans: maternal heterogeneity in reproduction and survival, Proc. R. Soc. Lond. (Biol.) 278 (125) (2011) 3755–3761.

[38] York White Rose. Interesting Facts About Twins, 2014.

[39] N.L. Segal, Entwined Lives: Twins and What They Tell us About Human Behavior, Plume, New York, (2000).

[40] K. Kleinhaus, M.C. Perrin, O. Manor, Y. Friedlander, R. Calderon-Margalit, S. Harlap, D. Malaspina, Paternal age and twinning in the Jerusalem Perinatal Study, Eur. J. Obstet. Gynecol. Reprod. Biol. 141 (2) (2008) 119–122.

[41] E.L. Abel, M.L. Kruger, Maternal and paternal age and twinning in the United States, 2004–2008, J. Perinat. Med. 40 (3) (2012) 237–239.

[42] K.I. Aston, C.M. Peterson, D.T. Carrell, Monozygotic twinning associated with assisted reproductive technologies: a review, Reproduction 136 (4) (2008) 377–386.

[43] J.A. Martin, B.E. Hamilton, M.J. Osterman, Three Decades of Twin Births in the United States, 1980-2009, US Department of Health and Human Services, Centers for Disease Control and Prevention, National Center for Health Statistics, NCHS Data Brief, No. 80, Hyattsville, MD, (2012) Pison et al. (2015).

[44] J.M. Knopman, L.C. Krey, C. Oh, J. Lee, C. McCaffrey, C.N. Noyes, What makes them split? Identifying risk factors that lead to monozygotic twins after in vitro fertilization, Fertil. Steril. 102 (1) (2014) 82–89.

[45] Available from: http://www.merriam-webster.com/dictionary/mirror%20image

[46] I.E.C. Sommer, N.F. Ramsey, A. Bouma, R.S. Kahn, Cerebral mirror-imaging in a monozygotic twin, Lancet 354 (9188) (1999) 1445–1446.

[47] G. Steinman, Mechanisms of twinning: II. Laterality and intercellular bonding in monozygotic twinning, J. Reprod. Med. 46 (5) (2001) 473–479.

[48] C. Derom, E. Thiery, R. Vlietinck, R. Loos, R. Derom, Handedness in twins according to zygosity and chorion type: a preliminary report, Behav. Genet. 26 (4) (1996) 407–408.

[49] D.K. Sokol, C.A. Moore, R.J. Rose, C.J. Williams, T. Reed, J.C. Christian, Intrapair differences in personality and cognitive ability among young monozygotic twins distinguished by chroion type, Behav. Genet. 25 (5) (1995) 457–466.

[50] N. Jacobs, S. Van Gestel, C. Derom, E. Thiery, P. Vernon, R. Derom, R. Vlietinck, Heritability estimates of intelligence in twins: effect of chorion type, Behav. Genet. 31 (2) (2001) 209–217.

[51] M.T. Liu, R.A. Iglesias, S.S. Sekhon, Y. Li, K. Larson, A. Totonchi, B. Guyuron, Factors contributing to facial asymmetry in identical twins, Plast. Reconstr. Surg. 134 (4) (2014) 638–646.

[52] L. Mealey, R. Bridgstock, G.C. Townsend, Symmetry and perceived facial attractiveness: a monozygotic co-twin comparison, J. Pers. Soc. Psychol. 76 (1) (1999) 157–165.

[53] S. Silva, Y. Martins, A. Matias, I. Blickstein, Why are monozygotic twins different?, J. Perinat. Med. 39 (2) (2011) 195–202.

[54] Z. Abbasi, Situs Inversus Totalis, 2013. Available from: http://situsinversustotalis.com

[55] R.E. Nisbett, Intelligence and How to Get it: Why Schools and Cultures Count, W.W. Norton, New York, (2009).

[56] Vasa Previa Foundation, Velamentous Cord Insertion. Available from: Vasaprevia.com

[57] D.K. Sokol, C.A. Moore, R.J. Rose, C.J. Williams, T. Reed, J.C. Christian, Intrapair differences in personality and cognitive ability among young monozygotic twins distinguished by chorion type, Behav. Genet. 25 (5) (1995) 457–466.

[58] D.J. Jamieson, J.S. Read, A.P. Kourtis, T.M. Durant, M.A. Lampe, K.L. Dominguez, Cesarean delivery for HIV-infected women: recommendations and controversies, Am. J. Obstet. Gynecol. 197 (3) (2007) S96–S100.

[59] L. Tazi, H. Imamichi, S. Hirschfeld, J.A. Metcalf, S. Orsega, M. Pérez-Losada, et al. HIV-1 infected monozygotic twins: a tale of two outcomes, BMC Evol. Biol. 11 (1) (2011) 62.

[60] N. Martin, D. Boomsma, G. Machin, A twin-pronged attack on complex traits, Nat. Genet. 17 (4) (1997) 387–392.

[61] G. Alheri, Zika Twins With One Microcephalic Baby Offering Clues to Doctors in Brazil, July 6, 2016. Available from: http://latino.foxnews.com/latino/health/2016/07/06/zika-twins-with-only-one-microcephalic-baby-offering-clues-to-doctors-in-brazil/

CHAPTER 4

Mythconceptions About Twin Conceptions—II

This chapter further explores some of the topics I discussed in Chapter 3, such as the various arrangements of twins' placentae and what causes the different types of twins. Some new subjects are also examined, including whether or not eating yams is linked to fraternal twinning, and the nature and frequency of vanishing twins.

1. *The time at which the fertilized egg (or zygote) divides determines whether identical twins have single or shared fetal membranes (amnions and chorions) and placentae.*
   Reality Check: Likely
   Short Answer: Nearly everyone—from physicians to families—claims that timing of the zygotic split is everything when it comes to identical twins' type of placentation (one placenta or two). I used to think so, too. However, I have become more cautious after looking at some revealing historical papers that strongly challenge this view [1]. I would now say that timing is *probably* everything. I miss the days when the timeline for twins' placental arrangements seemed certain—that is, when zygotic splitting before day 4 meant two placentae, and splitting after day 12 meant one—but it is exciting to have old notions challenged and fresh ideas proposed.

   We know that MZ twin pairs can have two chorions, two amnions, and two placentae—or they can have a single chorion and single placenta and two separate amnions—or (in rare cases) they can share a single chorion, amnion, and placenta. We also know that most DZ twins have two separate placentae, but the placentae fuse in nearly 50% of the pairs [2,3].

   Most professional and popular sources on multiple birth indicate that early splitting (within about the first 3 or 4 days after conception) produces MZ twins with two chorions and two amnions; later splitting (between 5 and 8 days after conception) produces MZ twins with one chorion and two amnions; and even later splitting (between 9 and 12–14 days after conception) produces the very rare MZ twins with just one chorion and one amnion. (These different outcomes were

Twin Mythconceptions
http://dx.doi.org/10.1016/B978-0-12-803994-6.00004-4

displayed in Chapter 1; Fig. 1.1.) However, this sequence of events is *theoretical, not proven*—it is inferential, based on what is known about the sequence of embryological events, but it is viewed as factual because it seems so plausible. Currently, it is impossible to insert a camera into the womb to capture these early events, or to even know in advance that a particular woman would conceive identical twins.

More of the Story: The Spanish physician Gonzalo Herranz calls the conventional MZ twinning/timing events introduced previously "the model," and urges serious rethinking of what actually happens [1]. The history of how this model developed is an insightful look at how the scientific process produces tentative findings that turn into "truth." The events responsible for this outcome are sometimes beyond investigators' control.

Herranz's fascinating discussion of the older twin literature traces how MZ twinning events (which no one has actually witnessed) came to be regarded as scientific truth. He cites a 1922 paper by researcher George W. Corner in which Corner introduced the idea of timing as possibly significant in the origins and placentation of MZ twins. However, Corner did not consider timing with regard to double chorion–double amnion (DC–DA) MZ twins because at that time it was believed that DC–DA twins were always fraternal or DZ twins.

Subsequent to Corner's work, but also in the 1920s, the German scientist Hermann W. Siemens showed that some MZ twins could be DC–DA, a discovery that required refinement of Corner's efforts. Then, in the early 1930s, the German investigator Helmut von Vershuer suggested that early zygotic splitting could produce DC–DA MZ twins. Following further developments, Corner authored a 1955 paper, addressing associations between the timing of the split and placental outcomes, while still acknowledging the theoretical nature of his MZ twinning model. Nevertheless, the model came to be regarded as fact in the years that followed, despite the absence of direct observation.

When events seem reasonable and rational we tend to regard them as facts—not just events in the world of science, but also the events happening in our daily lives. When our cars break down in the snow or we do poorly on an exam we blame it on the storm or a lack of sleep, when the actual explanations for these events could be very different. Perhaps our car stopped working because we failed to take it in for check-ups or we failed the exam because we spent more time in the local pub than at the college library. Humans have an inherent tendency to impose order and structure on their experiences and observations, even those that are not seen directly.

Herranz explains the transition from speculation to science by three key factors that worked together in sync: (1) Corner was a prestigious researcher with many well-respected achievements; (2) the model was plausible; and (3) Corner's original diagram and adaptations made the model seem correct to his colleagues.

As I indicated earlier, I now believe that timing probably explains everything when it comes to when the zygote splits, and what the chorions, amnions, and placentae look like. Science makes inferences based on available data and the weight of evidence favors Corner's work. Still, there could be unknown and/or unimagined events inside or outside the uterus that could trigger or hasten the formation of identical twins. Scientists cannot pinpoint the exact day that splitting results in one placenta or two, or one amnion or two; instead, most physicians and researchers reference a range, as indicated earlier.

I applaud Herranz's interest in telling the most truthful story about twins' earliest prenatal days. I believe his views should be taken seriously and that everyone can benefit from closer attention to MZ twins' unique and exquisite embryology. Some researchers have done so, suggesting that because "splitting" is not witnessed in the laboratory, the word (splitting) should be replaced by one that better captures the MZ twinning event. That is an interesting idea that may steer us closer to the truth. I would suggest "separation," "replication," or possibly "doubling," with the caveat that the resulting products are not two exact copies.

2. *Identical twins share exactly 100% of their alleles or gene forms.*
Reality Check: Unlikely
Short Answer: Similar to the myth of mirror-image twins, identical twins are not identical in every respect, even with regard to their genes. Some of my colleagues would like to replace the label "identical" with "monozygotic," a practice I favor. However, I realize it would be difficult to abandon the term "identical" given its greater simplicity than "monozygotic," as well as its widespread usage [4]. (I have used the term "identical" throughout this book for these reasons.) If we continue to call monozygotic twins "identical" then it should be done with the knowledge that these twins are not completely identical—no pair is.
More of the Story: Theoretically, identical twins *should* share 100% of their genes, having originated from the same fertilized egg. Some identical cotwins may actually place in this category, but they would be very rare

exceptions because of the wide range of biological events that move identical twins away from strict genetic and physical identity. Some of these events, introduced in Chapters 1–3, are examined along with others in greater detail next.

Somatic mutations are single gene changes that occur spontaneously, usually in one twin, but not the other. A change in the gene labeled *SCN1A,* for example, was found in one identical twin of a pair, causing that twin to have a rare form of epilepsy known as Dravet's syndrome. These twins had no family history of this condition [5].

A related event is *paradominant inheritance*, which occurs when a gene linked to an illness or disease is transmitted across family generations, but is not expressed for years. Then, like a bad cold or an annoying relative, it shows up unannounced. I was intrigued by a case report in which only one identical twin was affected with Klippel–Trénaunay syndrome. Individuals with this condition have capillary malformations that often affect the lower extremities, and cause enlargement of bones and soft tissue. In this case it seemed that both twins inherited a single copy of the gene from one parent, yet two copies are needed in order to have the condition. Apparently, a mutation in one twin transformed a healthy gene into this harmful one, giving her two copies, thus causing her to have the disorder [6,7].

Copy number variations (CNVs) are long sections of DNA that are duplicated for unknown reasons and could differ between cotwins if they occur *after* the fertilized egg divides. CNV differences (long sections of duplicated DNA) have been linked to disease differences between identical twins (e.g., schizophrenia and Parkinson's disease), as I explained in Chapter 2. CNV differences in an identical twin pair have also been linked to differences in attentional behaviors. In fact, the twin who had the high attention problem score had CNVs that tended to overlap with genes associated with attention deficit hyperactivity disorder (ADHD) and autism [8]. However, CNV differences between MZ cotwins are generally rare—it is only when MZ cotwins differ in a specific illness or trait that the CNVs may contain the genes underlying the difference [9].

Genomic imprinting is a process in which the expression of a child's gene is affected by whether the mother or the father passed along that particular form of the gene or allele. In some cases, a gene from the father may be active (expressed in a child), but the same gene or allele would be inactive (not expressed in a child) if it came from the mother. Of course, identical twins receive the same genes from both parents, but errors in their expression can cause differences between them.

Beckwith–Wiedemann syndrome (BWS) is a particularly interesting condition related to imprinting and to twins. Affected infants and children grow longer and taller than their peers, but their growth slows down by age 8 so as adults they are not unusually tall. Some children affected with BWS show abnormally large growth in some parts of their body, on one side or the other, and 10% may be at increased risk for cancers and tumors [10]. About 20% of children with BWS inherited a particular gene from their father that is active in these children.

The incidence of female identical twins with this condition is higher than that of the general population, suggesting that there could be a relationship between twinning and BWS; however, a relationship between BWS and twinning is not proven. More intriguing, most identical twins with BWS *do not* have an affected twin brother or twin sister—in one study, five affected twins had an imprinting defect that their unaffected cotwins did not have. It is possible that an imprinting defect occurred at a critical moment before implantation, and that the defect caused the fertilized egg to divide, resulting in MZ twins. Alternately, it is possible that whatever caused the fertilized egg to divide also caused one twin to have a defect in the BWS gene [11,12].

I actually corresponded with Dr. Beckwith by email on a different twin-related matter—that is coming up in this chapter—when I discovered his connection to this disorder. Perusing his resume, I saw that many of his publications concerned BWS, and when I asked him if this syndrome was named partly for him he replied, "Guilty as charged."

3. *Fraternal twins always have two chorions or outer fetal membranes.*
    Reality Check: False
    Short Answer: The great part about scientific inquiry and analysis is that new findings rattle old notions. This is exciting, but can also be disconcerting for researchers who must rethink existing explanations and propose fresh answers. As a result of this process, the long held belief that fraternal twins *always* have two separate chorions (outer cell membranes) is no longer tenable. Single-chorion (monochorionic) fraternal twins have been identified, but are probably rare because several large twin studies have detected only identical twins among the monochorionic pairs [13,14]. (Chorionicity can be detected by ultrasound at about 11–12 weeks gestation). But as I suspected, single-chorion DZ twins *are* more frequent in occurrence than researchers anticipated—a recent

review included 20 such cases [15] and 2 recent reports highlighted these exceptions to the "DZ two-chorion rule."

More of the Story: I value case reports because they go into great depth when it comes to individual cases, providing details that can generate new ideas about human conditions. A case study of a naturally conceived DZ twin pair reported that a 6-week ultrasound scan of these twins revealed one chorion and two amnions [16]. A second scan performed at 20 weeks confirmed these initial findings, but also showed a male and female fetus, inconsistent with MZ twinning. The twins, delivered at 37 weeks gestation, were healthy, although the female twin showed ambiguous genitalia (genitals that did not clearly identify her as male or female). Chimerism (the presence [in one individual] of cells originating from two different individuals) was also detected. In the case of fraternal twins, this may result from prenatal blood exchange. In fact, analysis of DNA derived from these twins' blood samples classified them as MZ with 99.9% probability. However, further DNA studies determined that the twins were, in fact, DZ.

In a second case study, a pair of naturally conceived twins showed a single chorion at 12 weeks, 19 weeks, and upon placental analysis after delivery at 37 weeks [17]. Given this evidence, the twins' parents were informed by hospital personnel that their male twins were identical. However, the family contacted the hospital when the twins turned 14 months old because of their sons' marked difference in physical appearance. Additional DNA testing confirmed that the twins were fraternal. (It is important to pay attention to parents!) In a third case (the first pair of monochorionic DZ twins identified in South Korea), the blood type of a male twin from an opposite-sex pair was wrongly diagnosed at birth. It turned out that this male twin carried a mixture of his own blood and the blood of his twin sister. These twins were conceived by in vitro fertilization-preembryo transfer (IVF-ET; preembryos refer to fertilized eggs that are in the stage between fertilization and implantation) [18]. Clearly, researchers are recognizing this unique class of fraternal twins that come with single chorions. How many more are out there is a tantalizing question. In 2016, my colleague, Jeffrey Craig at the Murdoch Childrens Hospital in Melbourne, Australia, identified three fraternal twin pairs out of 70 monochorionic sets, or 4.3% (Dr. J. Craig, Personal communication, July 16, 2016). More studies like this are needed.

What causes some DZ twins to have single chorions is speculative at this time. Fusion or partial fusion of the blastocysts (the hollow cell structures giving rise to the embryo) are possible mechanisms that may be involved. These mechanisms may be more likely to occur in assisted rather than natural conceptions [17,19].

4. *Twins conceived by assisted reproduction are more likely to have birth defects than those conceived naturally.*

Reality Check: Likely

Short Answer: There is some evidence that twins with two chorions, conceived by assisted reproductive technology (ART), are more likely to show birth defects than twins conceived naturally. Among these birth defects are cardiac difficulties (e.g., opening in the wall that divides the two upper chambers of the heart), musculoskeletal problems (e.g., foot and spine deformities), and urogenital abnormalities (e.g., hypospadias, in which the urethra or tube that drains urine from the bladder and body is on the underside of the penis) [20]. Aside from birth defects, ART twins have lower birth weights, but they do not show increased levels of problem behaviors, relative to naturally conceived twins.

More of the Story: Not all ART twins are destined to show birth defects—and the same birth defects found in ART twins have been found in naturally conceived twins and singletons. ART techniques have improved greatly over the years, increasing the likelihood of successful pregnancies and healthier infants.

Interestingly, fraternal twins conceived by ART have been found to resemble one another less often than naturally conceived fraternal twins in the areas of birth weight, internalizing behaviors (negative behaviors directed toward the self such as blame or anger), and antisocial behaviors, as rated by their parents. Their reduced resemblance may reflect greater differences in the preimplantation environments of ART twins (ART twins originate from embryos created and manipulated in laboratories), as compared to their naturally conceived counterparts [21].

Individuals engaging in research may wish to consider the biological origins of their fraternal twin participants [21]. Suppose that a classic identical–fraternal twin comparison of intelligence or personality were conducted and the fraternal group included a relatively high proportion of ART twin pairs who were less alike than non-ART pairs. It is, therefore, conceivable that these fraternal twin pairs could be much more different in weight or personality or problem behavior, compared with naturally conceived fraternal twins. Because greater genetic influence is indicated by a greater degree of difference between fraternal than identical twins, genetic influence might be inflated or exaggerated in this case [22].

The greatest benefit of ART, of course, is that when the procedure is effective it allows infertile couples to start families from their own bloodlines. No wonder that one successful mother of ART twins, Evan and Trevor, preferred the names: *Heaven and Treasure* [23].

5. *DZ twinning is influenced by yam consumption.*
   Reality Check: Likely
   Short Answer: Myths sometimes work in surprising ways. So far, some of the myths I have listed and discussed seemed logical at first, but were unlikely or untrue. However, I was shocked to discover that a widespread belief I had always regarded as untrue turned out to be pretty likely.

   A meaningful relationship between yam consumption and the high fraternal twinning rate among the Yorùbá people of southwestern Nigeria has been observed since the 1970s [24]. At first, it seemed hard to believe that an edible tuber could be implicated in the twinning frequency of a population—but the data and my conversation with New York University physician Fred Naftolin convinced me that it is likely. Note that the yam in question is the white yam (locally called *isu* [25]), common to Africa, not the golden variety typically served at Thanksgiving dinners, embellished with marshmallows, brown sugar, and/or brandy. In Nigeria, the white yam is commonly mashed and mixed with palm oil to form *fufu*, but is prepared in many forms and eaten regularly in this region [26].

   It is thought that the white yam has fertility-inducing properties. One possibility is that it fools the body into thinking that a woman's estrogen is low, causing the release of follicle-stimulating hormone (FSH) to promote ovulation.

   The Yorùbá people celebrate twins in many ways as I described in Chapter 1. Many different carved wooden figures have been created specially for this purpose (Fig. 4.1).
   More of the Story: The hormonal effects of the white yam have been seen in a study of rats, in that yam consumption causes the animals' FSH levels to rise (Dr. F. Naftolin, Personal communication, 2015). If true, this theory would agree with the finding that Yorùbán women bearing more than two twin pairs show elevated FSH levels, relative to those who deliver just one pair; and that women bearing one twin pair have higher FSH levels than those having singletons. Consistent with these findings, twinning rates are higher among lower socioeconomic Yorùbán women whose diets include higher proportions of the white yam, which they eat up to 4 times/day. Conversely, Yorùbán twinning rates have dropped when people moved from rural to urban areas and their diets became more westernized [27,28].

Figure 4.1 *These figures are from the exhibit,* **Double Fortune, Double Trouble: Art for Twins Among the Yorùbá.** *(Courtesy of the Fowler Museum at UCLA, displayed October 13, 2013–March 2, 2014. Photo credit: Josh White/JWPictures.com).*

I discussed the effects of the white yam on twinning with Dr. Fred Naftolin, from the Department of Obstetrics and Gynecology at New York University's Langone Medical Center. Naftolin and his student Obinwanne Ugwonali have studied factors affecting the high rate of DZ twins and triplets among the Yorùbá. Naftolin noted that women with dominant follicles (mature sacs that release an egg), as opposed to primordial follicles (sacs that may either mature and release an egg, or die away) [29], are more likely to conceive fraternal twins. Having dominant follicles can be interpreted as a stable condition, meaning that Yorùbán women maintain them throughout their reproductive periods. According to Naftolin, this situation would be consistent with the "string of multiple births" produced by some Nigerian women—some mothers produce eight or nine children from just three or four pregnancies.

Naftolin also explained that the reasons women vary in follicle type are unknown, but could be due to either genetic or epigenetic events. He also noted that aromatase (a substance converting androgens to estrogens), has a unique composition—three different forms of aromatase are found in Nigerian women, but only one form is found among Asian populations whose twinning rates are the lowest in the world. Of course, some of these findings are preliminary and require replication. Furthermore, the mechanism linking yams and twins has not been identified—but perhaps yam consumption augments the predisposition toward DZ twinning associated with the variety of estrogens that have been detected.

As I described in Chapter 1, DZ twinning has been associated with many factors. Rasak Tijani, Medical Director of Nigeria's Olugbon Hospital, disputes the yam's effects in favor of a genetic explanation of the high Yorùbán twinning rate. Tijani has claimed that residents of other Nigerian areas follow the same diet and culture, yet do not show the elevated twinning rate characteristic of the Yorùbá [30]. His view strikes me as impressionistic rather than research-based; however, I believe that both genetic *and* dietary factors could be implicated in twinning among the Yorùbán people.

An ideal study would introduce large quantities of white yams into the diets of non-Yorùbán women and monitor their tendencies toward twinning. (This study, as well as Naftolin's demographic, epidemiological, and genomic research on Yorùbán multiple births, were being prepared as a review at the time of this writing.) But caveat emptor! Suddenly eating large quantities of yams to conceive DZ twins may prove futile, given the many factors affecting DZ twin conceptions. Based on research done so far,

Yorùbán women appear to have a unique biological makeup, in addition to a unique diet that they have maintained for many years. As I write this I am aware that it is November 24, 2016, the United States' Thanksgiving holiday. I wonder how many women will order sweet potatoes along with their turkey, hoping for a double delivery in the New Year.

6. *Beyond yams: some dietary regimens increase the chances of conceiving DZ twins.*
Reality Check: Possible
Short Answer: Dietary supplements are often a source of controversy with regard to their health benefits, yet several studies have suggested that various food and vitamin regimens boost fraternal twin conceptions [31]. Women taking folic acid (a synthetic version of the naturally occurring folate, that is somewhat different chemically) and conceiving by IVF seem to show an increased rate of twinning, relative to those who do not take it. However, some researchers suspect that other factors, such as maternal age, are really causing this relationship, so additional research is needed [32].

The regular consumption of dairy products has been found to increase fraternal twinning by quite a bit [33,34]. In contrast, vegans (individuals whose diets do not include protein-rich animal products), show relatively low twinning rates. Some vegans rely largely on soy products, beans, and/or legumes for nutrition, so are likely to consume less protein than meat eaters [35].

These findings may sound encouraging to women wishing to add twins to their family, but I advise caution before changing one's diet in hopes of twinning success. Dietary findings apply to groups, not to all individuals in those groups. Women who, based on their diet, seem destined to deliver twins may be disappointed, and women such as vegans who seem unlikely to have twins may be surprised. Simply consuming large quantities of dairy products does not guarantee twins, nor does giving up meat predict singletons. Perhaps a touch of uncertainty makes family planning that much more intriguing—but for women who really want to have twins, it may be wise to follow better documented routes, for example, IVF and conception at a later age.

More of the Story: Dietary practices and twinning do not begin and end with dairy, vitamins, and meat—there's more. In particular, folate metabolism has been associated with twinning, and folate metabolism is affected by certain genes, for example, TT and CT. Therefore, the specific genes that a woman carries can make a difference between her having or not having twins. Chinese populations show a high occurrence of the TT genotype (presence of two T alleles) and a low frequency of DZ twinning. In contrast, Hungarian populations show a low frequency of the TT genotype (11%), as well as a higher frequency of the CT genotype (45%) and a higher frequency of DZ twinning. Among Hungarian women, the proportion of twin pregnancies was 1.52% among mothers who took postconception folic acid, a multivitamin, and folic acid plus multivitamin supplements—higher than the .78% found among mothers who did not take them [36]. However, subsequent studies have produced mixed evidence on the contributions of folic acid to twinning [32].

A benefit of folic acid taken during pregnancy is that it tends to reduce the chances of spinal defects in the newborn. One such condition is spina bifida which involves failure of the neural tube to close [37].

Consuming relatively higher quantities of dairy products appears to raise DZ twinning rates. (Exactly how much dairy food must be consumed to make a difference is unknown and, presumably, varies across individuals.) It is, therefore, worth noting that vegans show lower levels of *IGF-1* (insulin-like growth factor which is associated with early growth and development) than meat eaters. Soy, a food commonly consumed by vegans, has a lower protein content than milk.

It has also been noted that recombinant growth hormone is given to cattle in the United States (to increase meat and milk production), but not to cattle in the United Kingdom. This is important because twin births have increased in the United States to a greater degree than in the United Kingdom, with rates of 33.9/1000 (US, 2014) and 15.6/1000 (England and Wales, 2012) [38,39].

The availability of limited quantities of food can lower twinning rates, possibly reflecting lower maternal *IGF-1* levels [34]. Using preindustrial data from 1752–1850, a lower incidence of twinning was found on the Finnish mainland, compared with the archipelago formed by the islands of Åland and Åboland. The greater abundance and stability of food sources on the archipelago than on the mainland may have been responsible [40]. Of course, an ample diet and level of body fat are required for conception generally.

The foregoing findings are interesting, important, provocative—and open for discussion. We need to know if the women in the published studies who consumed dairy products were older than the women in the same studies who did not because of the association between older maternal age and increased DZ twinning. We also need to know the ethnic composition of the two groups (those who ate dairy regularly and those who did not) because DZ twinning is highest among Africans and lowest among Asians. These are just a few of the questions raised by reported associations between dietary practices and twinning.

7. *Conjoined twins result from delayed division of the fertilized egg.*
   Reality Check: Likely
   Short Answer: When people hear about twins who are physically connected to one another they often picture Chang and Eng, the famous Siamese twins born in Siam (now Thailand) in 1811. These male twins, who shared a liver and were connected by a band of flesh, were a popular attraction in P.T. Barnum's circus show, beginning in 1850 and lasting for 5 years [41]. The twins went on to marry two sisters, Sarah and Adelaide Yates, and to father 21 children between them [42].

   Two theories attempt to explain why conjoined twinning occurs. *Fission theory* states that conjoined twins result when the fertilized egg divides relatively late, at about 13–15 days after conception. *Fusion theory* claims that conjoined twins come from the merging of embryos (presumably identical). These opposing views have stirred a lively debate among embryologists and anatomists [43,44,45]. Most experts favor the fission theory (as do I), reasoning that conjoined twins are also identical and that mirror-imaging effects are more frequent among these presumably very late-splitting pairs than among ordinary late-splitting identical twins (about days 10–14 postconception). However, through email exchanges with anatomical expert, Dr. J. Bruce Beckwith (of Beckwith–Wiedemann syndrome fame; see number 2) I learned that fusion theory could account for a share of rare conjoined twin pairs. I have also discovered that some conjoined twins might possibly be fraternal [46], challenging the belief that all conjoined twins are identical.

   More of the (Fission and Fusion) Story: In the early 20th century, German researcher Hans Spemann and his graduate student Hilde Mangold, created conjoined twin salamanders. They did so by using a strand of hair "donated" by Spemann's infant daughter to constrict the developing embryo [47]. Their achievement supports the widely held view that delayed zygotic splitting results in conjoined twins (fission) [48]. But in 2003, the late Dr. Rowena Spencer authored a comprehensive volume with arguments to support fusion theory [49]. Her ideas have been less widely embraced, but seem to account for some curious cases, such as a rare pair of conjoined twins with a single amnion and separate chorions. (Note that fission theory would require that conjoined twins have a single chorion *and* a single amnion, because single structures are linked to late splitting of the fertilized egg. As such, while monoamniotic–dichorionic conjoined twins would be "theoretically improbable" such a case has been reported [50].)

Dr. J. Bruce Beckwith of Loma Linda University's Department of Pathology and Human Anatomy has studied what he calls the "wonderfully complex anatomy" of conjoined twins. He believes that fusion might be the best explanation for some conjoined twin pairs: "It is not too difficult to find examples of the sort of forehead conjunction of otherwise complete and normally formed individuals. … von Baers's (1845) plate 6 has a large outline drawing of twins 6 years of age who had such a small forehead connection … the same plate has a small reproduction of an infant pair joined in the forehead by a slightly larger connection" (J.B. Beckwith, Personal communication, November 19, 2015). It could be that the cotwins' foreheads touched some time during their prenatal development, establishing a permanent physical connection between them. Both pairs are female and presumably identical (J.B. Beckwith, Personal communication, June 26, 2016).

As mentioned earlier, it was with great interest that I learned about a fraternal twin pair whose physical connection *might* be explained by the fusion of two embryos. The actual biological events responsible for the fusion are, however, speculative [46]; after all, most researchers speak exclusively about conjoined *identical* twins. (It is also conceivable that two initially separated identical zygotes might fuse.) But it turns out that this particular fraternal pair may be part of a special class of conjoined twins, known as parasitic twins.

Parasitic twins are rare, occurring in approximately 1/1,000,000 births in the United States [51]. Some researchers classify such twins separately from conjoined twins who are both fully formed [52]. In fact, a continuum of parasitic twins that includes fetus-in-fetu (described later) acardiac twins (absence of the heart in one twin, usually the smaller one, when the cotwin receives the majority of the blood supply [53]) and teratomas (germ cell tumor or tissue with organ components [54]) has been recognized [55].

The twins that so intrigued me presented as a normally developed male infant with the lower half of a parasitic male twin attached to his chest. Parasitic twins develop in utero and are either partly formed, not functional or reliant upon the cotwin for sustenance [56]. Close implantation of the two embryos might have allowed fusion and resorption (selective uptake) of part of the parasitic twin partner.

Culture often captures what science cannot explain. In 1547, in Löwen, Germany, an illustrated handbill appeared depicting opposite-sex conjoined twins—two bodies beneath one head. The authenticity of this intriguing etching has not been confirmed, but many artists at that time produced medically correct renditions of conjoined twins based on description, rather than direct inspection or observation. Another pair of seemingly opposite-sex conjoined twins did not appear in the literature until 450 years later, in 1997. The origin of this more recent pair is speculative, but might have come from the fusion of a fertilized egg and polar body—one of the three smaller products resulting from the division of the primary and secondary egg cells [57,58].

I believe that both fission and fusion are viable theories of conjoined twinning, but I mostly support the former because virtually all conjoined twins are MZ and virtually all show evidence of mirror-image reversal. Fortunately today, high quality imaging techniques can diagnose conjoined twins during the first trimester of pregnancy. The latest procedure, known as virtual embryoscopy, creates a "hologram" of the three-dimensional ultrasound volume, with enhanced details of the embryonic and fetal structures [59]. This image allows physicians to get the best possible anatomical picture of conjoined twins to devise an optimal plan for managing the pregnancy.

During routine prenatal ultrasound the suspicion of conjoined twins is raised when there is a single placenta, failure to see a separating amniotic membrane or when only one yolk sac is present. Other indicators include the visibility of more than three vessels in the umbilical cord, no change in twins' movement after ultrasound scans, fewer limbs than expected, hyperflexion (bending of a body part beyond the normal limit) of the spine, bifid appearance of the fetal pole (notching of the widened thickening of the margin of the yolk sac) at about 6.5 weeks gestation, and increased nuchal translucency thickness (fluid accumulation behind the neck of the fetus, measured by ultrasound at 10–14 weeks gestation—an indicator of possible chromosomal abnormalities).

It is easier to distinguish single amnion MZ twins from conjoined twins at week 8 when fetal activity increases [59]. Given its technical advantages, virtual embryoscopy can help parents and physicians work more cooperatively toward the optimal management of these particular pregnancies. Operations performed on the rarest type of conjoined twins, the craniopagus twins who are joined at the head and may even share brain structures, have benefited greatly from such imaging procedures. A 20-year review shows that successful outcomes from surgeries on craniopagus twins are most likely when the twins show vertical conjoining (fusion of the twins at the top of the head, with the axis of the twins forming an obtuse angle), operations are completed in multiple stages, surgery is performed prior to the twins' first birthday, and the surgical team includes members from different disciplines [60,61].

8. *Conjoined twinning is more common as a result of ART.*
   Reality Check: Possibly
   Short Answer: Conjoined twins are rare, occurring in 1/200 identical twin births; see Chapter 1. However, since 2000, researchers have wondered if ART might increase the chances of producing conjoined twins. They reasoned that ART, by increasing the frequency of identical twins, may do the same for conjoined twins since the events causing the zygote to divide are essentially the same. A number of case reports of conjoined twins following ART have appeared in the medical literature, but it is too soon to say if ART contributes directly to conjoined twinning.
   More of the Story: In 2015, Finnish investigators reported the first known case of conjoined twins conceived after the transfer of a multinuclear embryo (an embryo containing cells with more than one nucleus) [62]. The mother, 33 years old and healthy, was referred to the clinic because her partner's infertility prevented the couple from conceiving. An eight-cell embryo with three multinuclear even-sized blastomeres (special cells formed after a zygote starts to divide) was transferred to her uterus at 2 days postovulation—more than one nucleus in a blastomere can result from uneven division of the embryo early on [63]. Thoracopagus conjoined twins (MZ twins joined from the upper chest to the lower belly) were confirmed at 12 weeks. A total of 16 conjoined twin pairs have been reported following assisted reproduction, but the presence or absence of multinuclear blastomeres was not provided.
   The researchers noted that multinuclear embryos are observed in 15–30% of embryos in nearly 80% of IVF or intracytoplasmic sperm injection (ICSI) cycles, so they are not uncommon in ART pregnancies. Such embryos are considered abnormal so they are usually not transferred; however, the birth of a healthy, normally developed singleton conceived with a multinuclear embryo has been reported. The criteria for assessing the "health" of embryos prior to implantation are based on appearance (form and structure). Different systems are used for scoring these criteria. The uniformity of blastomere size (which might reflect multinuclearity) has been thought to be of less significance than other features, such as fragmentation. However, the possibility that multinuclearity or other

characteristics reflecting the uneven distribution of genetic material may interfere with successful implantation has not been well studied—this may explain why multinuclear embryos haven't been implanted in the past. The need for additional investigations on embryo morphology and its relationship to twinning, conjoined twinning, and health is indicated [62,63].

9. *Vanishing twins occur in 10–15% of twin pregnancies.*
   Reality Check: Possibly
   Short Answer: The March 2013 "Interesting Facts About Twins" fact sheet from the York White Rose Mothers of Twins and Triplets Club caught my attention with the statement that 10–15% of twin pregnancies vanish. In other words, some multiple pregnancies become singleton pregnancies when one twin is resorped (for unknown reasons) by the cotwin or the mother; the absence of the second twin is usually detected by ultrasound during the first trimester. A chapter in a scholarly book about twins indicated that 12–15% of all live births (1 in 8 people) began as twins [64]. I took a closer look at this statement because I believe that the frequency of vanishing twins is less certain than these numbers imply. Indeed, the estimated percentages are quite scattered. In fact, as odd as it sounds, some "lost" twins, are never detected.
   More of the Story: The vanishing twin syndrome (VTS) involves the disappearance of one twin during the first trimester of pregnancy. This event is usually discovered by repeated ultrasonographic scanning—for example, a multiple pregnancy identified at week 6 of gestation may appear as a singleton pregnancy at week 12, with only one heartbeat detected. Reasons for the disappearance of one twin include natural spontaneous abortion or resorption of the twin by the mother, placenta, or cotwin fetus—although why this happens is unknown. It is suspected that the aborted or resorped fetus had a chromosomal anomaly or other congenital malformation and so is eliminated by various means.

   Different studies in the medical literature report different estimates for how often VTS occurs. These figures vary widely: 0.0% [65], 9.6% [66], 10.4% [67], 21%, 30% [68], and even 78% and 100%! [69]. Some of the variability is probably due to the different methods and different sized samples used in these studies. In addition, not all women conceiving twins undergo ultrasound scans so an unknown number of VTS cases will go undetected. It is also important to track VTS occurrences for natural and assisted conceptions because spontaneous abortions are more likely to happen in assisted pregnancies than in natural ones—early miscarriage occurs in 10–15% of *all* pregnancies, but in 22–63% of those that are assisted [70]. Unknown conditions in the womb might also cause fetuses to abort [71].

A twin study limited to pregnancies conceived either by IVF or ICSI identified 642 singleton twin survivors from vanishing twin pregnancies, 3678 twins from twin gestations, and 5237 singletons from singleton pregnancies. The aim of this research was to estimate the frequency of VTS with large numbers of participants. All of the mothers in this study had undergone ultrasound at 8 weeks gestation. This study found that 10.4% of the IVF/ICSI singletons had started out as twins.

This study also offered an opportunity to compare the health outcomes of the twins and singletons conceived by assisted methods. The surviving twins were not at greater risk for neurological difficulties compared with the IVF/ICSI singletons, but their risk for cerebral palsy was somewhat elevated [67].

There have been cases of suspected tumors in adults that, following surgical removal, appeared to be resorbed twins. In June 1999, an adult male was admitted for surgery to remove a large tumor from his stomach, but the growth proved to be a case of fetus-in-fetu (a rare occurrence of a fetus becoming trapped inside a cotwin). In April 2015, a woman underwent surgery for a brain tumor, but was later informed that the tumor was her embryonic twin [72,73].

Two other curious medical findings may help in the early detection of vanishing twins. A study from the Netherlands performed rheumatoid heart disease (RHD) screening in a large clinical sample of pregnant women and their fetuses. In a very small subset of cases the results for RHD were positive when based on maternal blood cells, but negative when based on cord blood. The possibility of VTS as an explanation for these perplexing results was raised—if one fraternal twin failed to develop early on, but fused with the remaining cotwin, a third cell line would be created, thereby explaining the conflicting findings [74].

Also of interest is a case report showing that the sex of a fetus based on DNA analysis did not match the sex of the fetus when the analysis was repeated during the first trimester [75]. The investigators wondered if the inconsistency in their diagnosis of the fetus's sex was due to VTS—perhaps the mother was unknowingly carrying male–female twins, the sex of one twin was determined, then that twin was lost along the way, leaving an opposite-sex cotwin survivor. Even though VTS could not be confirmed in this case, it could be a complicating factor in prenatal diagnosis. Such a problem could be very serious and here is why.

The presence of a Y chromosome indicates a male fetus, while the absence of a Y chromosome (actually the presence of two X chromosomes) indicates a female. Correct determination of fetal sex is crucial if, for example, a fetus carries a recessive X-linked gene for a debilitating condition like Duchenne muscular dystrophy (progressive weakness and wasting of muscles) or Lesch–Nyhan syndrome (abnormal involuntary movements and self-injurious behaviors). If these two conditions are carried on the X chromosome, this means that male infants (XY) will be affected since they only have one X chromosome. In contrast, given that the genes for these conditions are recessive, female infants (XX) would need to have the deleterious gene on *both* of their two X chromosomes in order to show the disorder; if they have only one copy of the gene they are called *carriers*, but they are unaffected. However, female carriers have a 50% chance of transmitting their one harmful gene to a daughter (she'd be a carrier) or to a son (he'd be affected). Therefore, medical personnel and parents need to determine fetal sex with complete certainty in order to provide informed guidance to couples weighing family planning options, especially when disorders and defects are involved.

VTS is a widely recognized, natural aspect of multiple pregnancies, but there is a great deal we do not know about its origin and frequency. Coming up with the correct calculations is challenging for many reasons—for example, triplet pregnancies may be spontaneously reduced to two, and a twin can be resorbed by the mother, placenta, or cotwin, to be discovered later in life, if at all. I agree with Professor Charles E. Boklage of East Carolina University that "an ideal study of natural conception" (p. 91) would include a large number of couples with known fertility histories [71]. Given the increased frequency of both identical and fraternal twins following reproductive assistance, a study of naturally conceived twins would be best suited to answer the question of how many people start out as a twin.

A related mythconception is relevant here: One early investigator suggested that all left-handed individuals began as a twin [76]. However, there is no scientific basis to support this claim—left-handedness (while it occurs more often among twins than singletons) has many explanations, including genetic transmission and adverse birth events, as well as possible delayed zygotic splitting.

Telling twins apart is complex and fascinating, not simple and routine. Knowing what type of twin you have or what type of twin you are have been hotly debated by families, twins, friends, relatives, and even physicians. That is the next topic to which I will turn. I wish I could find an illustrative cartoon that was once in my file—a woman reminds her husband not to ask their friends about the type of twins they have, or they will be discussing nothing else for the rest of the night!

REFERENCES

[1] G. Herranz, The timing of monozygotic twinning: a criticism of the common model, Zygote 23 (1) (2013) 27–40.

[2] M.G. Bulmer, The Biology of Twinning in Man, Clarendon Press, Oxford, 1970.

[3] R.J. Loos, C. Derom, R. Derom, R. Vlietinck, Birthweight in liveborn twins: the influence of the umbilical cord insertion and fusion of placentas, BJOG 108 (9) (2001) 943–948.

[4] N.L. Segal, Identical and fraternal: when words mislead, Twin Res. 3 (4) (2000) 338–343.

[5] L. Vadlamudi, L.M. Dibbens, K.M. Lawrence, X. Iona, J.M. McMahon, W. Murrell, S.F. Berkovic, Timing of de novo mutagenesis—a twin study of sodium-channel mutations, N. Engl. J. Med. 363 (14) (2010) 1335–1340.

[6] P.M. Steijlen, M.A. van Steensel, Paradominant inheritance, a hypothesis explaining occasional familial occurrence of sporadic syndromes, Am. J. Med. Genet. 85 (4) (1999) 359–360.

[7] T. Hofer, J. Frank, P.H. Itin, Klippel–Trénaunay syndrome in a monozygotic male twin: supportive evidence for the concept of paradominant inheritance, Eur. J. Dermatol. 15 (5) (2005) 341–343.

[8] E.A. Ehli, A. Abdellaoui, Y. Hu, J.J. Hottenga, M. Kattenberg, T. van Beijsterveldt, et al. De novo and inherited CNVs in MZ twin pairs selected for discordance and concordance on attention problems, Eur. J. Hum. Genet. 20 (10) (2012) 1037–1043.

[9] A.F. McRae, P.M. Visscher, G.W. Montgomery, N.G. Martin, Large autosomal copy-number differences within unselected monozygotic twin pairs are rare, Twin Res. Hum. Genet. 18 (1) (2015) 13–18.

[10] Beckwith–Wiedemann Syndrome. Available from: http://ghr.nlm.nih.gov/condition/beckwith-wiedemann-syndrome

[11] R. Weksberg, C. Shuman, O. Caluseriu, A.C. Smith, Y.L. Fei, J. Nishikawa, et al., Discordant KCNQ1OT1 imprinting in sets of monozygotic twins discordant for Beckwith–Wiedemann Syndrome, Hum. Mol. Genet. 11 (11) (2002) 1317–1325.

[12] S. Silva, Y. Martins, A. Matias, I. Blickstein, Why are monozygotic twins different? J. Perinat. Med. 39 (2) (2011) 195–202.

[13] R. Vlietinck, C. Derom, R. Derom, H. Van den Berghe, M. Thiery, The validity of Weinberg's rule in the East Flanders Prospective Twin Survey (EFPTS), Acta Genet. Med. Gemellol. 37 (2) (1988) 137–141.

[14] H. Husby, N.V. Holm, A. Gernow, S.G. Thomsen, K. Kock, H. Gurtler, Zygosity, placental membranes and Weinberg's rule in a Danish consecutive twin series, Acta Genet. Med. Gemellol. 40 (2) (1991) 147–151.

[15] H.C., McNamara, S. C., Kane, J.M. Craig, R.V., Short, M.P., Umstad, A review of the mechanisms and evidence for typical and atypical twinning, Am. J. Obstet. Gynecol. 214 (2) (2016) 172–191.

[16] V.L. Souter, R.P. Kapur, D.R. Nyholt, K. Skogerboe, D. Myerson, C.C. Ton, ... , I.A. Glass, A report of dizygous monochorionic twins. N. Engl. J. Med. 349 (2) (2003) 154–158.

[17] M.P. Umstad, R.V. Short, M. Wilson, J.M. Craig, Chimaeric twins: why monochorionicity does not guarantee monozygosity, Aust. NZ J. Obstet. Gynaecol. 52 (3) (2012) 305–307.

[18] O.J. Lee, D. Cho, M.G. Shin, S.O. Kim, J.T. Park, H.K. Kim, D.W. Ryang, The first known case of blood group chimerism in monochorionic dizygotic twins in Korea, Ann. Lab. Med. 34 (3) (2014) 259–262.

[19] R.W. Redline, Nonidentical twins with a single placenta—disproving dogma in perinatal pathology, N. Engl. J. Med. **349** (2) (2003) 111–114.

[20] T. Kuwata, S. Matsubara, A. Ohkuchi, T. Watanabe, A. Izumi, Y. Honma, et al. The risk of birth defects in dichorionic twins conceived by assisted reproductive technology, Twin Res. 7 (3) (2004) 223–227.

[21] A. Goody, F. Rice, J. Boivin, G.T. Harold, D.F. Hay, A. Thapar, Twins born following fertility treatment: implications for quantitative genetic studies, Twin Res. Hum. Genet. 8 (4) (2005) 337–345.

[22] N.L. Segal, Entwined lives: twins and what they tell us about human behavior, Plume, New York, NY, (2000).

[23] New York Magazine, December 1, 1997. Available from: https://books.google.com/bo oks?id=DOgCAAAAMBAJ&pg=PA21&lpg=PA21&dq=twins+heaven+treasure+tre vor&source=bl&ots=kzistc1ubN&sig=pCBe09c5G5UFtk8vVeqtcwtib3U&hl=en&sa =X&ved=0ahUKEwjX9dPwy6zJAhXFeT4KHeOQCCUQ6AEIFDAA#v=onepage &q=twins%20heaven%20treasure%20trevor&f=false

[24] P.P.S. Nylander, The twinning incidence in Nigeria, Acta Genet. Med. Gemellol. 28 (4) (1979) 261–263.

[25] E. Ibagere, Nigeria Boasts World's Twin Capital, BBC News, World Edition, 2002. Available from: http://news.bbc/co.uk/2/hi/Africa/2253845.stm

[26] Yams. Available from: http://www.marksdailyapple.com/difference-yams-sweet-potatoes/#axzz3rELkDtXG

[27] What's in a Yam? Clues to Fertility, A Student Discovers. Available from: http://yale-medicine.yale.edu/summer1999/news/scope/60951/

[28] Wonali, O.F.C., Okonofua, F.E., Odunsi, K., Jekel, J., Wyshak, G., Naftolin, F. White yams (dioscorea rotundata) and socioeconomic status as risk factors for twin births in southwest Nigeria. Twin Res. 1 (3) (1998) (Abstract) Ninth International Congress of Twin Studies, Helsinki, Finland, 164.

[29] G.F. Erickson, Follicle Growth and Development, Global Library of Women's Medicine, 2008, ISSN: 1756-2228, DOI 10.3843/GLOWEN.10289. The Foundation for the Global Library of Women's Medicine Ltd. Albyfield House, Wetheral, Carlisle CA4 8ET, UK.

[30] E. Ibagere, Follicle growth and development, Global Library of Women's Medicine, The Foundation for the Global Library of Women's Medicine Ltd., Albyfield House, Wetheral, Carlisle CA4 8ET, UK ISSN: 1756-2228 (2002).

[31] P. Haggarty, H. McCallum, H. McBain, K. Andrews, S. Duthie, G. McNeill, et al. Effect of B vitamins and genetics on success of in-vitro fertilisation: prospective cohort study, Lancet 367 (9521) (2006) 1513–1519.

[32] C. Hoekstra, Z.Z. Zhao, C.B. Lambalk, G. Willemsen, N.G., Martin, D.I. Boomsma, G.W. Montgomery, Dizygotic twinning. Hum. Reprod Update 14 (1) (2008) 37–47.

[33] N. Bakalar, Rise in Rate of twin Births May be Tied to Dairy Case, New York Times, May 30, 2006.

[34] G. Steinman, Mechanisms of twinning VII. Effects of diet and heredity on the human twinning rate, J. Hum. Reprod. **51** (5) (2006) 405–410. The estimated proportion of dairy products in the diets of multiple birth mothers was 2.9 on a 4-point scale, in which 4 indicated "much" and "1 indicated none." However, none of these mothers avoided milk products entirely.

[35] R. Mangels, Protein in the vegan diet, Simply Vegan, fifth ed., 2014. Available from: http://www.vrg.org/nutrition/protein.php

[36] A.E. Czeizel, P. Vargha, Periconceptional folic acid/multivitamin supplementation and twin pregnancy, Am. J. Obstet. Gynecol. 191 (3) (2004) 790–794.

[37] M. Eichholzer, O. Tönz, R. Zimmermann, Folic acid: a Public-health challenge, Lancet 367 (9519) (2006) 1352–1361.

[38] C. Storrs, D. Goldschmidt, U.S. Twin Birth Rate Hits Record High, December 23, 2015. Available from: http://www.cnn.com/2015/12/23/health/twin-birth-rate-record-ivf/

[39] Twins 2 UK, Multiple Birth Statistics 2012, 2014. Available from: http://www.twinsuk.co.uk/twinstips/18/9934205/multiple-birth-statistics,-facts-&-trivia/multiple-birth-statistics-2012-(released-2014)/

[40] V. Luumma, E. Haukioja, R. Lemmeetyinen, M. Pikkola, Natural selection on human twinning, Nature 394 (6693) (1998) 533–534.

[41] J.T. Pednaud, The Siamese Twins—Chang and Eng Bunker, 2014. Available from: http://www.thehumanmarvels.com/the-siamese-twins-chang-and-eng-bunker/

[42] I. Wallace, A. Wallace, The Two, Simon and Schuster, New York, NY, (1978).

[43] L. Spitz, Conjoined twins, J. Am. Med. Assoc. 289 (10) (2003) 1307–1310.

[44] G.A. Machin, Heteropagus conjoined twins due to fusion of two embryos, Am. J. Med. Genet. 78 (4) (1998) 388–389.

[45] R. Logrono, C. Garcia-Lithgow, C. Harris, M. Kent, L. Meisner, Reply to Geoffrey A. Machin, Am. J. Med. Genet. 78 (4) (1998) 390.

[46] R. Logrono, C. Garcia-Lithgow, C. Harris, M. Kent, L. Meisner, Heteropagus conjoined twins due to fusion of two embryos: report and review, Am. J. Med. Genet. 73 (3) (1997) 239–243.

[47] M. Costandi, How to Create Siamese Twins or an Embryo With Two Heads, December 20, 2006. Available from: https://neurophilosophy.wordpress.com/2006/12/20/how-to-create-siamese-twins-or-an-embryo-with-2-heads/

[48] M.H. Kaufman, The embryology of conjoined twins, Childs. Nerv. Syst. 20 (8–9) (2004) 508–525.

[49] R. Spencer, Conjoined Twins: Developmental Malformations and Clinical Implications, Johns Hopkins University Press, Baltimore, MD, (2003).

[50] C.C. DeStephano, M. Meena, D.L. Brown, N.P. Davies, B.C. Brost, Sonographic diagnosis of conjoined diamniotic monochorionic twins, Am. J. Obstet. Gynecol. 203 (6) (2010) e4–e6.

[51] G. Sharma, S.S.N. Mobin, M. Lypka, M. Urata, Heteropagus (parasitic) twins: a review, J. Pediatr. Surg. 45 (12) (2010) 2454–2463.

[52] O.M. Mutchinick, L. Luna-Muñoz, E. Amar, M.K. Bakker, M. Clementi, G. Cocchi, et al. Conjoined twins: a worldwide collaborative epidemiological study of the International Clearinghouse for Birth Defects Surveillance and Research, Am. J. Med. Genet. C 157 (4) (2011) 274–287.

[53] Acardia in Medicine. Available from: http://dictionary.reference.com/browse/acardia

[54] Teratoma, 2015. Available from: http://medical-dictionary.thefreedictionary.com/teratoma

[55] R. Spender, Parasitic conjoined twins: external, internal (fetuses in fetu and teratomas), and detached (acardiacs), Clin. Anat. 14 (6) (2001) 428–444.

[56] C. DeRuiter, Parasitic twins, in: Embryo Project Encyclopedia, 2011. Available from: http://embryo.asu.edu/handle/10776/2290, https://embryo.asu.edu/pages/parasitic-twins#sthash.y4LDhUlP.dpuf

[57] I. Blickstein, The conjoined twins of Löwen, Twin Res. 3 (4), 2000, 185–188.

[58] R. Maymon, S. Mendelovic, M. Schachter, R. Ron-El, Z. Weinraub, A. Herman, Diagnosis of conjoined twins before 16 weeks' gestation: the 4-year experience of one medical center, Prenat. Diagn. 25 (9) (2005) 839–843.

[59] L. Baken, M. Rousian, E.J. Kompanje, A.H. Koning, P.J. van der Spek, E.A. Steegers, N. Exalto, Diagnostic techniques and criteria for first-trimester conjoined twin documentation: a review of the literature illustrated by three recent cases, Obstet. Gynecol. Surv. 68 (11) (2013) 743–752.

[60] D.J. Harvey, A. Totonchi, A.E. Gosain, Separation of craniopagus twins over the past 20 years: a systematic review of the variables that lead to successful separation, Plast. Reconstr. Surg. 138 (1) (2016) 190–200.

[61] M. Walker, S.R. Browd, Craniopagus Twins: Embryology, Classification, Surgical Anatomy, and Separation, Childs. Nerv. Syst. 20 (8–9) (2004) 554–566.

[62] H. Mankonen, J. Seikkula, T. Jüarenpää, V. Jokimaa, A case of conjoined twins after a transfer of a multinuclear embryo, Clin. Case Rep. 3 (4) (2015) 260–265.

[63] T. Hardarson, C. Hanson, A. Sjögren, K. Lundin, Human embryos with unevenly sized blastomeres have lower pregnancy and implantation rates: indications for aneuploidy and multinucleation, Hum. Reprod. 16 (2) (2001) 313–318.

[64] C.E. Boklage, The frequency and survival probability of natural twin conceptions, in: L.G. Keith, E. Papiernik, D.M. Keith, B. Luke (Eds.), Multiple Pregnancy: Epidemiology, Gestation and Perinatal Outcome, Parthenon Publishing Group, London, 1995, pp. 41–50.

[65] H.J. Landy, L.G. Keith, The vanishing twin: a review, Hum. Reprod. Update 4 (2) (1998) 177–183.

[66] F.F. Thurik, A. Ait Soussan, B. Bossers, H. Woortmeijer, B. Veldhuisen, G.C. Page-Christiaens, M. de Haas, et al. Analysis of false-positive results of fetal RHD typing in a national screening program reveals vanishing twins as potential cause for discrepancy, Prenat. Diagn. 35 (8) (2015) 754–760.

[67] A. Pinborg, O. Lidegaard, N. la Cour Freiesleben and A.N. Andersen, Consequences of vanishing twins in IVF/ICSI pregnancies, *Hum. Reprod.* **20** (10) (2005) 2821–2829

[68] American Pregnancy Association, Vanishing Twin Syndrome, 2015. Available from: http://americanpregnancy.org/multiples/vanishing-twin-syndrome/

[69] H.J. Landy, L. Keith, D. Keith, D., The vanishing twin, Acta. Genet. Med. Gemellol. (Roma). 31 (3–4) (1982) 179–194.

[70] J.Z. Qin, L.H. Pang, M.Q. Li, J. Xu, X. Zhou, Risk of chromosomal abnormalities in early spontaneous abortion after assisted reproductive technology: a meta-analysis, PLoS One 8 (10) (2013) e75953.

[71] C.E. Boklage, Survival probability of human conceptions from fertilization to term, Int. J. Fertil. 35 (2) (1990) 75.

[72] ABC News, Man With Twin Living Inside Him—A Medical Mystery Classic, 1999. Available from: http://abcnews.go.com/Health/man-twin-living-inside-medical-mystery-classic/story?id=2346476

[73] B. Hooper, Los Angeles Surgeons Find Brain 'Tumor' Was Embryonic Twin, April 22, 2015. Available from: http://www.upi.com/Odd_News/2015/04/22/Los-Angeles-surgeons-find-brain-tumor-was-embryonic-twin/1781429717584/

[74] F.F. Thurik, A. Ait Soussan, B. Bossers, H. Woortmeijer, B. Veldhuisen, G.C. Page-Christiaens, et al. Analysis of false-positive results of fetal RHD typing in a national screening program reveals vanishing twins as potential cause for discrepancy, Prenat. Diagn. 35 (8) (2015) 754–760.

[75] B. Vlková, J. Hodosy, Vanishing twin as a potential source of bias in non-invasive fetal sex determination: a case report, J. Obstet. Gynaecol. Res. 40 (4) (2014) 1128–1131.

[76] C.E. Lauterbach, Studies in twin resemblance, Genetics 10 (6) (1925) 525–568.

CHAPTER 5

Identical or Fraternal? Telling Twins Apart

There are more mythconceptions about twins than those surrounding their earliest development. For example, some parents and physicians argue that it is better to *not know* one's twin type or the twin type of one's children once they are born. Many people also assume (understandably) that because identical twins have identical DNA, a twin who is guilty of a crime could place blame on an innocent cotwin if a hair or blood sample were found at the scene. In fact, a lot of people assume that identical twins have identical fingerprints, another feature that would allow them to shift blame for wrongdoing or get through a fingerprint scanner at their twin's workplace. In this chapter I will examine these and other mythconceptions about telling twins apart.

1. *Twin-type testing (zygosity diagnosis) should not be routinely performed on same-sex twins.*
    Reality Check: False
    Short Answer: I love the following cartoon from Ms. Peach, shown in Fig. 5.1. I actually included this comic strip in my written doctoral candidacy exam at the University of Chicago to highlight two important ideas: (1) twins and their families benefit greatly from knowledge of twin type, and (2) misconceptions about twin type can be harmful.

    I strongly advocate routine DNA testing of same-sex twins in order to establish their twin type with scientific certainty. (Opposite-sex twins are typically diagnosed as fraternal without such testing, based on their obvious observable sex difference.) My colleagues and I addressed the benefits of twin-type testing in a 2015 letter to the *British Journal of Obstetrics and Gynaecology* [1]. Optimal management of twin pregnancies for both the mothers and fetuses (especially single-chorion MZ twins who may be affected by twin-to-twin transfusion syndrome) were among the advantages of testing. Single chorion twins can be detected by ultrasound during the first trimester and their very likely monozygosity confirmed by placental examination or DNA testing at birth; however, recall that rare cases of DZ twins with single chorions

Twin Mythconceptions
http://dx.doi.org/10.1016/B978-0-12-803994-6.00005-6

Figure 5.1 Lively discussion of twin types enters into comic strips and suggests how inaccuracies (the two twin types being benevolent and malicious) enter the public arena. *(Reprinted with permission from Mell Lazarus and Creators Syndicate, Inc.).*

have been discovered. We also described the benefits of having more informed perspectives on disease risk if one twin expresses a particular condition, the greater understanding of twins' physical and behavioral similarities and differences, and the peace of mind enjoyed by parents and twins when issues of identity and self-concept arise. Most other researchers have concurred with our conclusions [2,3].

More of the Story: These days DNA tests are simple to conduct, requiring saliva samples that can be easily collected at home and mailed to a genetics laboratory for analysis. The results are typically available within 2–3 weeks. Given the ease of DNA testing and the steady reduction in its cost, the knowledge gains are well worth the time, effort, and expense. As a researcher, I have experienced a lot of satisfaction from guiding twins and their families through this process and explaining the findings. Twins and their parents are variously delighted, relieved, and/or surprised to finally learn the truth.

Consider the following comment from Tiffany Brown, a mother and judicial law clerk, upon discovering that her 2-year-old "fraternal" twin girls were actually identical:

Instantly, my world turned upside down; this was a case of mistaken identity... I felt a sense of relief receiving the news... I was rattled at the thought that my pride and stubbornness in refusing to entertain the possibility that my girls were identical could have resulted in my daughters not fully appreciating who they are—their very identity [4].

In Chapter 1 I discussed the twin type dilemma of identical twin, Barbara McDowell. (Barbara is the former Director of the Women's Center at California State University, Fullerton where I am a professor.) Recall that Barbara and her twin sister Betsy had been told by their mother that they were fraternal twins. However, they always suspected otherwise because of their similar appearance and personalities. I arranged a DNA test for these twins when they were in their 60s. Several weeks later I forwarded the results in an email message to Barbara: identical.

So we read it together and we both burst into tears! So very much to say about this...

On the medical side, WGBH-TV in Boston produced an informative scientific television documentary, *Body Watch* (January 31, 1987), showing identical twins, one of whom had diabetes. Doctors continued to track the well twin for disease symptoms through yearly blood tests designed to detect warning signs. If symptoms of diabetes appeared in the well twin the advantage would be early discovery and early treatment. If the well twin never developed any symptoms, nontwins would benefit if researchers found a biological and/or environmental factor that explained why one twin was affected and the other was not. If the twins featured in *Body Watch* did not know they were identical and that both were predisposed to the disease, then the unaffected sister might not have been as health conscious as she was and might have ignored suspicious signs.

One more thing—a mother of young twin boys was told (and believed) that her sons were fraternal, even though she, her husband, and others mixed them up. She posted the following comment on the Internet: "And why would we waste the 160 bucks plus shipping when we never mix them up anymore?! Okay, so there was that *one* time last month ..." [5]. I could not disagree with her more for the reasons I have given earlier.

Parents of twins are wonderful sources of information, both for researchers and for each other. I would urge all current and prospective parents of twins to read the mother-authored blog, "Why Don't Identical Twins Always Look Alike?" The article focuses on two beautiful dark-haired identical twin girls, J and M, one of whom has frontonasal dysplasia (FND) [6]. FND is a condition linked to a specific gene mutation, causing abnormal head and facial development before birth [7,8]. Affected individuals show widely spaced eyes and a broad nose. Six other moms chimed in with accounts of differences between their identical multiples, several indicating a gene mutation in one of their twin children that caused the child to have primordial dwarfism (pre- and postnatal growth retardation, microcephaly, and distinct facial appearance). I believe these narratives are insightful examples of how identical twins can differ in some fundamental ways, underlining parents' need to know what type of twins they are raising. In other words, if twins are identical, what are the chances that an unaffected twin might eventually show the same medical condition as his or her affected cotwin? A physical difference due to a genetic mutation does *not* necessarily identify fraternal twins.

Subsequent to the publication of our letter in the *British Journal of Obstetrics and Gynaecology,* another researcher took the opposing view, arguing that knowledge of twin type rarely leads to improved pregnancy management [9]. This statement is blatantly false as evidenced in the obstetrical and gynecological literature, especially as it concerns single-chorion MZ twins who may suffer from transfusion syndrome, which you will recall involves the dangerous mutual circulation between identical twin fetuses. The letter also asserted that twins may suffer unnecessary stress if their identical cotwin contracts diseases, such as breast cancer or diabetes, both of which have a genetic component (20 and 50% of identical twins will have breast cancer and diabetes, respectively, if their cotwin is affected). I would argue, instead, that knowing one's twin type (like the twins who differed in diabetes, described earlier) and the risk of a particular disease allows more informed lifestyle choices, such as following certain diets and exercise routines that minimize disease risk. Another advantage is increased sensitivity to, and awareness of, possible symptoms, allowing treatment to begin as soon as possible. And another is the comfort afforded to families and twins from knowing that an available test can reveal the twins' biological origins, allowing them to better understand twins' behaviors, identities, and needs.

The researchers' opposing letter also stated that knowledge of twin type inflicts emotional stress on an identical twin if his or her organ is needed by the cotwin. (Organ donation/transplantation has an excellent prognosis if performed between identical twins; however, some fraternal twins can also be good genetic matches. I will return to this topic later.) Being an identical twin does *not* obligate one to donate an organ to a cotwin. Instead, I would argue that such decisions, while based on many factors, should be made privately by individuals, in consultation with their physicians. The fact that close genetic relatedness is a key contributor to successful organ transplantation is one of many decisive factors.

The final argument levied against twin typing by the opposing research team was that the procedure should not be paid for by public healthcare, an issue we had not addressed in our letter. The cost of DNA testing for twins has dropped to about $150 in recent years and will probably go down even more, but this may still be prohibitive for some twins and families. I believe that health insurance *should* cover this cost for families in need. It is mandatory that twins and parents of twins have accurate twin-type information for the reasons I have stated earlier.

Of course, adult twins and parents of twin children can freely decide if DNA analysis is something they desire. However, it is important that they fully understand the benefits of knowing their own twin type or their children's twin type, and the consequences of not knowing.

2. *Dogs can tell identical twins apart, based on their body odors.*
Reality Check: Likely
Short Answer: It is true that highly trained dogs can distinguish between the body odors of identical twins, even when the twins are living at home and eating the same foods [10]. Furthermore, I always suspected that identical twins growing up with a dog might not be able to fool their pet for long because the dog would eventually have plenty of experience with each twin—and might identify certain physical or behavioral cues that the twins did not share. The following story from identical twin and University of Tennessee's Professor of Plant Sciences, Dean A. Kopsell, confirms my suspicion—his family's dog Peggy was confused at first, running back and forth between Dean and his twin brother David when both newborn twins were present. Peggy's confused behavior eventually stopped, suggesting that the pet picked up a difference between them. Dean and David participated in my doctoral dissertation twin research when they were 9 years old. Dean recalled:

> If you remember our story, Dave came home about a week before I did. I was about a 1/2 pound lighter and needed extra time in the hospital. The dog we had at the time was a white female German Shepherd. My folks told me that she smelled Dave up and down when they brought him home. When I arrived several days later, they said the dog was very surprised! They separated us into two cribs, one on each side of the room. The dog could not get to me, so my Dad put an ottoman close to my crib. He told me the dog routed me with her nose for several minutes, and then ran over to Dave's crib and did the same thing… It sure sounds to me that the dog was scenting us both. It took some time, but the dog eventually calmed down and stopped going back and forth.

Peggy's sniffing behavior suggests that she finally distinguished between the twins on the basis of their body odors. A series of twin studies have addressed this interesting question and most of them agree.
More of the Story: The possibility that dogs can use identical twins' body scents to distinguish between them has been of interest ever since Galton

began working with twins in England in the 1870s. Unfortunately, 80 years passed before H. Kalmus from the Galton Laboratory in London revisited this question. Kalmus [11] began with a compelling anecdote:

In a prospector's camp in Northern Ontario [Canada] was a nearly blind Great Dane, Silvia. She was not a friendly dog, but she had a passion for one prospector and fawned on him delightedly whenever he came to camp. One day a stranger appeared for the first time and to the great surprise of those present, Silvia greeted him with great affection. Upon enquiry by the camp crew it was found that the stranger was the identical twin of the particular prospector, whom Silvia had such a passion for, and that he had never been there before nor seen the dog before." (p. 25).

It is reasonable to expect that dogs, whose sense of smell is very well developed, are able to distinguish between identical twins. However, experiments along these lines have provided mixed results, possibly due to different methods for dog training and other procedures. For example, Kalmus found that dogs could match a twin's hand scent to a handkerchief, but if both twins' handkerchiefs were present the dog chose the one encountered first. Thus, the dog did not appear to tell the twins apart. Dogs could, however, track (follow) the odor of one twin, based on a garment, even if the other twin's scent was present, indicating discrimination [11]. In another study, dogs could tell twins apart if they were fraternal and living together or identical and living apart—but not if they were identical *and* living together [12].

A 2011 study showed that highly trained police dogs *could* distinguish between identical twins even if they were living at home *and* eating the same foods. The dogs came from three Czech Republic Police Regional Headquarters and the twins consisted of two identical pairs and two fraternal pairs, between 5 and 13 years of age. The dogs matched the scents of each individual to him or herself, and to that person's cotwin, but discriminated successfully between the two twins in every pair [10].

What about insect bites? Twin studies have shown that identical twins are more likely than fraternal twins to be similarly attractive to or "rejected by" mosquitoes, confirming genetic influence on body odor [13,14]. This does not surprise me—when my fraternal twin sister Anne and I went to summer camp together as children, I was rarely bothered by mosquitoes, but Anne was bitten. However, my being less susceptible to mosquitoes than my twin sister did not prevent me from covering my body with strong insect repellent when I visited Brazil in February 2016 when worries over the Zika virus, carried by the *Aedes aegypti* mosquito, were at a peak. The Zika virus has been linked to both microcephaly (small head with consequent cognitive and physical problems) in babies born to infected pregnant women, and Guillain–Barré syndrome (temporary paralysis) in some infected adults [15,16].

Human body odors are individualized and partly genetically based. They are regulated by the human leukocyte antigen (HLA) genes (the immune system that affects outcomes from transplantation and transfusion). Odors are also affected by the microbiota (microorganisms) on our skin; in fact, human sweat is odorless in the absence of microbiota [17]. Evidence that people can distinguish biological relatives from nonrelatives or close relatives from distant relatives, based on odors from garments worn by these individuals under standard conditions, has been reported. However, the degree of social contact between people can mediate these associations, underlining the complexity of human kin recognition mechanisms [18]. Human body odors have also been linked to various characteristics and conditions, such as physical attractiveness and medical illness [19,20].

3. *Identical twins have identical fingerprints.*
   Reality Check: False
   Short Answer: I am often asked if identical twins have identical fingerprints—but before I can answer, the person questioning me often jokes that perhaps one twin could "substitute" for the other twin in crime. Based on what is known about fingerprint evidence, the answers to the question and the punchline are "no" and "no." Identical twins do have more similar fingerprints than fraternal twins, which is expected because fingerprints are partly affected by genetic factors. However, only a rare pair of identical twins might possibly have prints that match exactly. According to internal medicine specialist Dr. Michael Roizen, "The entire development process [of fingerprints] is so chaotic that, in the entire course of human history, there is virtually no chance of the same exact pattern forming twice [21,22]."

   Likewise, identical twins have similar, but not identical teeth. At one time, similarity in dental characteristics was a key determinant of twin type, but that is no longer the case [23]. Tooth decay, displacements (movement of a tooth from its normal position), and number of teeth present at examination are more alike in identical than fraternal twins, evidence of genetic influence [24,25]. But identical twins' teeth vary, just like their fingerprints.

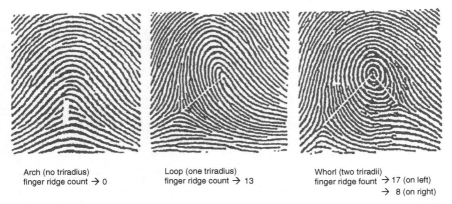

Arch (no triradius)
finger ridge count → 0

Loop (one triradius)
finger ridge count → 13

Whorl (two triradii)
finger ridge fount → 17 (on left)
→ 8 (on right)

Figure 5.2 Three main types of dermatoglyphic (fingerpint) patterns. *(Reprinted with permission from R. Vonk, A.C. van der Schot, G.C.M. van Baal, C.J. van Oel, W.A. Nolen, R.S. Kahn, Dermatoglyphics in relation to brain volumes in twins concordant and discordant for bipolar disorder. Eur. Neuropsychopharmacol. 24(12) (2014) 1885–1895. Elsevier Press).*

More of the Story: The scientific study of fingerprints, as well as hand-prints and footprints, is called *dermatoglyphics.* Dermatoglyphic finger-print studies involve analyzing the number of ridges (the slightly raised lines that appear on the palm-side tips of each of the 10 fingers), as well as examining the patterns formed by these ridges. Fingerprint ridge count represents the total number, or *sum*, of the ridges across all 10 fingers. The three main pattern types are arches, loops, and whorls, although variations (e.g., tented arches and double loops) are possible, yielding eight subtypes [22]. The ridges that form arches are not included in the total ridge count because arches lack the necessary features (core and delta) that allow for the counting of ridges. In the case of whorls the larger of the two counts is typically used [26,27]. The three main pattern types and sample ridge counts are displayed in Fig. 5.2.

The ridges that run across the 10 fingers, as well as the patterns that they form, are permanent features. They do not change over time, although some drugs, chemicals, rashes, burns, and abrasions—even poison ivy—can cause modifications, but such afflictions are usually temporary. Bricklayers whose fingers experience a lot of friction from building materials and machinery are especially susceptible to short-lived fingerprint changes. Unless one is trying to escape the law by surgically altering or mutilating his or her fingerprints, the prints and patterns he or she are born with are there for life [28].

Fingerprint patterns are under the influence of seven or more different genes [22]. MZ (identical) twins are generally more alike on dermatoglyphic measures than DZ (fraternal) twins, demonstrating genetic influence on these characteristics [29]. However, despite their genetic overlap, MZ twins do not match precisely on either the fingerprint ridge count or pattern types, and some MZ twins show marked differences. These differences are due to various idiosyncratic prenatal influences that MZ cotwins experience, such as temperature, sounds, position in the uterus, and the composition and density of amniotic fluid near the fingers [30,31]. And different womb locations mean that pressures on the two developing fetuses will not be the same, causing fine fingerprint details to differ. Given all this biological activity, it is not surprising that identical twins' fingerprints differ—instead, it is very surprising that some identical twins' prints are alike at all.

Marked dermatoglyphic or fingerprint differences have been observed in MZ twin pairs in which one cotwin is affected by a particular medical condition. Twin research has shown a higher than normal a–b ridgecount (the number of ridges below the second and third finger, summed across both hands) on the palms of the hands and a smaller brain volume in individuals at risk for bipolar disorder [32]. A twin study of schizophrenia showed a different total ridge count between affected and unaffected cotwins. Viruses, such as rubella (German measles) can alter children's dermatoglyphic features if their mothers are infected during pregnancy [33].

Now that we know that twins' fingerprints vary, how and when do fingerprints actually form? Volar pads, the swollen areas under the fingers where the ridges and patterns appear, develop some time after the 4th week of gestation. The processes by which fingerprint ridges form have been explained by competing theories, but the general scientific consensus is that the initial ridge formation occurs at about 10.5 weeks gestation, with primary ridge formation occurring until about week 16 or 17. During this time, the fingers are growing, ridges are forming, existing ridges are separating, and sweat glands are developing. Secondary ridges appear at about 14 weeks' gestation and continue developing between weeks 16 and 24. Secondary ridges form continuously until one secondary ridge appears between all the existing primary ridges. The fingerprint ridge achieves its final unchanging state by about week 24 or 25 [34,35].

It is possible for identical twins to show mirror-imaging effects in some fingerprint characteristics. An arch on the left thumb of one twin might be mirrored on the right thumb of his or her cotwin. In fact, the patterns on the left hand of one twin might show greater resemblance to those on his or her cotwin's right hand than to those on his or her own right hand.

On a different but related topic, correctly linking a new mother with her newborn baby (and not someone else's) in a busy hospital is usually accomplished by attaching matching identification bracelets to the mother and baby's wrist and ankle. My colleague, the distinguished Dr. Antonio Garrido-Lestache from the *Hospital del Nino Jesus,* in Madrid, Spain, has made a strong case for using mothers' and babies' fingerprints instead, and I support this idea. Dr. Garrido-Lestache asserts that fingerprints are durable biological characteristics that can be easily, safely, and inexpensively obtained from mothers and newborns [36], whereas bracelets can be altered or removed. I will return to this important topic later in the book.

4. *Twins must be fraternal if they write with their opposite hands.*
   Reality Check: False
   Short Answer: Lisa Holland, mother of identical twins Susan and Anna, believed that her twin daughters were fraternal because one girl drew pictures with her right hand and the other girl drew pictures with her left hand. As indicated in Chapter 1, about 25% of identical twins show some form of mirror-image reversal. Fraternal twins can also show opposite-handedness (one being right-handed, the other being left-handed), and I have known several such sets over the years. The key point is that twin type *cannot* be diagnosed simply by knowing whether or not cotwins favor the same hand or the opposite hand—only DNA tests can do that for us.
   More of the Story: Increased left-handedness among twins (14.5%), relative to nontwins (9.9%), has been reported by many studies. One possible explanation of several is that the elevated frequency of left-handedness among identical twins involves delayed splitting of the fertilized egg, a process thought by some researchers to affect sidedness. However, links between a family history of left-handedness and twinning, and the difficult deliveries to which twins are often subject could elevate left-handedness among both types of twins. Interestingly, the frequency of left-handedness appears to be equally elevated among identical and fraternal twins even though fraternal twins do not experience one of the

presumed causes of left-handedness in MZ twins, that is, delayed zygotic splitting. (It is conceivable that polar body twinning—the fertilization of a mature ovum and a polar body which splits off from the egg as it undergoes maturation—could be implicated in opposite-handedness among nonidentical polar body twins, but this possibility has never been investigated [37].)

Most people think of themselves as right-handed or left-handed, but there are *degrees* of handedness. Most of us are strong right-handers or strong left-handers, but some individuals are able to perform certain tasks equally well with both hands, or perform certain tasks with their right hand and other tasks with their left hand. In order to classify twins with respect to hand preference, I observe twins as they perform a series of activities, such as holding a bottle while opening it, holding a needle while threading it, and holding a dish while drying it. I then record their hand preference on each task: right always, right mostly, equally, left mostly, and left always. The 14 activities I use come from a standard self-report questionnaire [38], but comparing the two shows that an actual behavioral assessment provides more valid information—people sometimes just guess as to which hand they favor while doing a particular task. The handedness questionnaire and scoring procedure are reproduced in Appendix 2 for individuals interested in knowing how right-handed or left-handed they or their twins are.

5. *One identical twin always has a rounder or longer face than his or her cotwin.*
   Reality Check: Possibly
   Short Answer: Twins' immediate family members rarely have trouble telling identical twins apart because these relatives are familiar with the twins' fine physical differences that others miss. Some people (twins' kin and nonkin acquaintances) have insisted to me that one identical twin always has a rounder or a longer face, but this has never been scientifically demonstrated. It is possible that weight differences make one twin appear slightly heavier than the other, or that unknown prenatal effects might elongate one twin's face just slightly. Of course, a slimmer twin might seem to have a longer face even when their two head lengths match.
   More of the Story: There is a modest, but fascinating body of work comparing twins' facial features. My late friend and colleague Dr. Linda Mealey used photographs to obtain measures of identical twins' facial asymmetry, that is, the difference between the left and right sides of each twin's face, relative to a midline [39]. Next, she had people rate each twin for physical attractiveness. She found that the more symmetric twin

in a pair was perceived as more attractive than his or her cotwin, and that the greater the twins' difference in symmetry, the greater their difference in attractiveness. This finding agrees with many, but not all, related studies that have examined facial asymmetry in relation to perceptions of physical attractiveness [40].

The composition of twins' facial features is not limited to what we can see. Everyone, including identical twins, has a unique pattern of blood vessels lying beneath the surface of the skin. These unique patterns can be captured in thermograms, images created when an infrared camera picks up the heat generated from the face. Contrary to what some people think, genetically identical twins are no exception—they can be differentiated from one another by these unique patterns, which presumably are affected by random developmental events either before or after birth [41]. Heredity plays a role, but circulation and sun exposure can alter the appearance and functioning of veins lining the face. Identical twins have also been distinguished by detection of facial markings (light and dark) made by radial symmetry transform (that converts facial marking to light and dark spots) and three-dimensional stereo photogrammetric devices (that analyze and compare twins' facial regions) [42,43].

On the topic of twins' physical differences and similarities I would like to share a compelling anecdote. One day I discovered an identical twin student sitting outside my laboratory who proudly showed me that he could unlock his laptop computer with his eyes. A biometric device in the computer had been set up to recognize the fine patterns on the iris that are highly unique across individuals, creating a security feature that is difficult to breach [44]. I invited his twin brother to visit my lab to see if he could also unlock his brother's computer—he did. I captured this extraordinary sequence on my iphone, both to impress people and to convince skeptics that twins' genetic identity underlies so many of their matched behaviors.

It turns out that the iris begins to form at the 3rd month of gestation, a process that is complete by the 8th month. Development is random so not even identical twins have exactly the same patterns [45]. However, the patterns must be close in some cases, as shown by the twins in my lab—perhaps the technology is not yet sensitive enough to distinguish between them.

6. *DNA tests tell us if twins are identical or fraternal with 100% certainty.*
Reality Check: Likely

Short Answer: As I explained in Chapter 1, DNA testing for twin type involves comparing cotwins across about 15 unique DNA regions. Two individuals must match across all of these regions in order to be classified as identical. The chance of two fraternal twins showing perfect similarity is theoretically possible because fraternal twins have the same parents, but it is statistically and practically impossible because there is too much variation at each region—it would be like winning the lottery twice. The key point is that if cotwins' DNA tests show differences in any markers, then the twins are classified as DZ with 100% certainty—any mismatch reflects the presence of different genes. However, if the DNA tests match across all the tested markers then the twins are classified as MZ with virtually 100% certainty.

If parents or twins strongly believe that laboratory results do not agree with their perceptions, I advise them to repeat the test, perhaps using a different laboratory. (Recall that parents discussed in the previous chapter questioned their twin's zygosity report and they were right.) There is always a remote chance of human error, ranging from using an inadvertently switched saliva sample to contamination from handling or exposure.

I recall two experiences in which reports I received from different twin-typing laboratories were questionable. In one case, two little girls who had been born in China, were adopted by different families in the United States [46]. Their mothers had been part of the same group of parents who traveled to China to receive their daughters. They and the other members of their group could not help noticing the girls' striking physical resemblance—brown hair, rounded eyes, tiny chins, and short stature. The families asked for my help in determining if their girls were identical twins. The DNA testing laboratory returned several conflicting reports, owing to human error, but a final analysis performed at a different location showed no biological relationship between them. One mother was clearly disappointed that the girls were unrelated and asked, "Perhaps they could be cousins?" In the other case, two young twins whom I had studied as part of my doctoral research were clearly fraternal, based on their different eye color (one twin blue, one twin hazel), height difference (one twin 4 ft. 10.5 in. tall, one twin 4 ft. 6.5 in. tall), and hair color (one twin dark brown, one twin light brown). Much to my surprise, they were diagnosed as identical, based on their match across a series of blood groups. I asked the laboratory to repeat the analysis and this time the result was fraternal. It seemed that a particular test in the blood-typing series was weak—had I not seen the twins myself this error would not have been detected.

More of the Story: Until about the early 1990s, twin type was determined by whether or not twins matched across an extensive series of blood groups. But in an exceptional 1940s case in Switzerland of an identical twin switched at birth with an unrelated infant, blood typing was not all that informative because fewer blood groups had been identified at the time. So the doctors in Geneva performed reciprocal skin grafts between the twins and nontwin to see which grafts were accepted and which were rejected. After watching and waiting, it turned out that the only successful skin graft was the one between the separated identical twins [47]. This was not the first successful skin grafting procedure performed between MZ twins (the first one was reported in 1937 [48]), but it was the first time one was performed for zygosity determination.

In addition to the commonly known blood groups (A, B, and O), twins in some studies conducted prior to the 1990s were tested to see if they matched across eight blood group systems, four serum proteins, and six red blood cell enzymes. My late Minnesota colleague, Dr. David T. Lykken, showed that if this information was combined with twin similarity on fingerprint ridge count, ponderal index [weight in kilograms/(height in meters)^3], and cephalic index [(head width × 100)/head length], then the probability of coming up with the wrong diagnosis was less than .001 [49].

DNA analysis, using cells derived from saliva samples, is an easier and more convenient method for performing twin zygosity tests than blood group analysis. I know this firsthand—when I conducted my dissertation research, DNA testing was not available; therefore, I relied on extensive blood-typing and questionnaires to classify the 105 pairs of Chicago and New York twins who took part in my research. Many of the mothers confessed to me that they had to bribe their twin children, usually with ice cream or other sweet treats, to have them undergo the painful needle prick. My research grant paid for the procedure, so it was an opportunity that the twins' parents did not want to miss.

7. *Identical cotwins can differ in congenital anomalies.*
    Reality Check: True
    Short Answer: It is logical to think that genetically identical twins should have the same congenital anomaly or developmental irregularity, but that is often *not* the way it works. A report involving one MZ female twin diagnosed prenatally with cloacal dysgenesis [50]—a malformation

in which the vagina, rectum, and urinary tract merge into a common channel—illustrates this curious finding. It was suspected in this case that the malformation in the affected twin was related to the twinning event. In other words, whatever triggered the fertilized egg to divide also caused each twin to receive an unequal number of stem cells (cells that have the potential to develop into specific tissues and organs). The unequal distribution of cells could have been linked to the disorder in the cotwin with the deficient number of cells.

It has been estimated that congenital anomalies occur in about 10% of MZ twins [51]. This figure includes cases in which one twin, or both twins, are affected. It has been estimated that in 15% of the cases that involve identical twins, both twins are born with a structural anomaly, while only one cotwin is affected about 85% of the time.

More of the Story: Congenital anomalies can be classified as malformations, disruptions, or deformations [51]. *Malformations* (structural defect in a body part) may occur when normal development fails, as in cases of neural tube defects and cardiac difficulties—in fact, discordance (cotwin difference) for these two malformations is more common than concordance (cotwin similarity) [52]. Other malformations, often of the midline (the imaginary line that divides the body into right and left halves) may be associated with twinning events, such as conjoined twinning and acardiac twins. Acardiac twins develop without a heart or with an underdeveloped heart and usually neither twin survives. These twins result from twin reversed arterial perfusion (TRAP), a situation in which blood enters the disadvantaged twin through vessels in the wrong direction [53]. In some cases of TRAP, twins with acardiac cotwins suffer from milder forms of the condition—that is because in the TRAP sequence, this twin pumps blood for both twins so may also be at some risk for heart failure. If the acardiac twin's weight is 50% higher than the weight of the cotwin then the cotwin has only a 10% chance of survival.

Some cotwins show similar, but not identical, dental anomalies also linked to twinning events, i.e., possibly delayed zygotic division and consequent laterality disturbance (departure from normal body development along the midline). Such disturbances may be minor as in the case of dental anomalies, but may be serious as in the case of spina bifida [23]. *Disruptions*, such as limb defects, may result from unequally shared circulation in utero or the death of one twin. *Deformities*, such as clubfoot and dislocated hips, may come from intrauterine crowding in which two babies occupy space intended for one.

Cardiac malformations occur 4 times as often in identical twins as in singletons [54]. Twins with shared chorions (mostly MZ) are at twice the risk for congenital anomalies as twins with separate chorions, and twins with separate chorions are at higher risk than singletons. Congenital anomalies occur in about 2–3% of fraternal twins, which is about the same percentage as nontwins. Twins are, however, not at higher risk for chromosomal anomalies than nontwins, such as Down syndrome (trisomy 21) [55]. Interestingly, a few rare identical pairs (1/385,000 cases) have included one unaffected twin and one twin affected with Down syndrome. A series of complex prenatal events, including nondisjunction (failure of chromosomes to line up properly as the primitive egg cell and sperm cells mature) and recombination (exchange of genetic material between chromosomes), are thought to be responsible [56,57].

8. *Twins are always born on the same day—or month or year.*
    Reality Check: False
    Short Answer: Not all twins are born on the same day—in fact, the current world record for the longest interval between twin births belongs to Amy and Katie Elliot from Waterford, Ireland, who were born 87 days apart [58]. Amy was born on June 1, 2012 when her mothers' water broke at 23 weeks, and her sister Katie followed on August 27. Amy was 4 months premature and weighed just a little over 1 lb. The twins' mother was induced to deliver Katie in her 36th week. Prior to the birth of these twins, the *Guinness World Records (GWR)* identified Hannah and Eric Lynn from Huntingdon, Pennsylvania, as the world's longest separated pair at 84 days.
    More of the Story: Unusual prenatal events are not required for twins to have different birthdays. Twins can be born naturally on different days, months, and even years if one twin arrives just before midnight and the other arrives just afterward. A difference of minutes, however, can have lifelong implications for a given pair. At the University of Minnesota, I studied reared-apart fraternal female twins who were born, respectively, on November 30 and December 1, 1941. At age 44 when they participated in the Minnesota Study of Twins Reared Apart, they told us that their different birthdays delayed their reunion for years—because the twin who initiated the search was understandably looking for someone with the same birthday. British twins Lexus and Amber Conway were born 45 minutes apart on August 31 and September 1, 2008, meaning that one twin would enter school a year before her twin sister, a policy that the twins' parents intended to fight. In fact, their father announced

that if school officials insisted on separation, either the twins would be home schooled or the family might move to Spain [59,60]. (My attempts to learn what was finally decided yielded no new information.) And on New Year's Eve 2011, six babies comprising three sets of United States twins were born straddling the transition from 2011 to 2012 [61]. We can only imagine how this twist of fate has, or will, affect these different birth year twins.

Even though some twins miss sharing their birthdays by minutes or by months I still consider them to be twins, and I believe most people would. That is because most twins (with the possible exception of superfecundated and superfetated twins) were conceived together and carried together—for the most part. The intervening events working against them, which interfere with shared birthdates, occurred naturally.

9. *Twins are always born in the same country.*
   Reality Check: False
   Short Answer: In 2014, I had the privilege of consulting for the 2016 *Guinness World Records (GWR)* book for its special two-page coverage of twin-related records. This experience was not only informative, but a great deal of fun.

   I was astonished to learn about a pair of twins born in different countries within the United Kingdom [62,63]. The twins are Dylan and Hannah Fox, born in 2012. Dylan was born first at his grandparents' home in Wooler, Northumberland in the United Kingdom when his mother, Donna Keenan, went into early labor on July 1, 2012. Donna and her partner, Joe Fox, were watching the Euro 2012 football tournament final at the time Donna's labor started. However, even though Dylan was delivered, Hannah was not ready to be born—so Donna was brought by ambulance to the Borders General Hospital across the border from Northumberland, to Melrose, Scotland, about 45 miles away. The trip took 1 hour and Hannah was born 90 minutes after her twin brother—in Scotland.

   More of the Story: After an exhaustive search turned up no other cases of twins born across national borders, I believed that Dylan and Hannah were the first "international twins." They were entered as such into the 2016 *GWR*, but they turned out not to be. This news was revealed in January 2016 when 39-year-old Heidi Gannon and Jo Baines (née Roberts) spotted the *GWR* entry and came forward to claim their title [64]. The twins' mother, Carol, unaware that she was having twins, delivered Heidi at 9:05 a.m. on September 23, 1976, at the Welshpool

Hospital in Wales. When a twin delivery was finally recognized there were potential complications, so Carol was rushed to Copthorne Hospital in Shrewsbury, England. Jo was born nearly 2 hours later at 10:45, becoming the first English member of her family. Both twins' passports identify them as British citizens, but Jo enters "England" on official forms that ask for her country of birth, while Heidi enters "Wales." Heidi confessed to me, "I tease Jo calling her the 'English twin,' but she says she was only born there so as far as she's concerned she is Welsh."

Heidi and Jo's mother always believed that her twins were identical, but Heidi and Jo had doubts. There is a 3-inch height difference between them and in pictures they look just different enough to qualify as similar-looking fraternal twins. When I learned that the twins' mother is left-handed (a risk factor for having twins) *and* that Heidi and Jo are not only opposite handed, but have hair whorls on opposite sides of their heads, I seriously wondered if they could be identical. The twins had always wanted to have a DNA test done to be certain of their twin type and I encouraged them to do so. When the results came back showing that they were identical twins, Heidi wrote, "Wow, that's fantastic news!!! I've just told mum and she's crying saying she knew it all along!" And according to Heidi, Jo was "over the moon." I suspect that their sizeable height difference is partly explained by Jo's stressful delivery over the border—Jo is the second-born twin and the shorter of the two sisters. This update on the first twins born in different countries appeared in the *Stop Press* pages of the *GWR*, 2016.

10. *DZ twins share exactly 50% of their genes.*
    Reality Check: False
    Short Answer: DZ twins share the same genetic relationship as nontwin brothers and sisters. That is to say they share 50% of their genes, *on average, by descent.* (These genes are the ones that vary among people. We all have genes for hair color, but some people have alleles coding for red hair, while others have alleles coding for brown hair). It is also true that DZ twins *do not* share exactly 50% of their genes. It was once thought that most DZ twins and full siblings have somewhere between 25% and 75% of their genes in common [65]. However, those figures were reported in the 1970s, prior to the development of sophisticated molecular genetic methods. It is now believed that DZ twins share between 42% and 58% of their genes by descent [66]. Consequently, some pairs will look and act more alike than others in specific traits.

More of the Story: The concepts "on average" and "by descent" are interesting and important for understanding the biological relatedness of fraternal twins, as well as full siblings. Each parent transmits just one of his or her two gene forms or alleles (say gene A or gene B) that reside on corresponding places (loci) on each of their 23 chromosome pairs.

Consider that a mother has a .5 or 50% chance of transmitting gene A to her first fraternal twin (or first child) and a .5 or 50% chance of transmitting the same gene to her second fraternal twin (or second child). These probabilities are combined by multiplying them together, giving us .5 × .5 = .25 or 25%. The same applies to the twins' (and siblings') father, so adding these probabilities give us 25 + 25% = 50% for this gene.

There is another way to think about this. Let's say that a mother has genes A and B and a father has the corresponding genes C and D. Lets' also say that the couple's first twin (or first child) is AC. If their second twin (or second child) is also AC, then the two children are related by 100% for those two genes. However, if their second twin (or second child) is AD or BC, the two fraternal cotwins (or full siblings) are related by 50% for that particular gene because they would share the A gene or the C gene. However, if their second twin (or second child) is BD, then the twins (or siblings) have 0% relatedness for those two genes because one child would be AC and the other BD. Averaging these figures gives us (100 + 50 + 50 + 0%)/4 = 50%.

It is theoretically possible, but practically impossible, for fraternal twins and full siblings to share (on the extreme ends of the spectrum) *all* or *none* of their genes. Think about the couple mentioned previously whose two children did not match at all for a certain pair of genes (AC and BD). If this nonmatched random occurrence happened for every single gene pair, then the children would share none of their genes, despite having the same parents. Conversely, the same couple could have two children who both had genes AC. If this match happened for every single gene pair then the fraternal twins or siblings would be like identical twins genetically, but without undergoing division of the fertilized egg. Of course, these unusual events are just theoretical and never happen in real life—as far as we know.

Fraternal twins and siblings share some genes *by descent* because they have the same parents who will transmit some of the same genes to both of their children. Two unrelated people can both have genes for blue eyes or genes for straight hair, but they would *not* share these genes by descent—they would have received these genes from different parents.

Twins' biological complexities are far-reaching. I take a hard look at the myths and realities of more of them in the next chapter.

REFERENCES

[1] J.M. Craig, N.L. Segal, M.P. Umstad, BJOG Debateet al. Zygosity testing should be recommended for all same sex twins, Br. J. Obstet. Gynecol. 122 (12) (2015) 1641.

[2] J.M. Knopman, L.C. Krey, C. Oh, J. Lee, C. McCaffrey, N. Noyes, What makes them split? Identifying risk factors that lead to monozygotic twins after in vitro fertilization, Fertil. Steril. 102 (1) (2014) 82–89.

[3] K.I. Aston, C.M. Peterson, D.T. Carrell, Monozygotic twinning associated with assisted reproductive technologies: a review, Reproduction 136 (4) (2008) 377–386.

[4] N.L. Segal, Zygosity diagnosis: when physicians and DNA disagree, Twin Res. Hum. Genet. 18 (5) (2015) 613–618.

[5] Tracey, The Incredible Identical Fraternal, Twins, 2008. Available from: http://hdydi.com/2008/04/16/the-incredible-identical-fraternal-twins/

[6] Sadia, Why Don't Identical Twins Always look Alike?, 2013. Available from: http://hdydi.com/2013/09/11/why-dont-identical-twins-always-look-alike/

[7] Genetics Home Reference, Frontonasal Dysplasia, 2016. Available from: http://ghr.nlm.nih.gov/condition/frontonasal-dysplasia

[8] S.N. Mohammed, M.C. Swan, S.A. Wall, A.O. Wilkie, Monozygotic twins discordant for frontonasal malformation, Am. J. Med. Genet. Part A 130 (4) (2004) 384–388.

[9] R. Brown, Zygosity testing should be encouraged for all same-sex twins, BJOG 122 (12) (2015) 1641–11641.

[10] L. Pinc, L. Bartoš, A. Reslova, R. Kotrba, Dogs discriminate identical twins, PloS One 6 (6) (2011) e20704.

[11] H. Kalmus, The discrimination by the nose of the dog of individual human odours and in particular of the odours of twins, Br. J. Anim. Behav. 3 (1) (1955) 25–31.

[12] P.G. Hepper, The discrimination of human odour by the dog, Perception 17 (4) (1988) 549–554.

[13] K.M. Kirk, L.J. Eaves, J.M. Meyer, A. Saul, N.G. Martin, Twin study of adolescent genetic susceptibility to mosquito bites using ordinal and comparative rating data, Genet. Epidemiol. 19 (2) (2000) 178–190.

[14] G.M. Fernandez-Grandon, S.A. Gezan, J.A.L. Armour, J.A. Pickett, J.G. Logan, Heritability of attractiveness to mosquitoes, PLoS One 10 (4) (2015) e0122716.

[15] M. Cheng, Zika May Cause Temporary Paralysis: Study, Toronto Sun, March 1, 2016. Available from: http://www.torontosun.com/2016/03/01/zika-may-cause-temporary-paralysis-study

[16] T. Stelloh, *Aedes aegypti*: Meet the Mosquito Spreading Zika Virus Panic, NBC News, January 26, 2016. Available from: http://www.nbcnews.com/health/health-news/aedes-aegypti-meet-mosquito-spreading-zika-virus-panic-n504026

[17] N.O. Verhulst, H. Beijleveld, Y.T. Qiu, C. Maliepaard, W. Verduyn, G.W. Haasnoot, et al. Relation between HLA genes, human skin volatiles and attractiveness of humans to malaria mosquitoes, Infect. Genet. Evol. 18 (August 2013) 87–93.

[18] G.E. Weisfeld, T. Czilli, K.A. Phillips, J.A. Gall, C.M. Lichtman, Possible olfaction-based mechanisms in human kin recognition and inbreeding avoidance, J. Exp. Child Psychol. 85 (3) (2003) 279–295.

[19] S.C. Roberts, A. Kralevich, C. Ferdenzi, T.K. Saxton, B.C. Jones, L.M. DeBruine, et al., Body odor quality predicts behavioral attractiveness in humans, Arch. Sex. Behav. 40 (6) (2011) 1111–1117.

[20] M. Shirasu, K. Touhara, The scent of disease: volatile organic compounds of the human body related to disease and disorder, J. Biochem. 150 (3) (2011) 257–266.

[21] How Are Fingerprints Formed in the Womb? Available from: https://www.sharecare.com/health/fetal-development-basics-pregnancy/how-fingerprints-formed-in-womb

[22] G. Steinman, Mechanisms of Twinning. I. Effect of Environmental Diversity on Genetic Expression in Monozygotic Multifetal Pregnancies, J. Reprod. Med. 46 (5) (2001) 467–472.

[23] G.H. Sperber, G.A. Machin, F.J. Bamforth, Mirror-image dental fusion and discordance in monozygotic twins, Am. J. Med. Genet. 51 (1) (1994) 41–45.

[24] J.C. Boraas, L.B. Messer, M.J. Till, A genetic contribution to dental caries, occlusion, and morphology as demonstrated by twins reared apart, J. Dent. Res. 67 (9) (1998) 1150–1155.

[25] G.C. Townsend, S.K. Pinkerton, J.R. Rogers, M.R. Bockmann, T.E. Hughes, Twin Studies: Research in Genes, Teeth and Faces, University of Adelaide Press, Adelaide, Australia, (2015).

[26] H.C. Allison, Personal Identification, Holbrook Press, Inc, Boston, (1976).

[27] J.J. Yunis, Human Chromosome Methodology, second ed., Academic Press, New York, (1974).

[28] K. Harmon, Can you lose your fingerprints? Scientific American, 2009. Available from: http://www.scientificamerican.com/article/lose-your-fingerprints/

[29] X. Tao, X. Chen, X. Yang, J. Tian, Fingerprint recognition with identical twin fingerprints, PloS One 7 (4) (2012) 61.

[30] How Are Fingerprints Formed in the Womb? Available from: https://www.sharecare.com/health/fetal-development-basics-pregnancy/how-fingerprints-formed-in-womb

[31] Steinman (2001); see ref note 16. A.K. Jain, S. Prabhakar, S. Pankanti, On the similarity of identical twin fingerprints, Pattern Recognit 35 (11) (2002) 2653–2663.

[32] R. Vonk, A.C. van der Schot, G.C.M. van Baal, C.J. van Oel, W.A. Nolen, R.S. Kahn, Dermatoglyphics in relation to brain volumes in twins concordant and discordant for bipolar disorder, Eur. Neuropsychopharmacol. 24 (12) (2014) 1885–1895.

[33] E.F. Torrey, A.E. Bowler, E.H. Taylor, I.I. Gottesman, Schizophrenia and Manic–Depressive Disorder: The Biological Roots of Mental Illness as Revealed by the Landmark Study of Identical Twins, Basic Books, New York, (1994).

[34] W.J. Babler, Quantitative differences in morphogenesis of human epidermal ridges, Birth Defects Original Article Series 15 (6) (1979) 199–208.

[35] K. Wertheim, A. Maceo, The critical stage of friction ridge and pattern formation, J. Forensic Identif. 52 (1) (2002) 35–85.

[36] N.L. Segal, Someone Else's Twin: The True Story of Babies Switched at Birth, Prometheus Books, Amherst, NY, (2011).

[37] C.E. Boklage, On the distribution of nonrighthandedness among twins and their families, Acta Genet. Med. Gemellol. 30 (3) (1981) 167–187.

[38] H.F. Crovitz, K. Zener, A group-test for assessing hand-and eye-dominance, Am. J. Psychol. 75 (2) (1962) 271–276.

[39] L. Mealey, R. Bridgstock, G.C. Townsend, Symmetry and perceived facial attractiveness: a monozygotic co-twin comparison, J. Pers. Soc. Psychol. 76 (1) (1999) 151.

[40] S.W. Gangestad, R. Thornhill, Human sexual selection and developmental stability, in: J.S. Simpson, D.T. Kendrick (Eds.), Evolutionary Social Psychology, Lawrence Erlbaum Associates, Mahwah, NJ, 1997, pp. 160–195.

[41] R.E. Ross, I Can Read Your Face, Forbes 154 (1994) 304–205; How Facial Veins Develop. Available from: http://www.skincareguide.com/article/skin-conditions/varicose-veins/how-facial-veins-develop.

[42] N. Srinivas, G. Aggarwal, P.J. Flynn, R.W. Vorder Bruegge, Analysis of facial marks to distinguish between identical twins, IEEE Transactions on Information Forensics and Security 7 (5) (2012) 1536–1550.

[43] V. Vuollo, M. Sidlauskas, A. Sidlauskas, V. Harila, L. Salomskiene, A. Zhurov, et al. Comparing facial 3D analysis with DNA testing to determine zygosities of twins, Twin Res. Hum. Genet. 18 (3) (2015) 306–313.

[44] M. Honoroff, J. Scharr, Eyelock Myris Secures Computer With Eye Scan in Place of Password. Tom's Guide, January 6, 2014. Available from: http://www.tomsguide.com/us/eyelock-myris-secures-pcs,news-18098.html

[45] Iris Recognition. Available from: http://www.biometric-solutions.com/solutions/index.php?story=iris_recognition

[46] N.L. Segal, Laboratory findings: not twin, twins, not twins, Twin Res. Hum. Genet. 9 (2) (2006) 303–308.

[47] A. McIndoe, A. Franceschetti, Reciprocal skin homografts in a medico-legal case of familial identification of exchanged identical twins, Br. J. Plast. Surg. 2 (4) (1940-1950) 283–289.

[48] J.B. Brown, Homografting of skin: with report of success in identical twins, Surgery 1 (4) (1937) 558–563.

[49] D.T. Lykken, The diagnosis of zygosity in twins, Behav. Genet. 8 (5) (1978) 437–473.

[50] Y. Chitrit, E. Vuillard, S. Khung, N. Belarbi, F. Guimiot, F. Muller, et al. Cloaca in discordant nonoamniotic twins: prenatal diagnosis and consequence for fetal lung development, AJP Rep. 4 (1) (2014) 33–36.

[51] S. Silva, Y. Martins, A. Matias, I. Blickstein, Why are monozygotic twins different?, J. Perinat. Med. 39 (2) (2011) 195–202.

[52] G. Machin, Non-identical monozygotic twins, intermediate twin types, zygosity testing, and the non-random nature of monozygotic twinning: A review, Am. J. Med. Genet. 151 (2) (2009) 110–117.

[53] C.S. Mott Children's Hospital, Twin Reversed Arterial Perfusion Sequence, 2015. Available from: http://www.mottchildren.org/conditions-treatments/twin-reversed-arterial-perfusion-sequence

[54] M.A. Rustico, M.G. Baietti, D. Coviello, E. Orlandi, U. Nicolini, Managing twins discordant for fetal anomaly, Prenat. Diagn. 25 (9) (2005) 766–771.

[55] S.V. Glinianaia, J. Rankin, C. Wright, Congenital anomalies in twins: a register-based study, Hum. Reprod. 23 (6) (2008) 1306–1311.

[56] S. Dahoun, S. Gagos, M. Gagnebin, C. Gehrig, C. Burgi, F. Simon, et al. Monozygotic twins discordant for trisomy 21 and maternal 21q inheritance: a complex series of events, Am. J. Med. Genet. Part A 146 (16) (2008) 2086–2093.

[57] A. Letourneau, F.A. Santoni, X. Bonilla, M.R. Sailani, D. Gonzalez, J. Kind, et al. Domains of genome-wide gene expression dysregulation in Down's syndrome, Nature 508 (7496) (2014) 345–350.

[58] M. Bennett-Smith, Huffington Post. Available from: http://www.huffingtonpost.com/2013/04/30/twins-born-87-days-apart-ireland-guiness-record_n_3186135.html. N.L. Segal, Between twins: birth intervals, Twin Res. 6 (6) (2003) 498–501.

[59] Available from: http://www.dailymail.co.uk/news/article-1053718/Twin-girls-born-midnight-split-school--fall-different-academic-years.html

[60] Available from: http://www.upi.com/Odd_News/2008/09/10/Twins-may-face-different-school-years/81951221085638/

[61] Available from: http://www.huffingtonpost.com/2012/01/03/twins-born-in-different-years_n_1181373.html

[62] O. Williams, Daily Mail. Available from: http://www.dailymail.co.uk/news/article-2351937/The-twins-born-different-countries-Mother-gives-birth-boy-England--Scotland.html

[63] P. Jeeves, Express. Available from: http://www.express.co.uk/news/uk/511723/Twins-Dylan-and-Hannah-born-on-opposite-sides-of-the-border

[64] County Times, Borderline Case of the Welshpool Twins, October 2, 1976.

[65] A. Pakstis, S. Scarr-Salapatek, R.C. Elston, R. Siervogel, Genetic contributions to morphological and behavioral similarities among sibs and dizygotic twins: Linkages and allelic differences, Soc. Biol. 19 (2) (1972) 185–192.

[66] Dr. N. Martin, personal communication, July 19, 2016. Also see an analysis of height heritability, based on the actual degree to which DZ twins and full siblings share genes identical by descent: P.M. Visscher, S.E. Medland, M.A. Ferreira, K.I. Morley, G. Zhu, G., B.K. Cornes et al., Assumption-free estimation of heritability from genome-wide identity-by-descent sharing between full siblings, PLoS Genet. 2 (3) (2006) e41.

CHAPTER 6

Biological Complexities, Myths, and Realities

"We must be the third type of twin!" or "Our kids are somewhere between identical and fraternal twins." I hear these appraisals from twins and parents all the time. There are, however, many misconceptions about this "third type" of twin (polar body pairs) that have taken root and it is time to weed them out. It is also important to contrast what is believed and what is known about some seemingly rare, but possibly common types of fraternal twins. And does it matter if twins exit the womb first or second? It does, but not in the way that many people suppose. In this chapter I will address these issues and questions, as well as other biological complexities, myths, and realities surrounding identical and fraternal twinning.

1. *Polar body twins are less alike than identical twins, but more alike than fraternal twins.*

   Reality Check: False … but with a few exceptions

   Short Answer: Polar body twinning (i.e., the fertilization of the mature egg and one of the three polar bodies that form when the primitive egg divides on its way to maturity) has been labeled the "third type of twin" in popular magazines and multiple birth websites. Twins and parents of twins who are uncertain about twins' being identical or fraternal (because the two look somewhat alike, but not *exactly* alike), often decide that the twins belong to this "third category." (Even if people have never heard of polar body twinning, most have heard that there is a third twin type that lies somewhere between identical and fraternal twins, at least with regard to appearance.) However, they would be wrong to make that determination on looks alone. One reason is that there are several types of polar body twins and *only one type* is more alike genetically than ordinary fraternal twins and less alike than identical twins. Moreover, genes work in mysterious ways, underlying both similarities and differences between family members. It is perfectly possible for fraternal twins to look or act somewhat alike, but not exactly alike, just as ordinary siblings sometimes do. Parents and twins who are uncertain about twin type should seek DNA testing, as I explained earlier.

Twin Mythconceptions
http://dx.doi.org/10.1016/B978-0-12-803994-6.00006-8

More of the Story: Polar body twins result when a mature egg and a polar body are each fertilized by two separate sperm. The possibility that polar body twinning has occurred is not determined by twins' looks alone as many people suppose; its occurrence must be established by genetic analysis using DNA from both parents and both twins. DNA testing allows scientists to track the transmission of genes from parent to child, to see if the twins' genes appear to come from the fertilization of the mature egg and a polar body.

The actual frequency of polar body twinning is presumed to be rare, although this has not been confirmed because suspected cases do not usually undergo DNA testing. That is because the expense of the procedure (it is more costly than ordinary DNA analysis) or the lack of knowledge about where to get the testing done (a professional genetics laboratory) may deter some twins and their families. Most importantly, there are several theoretically possible varieties of polar body twinning that could produce twins who range from very similar to very dissimilar [1]. In fact, one type of polar body twinning yields twins that would be *less* alike, on average, than ordinary fraternal twins, but more alike than two unrelated individuals. These twins are called *primary oocytary* and could result from unusual events occurring as the immature ovum develops into a mature egg. The upshot is that the two ova produced would be more alike than two ova from different women, but less alike than two independent ova typically produced by the same woman on her way to becoming a multiple birth mother.

The varieties and complexities of polar body twinning, complete with illustrative diagrams, are further examined in Appendix 3. I believe that the material in this section will enlighten people who think they are polar body twins, parents who think they have polar body twins, and anyone who is curious to know more about the "third type of twin."

2. *Superfecundation and superfetation are rare fraternal twinning events.*
Reality Check: Unlikely
Short Story: As I discussed in Chapter 1, some fraternal twins are really "genetic half-siblings" because they have different fathers. These superfecundated pairs (twins conceived days apart within the same menstrual cycle) and superfetated pairs (twins conceived weeks apart within different menstrual cycles) would share 25% of their genes, on average—less than the average 50% shared by ordinary fraternal twins and full siblings. The medical world has known about these extraordinary cases since 1810 when a mother delivered a curious pair of twins—one Caucasian

and one of mixed race. Two hundred years later, in May 2012, another such pair (albeit twins of the same ethnicity) drew public attention when a New Jersey woman sought child support for her infant twin daughters. Recall (from Chapter 1) that DNA evidence found that the alleged dad had fathered only one twin, so the man was held financially responsible for just "his" child [2].

A 1992 medical review was the most recent scientific paper I could find that focused exclusively on this subject. The review reported that the frequency of superfecundation in fraternal twins whose parents were involved in paternity suits was 2.4% [3]. This finding suggests that such twins are rare, but I believe that the number of fraternal twins with different fathers is higher since not all questions of nonpaternity in fraternal twins are handled in the courts—some cases may be resolved privately between couples. And not all cases are discovered—if the two fathers were of the same ethnicity, "twin evidence" of a woman's extramarital affair might be hidden and suspicion of one twin's nonpaternity would never be raised. Moreover, aside from paternity suits, there is no reason to routinely perform paternity testing on fraternal twins and their fathers—ordinary fraternal twins generally look physically different from one another, and one or both twins may resemble one parent more than the other, due to their different genes and gene combinations. That alone is not sufficient reason for a man to worry about his partner's fidelity [4]. Of course, some superfecundated twins might look less alike than ordinary fraternal twins since they only have one parent in common, and one child may not resemble his or her alleged father at all.

I suspect that the number of superfecundated twins will rise—not only because infidelity is more common today, but because we have better methods for examining and detecting suspected occurrences [5]. Add to this the fact that more people now know that this type of twinning exists. *Some Reassurance*: Most superfecundated and superfetated twins are likely to have the same father since paternity rates (the frequency of men being the biological fathers of their children) are higher than nonpaternity rates (the frequency of men not being the biological fathers of their children). As such, husbands and partners are more likely to father children in a family than are lovers and acquaintances.

More of the Story: I believe that the frequency of superfecundated twins with different fathers probably approximates that of extramarital births. In 2010, 40.8% of births in the United States were to unmarried women [6]. Of course, nonpaternity rates vary across populations and regions, ranging from .8% (Switzerland) to 30% (United Kingdom), centered on a median value of 3.7%. These values are based on seventeen studies in which the samples were not specifically chosen for disputed paternity. (Studies using samples identified for disputed paternity tend to yield higher, possibly overestimated rates.) These results, while not based on population surveys, do suggest that the widely cited nonpaternity figure of 10% is an overestimate, and that reported rates equal to or exceeding this figure are questionable [7].

Interestingly, a study in Great Britain found a link between greater frequency of sexual activity and fraternal twinning, based partly on an elevated frequency of illegitimately conceived fraternal twins [8]. An earlier study did not find differences in coital frequency among parents of monozygotic (MZ) twins, DZ twins, and singletons, [9] but the participants in this study were married couples—sexual relations with more than one partner (especially among the parents of the fraternal twins) probably occurred less often.

Some populations are good at "concealing" superfecundated twins. Nations, such as Japan and South Korea are good examples of this because hair color and eye color show less variability among the populace, shielding superfecundated newborn twins from detection. A likely case of superfecundation in Japan came to light only because a sonogram taken at 13 weeks gestation showed a marked difference (23 mm) in the twins' crown-to-rump lengths (75 mm for one twin and 52 mm for the other twin). Cotwin differences of this magnitude were also detected from weeks 10 to 35 of the pregnancy [10]. This is important prenatal information because cotwin differences exceeding 11% (calculated as the crown-to-rump length difference between the twins, divided by the value for the larger twin; in this case $75 - 52/75 = 30.7\%$) have been linked to brain and respiratory complications in some twin pregnancies [11].

3. *Male–female twins can be identical MZ.*
   Reality Check: False, but …
   Short Answer: Parents and students sometimes ask me if male–female twins can be identical. The answer to this question is *no*. Identical twins share (virtually) all of their genes, so they cannot differ in sex—a characteristic decided by whether or not a child inherits two X chromosomes (XX, female) or one X chromosome and one Y chromosome (XY, male).

   Male–female twins result when a woman releases two eggs that are fertilized by two separate sperm. In this case, one egg is fertilized by an X-bearing sperm (resulting in a female cotwin) and the other egg is fertilized by a Y-bearing sperm (resulting in a male cotwin). Women have two X chromosomes so they can only transmit an X chromosome to a child. In contrast, men can pass on either an X chromosome or a Y chromosome to a child, giving rise to the myth that men solely "determine" the sex of their child. That is not necessarily so, a myth I explore in *More of the Story*. I will also discuss some unusual medical exceptions in which twins starting out as identical end up as a male and a female—the "but" in the Reality Check.

More of the Story: There are some exceptional medical reports of identical twins who differ in sex, but this only occurs because of an error in how the chromosomes aligned very early after conception. If an X chromosome ends up in a nonfertilized polar body, or a Y chromosome ends up in a sperm cell that does not fertilize the egg, then the twins may differ in sex, but would otherwise be genetically identical. For example, if both twins were initially male (XY) and one twin lost a Y chromosome soon after conception, the pair would include a normal male (XY) and a Turner's syndrome female (XO). Turner's syndrome, a condition affecting about 1/2500 individuals, [12] variously includes a webbed neck, relatively short stature, impaired spatial visualization, infertility, and possible cardiac difficulties. A dramatic case, such as this affecting one MZ male triplet was reported in 1985 in Italy [13]. The male triplet was diagnosed with Turner's syndrome and would be considered a female because of the absence of a Y chromosome. In another case, mosaicism (in which an individual shows two different cell lines) was responsible for sex chromosome differences in an identical female (XX) twin pair—one cotwin showed only XX chromosomes, while her cotwin showed a mix of XX and XO [14]. Thus, such twins would start out being genetically identical, but would quickly diverge.

Some male and female children as young as 3 years of age identify strongly with the opposite sex, irrespective of their biological sex or anatomy. These children prefer clothes, toys, and playmates that reflect these feelings. Some twins in these pairs eventually undergo sex reassignment surgery to bring their bodies in line with their gender identities [15]. I believe that these twins are still identical in a biological sense, despite their sex change, because their genes have not been altered in any way. However, some transgendered pairs do not identify as identical twins after their cotwin transitions to the opposite sex and some never did (even prior to their twin's transition), so it is important to respect their perspective in a psychological sense [16,17]. I will return to a discussion of transgendered twins later in the book.

It is also wrong to think that males determine the sex of a child simply because they can transmit either X-bearing or Y-bearing sperm.

There is some evidence, generated by the maternal dominance hypothesis, that dominant woman are more likely to conceive sons than women who are less dominant [18]. Dominance is a personality trait that is influenced by testosterone levels, as well as by various psychological, physical, and social factors. Some women seem to produce eggs that are more or less likely to be fertilized by an X-bearing sperm (so-called "girl mothers") or a Y-bearing sperm (so-called "boy mothers")—so women seem to have a significant, and probably equal "say" as to the sex of their child. In other words, many X- and Y-bearing sperm have a chance to fertilize an egg, but the state of the egg may favor one type of sperm over another. Selective implantation, miscarriage (S. Kanazawa, Personal communication, December 9, 2015), and even mothers' personality might also play a role in influencing a child's biological sex.

The maternal dominance hypothesis has been supported by several human studies, but more are clearly needed. As a test, I would suggest comparing the number of male and female children born to identical twin mothers and fraternal twin mothers. Identical twins show greater match in personality traits than fraternal twins, but their degree of similarity is not perfect. The maternal dominance hypothesis would predict that (1) identical twin women should conceive more children of the same sex than fraternal twin women, and (2) when identical twins differ in dominance, the more dominant twin should produce more male children. It is also theoretically possible that a very early prenatal mutation in the *SRY* (sex-determining region-Y chromosome) gene in one MZ male cotwin could cause that twin to develop as a female. An *SRY* gene mutation has been identified in 15% of individuals with Swyer's syndrome, a condition preventing the production of an essential male-determining protein, leading to female sexual differentiation [19].

4. *Identical twins can differ in gender identity.*
    Reality Check: True (but in rare cases)
    Short Story: Identical twins can differ in whether they identify with the biological sex they were born with, even from a very early age. My first encounter with such a pair occurred in 2002, when the media contacted me about an identical female twin undergoing sex reassignment surgery to become a male. Since then, I have met and studied several such pairs, and discussed their memorable life stories on the *Oprah Winfrey Show* in 2005.

    Most of the twins I've met whose identity and anatomy did not correspond sensed this mismatch as very young children, as early as 3 years of age. Based on the available studies, many of my colleagues and I believe that parenting practices and other life experiences are *not* responsible for this fundamental difference between cotwins. Factors underlying gender identity most likely originated at conception or in the womb, in the form of genetic, hormonal, developmental, and/or epigenetic events. It is true that the parents of transgender children probably treat them differently from their cotwin—but it is ultimately a little girl's attraction to trucks or a little boy's desire for dresses that shapes their parents' behaviors, not the other way around.

More of the Story: Genetic influences on gender identity development have been reported by a growing number of twin studies [20,21]. An analysis of adult transsexual twins showed that a higher proportion of identical male twins transitioned from male to female (33.3%), relative to identical female twins who transitioned from female to male (22.9%). This finding is important because it matches the male-to-female and female-to-male difference among nontwin transsexuals. A case study I conducted with my colleague Dr. Milton Diamond, from the University of Hawaii, concerned identical reared-apart twins who decided to transition from male to female independently *without their cotwin knowing about it*; this report further demonstrates genetic influence on gender identity [22]. In marked contrast, the percentage of fraternal male and female twin pairs in which both cotwins change sex is zero or close to zero [23].

Transsexualism is rare, affecting about 1/8,300–1/4,000,000 females and 1/2,900–1/100,000 males internationally [24]. Applications for sex reassignment have risen from 1960 to 2010 in Sweden, most likely because of improved medical techniques and greater societal acceptance. Gender identity is clearly complex, affected by many factors. Some brain structures, notably the stria terminalis (BSTc), which is involved in involuntary, neuroendocrine and behavioral responses, appear reduced in size among male-to-female transsexuals [25,26]. A comparable study has not been conducted among females, but an examination of the brain of one female-to-male transsexual revealed the typical heterosexual male volume and neuron number [27]. An informative study would compare the size of the BSTc in identical cotwins who differ in their gender identity; however, these studies are complicated because they can be performed only on the brains of deceased individuals. Possible environmental, experiential, and rearing effects on transsexualism (e.g., paternal distance from daughters, maternal closeness to sons, religious practices, and/or sexual abuse) are not denied by these biological findings, but their causal effects in place of genetic predisposition cannot be assumed [28].

Insight into how one family manages and copes with having one identical twin who transitioned from male to female is available in the 2015 book, *Becoming Nicole* [29,30]. The twins, Jonas and Wyatt, while identical in appearance, were not identical in every way. Wyatt identified as a female from an early age and, despite having a mother who was very supportive of his preferred gender expression, suffered from classmates' cruel remarks and schools' policies regarding bathroom use in elementary school and beyond. The family fought hard to introduce legislation to accommodate transgender individuals in public facilities, and was ultimately successful. In 2015, the twins became undergraduate students at the University of Maine, in Orono, where Wyatt is no longer Wyatt, but is completely Nicole.

5. *Identical cotwins are perfect organ donors and recipients for one another.*
   Reality Check: Mostly true
   Short Answer: Drs Rafael and Robert Mendez have a unique surgical practice. I believe they are the only identical twin doctors to perform organ transplants as a team—Rafael removes a healthy organ from a donor, while Robert places it into the new recipient. In January 1999, at the University of Southern California Hospital in Los Angeles, these twin doctors performed a kidney transplant on identical female twins Anna and Petra Martinez [31]. This operation—twins operating on twins—may be the first and only one of its kind. Identical twins are excellent partners for organ transplantation, but their genetic relationship does not always guarantee unsullied success.
   More of the Story: There is a common belief that identical twins are perfect organ donors for one another, based on their genetic identity [32]. Barring infection, it is assumed that organ rejection will not occur because organ transplantation between identical twins is like replacing the recipient's diseased organ with an identical healthy copy. The truth is that identical twins are *nearly* perfect partners for organ transplantation because even with a genetic match there can be complications. Varying prenatal effects, such as different mutations, X-inactivation in one female twin, and gene methylation differences (see Chapters 1 and 2), may produce genetic or epigenetic differences between identical cotwins that could interfere with acceptance of the new organ. It is also possible that unique life experiences may cause a recipient to build up

antibodies (proteins produced by the immune system) to antigens (foreign substances) that could cause rejection [33]. For this reason, treatment (immunosuppressive medication) that will help an individual accept an organ is sometimes, but not always, administered to identical twin recipients. A case report indicated that immunosuppressive drugs were *not* needed for an identical twin who received skin grafts from his brother following serious burns over 70% of his body [34].

The very first identical twin organ transplant operation took place in 1954, when a kidney was successfully accepted by a recipient twin. The recipient twin remained healthy for 9 years without immunosuppressive treatment, until he passed away from a cardiac condition [35]. In 1978, a testis from one identical twin male was transplanted into his cotwin who was born without testes, a condition called anorchia. (The possibility that the anorchic twin was born with testes that degenerated in utero was raised by the investigators) (Silber, Personal communication, December 23, 2015) [36,37]. Remarkably, the recipient twin successfully fathered a child at a later date. (The identity of the true father could be debated, but I would pick the recipient since his coital act resulted in conception.) The surgical procedure that took place when the twins were aged 30 was performed without immunosuppressive medication. The recipient twin lived for another 30 years, dying of natural causes in his 60s.

In a subsequent study by this same research team, 8 out of 10 identical female twin pairs discordant for ovarian failure underwent twin-to-twin ovarian transplant surgery. The women were between 24 and 37 years of age at the time. The surgery, performed without immunosuppressive medication, restored ovarian function and produced a number of successful pregnancies [38].

A case study by a different research team is also provocative [39]. Following ingestion of poisonous mushrooms, a presumably fraternal male twin developed interstitial nephritis with renal failure (a serious kidney disorder). Part of his treatment included a kidney transplant from his twin brother, with immunosuppressive therapy to guard against rejection. Fifteen years later the twin type of this pair was questioned by a leading researcher, due to the cotwins' very similar (but not identical) appearance. DNA analysis showed that the brothers were identical twins, not fraternal twins, as they and their family had always assumed. Immunosuppression was discontinued and the recipient twin remained well. This case is a key addition to the medical literature because it (1) illustrates the biological compatibility of identical twins for solid organ transplantation, and (2) underlines the importance of knowing the twin type of each and every pair.

However, such favorable results do not always happen—a 1986 follow-up study of 30 identical twin transplant cases showed that graft survival success was 84% after 1 year and down to 72% after 5 years [40]. It is, therefore, recommended that each identical twin pairs' condition be evaluated individually with the administration, type, and duration of immunosuppressive treatment decided on a case-by-case basis. The same applies to fraternal twins and siblings who donate organs to their brothers and sisters (S.J. Silber, Personal communication, December 10, 2015).

6. *DNA evidence cannot distinguish a guilty identical twin from his or her innocent cotwin.*

   Reality Check: False

   Short Answer: A number of years ago I was contacted by a lawyer grappling with an extraordinary case. Her client was an identical male twin who had been accused of fathering a child—but because both he and his twin brother had had a sexual relationship with the baby's mother, paternity could not be assigned. At the time, there was no definitive test to identify the true father. Ironically, I realized that while the identity of the child's father was in dispute, the identity of the child's paternal grandmother was certain!

   Advances in genetic research have completely changed this situation. It is now possible to identify the guilty twin in any misdemeanor or criminal case as long as DNA evidence is available.

   More of the Story: In 2014, researchers at *Eurofins Genomics Campus* in Ebersberg, Germany developed a way to distinguish between identical cotwins through DNA analysis [41]. Their test is based on examination of a person's full set of genes in search of unusual de novo mutations (mutated genes that arise in a person that are not present in his or her parents [42]). This task was accomplished with the help of four people: an adult male identical twin pair and the wife and child of one of the twins. The researchers were told in advance which twin was the child's father and set about to show that this was true.

   DNA was obtained from blood samples provided by the mother and child, and from blood, cheek cells, and sperm samples taken from the two potential twin fathers. First, the twins' zygosity (twin-type) and parent–child paternity were confirmed by standard methods. (At this first stage either of the twins could have been identified as the child's father.) Then, DNA from each twins' sperm sample and DNA from the child's blood were used to identify inherited germline (sex cell)/somatic cell (body cell) mutations that occurred after the twinning event took place. Different mutations can appear in twins, and could be used to link the biological twin father and his child. Ultimately, five single nucleotide polymorphisms (SNPs, a common type of genetic variation) were detected in one of the twins (ultimately determined to be the father because they were also found in his son). These mutations were not detected in the child's uncle (the father's identical cotwin).

This study has four key points: (1) rare mutations can arise soon after the blastocyst divides to create MZ twins. Mutations can also occur in sex cells after birth and can be transmitted to children. (2) These rare mutations can be transmitted into somatic tissue and the germline. (3) Legal cases involving MZ twins' paternity, criminality, or other issues can now be resolved through genetic testing. (4) MZ cotwins are not strictly biologically interchangeable, meaning that one twin cannot substitute for the other twin in every circumstance. For example, if an identical male twin secretly fathered a child with his twin's wife, the identity of the father can now be known if nonpaternity is suspected. Identical twins can no longer be regarded, or treated, as strict genetic understudies for one another.

Of course, if a set of MZ cotwins showed no mutational differences, then differentiating between them on that basis might not be possible. Up to five mutational differences have been identified between MZ cotwins, but few pairs have undergone complete genomic sequencing (J. Craig, Personal communication, July 20, 2016).

7. *Chimeric fraternal twins can accept skin grafts from one another.*
   Reality Check: Possibly
   Short Answer: Recall that chimerism is the presence of more than one cell line in an individual that originated from different sources, such as a blood exchange between fraternal twins while they are in the womb. This same phenomenon occurs naturally between twin cattle, and experimentally between mice. In the case of nonhuman chimerism, when skin has been grafted from one animal to another the new skin has been accepted [43]. There have, however, been no known cases of skin grafting, organ transplantation, or postnatal blood transfusion between chimeric human twins (Dr. M. Sykes, Personal communication, December 10, 2015).
   More of the Story: Theoretically, organ transplantation and related procedures should be successful between DZ twins who share a chorion

and/or who have exchanged cells while in the womb. According to one researcher, "Obviously, the immunological tolerance during fetal life can be maintained in these cases, preventing a graft (donor) versus host (recipient) reaction for the rest of the individual's life" [44] (p. 57). If such twins did acquire immunological tolerance, as expected, it might not be to the same degree for both twins [45]. In other words, DZ cotwins who receive cells from one another prenatally might eventually serve as organ donors and recipients for one another. Given the biological complexities of this process, one cotwin might be better able to tolerate a foreign organ than the other.

8. *Identical twins live longer than fraternal twins.*
    Reality Check: Possibly
    Short Story: There is some evidence that identical twins outlive fraternal twins—at least among male twins who survive to the age of 35, but especially among twins who survive to the age of 50 [46]. More frequent communication between identical than fraternal twins has been associated with their longer life span, but this only made a difference if cotwins were in contact at least 1 time/month. Interestingly, twins' relationships with friends and relatives did not affect the length of their life span. And for some reason, reduced smoking and being married extended identical twins' lives to a greater degree than those of fraternal twins.

    Now there is more to this story: based on data gathered in 2016, it seems that both identical *and* fraternal twins outlive their nontwin counterparts. Identical twins continue to outlive fraternal twins, but the events responsible for this difference and the timing of these events are not the same for males and females [47].

    More of the Story: Twin research shows that genetic factors make a difference when it comes to our longevity, but mostly after the age of 60. These findings come from a study of Danish, Finnish, and Swedish twins showing that the mean life span of identical male twins increased by .39 years for every year that their cotwin lived past 60, while the mean life span of fraternal male twins increased by .21 years. These rates were similar for males and females, although females survived longer than males [48]. Why genetic effects on the life span seem to be greatest at older ages is uncertain, but could reflect the expression of specific genes later in life—however, identical–fraternal twin differences in this regard seem unlikely.

    A 2016 study of Danish twins extended these findings by showing that identical twins live longer than fraternal twins, *both* of whom live longer than singletons [47]. What lies behind these differences offers clues to understanding the length of the life span. Extrinsic mortality processes refer to environmental factors affecting the life span (e.g., quality and availability of support systems). Intrinsic mortality processes refer to biological factors affecting the life span (e.g., the particular genes passed down in one's family). A "twin protection effect" was seen at all ages for female twins—identical–fraternal twin differences in intrinsic mortality (i.e., death due to biological events, such as a genetically influenced disease) were not seen, but the identical twins showed lower extrinsic mortality (i.e., death due to environmental events, such as accidents). The protective effect for males was explained by lower extrinsic mortality through age 65 or 70, during which time the identical twins showed a longevity advantage over fraternal twins and nontwins. It was suggested that, at most ages (but especially among middle-aged identical male twins), the close social bond for which identical twins are famous shields them from risky behaviors, facilitates access to assistance in times of stress, and encourages behaviors promoting good health. It was further suggested that the identical male twin advantage at older ages was due to lower intrinsic mortality, possibly reflecting the cumulative health benefits linked to the social closeness of their earlier years.

A kind of twin protection effect is also provided by the marital relationship that tends to benefit males more than females. This effect was mirrored in the twin data, which showed that males benefited more from extrinsic processes than females. However, the direction of the marriage effect is at issue—does marriage make people healthier, or are healthier people more likely to marry? As the researchers noted, studying twins removes this effect because people do not choose to be twins [49].

An interesting twist to both these stories is that many genetically influenced conditions, such as type 2 diabetes, Alzheimer's disease, and breast cancer, may affect one or both identical twins. Even twins who are both affected sometimes show different degrees of severity—this is especially true of psychiatric conditions, such as bipolar disorder and schizophrenia [50]. Discordance between twins for these conditions might be linked to differences in the cotwins' life span. It could be that one twin passes away before he or she develops a certain condition, giving the appearance of twin discordance. I have discussed various reasons for such differences in earlier chapters; among them are prenatal factors, X chromosome inactivation, and epigenetic events.

9. *Twins' birth order matters.*

Reality Check: True—but not the way many people think it does

Short (But Somewhat Long) Answer: In the introduction to this volume, I wrote that my mother did not reveal which twin (my sister or me) was the firstborn until we turned 7—she said that she kept this information quiet to avoid a within-pair battle. Regardless, I always believed that my twin sister Anne had been born first because she was bigger and stronger than I—older children *are* bigger than younger ones. Anne was even allowed to ride the New York City subway before I was, possibly because she *seemed* older. So when we learned that I had been the first twin to enter the world (via a natural delivery) I experienced a moment of glee! Actually ecstasy—but this feeling lasted for only a few minutes. This new information changed nothing about who we were then, or how we think about ourselves as individuals and as twins today. It is possible that other newly self-discovered firstborn twins might react differently, but I think that is improbable—knowledge of birth order is unlikely to alter years of intertwin relations.

Still, who goes first or chooses first in games or other daily activities is something many young twins monitor closely—as conveyed by the fictional twins show in Fig. 6.1.

A few early, modest-size studies found that parents and teachers judged firstborn twins from same-sex pairs to be the more dominant cotwin [51,52]. The tendency for firstborn twins to be heavier at birth and at school entrance than second born twins may partly explain this finding. In contrast, female twins from opposite-sex pairs were judged to be *more* dominant than their brothers who were usually firstborn and bigger, an interesting situation I will revisit later. However, a study of several hundred twin pairs found that birth order was unrelated to personality traits including sociability, responsibility—and dominance [53]. And an analysis of birth order and intellect among Japanese 12-year olds did not find that second born twins performed less well than firstborn twins, despite the second born's birth complications, such as cyanosis (skin discoloration due to low oxygen in the blood) or breech (foot-first) presentation [54].

There is nothing psychologically significant about being the first or second born twin *unless others make that difference meaningful.* I have known parents who gave the "older" twin the respected task of carrying the house keys, and parents who chose the "older" twin to perform religious rituals in the home. Age connotes authority, wisdom, and responsibility, so making

Figure 6.1 *You go out first. Signal me if it's safe!! (Reprinted with permission. Image source: Cartoonstock.com).*

birth order distinctions between twins may unfairly (and unjustifiably) promote superiority and inferiority feelings between Twin 1 and Twin 2, respectively. Such scenarios should be avoided—in fact, birth order is often decided arbitrarily in cesarean section deliveries, so it is truly without meaning. Even when twins are delivered naturally, I would urge parents to conceal the identity of their first and second born twins until they are old enough to know that birth order has little psychological meaning apart from what others may think, or how others might act toward each twin.

In contrast, birth order can spell important biological and medical differences between twins. Naturally delivered second born twins are at a higher risk for health problems, such as respiratory distress, neonatal trauma, and infection than firstborns. Second born twins are also at greater risk for newborn death [55,56]. These problems are partly associated with the decreased size of the uterus after the delivery of the first twin. In addition, longer delivery intervals between first and second born twins predict less favorable outcomes for the second born twin who may need immediate assistance. Of course, not all second born twins have difficult births, but their average risk is higher.

More of the Story: Psychologist Frank Sulloway had an intriguing theory that tied personality traits to birth order [57]. He reasoned that first-borns would benefit by adopting their family's values and practices to secure their role as successor. He also reasoned that later borns should be more rebellious and less compliant in order to establish a special niche in the family structure. Attempts to replicate the findings from his 1996 investigation have been mixed, with calls for new ways to study birth order. So in 2008 I decided to test Sulloway's theory using identical twins reared apart [58]. The theory predicts that if Twin A was the eldest and Twin B was the youngest within their different adoptive homes, then Twin A should be more of a "conformist" and Twin B should be more of a "revolutionary." Unfortunately, the limited number of separated twins raised in these different birth orders only allowed me to compare the personalities of twins who occupied the same versus different positions in their respective pecking orders. I found that twins raised in different birth order positions *did not* differ appreciably from one another in personality, but firm conclusions could not be drawn from this modest study. I still find this idea very exciting because it might highlight an environmental measure that is not shared between twins, and that affects personality development in a meaningful way. I hope that I or someone else can carry out this analysis in the future.

There are stacks of studies comparing the health outcomes of first and second newborn twins [55,56,59]. The most consistent finding is that newly delivered second born twins are at great physical risk than their firstborn cotwins. The risk to Twin 2 appears to be unrelated to presentation (vertex or breech), chorionicity (separate or shared membranes), or infant sex. But the risk may be increased when mothers and physicians jointly plan for a vaginal delivery, when there is a 20–40% difference in birth weight (especially when the second born twin is heavier than the firstborn twin) and when the birth interval is relatively long (15–30 min). In addition, during vaginal delivery the status of the umbilical cord blood gas drops for first and second born twins, but more so for the second born, mandating the timely delivery of Twin 2 [60].

Interestingly, when twins are both in the vertex position a vaginal delivery is safer for the firstborn twin, while delivering the second twin vaginally or by cesarean section does not differ with respect to physical problems. However, the risk of fetal death is somewhat lower for the second twin (vertex or breech) if delivered vaginally *and* promptly—benefits to the first twin from vaginal delivery may be outweighed if there is an extended delay, possibly necessitating a combined vaginal/cesarean section delivery.

According to a large 2015 study of Australian mothers, twins born at 32 weeks or beyond fare best when the delivery is vaginal and uncomplicated for both twins, or is done by elective cesarean section. However, only 14.8% of these women delivered both twins vaginally without the need for intervention [61].

I came across a related mythconception about twins' birth order that I hadn't anticipated: it seems that many obstetricians, neonatologists, and parents assume that the birth order diagnosed by ultrasound corresponds to the birth order at delivery [62]. That's just not so. Twins may change their womb position for a number of reasons, either naturally before or during labor, or possibly because the membranes surrounding each twin can rupture, affecting their positioning relative to the birth canal. Analyses of 149 opposite-sex twin pairs revealed discrepancies between predicted and actual birth order in 37.6% of cases based on fetal sex and 36% of cases based on weight discordance. In contrast, chorionicity, the scan-to-delivery interval, gestation at scan, and gestation at delivery were not meaningful predictors of twins' birth order. This is especially important information for doctors who must provide optimal care when delivering twins discordant for fetal anomalies, size, or other conditions; however, additional studies assessing a broader range of factors thought to affect twins' delivery status are required. It is also vital that families understand that predicting twins' birth order is not an exact science or their faith in physicians might be challenged.

Finally, much has been made of the tendency for firstborn twins to be bigger at birth. That may be, but interestingly, a 2016 international collaborative study involving thousands of twins showed that firstborn twins were larger as measured by body mass index (weight in kilograms/height in meters) in childhood and adolescence, and also slightly taller in childhood [2]. However, the birth order differences in size were quite modest for both male and female pairs, and for identical and fraternal pairs [63]. It is also the case that, during development, initially smaller twins may engage in games of "catch-up" en route to childhood and adolescence, and may even "outsize" their initially larger cotwin from time to time [64]. This is a great example of how prenatal factors constraining early growth can be overcome.

10. *Twin research applies only to twins, not to anyone else.*

Reality Check: False

Short Answer: I am surprised that so many psychological scientists still believe that twin research findings cannot be applied to the general population [65,66]. They claim that because twins and singletons experience different prenatal and postnatal biological and social conditions, twin research applies only to twins. That is just not correct— the truth is that the vast majority of findings from twin studies (with the exceptions that I discuss later) have far reaching implications for the nontwin population. If identical twins are more alike in language skills, running speed, and visual acuity than fraternal twins, this shows that genes (as well as the environment) affect the development of these traits. This information can help everyone understand why they resemble all, some, or none of their family members because genes explain both similarities and differences between relatives living together. For example, fraternal twins and siblings may both benefit physically from healthy meals served at home, but one child may benefit more than another because of his or her genetic makeup.

The usefulness of twin studies does not end there. When one identical twin outperforms his cotwin (like former major league baseball player José Canseco, who enjoyed a more illustrious career than his twin brother Ozzie), or one twin develops Alzheimer's disease (like the renowned photographer of twins, Frances McLauglin-Gill, whose identical twin sister and collaborator Kathryn Abbe stayed healthy), scientists aim to find the biological and environmental events at the root of these differences. This is information that helps everyone.

More of the Story: In 1995, researchers in Denmark took a close look at the generalizability of twin research findings to the general public. The twins they studied came from the national Danish Twin Registry, established in 1954. Information regarding similarity in genetically influenced traits, such as hair color and eye color, was needed to make accurate assessments of twin type. Therefore, if one or both twins had passed away or emigrated before the age of 6 they were not included in the study, leaving about one-third of the twins who were originally registered. It turned out that disease incidence and mortality were comparable for twins and singletons, a finding confirmed for most of the behavioral and physical measures [67]. It is also the case that neurodevelopmental problems, such as those involving word comprehension, motor coordination, and visual perception, are increased among very low birth weight children [68].Therefore, twins may be overrepresented among such children until birth weight and gestational age are accounted for. In Chapter 7 I note that twin–singleton differences in IQ diminish when the effects of twins' birth weight on IQ are considered.

More recently, in 2014, an interdisciplinary team defended the methods and assumptions of twin research against comments from critics. These researchers concluded that, "There is still much to be gained from heritability studies (analyses of genetic and environmental influences on human traits) and the classical twin design" (p. 616) [69]. I completely agree.

Before I weigh in further on this topic, it is important to recall and distinguish between the two twin-related research tracks; I have called them Track One and Track Two. Track One uses MZ and DZ twins as a research design or model for examining genetic environmental influences on behavior and disease. (I described the various ways in which twins are used in research in Chapter 2.) Track One researchers explore factors underlying individual differences in general intelligence, personality profiles, social attitudes, and job satisfaction, among other things. They would also study identical twins who differ in schizophrenia, diabetes, or depression, with the aim of finding factors that might have triggered the disorder in one twin and prevented it in the other. This information can help nontwins who are trying to understand the origins of an illness and the ways in which they might prevent it. Findings from Track One studies are generalizable to the nontwin population, or they would not be worth conducting.

Track Two researchers approach twins and their families as a unique population, and conduct research dedicated to specific twin-related topics. Track Two researchers might examine the wisdom of separating twins at school, dressing twins alike, or telling twins which of the two was born first. Twins' shorter gestational period and higher frequency of congenital anomalies, relative to singletons, would also be of interest to parents and physicians for detecting and managing twin-related problems and their treatment [70]. Findings from Track Two studies would *not* be generalizable to the nontwin population because they focus on characteristics specific to twins.

There are physical and behavioral characteristics unique to twins and twin pregnancies that do *not* apply to singletons and singleton pregnancies. For example, congenital heart defects occur more frequently among twins than nontwins [71]. And both MZ and DZ twins' growth patterns differ from those of nontwins. Beginning at about 30 weeks' gestation, more twins than singletons tend to be small for their gestational age [72]. The growth patterns of twins and singletons become even more marked by 35 weeks in utero. In addition, the peak growth for twins is 175 g/week at 31 weeks, but 250 g/week for singletons at 33 weeks. And twins' birth weight continues to fall behind that of nontwins—by 38 weeks, twins in the 50th percentile are equivalent to nontwins in the 10th percentile. In fact, twins delivered at or after 40 weeks may show growth retardation, such that they are lighter in weight than twins delivered at 38–39 weeks [73]. These findings show that the birth size of twins cannot be properly evaluated using nontwin standards.

Both twin and nontwin pregnancies may be complicated by a mother's preexisting diabetes mellitus (90–95% of adult cases of diabetes are type 2, in which the body manufactures too little insulin or is unable to use available insulin, interfering with the use of blood sugar for energy [74]), but adverse outcomes in these two groups are not the same. For example, stillbirths, large-for-gestational-age infants, and congenital anomalies are more common among twin pregnancies; cesarean delivery, large-for-gestational-age infants, and preeclampsia (high maternal blood pressure and protein in the urine) are more common among nontwin pregnancies [75]. The pregnancy experience and medical complications of multiple births are unique and *not* generalizable to mothers bearing just one child.

One More Point: As I explained in Chapter 1, about 25% of identical twin pairs include cotwins who show opposite hand preference. Handedness has a genetic component as shown by biological and adoptive parent–child research, but a classic twin study would suggest otherwise. That is because a substantial minority of identical twins would differ in handedness, *but not for genetic reasons*. Opposite-handedness in identical twins has been explained by events that would not apply equally or at all to nontwins, such as increased birth difficulties and possible delayed zygotic splitting—recall that the consequences of early versus late division of the fertilized egg are uncertain. Regardless, the key point is that some prenatal and physical features argue against applying *selected twin findings* to nontwins.

11. *Twins' average birth weight is 5 lbs, 5 oz. and applies to all twins.*
Reality Check: False
Short Answer: I was alarmed to find this birth weight statistic masquerading as a hard fact because twins' average birth weight depends on

the length of the pregnancy, the sex of the newborn, and whether or not the mother has had previous deliveries. According to a large-scale 2013 study, 4 lbs, 15.68 oz. is the average weight of male twins born at 34 weeks, and 5 lbs., 2.72 oz. is the average weight of female twins born at 35 weeks [76]. *These average weights do not apply to all twins.*

More of the Story: Population-based birth weight data from Finland are available for both twins and singletons, organized according to sex, gestational length, and mother's childbearing history (primapara or first birth; multipara or later birth). Evaluating twins' birth weight is most informative when done in reference to these factors. Male twins typically weigh more than female twins, and twins born at 37 weeks weigh more than twins born at 32 weeks. And mothers who have given birth previously tend to have heavier birth weight twins. However, even these recent population-based figures, based on 533,666 newborn twins, are somewhat misleading because chorion type was not considered in these calculations [76].

There is a reason that chorion type (one chorion or two) matters when it comes to twins' birth weight. Identical twins with single chorions are at high risk for low birth weight because of their earlier delivery. Dichorionic identical twins and fraternal twins tend to be heaviest, while dichorionic MZ twins do not differ from DZ twins in early outcome. This suggests that chorion type is a more significant influence on birth weight than twin type [77,78]. Monochorionic twins are delivered earlier than dichorionic twins (34.2 weeks vs. 35.0 weeks) and remain in the hospital for longer periods before going home (13.7 days vs. 10.8 days), [79] consistent with their relatively lower birth weights.

12. *The real incidence of twin-to-twin transfusion syndrome (TTTS) is uncertain.*
   Reality Check: True
   Short Answer: TTTS involves the unequal sharing of a single placenta in which blood flow is unidirectional, flowing from a donor twin to a recipient twin, resulting in the restricted growth and the death of one or both twins. The real incidence of TTTS is unknown because some affected twins are lost through miscarriage in the second trimester of pregnancy or the vanishing twin syndrome in the first trimester. Estimates of how often TTTS occurs vary from between 9% and 20% [80,81] to 10–15% among monochorionic MZ twins [82]. However, twins at *potential* risk for TTTS are the approximately 70% of MZ twins with a single chorion. TTTS is confirmed by ultrasound based on suspicious signs, such as marked size discordance

between the cotwins. A few rare cases of TTTS in monochorionic fraternal twins have been reported [83].

More of the Story: As indicated earlier, TTTS involves the sharing of a single placenta, in which blood flow is unidirectional, a situation posing serious risks to both twins. Severe TTTS may be identified when the pregnancy has advanced to between 16 and 24 weeks, eventuating in oligohydramnios (insufficient amniotic fluid surrounding the donor twin) and polyhydramnios (excess amniotic fluid surrounding the recipient twin). TTTS is established when a difference in amniotic fluid is observed on the two sides of the membrane (amnion) separating the twins. Fetal growth restriction is another clue to the presence of TTTS.

Once TTTS has been diagnosed, its progression and severity can be established according to the Quintero staging system that applies various criteria (e.g., inability to see the fetal bladder on a scan for longer than 60 seconds; folding of the intertwin membrane) to assist the diagnosis and management of each case [82].

Marked discordance in estimated fetal weight does not always mean that twins have TTTS, although it does have medical significance. The growth difference between twins can be calculated as: (birth weight of the larger twin − birth weight of the smaller twin)/(birth weight of the larger twin) × 100. If the larger twin weighs 5 lbs and the smaller twin weighs 3 lbs, the twins' weight differential would be 40% (2/5 or .4 × 100 = 40%). A birth weight difference of 20% or greater has been associated with higher neonatal death, but opinions vary. Some physicians believe that a 15% birth weight difference poses serious risk, while others believe that risks begin when cotwins' birth weight difference reaches 29% [82,84].

TTTS should not be diagnosed by the cotwins' birth weight difference alone, but it can be a clue to this condition. Identifying more precise degrees of risk linked to the percentage by which twins' birth weight differs is an important goal. Other factors associated with birth weight, such as parental education (presumably associated with greater knowledge and understanding of twins and twinning), socioeconomic status, race, and foreign-born status need to be considered [85].

A special issue of the journal *Twin Research and Human Genetics* (2016), devoted to the TTTS, includes an extraordinary compilation of papers on the development, detection, consequences, and treatment of this condition [86].

13. *Twins' average length of gestation (twin pregnancy) is less than 37 weeks.*
Reality Check: True

Short Answer: The average length of a twin pregnancy is 35 weeks, about 4 weeks less than the average length of a nontwin pregnancy (38.9 weeks—longer than what most people think). However, 61.6% of twins are born at 36 weeks or less, and among those 10.5% are born before 31 weeks, and 4.1% are born between 20 and 27 weeks. It is very rare for twins to be born after 41 weeks [87].

Conventional wisdom suggests that efforts toward extending multiple pregnancies for as long as possible guarantees the best health outcomes for newborn twins. This is *not* so, as I explain next.

More of the Story: There are heightened risks for women whose twin pregnancies last beyond 37 weeks, such as newborn morbidity (diseased condition) and newborn mortality (susceptibility to death) at or around the time of birth. Population-based studies show that risks such as these are lowest when twins are born between 36 and 38 weeks. Another large-scale study found that 70% of "ideal twin pregnancies" lasted between 35 and 38 weeks. These findings have encouraged physicians to reconsider what it means to carry twins postterm, or later than expected—twins' new postterm benchmark may be 38 weeks, whereas it remains at 41+ weeks for singletons [73,88]. In part, this has to do with the fact that twins' maturation in the womb is faster than that of nontwins. The aging of the twin placenta is quicker and twins' average lecithin/sphingomyelin ratio (test of fetal amniotic fluid to assess lung maturity) is achieved sooner than that of singletons [73]. Twins' accelerated prenatal development may be due to their shorter gestation times [89].

In order to determine the optimal delivery time for twins, infant outcomes were compared between women randomly select to be part of an elective or standard care delivery group. Women in the elective group delivered twins at 37 weeks, either vaginally by labor induction or by cesarean section, based on consultation with their physician. Women in the standard care group delivered twins at 38 weeks or later, either vaginally following spontaneous labor or labor induction, or by elective cesarean section. Fewer unfavorable outcomes (especially those associated with lower birth weight) were observed among the twins born to the 37-week delivery group. It appears that when multiple birth pregnancies are without complications, elective delivery at 37 weeks is in the best interest of newborn twins [88].

Mythconceptions about twins are not limited to what goes on inside the womb, nor to theories about what distinguishes identical twins from fraternal twins. Many popular, but poorly conceived impressions also surround the way identical and fraternal twins think and act. A look into the minds and thoughts of twins is my next task—and the extent to which what *is true* squares with what *is thought to be true* is my mission.

REFERENCES

[1] M.G. Bulmer, The Biology of Twinning in Man, Clarendon Press, Oxford, (1970) V.J. Baldwin, Pathology of Multiple Pregnancy, Springer-Verlag, New York, NY, 1994.

[2] Associated Press, Correction: Twin-2 Dads Story, Associated Press, May 8, 2015. Available from: http://www.apnewsarchive.com/2015/Correction-Twins-2-Dads-story/id-2684b32fb9c7449491ecf3e8bff7e70e

[3] R.E. Wenk, T. Houtz, M. Brooks, F.A. Chiafari, How frequent is heteropaternal superfecundation?, Acta Genet. Med. Gemellol. 41 (1) (1992) 43–47.

[4] H. Assefa, New Jersey Judge Rules Twin Girls Have Different Fathers, May 8, 2015. Available from: http://www.cnn.com/2015/05/08/us/new-jersey-twins-two-fathers/index.html

[5] H.C. McNamara, S.C. Kane, J.M. Craig, R.V. Short, M.P. Umstad, A review of the mechanisms and evidence for typical and atypical twinning, Am. J. Obstet. Gynecol. 241 (2) (2015) 172–191.

[6] Economist, The Fraying Knot, Economist, January 12, 2013. Available from: http://www.economist.com/news/united-states/21569433-americas-marriage-rate-falling-and-its-out-wedlock-birth-rate-soaring-fraying

[7] M.A. Bellis, K. Hughes, S. Hughes, J.R. Ashton, Measuring paternal discrepancy and its public health consequences, J. Epidemiol. Commun. Health 59 (9) (2005) 749–754.

[8] W.H. James, Coital frequency and twinning–a comment, J. Biosoc. Sci. 24 (1) (1992) 135–136.

[9] B. Bonnelyke, J. Olsen, J. Nielsen, Coital frequency and twinning, J. Biosoc. Sci. 22 (2) (1990) 191–196.

[10] Okamura, et al. A probably case of superfecundation, Fetal Diagn. Ther. 7 (1) (1992) 717–720.

[11] Z. Shahshahan, M. Hashemi, Crown-rump length discordance in twins in the first trimester and its correlation with perinatal complications, J. Res. Med. Sci. 16 (9) (2011) 1224–1227.

[12] H.K. Kim, W. Gottliebson, K. Hor, P. Backeljauw, I. Gutmark-Little, S.R. Salisbury, R. Fleck, Cardiovascular anomalies in Turner syndrome: spectrum, prevalence, and cardiac MRI findings in a pediatric and young adult population, Am. J. Roentgenol. 196 (2) (2011) 454–460.

[13] B. Dallapiccola, C. Stomeo, G. Ferranti, A. Di Lecce, M. Purpura, Discordant sex in one of three triplets, J. Med. Genet. 22 (1) (1985) 6–11.

[14] J.H. Edwards, T. Dent, J. Kahn, Monozygotic twins of different sex, J. Med. Genet. 3 (2) (1966) 117–123.

[15] M. Diamond, Transsexuality among twins: identity concordance, transition, rearing and orientation, Int. J. Transgend. 14 (1) (2013) 24–38.

[16] N.L. Segal, Indivisible by Two: Lives of Extraordinary Twins, Harvard University Press, Cambridge, MA, (2007).

[17] A.E. Nutt, Becoming Nicole: The Transformation of an American Family, Random House, New York, NY, (2015).

[18] V.J. Grant, Sex determination and the maternal dominance hypothesis, Hum. Reprod. 11 (11) (1996) 2371–2375.

[19] NIH, Swyer's Syndrome, 2016. Available from: https://ghr.nlm.nih.gov/condition/swyer-syndrome#genes

[20] G. Heylens, G. De Cuypere, K.J. Zucker, C. Schelfaut, E. Elaut, H.Vanden Bossche, et al. Gender identity disorder in twins: a review of the case report literature, J. Sex. Med. 9 (3) (2012) 751–757.

[21] A. Knafo, A.C. Iervolino, R. Plomin, Masculine girls and feminine boys: genetic and environmental contributions to atypical gender development in early childhood, J. Pers. Soc. Psychol. 88 (2) (2005) 400–412.

[22] N.L. Segal, M. Diamond, Identical reared apart twins concordant for transsexuality, J. Exp. Clin. Med. 6 (2) (2014) 74.

[23] M. Diamond, Transsexuality among twins: identity concordance, transition, rearing and orientation, Int. J. Transsexualism 14 (24) (2013) 38.

[24] C. Dhejne, K. Öberg, S. Arver, M. Landén, An analysis of all applications for sex reassignment surgery in Sweden, 1960–2010: prevalence, incidence, and regrets, Arch. Sex. Behav. 43 (8) (2014) 1535–1545.

[25] J. Zhou, M.A. Hofman, L.J. Gooren, D.F. Swaab, A sex difference in the human brain and its relation to transsexuality, Nature 378 (1995) 68–70.

[26] C.C. Crestani, F.H. Alves, F.V. Gomes, L.B. Resstel, F.M. Correa, J.P. Herman, Mechanisms in the bed nucleus of the stria terminalis involved in control of autonomic and neuroendocrine functions: a review, Curr. Neuropharmacol. 11 (2) (2013) 141–159.

[27] W.C. Chung, G.J. De Vries, D.F. Swaab, Sexual differentiation of the bed nucleus of the stria terminalis in humans may extend into adulthood, J. Neurosci. 22 (3) (2002) 1027–1033.

[28] N.L. Segal, Two monozygotic twin pairs discordant for female-to-male transsexualism, Arch. Sex. Behav. 35 (3) (2006) 347–358.

[29] A. McNutt, Becoming Nicole: The Transformation of an American Family, Random House, New York, NY.

[30] Becoming Nicole, Washington Post, October 19, 2015. Available from: http://www.washingtonpost.com/sf/national/2015/10/19/becoming-nicole/

[31] B. Pool, Twin Doctors and Their Twin Patients Celebrate, Los Angeles Times, p. A13R, January 26, 1999.

[32] Y. Einahas, May 25, 2010. Available from: http://ezinearticles.com/?Organ-Transplantation!-What-Are-the-Difficulties?&id=4360825

[33] A. Hauch, J. Heneghan, M. Killackey, et al. Living-related kidney transplant in two sets of HLA identical twins, J. Surg. Transplant. Sci. 1 (1) (2013) 1003–1005.

[34] E. Turk, E. Karagulle, H. Turan, H. Oguz, E.S. Abali, N. Ozcay, et al. Successful skin homografting from an identical twin in a severely burned patient, J. Burn Care Res. 35 (3) (2014) e177–e179.

[35] J.P. Merrill, J.E. Murray, J.H. Harrison, W.R. Guild, Successful homotransplantation of the human kidney between identical twins, J. Am. Med. Assoc. 160 (4) (1956) 277–282.

[36] S.L. Silber, Transplantation of a human testis for anorchia, Fertil. Steril. 30 (2) (1978) 181–187.

[37] S.J. Silber, L.J. Rodriguez-Rigau, Pregnancy after testicular transplant: importance of treating the couple, Fertil. Steril. 33 (2) (1980) 454–455.

[38] S.J. Silber, M. DeRosa, J.E. Pineda, K. Lenahan, D. Grenia, K. Gorman, R.G. Gosden, A series of monozygotic twins discordant for ovarian failure: ovary transplantation (cortical versus microvascular) and cryopreservation, Hum. Reprod. 23 (7) (2008) 1531–1537.

[39] D.M. St. Clair, J.B. St. Clair, C.P. Swainson, F. Bamforth, G.A. Machin, Twin zygosity testing for medical purposes, Am. J. Med. Genet. 77 (5) (1998) 412–414.

[40] N.L. Tilney, Renal transplantation between identical twins: a review, World J. Surg. 10 (3) (1986) 381–388.

[41] J. Weber-Lehman, E. Schilling, G. Gradl, D.C. Richter, J. Wiehler, B. Rolf, Finding the needle in the haystack: differentiating "identical" twins in paternity testing and forensics by ultra-deep next generation sequencing, Forensic Sci. Int. 9 (March) (2014) 42–46.

[42] D. Kobalt, De Novo Mutations and Human Disease, Mass Genom. (2012) http://massgenomics.org/2012/08/de-novo-mutations-and-human-disease.html

[43] D. Ribatti, Peter Brian Medawar and the discovery of acquired immunological tolerance, Immunol. Lett. 167 (2) (2015) 63–66.

[44] R. Sudik, S. Jakubiczka, F. Nawroth, E. Gilberg, P.F. Wieacker, Chimerism in a fertile woman with 46, XY karyotype and female phenotype: case report, Hum. Reprod. 16 (1) (2001) 56–58.

[45] G. Machin, Non-identical monozygotic twins, intermediate twin types, zygosity testing, and the non-random nature of monozygotic twinning: a review, Am. J. Med. Genet. C 151 (2) (2009) 110–127.

[46] M.D. Zaretsky, Communication between identical twins: health behavior and social factors are associated with longevity that is greater among identical than fraternal US World War II veteran twins, J. Gerontol. A 58 (6) (2003) M566–M572.

[47] D.J. Sharrow, J.J. Anderson, A twin protection effect? Explaining twin survival advantages with a two-process mortality model, PLoS One 11 (5) (2016) e0154774 http://journals.plos.org/plosone/article?id=info%3Adoi%2F10.1371%2Fjournal.pone.0154774.

[48] J.V.B. Hjelmborg, I. Iachine, A. Skythe, J.W. Vaupel, M. McGue, M. Koskenvuo, J. Kaprio, et al. Genetic influence on human lifespan and longevity, Hum. Genet. 119 (3) (2006) 312–321.

[49] University of Washington, Twins, Especially Identical Male Twins, Live Longer, Science News, August 18, 2016. Available from: https://www.sciencedaily.com/releases/2016/08/160818170156.htm

[50] E. Cevenini, L. Invidia, F. Lescai, S. Salvioli, P. Tieri, G. Castellani, C. Franceschi, Human models of aging and longevity, Expert Opin. Biol. Ther. 8 (9) (2008) 1393–1405.

[51] P.S. Very, N.P. Van Hine, Effects of birth order upon personality development of twins, J. Genet. Psychol. 114 (1) (1969) 93–95.

[52] H.L. Koch, Twins and twin relations, University of Chicago Press, Chicago, (1966).

[53] J.C. Loehlin, R.C. Nichols, Heredity, Environment, and Personality: A Study of 850 Sets of Twins, University of Texas Press, Austin, TX, (1976).

[54] A. Asaka, S. Ooki, K. Yamada, The influence of birth injuries in first-born and second-born twins, Acta Genet. Med. Gemellol. 39 (3) (1990) 409–412.

[55] R.S. Hartley, J. Hitti, Birth order and delivery interval: analysis of twin pair perinatal outcomes, J. Matern. Fetal Neonatal Med. 17 (6) (2005) 375–380.

[56] B.A. Armson, C. O'Connell, V. Persad, K.S. Joseph, D.C. Young, T.F. Baskett, Determinants of perinatal mortality and serious neonatal morbidity in the second twin, Obstet. Gynecol. 108 (3 Pt. 1) (2006) 556–564.

[57] F.J. Sulloway, Born to Rebel: Birth Order, Family Dynamics and Creative Lives, Pantheon, New York, NY, (1996).

[58] N.L. Segal, Personality and birth order in monozygotic twins adopted apart: a test of Sulloway's theory, Twin Res. Hum. Genet. 11 (1) (2008) 103–107.

[59] A.C. Rossi, P.M. Mullin, R.H. Chmait, Neonatal outcomes of twins according to birth order, presentation and mode of delivery: a systematic review and meta-analysis, BJOG 118 (5) (2011) 523–532.

[60] T.Y. Leung, I.H. Lok, W.H. Tam, T.N. Leung, T.K. Lau, Deterioration in cord blood gas status during the second stage of labour is more rapid in the second twin than in the first twin, BJOG 111 (6) (2004) 546–549.

[61] S. Soong, R.M. Greer, G. Gardener, V. Flenady, S. Kumar, Impact of mode of delivery after 32 weeks' gestation on neonatal outcome in dichorionic diamniotic twins, J. Obstet. Gynaecol. Res. 42 (4) (2015) 392–398.

[62] F. D'Antonio, T. Dias, B. Thilaganathan, Does antenatal ultrasound labeling predict birth order in twin pregnancies?, Ultrasound Obstet. Gynecol. 41 (3) (2013) 274–277.

[63] Y. Yokoyama, A. Jelenkovic, R. Sund, J. Sung, J.L. Hopper, S. Ooki, Twin's birth-order differences in height and body mass index from birth to old age: a pooled study of 26 twin cohorts participating in the CODA twins project, Twin Res. Hum. Genet. 19 (2) (2016) 112–124.

[64] R.S. Wilson, Twin growth: initial deficit, recovery, and trends in concordance from birth to nine years, Ann. Hum. Biol. 6 (3) (1979) 205–220.

[65] S.L. Farber, Identical Twins Reared Apart, Basic Books, New York, NY, (1981).

[66] C.H. Burt, R.L. Simons, Pulling back the curtain on heritability studies: biosocial criminology in the postgenomic era, Criminology 52 (2) (2014) 223–262.

[67] K. Christensen, J.W. Vaupel, N.V. Holm, A.I. Yashin, Mortality among twins after age 6: fetal origins hypothesis versus twin method, Br. Med. J. 310 (6977) (1995) 432–436.

[68] G. Verkerk, M. Jeukens-Visser, A. van Wassenaer-Leemhuis, J. Kok, F. Nollet, The relationship between multiple developmental difficulties in very low birth weight children at 3½ years of age and the need for learning support at 5 years of age, Res. Dev. Disabil. 35 (1) (2014) 185–191.

[69] J.C. Barnes, J.P. Wright, B.B. Boutwell, J.A. Schwartz, E.J. Connolly, J.L. Nedelec, K.M. Beaver, Demonstrating the validity of twin research in criminology, Criminology 52 (4) (2014) 588–626.

[70] M.A. Weber, N.J. Sebire, Genetics and developmental pathology of twinning, Semin. Fetal Neonatal Med. 15 (6) (2010) 313–318.

[71] A.M. Herskind, D.A. Pedersen, K. Christensen, Increased prevalence of congenital heart defects in monozygotic and dizygotic twins, Circulation 128 (11) (2013) 1182–1188.

[72] J.G. Hall, Twinning, Lancet 362 (9385) (2003) 735–743.

[73] B. Luke, J. Minogue, F.R. Witter, L.G. Keith, T.R. Johnson, The ideal twin pregnancy: patterns of weight gain, discordancy, and length of gestation, Am. J. Obstet. Gynecol. 169 (3) (1993) 588–597.

[74] A. Santo-Longhurst, Type 2 Diabetes Statistics and Facts, 2016. Available from: http://www.healthline.com/health/type-2-diabetes/statistics

[75] F.Y. Lai, J.A. Johnson, D. Dover, P. Kaul, Outcomes of singleton and twin pregnancies complicated by pre-existing diabetes and gestational diabetes: a population-based study in Alberta, Canada, 2005–11, J. Diabetes 8 (1) (2015) 45–55.

[76] U. Sankilampi, M.L. Hannila, A. Saari, M. Gissler, L. Dunkel, New population-based references for birth weight, length, and head circumference in singletons and twins from 23 to 43 gestation weeks, Ann. Med. 45 (5-6) (2013) 446–454.

[77] M.A. Ramos-Arroyo, T.M. Ulbright, P.L. Yu, J.C. Christian, Twin study: relationship between birth weight, zygosity, placentation, and pathologic placental changes, Acta Genet. Med. Gemellol. 37 (3-4) (1988) 229–238.

[78] J. Dube, L. Dodds, B.A. Armson, Does chorionicity or zygosity predict adverse perinatal outcomes in twins?, Am. J. Obstet. Gynecol. 186 (3) (2002) 579–583.

[79] E.B. Carter, K.C. Bishop, K.R. Goetzinger, M.G. Tuuli, A.G. Cahill, The impact of chorionicity on maternal pregnancy outcomes, Am. J. Obstet. Gynecol. 213 (3) (2015) 390e1–390e7.

[80] A. Johnson, Diagnosis and management of twin–twin transfusion syndrome, Clin. Obstet. Gynecol. 58 (3) (2015) 611–631.

[81] U.F. Harkness, T.M. Crombleholme, Twin–twin transfusion syndrome: where do we go from here?, Semin. Perinatol. 29 (5) (2005) 296–304.

[82] S.A. Durbin, A sonographer's perspective: Quintero staging system for twin-to-twin transfusion syndrome in monochorionic twins, J. Diagn. Med. Sonogr. 27 (3) (2011) 122–125.

[83] K. Chen, R.H. Chmait, D. Vanderbilt, S. Wu, L. Randolph, Chimerism in mono-chorionic dizygotic twins: case study and review, Am. J. Med. Genet. 161 (7) (2013) 1817–1824.

[84] H.R. Yalçin, C.G. Zorlu, A. Lembet, S. Özden, O. Gökmen, The significance of birth weight difference in discordant twins: a level to standardize?, Acta Obstet. Gynecol. Scand. 77 (1) (1998) 28–31.

[85] D. Acevedo-Garcia, M.J. Soobader, L.F. Berkman, The differential effect of foreign-born status on low birth weight by race/ethnicity and education, Pediatrics 115 (1) (2005) e20–e30.

[86] M.P. Umstad, R. Palma-Dias, A. Khalil, Editorial—special issue on twin-to-twin trans-fusion syndrome, Twin Res. Hum. Genet. 19 (3) (2016) 167–291.

[87] L. Hilder, Z. Zhichao, M. Parker, S. Jahan, G.M. Chambers, Australia's mothers and babies 2012, Perinatal Statistics Series, vol. 30 (69), AIHW, Canberra, 2014.

[88] J.M. Dodd, C.A. Crowther, R.R. Haslam, J.S. Robinson, Elective birth at 37 weeks of gestation versus standard care for women with an uncomplicated twin pregnancy at term: the Twins Timing of Birth Randomised Trial, BJOG 119 (8) (2012) 964–974.

[89] G. Othel, M. Granat, D. Zeevi, A. Golan, S. Wexler, M.P. David, J.G. Schenker, Advanced ultrasonic placental maturation in twin pregnancies, Am. J. Obstet. Gynecol. 156 (1) (1987) 76078.

CHAPTER 7

Mind Readers? Twin Telepathy, Intelligence, and Elite Performance

Like most people I am stunned when some twins and their parents share extraordinary experiences with me. I have heard from an identical female twin who said she suffered from her sister's labor pains, an identical female twin who said she knew the moment that her sister died, and a mother of identical twins who said she observed a red spot on one twin's arm when her cotwin received an inoculation. I have combed the literature trying to find explanations for these incredible occurrences. I will summarize these findings, but first I want to share some incredible experiences—this time personal ones.

About 20 years ago I was a guest on a television talk show along with a physician who was an identical twin. The host asked both of us if we thought that twins could communicate telepathically—that is, can twins send and receive information by means other than the usual sensory channels of speaking and listening? I answered that there is no conclusive scientific evidence that thoughts can be transferred from one twin to the next (telepathy), a behavior included under extrasensory perception (ESP), or the "sixth sense [1]." I also indicated that there are other scientifically based reasons for why many twins seem to "know" what his or her cotwin is thinking or doing at a given time (and I will spell them out in this chapter). My answer was not well received by the audience that was filled mostly with identical twins. The physician, who spoke next, disagreed with me, claiming instead that twins *are* able to read each other's minds—he claimed that ESP is real because he engaged in such behavior with his identical twin brother. The physician received wild applause for his answer.

The next story I am about to tell will be interesting in light of my television experience. It concerns about 10 pairs of identical twin students who were charged with cheating on class assignments and examinations. (Since the mid-1990s I have served as a consultant and expert witness for some of these twins when their parents sought advice and legal assistance to defend their children.) These twins' nearly identical words and phrases, short

Twin Mythconceptions
http://dx.doi.org/10.1016/B978-0-12-803994-6.00007-X

143

answers, unusual mistakes, and overall test scores brought accusations of dishonest collaboration from their high school teachers and college professors. Some of these charges were later dismissed, others ended in probation or expulsion, but all brought deep shame to the twins and their families. As an example, in 2016 I studied a pair of college juniors whose former professor accused them of collaborating during completion of an online class assignment. Too terrified to contest the charge, both twins accepted a "0" grade for their work, lowering their A averages to a B.

With one exception that I discuss later, twins in these situations were *not* accused of having ESP or of "reading each other's minds." Instead, research shows that each twin was reading his or her *own* mind, but in doing so was unknowingly solving problems or answering questions in the same way as his or her cotwin. That is because identical twins tend to bring the same skills and approaches to a given task. I did wonder why these twins had not been accused of cheating earlier in life, but perhaps more advanced assignments and tests make identical answers and unusual mistakes by twin students more obvious.

Note: In January 2016, a 34-year-old identical twin sent me the following email message: "[My twin and I] once got put on detention for communicating telepathically during an exam." This was the only case I have encountered in which twin telepathy was actually held responsible for the twins' identical test performance. I wish I had heard the teacher's rationale for such a charge because such information might have helped these twins and others—and me to understand this phenomenon. However, this case did not receive legal attention and I was not involved with it at any level. Had it gone to court, I believe it is likely that charges of twin telepathy would have been dismissed because the available evidence is less persuasive than the research showing genetic effects on twins' mental abilities and information-processing skills.

In this chapter I will explore mythconceptions about twins' thoughts, minds, and behaviors. I will also examine popular beliefs about their intellectual skills, outstanding achievements, and other characteristics. And I will clarify several concepts and terms relating to twin research that have been used carelessly in the scientific and popular press, perpetuating and propagating more myths and mythconceptions. As always, I will provide a reality check, short answer, and detailed explanation. I will begin by continuing the discussion of twin telepathy (Fig. 7.1).

1. *Twins communicate telepathically.*
   Reality Check: Unlikely

Figure 7.1 *Identical twins' think about each other while separated at school—preoccupation, not communication. (Photo courtesy: Kathryn Whiteley. Reprinted with permission from the owner of this illustration).*

Short (but Somewhat Long) Answer. I began this chapter with an example of how my perspective on telepathic communication is at odds with those of some twins and medical professionals. I am also frequently contacted by members of the media who report scientific findings and human interest stories about twins. A topic on which I am often asked to comment concerns (mostly identical) twins' psychic phenomena, known widely as ESP. ESP is the acquisition of information by means other than one of the five senses, hence *extrasensory*. In my view, there is not enough scientific evidence that twins purposefully (or otherwise) transmit mental messages from one to the other.

I know that newspaper journalists and television producers are often disappointed to hear me say this because "evidence" of mental communication in twins guarantees enthusiastic audiences. A 2015 issue of *Orange Coast Magazine*, a glossy publication that covers local news and social events in Orange County, California (where I live) featured twins and triplets who work together [2]. The description of twin musicians, Jared and Jonathan Mattson, included the following: "Twin telepathy— an important component of their music. It happens especially during improvisations." I would argue instead that their comparable talent and years of playing together better explain their successful impromptu performances than telepathic exchange.

Beliefs about "twin telepathy" most likely originated because some twins *behave as if* they can read each other's minds. When twins "know" that their cotwin is calling, "know" that their twin is in trouble, "know" that their twin is in labor, or just think about how their twin is doing, they are expressing the constant concern and caring that is the hallmark of most identical twin relationships—like the students in the cartoon shown in Fig. 7.1. When twins are in frequent communication with one another the odds are high that if their cell phone rings, it is their cotwin calling. And when reared-apart identical twins independently read the same books, enjoy the same hobby, or scatter love notes around the house, they cannot be communicating because they are often unaware that the other twin exists—instead, they are reflecting their matched abilities, tastes, and temperaments. Their similarities could be misconstrued as a kind of psychic connection, but as I have indicated previously and will do so further later in this chapter and others, many twin studies support a genetic basis to intellect, interests, and personality [3]. In contrast, studies of twins and ESP are open to interpretation, and events are usually reported after the fact and without independent corroboration. Add to this the fact that we tend to only hear about the "hits," never about the "misses" with regard to nonverbal communication and coincidence.

As a researcher, my conclusions about human behavior are guided by results from carefully gathered data that show similar outcomes across studies. In the event that future ESP research using twins provides more persuasive findings, I am willing to take another look. A lack of scientific evidence does not mean that something does not exist—people waited years for proof that the world is round, that the earth circles the sun, and that there are two types of twins.

In the section that follows, I examine twin studies of ESP. I also describe *folie à deux*, a French term that translates literally into *double madness*.

More of the Story: A comprehensive review of twin research looking into telepathic phenomena argues that such studies are few, and most were poorly executed [4]. The author of this review also regrets that this area of interest, which has been around since the mid-1850s, has been neglected by twin researchers and covered more often in the press. I believe that several of these studies are worth examining in more detail as they had, or promise to have, impact on thinking about the question of telepathy between twins. But I do not agree with the contention that

twin telepathy is "swept aside as if it were taboo" (p. 94)—some repu-
table twin researchers have completed serious studies on this topic (see
later in the chapter). Twin researchers are interested in *all* aspects of twin
behavior, but have provided other explanations (e.g., genetic common-
ality and shared experiences) for some twins' unusual experiences and
recollections. And twin researchers are not the only ones reporting negative findings—some researchers who typically do not study twins have
also failed to find supportive evidence of twins' psychic connections. In
addition, psychological studies have confirmed that human memory is
fallible and flawed, so it is important to evaluate reports of ESP quite
carefully [5,6].

In 1965, a provocative twin study was reported in the prestigious
journal *Science*. Researchers in Philadelphia claimed to have demonstrated *extrasensory induction* (EI) in 2 out of 15 identical twin pairs [7].
EI is the presence of a certain brainwave (in this case alpha rhythm) in
one person that has been purposefully evoked in another person. This
study was highly criticized in journal correspondence, to which the
investigators responded by acknowledging a number of methodological
flaws [8,9]. One critic wrote, "If they have indeed established that alpha
rhythm can be made to appear in one twin as a result of evoking it in
the other, this finding is surely the most profound scientific discovery of
the present century...one comes to expect a higher standard of reporting." Another scientist noted, "The report...has so heated the mail to my
usually quiet ivory tower that I now need insurance" (p. 1244). Unfortunately, this study was never replicated despite promises that it would be.

A 1993 review of twin studies indicated that, "Research on ESP in
twins has been limited and sporadic" (p. 89). In an attempt to address
this weakness, experiments assessing *thought concordance* (similar thinking) and telepathy in twin and sibling pairs were conducted. The twin
and sibling partners assumed roles as the sender or receiver of pictures,
numbers, and drawings. It was concluded that thought concordance explained the more frequently observed similarities among the twins than
the nontwin siblings, behavior that could be *mistaken* for twin telepathy
in everyday life [10]. Another study also using a sender–receiver para-
digm had the sender watch film clips and describe the imagery, then
ask the receiver to choose the matching clip. This study failed to find
evidence of psychic behaviors expressed by these twin participants who
claimed to have them. Subsequent pilot work by this same researcher
(using four MZ twin pairs) recorded the physiological responses in one

twin while the cotwin was exposed to various stimuli (e.g., immersing an arm into an ice container and hearing the sound of plates crashing to the floor), chosen to evoke shock and surprise. The results generally did not support ESP-like behaviors, with the exception of one twin pair with highly matched reactions to the stimuli [11,12].

A problem that concerns me with nearly all these studies is their failure to document the methods by which the zygosity (identical or fraternal) of the twin pairs was established. Findings from such studies cannot be trusted on that basis alone. Suppose ESP occurs mostly among identical twins, but many of the pairs who participated in the studies were *fraternal*—the lack of evidence for ESP would lead to the conclusion that ESP does not exist among identical twins, or perhaps anyone else, and it would be wrong. All sound scientific twin studies of any behavioral or physical trait must describe the twin-typing methods in full.

I was excited to see a fairly recent 2013 study of "exceptional experiences" among zygosity-tested twins, based on considerable data about their possible telepathic incidents [13]. A new angle on this issue involved looking at relationships between twins' attachment (emotional closeness) to one another and their frequency of ESP experiences. Among the 224 twins (112 pairs) who completed a survey at a twin festival, 60% reported having had telepathic experiences, 11% of whom had them often, and 56% noted remarkable coincidences. Among the 77 individual twins who completed the survey by mail (out of 7518 who received it), 91% reported telepathic experiences, with 10% experiencing them frequently. Identical twins indicated such exceptional experiences more often than fraternal twins *and* were more closely attached to one another. These findings are of interest, yet can be challenged on the basis of unrepresentative samples, because only a small fraction of the pairs invited to participate in the study did so. The possibility of after-the-fact responding—twins' reporting of exceptional experiences long after they occurred, and possibly embellishing or distorting these events—do not make the results persuasive. Some twins' recollections of similar clothing and gift choices are, as the authors correctly noted, a probable reflection of "concordance," or genetically influenced tendencies, rather than telepathy.

There is another behavior of interest. *Folie à deux* (double madness) is a rare shared delusional disorder. (Delusions are strongly held beliefs about someone or something despite evidence to the contrary.) *Folie à deux* was first described in 1877 as the transfer of delusional ideas from one person to another person with whom they are closely affiliated. According to the 2013 *Diagnostic Statistical Manual-V*: "In the context of a relationship, the delusional material from the dominant partner provides content for delusional belief by the individual who may not otherwise entirely meet criteria for delusional disorder." Criteria for this condition include intimate association between the partners, identical delusional content between them, and the sharing, support, and acceptance of one's own delusion and that of their partner.

In most cases, folie à deux occurs when the individuals involved are relatively isolated from others. Various subtypes have been recognized, such as the imposition of delusions on the submissive partner by the dominant partner, and the acquisition and persistence of delusions by one individual following resistance. A case report of folie à deux in identical twin sisters with cerebral palsy illustrates the second subtype [14,15]. This behavior could conceivably be seen as telepathic in nature by some people.

Folie à deux is sometimes casually linked to identical twins who display unusual behaviors, carry out extraordinary schemes, or display exceptional intimacy. This is unfortunate because it paints an unfair and unfavorable portrait of twins and their relationships. Furthermore, folie à deux is a rare condition to which twins do not appear to be more prone than nontwins—but folie à deux in identical twins may be quite likely to attract attention, due to the twins' matched appearance, behaviors, and antics. As early as 1957, the idea that an identical twin might "catch" or copy a delusion or illness from a cotwin was disputed in favor of a genetic predisposition or susceptibility, in conjunction with environmental factors, and more recent work in this area concurs [16–19]. This second view is reasonable, especially in light of cases of identical twins reared (or living) apart who develop similar psychotic behaviors and psychoses, and fraternal twins reared (or living) together who do not [3].

Scientists must be open to new findings that challenge old interpretations. I believe that the best evidence we have so far shows that twins do not read each other's minds. I do not doubt the amazing stories twin have to tell, I only question how to explain them. As I have indicated, twin research has shown that the incredibly matched behaviors some twins display can be explained by their common genes, predisposing them to act and react in similar ways to similar events. I am, however, ready and willing to take another look at the next generation of studies that come long—and to change my mind if twin telepathy is demonstrated beyond a reasonable doubt.

Everything about twins is fascinating, but the way that their minds work ranks close to the top. Ideas about how twins think, speak, and act, relative to nontwins, have circulated among professionals and the public, many of which have proven to be myths. Taking a look at twins' general intelligence, achievements, and language skills, and how they compare with those of nontwins, is my next task. The critical question: Should twins be assigned to the same classroom or separate classrooms comes up in Chapter 8.

2. *Twins score below singletons on general intelligence tests.*
   Reality Check: Possible
   Short Answer: There is a notion that twins are not as smart as nontwins, based on standard intelligence tests. Some individual studies find no difference between them, while other studies find that twins perform better academically than singletons at certain ages—still, some evidence suggests that twins' test scores may be *slightly* lower, explaining my reality check of *possible.* I have also heard rumors that twins are underrepresented in government leadership and academia, but I have never seen persuasive reports. Here is what I have discovered.

An analysis that combined results from 19 twin studies showed that twins score somewhat below singletons in their *average level* of performance on general intelligence tests [20]. This *does not* mean that all twins score below all singletons—in fact, some twins score *above* some singletons on these tests. The data just mean that twins *as a group* score several IQ points below nontwins when the scores of the two groups are each averaged and compared. However, the difference between the average scores of twins and nontwins is *not* large (about 4–5 points) and in some studies this gap closed when the children all turned 12.

The combined analysis also showed that twins' lower IQ was often linked to their lower birth weight—but when the effects of birth weight on IQ were statistically removed from the data, the twin–singleton difference dropped to about 2.6 IQ points. And when researchers looked at studies including only the most recently born twins (twins born during the 1980s and 1990s), the difference dropped to just one-half (.5) of an IQ point. I believe that improvements in the prenatal and postnatal care of the most recently born twins partly explains this narrowing of the twin–singleton difference among younger twins.

Note: It is unlikely that one-half (.5) of an IQ point significantly affects academic performance and/or occupational achievement. And not all studies have found twin–singleton differences in intelligence.

More of the Story: Early twin studies, conducted in the 1970s, showed that twins scored 5–10 points below nontwins on general intelligence tests [21]. A cleverly executed British study conducted during those years showed that 11-year-old twins whose cotwins passed away either at, or near, birth scored considerably higher on a verbal reasoning test than twins who had grown up together [22]. This finding implicated the twin relationship in the reared-together twins' lower test scores— it was suggested that twins growing up together have reduced opportunities for verbal interaction with individuals other than their twin, such as peers, siblings, and parents, thereby depressing their language development. In contrast, individuals born as twins *but raised as singletons* enjoyed more frequent and varied social experience, thereby elevating their performance.

Still, the singly raised twins scored slightly below a group of non-twins, suggesting that the adverse events responsible for the cotwin's demise also affected the cognitive abilities of the surviving twin, albeit less severely. A subsequent 1976 study conducted in the United States showed no difference in IQ between singly raised twins and raised-together twins, but did show that both groups scored below nontwins [23]. It was suggested that the poorer quality of the twins' prenatal environments (which might have included competition for nutrition or fetal crowding) was responsible for the lower IQ scores of both twin groups.

In contrast with the older research, several studies published in 2000 and beyond did *not* find twin–singleton differences in intelligence. A Dutch study compared adult twins' scores to those of their nontwin siblings, while a Danish study compared 15- and 16-year-old twins' scores to those of their peers [24,25]. A second Dutch study expanded upon the first one by tracking the intellectual progress of a separate group of twin children between the ages of 6 and 12 and taking another look at the previous adult sample [26]. The young twins in this second Dutch study scored significantly below nontwins in language and arithmetic at age 6, but the difference continually decreased until age 12 when the twins *outscored* the nontwins. When it came to IQ scores, the twins scored .09 points lower than the nontwins at age 8, .83 points lower at age 10, and .14 points higher at age 12. It seems that the twins' small intellectual deficit at age 6 had vanished by age 12. Their recovery could variously reflect "buffering mechanisms" that work to protect individuals from the lasting effects of prenatal difficulties. For example, genetic factors may make some twins more resistant to prenatal stress than others. And the later the insult occurs and the shorter it lasts may assist prenatal and postnatal recovery [27]. Increased experiences with people outside the twinship could also work to raise twins' mental performance [28]. The lack of IQ difference between the adult twins and singletons confirms this notion.

Some more recent studies have, however, reported a lower average IQ score for twins as compared to singletons, consistent with the older research [29,30]. A Scottish twin study found that at ages 7 and 9 twins scored 5–6 points below their nontwin siblings—although (as indicated in my Short Answer) this difference dropped to 2.5 points when birth weight and gestational age were statistically controlled. A second Scottish twin study reported a singleton advantage of five IQ points, also consistent with the older reports. But unlike the Dutch and Danish studies that sampled twins born in the 1960s through the late 1980s, the Scottish studies sampled twins born in the 1930s to the 1950s when twins and twin pregnancies were detected later and managed less effectively, due to less sophisticated medical techniques. In addition to better healthcare, I believe that greater awareness and knowledge of twins' educational needs also explain the more recent convergence of twins' and nontwins' intelligence test scores.

3. *Twins are underrepresented when it comes to expert or elite performance.*
Reality Check: Unlikely
Short Answer: The belief that proportionally fewer twins than singletons achieve expert or elite status in a given field has circulated throughout academia for some time. Some difficulties in assessing this notion are that definitions of elite performance vary greatly, and whether or not an "elite" individual is or is not a twin may not be widely known. As such, this issue has *not* been fully resolved, but I believe twins' underrepresentation among expert and elite performers is unlikely.

By way of illustration, one of the few scientific papers on this subject looked for twins among Nobel Prize winners and concluded that, "there are no twins, monozygotic [identical] or dizygotic [fraternal], among Nobel laureates in the sciences" (p. 30) [31]. I instantly knew that this statement was incorrect, having met the late fraternal twin, Rita Levi-Montalcini, in Rome, at the 1989 *International Congress of Twin Studies*. Levi-Montalcini shared the 1986 Nobel Prize in Medicine with Stanley

Cohen for the discovery of nerve growth factor (NGF) and epidermal growth factor (EGF) [32]. I strongly suspect that there are other hidden twins mingling among the elite. These twins are not intentionally concealing their twinship—but asking a new acquaintance or coworker if they are a twin or singleton is not a common practice. And a question about being born a multiple is rarely included on a medical form, which is surprising because it might explain a person's multiple blood group lines (in the event of prenatal blood exchange; see Chapter 1) or susceptibility to diabetes or weight gain (based on the cotwin's medical history). Most people never learn that I am a fraternal twin until they ask me how I became involved in twin research.

More of the Story: A 2014 paper posed the question, "Why are there so few twins that exhibit expert and elite performance?" as if this issue had already been settled [33]. I understand the bases of this view. A 1978 study found few twins among 300 eminent individuals, as did the 2004 update of 700—the only twins included were the Mexican painter, Diego Rivera and the musician, Elvis Presley; but because Presley was *not* listed as a twin in the text it is likely that other twins were also missed. (Presley's twin brother Jesse Garon was delivered stillborn 35 minutes before him.) [34–36]. It may also be that the authors' criteria for eminence were too limiting, causing them to overlook qualified individuals. To be considered eminent, a person from America had to have had two books written about them, while a person outside America had to have had one book written about them. These books also had to be available in the Montclair, New Jersey Public Library. And in order to be chosen, these individuals had to have lived into the 20th century and been included in a standard reference work.

Other studies of eminence also used methods that may have overlooked qualified people. A 1991 study that surveyed the lives of 2206 scientists, identified by their inclusion in one of three selective biographical dictionaries, found only one twin in the group, the Swiss inventor and explorer, Auguste Piccard [37]. Given that the United States' twinning rate between 1915 and 1980 remained stable at 1/50 or 2% of all births in a given year [38], approximately 44 twins should have been identified by the 1991 study. Allowing for twins who did not survive due to less advanced medical care, I believe that the final tally should have been higher than just one.

Examining the lives and accomplishments of contributors from diverse fields (e.g., science and sports) and applying different evaluative schemes (e.g., number of citations in the professional literature; honors earned aside from the Nobel prize, such as the prestigious Lasker Award) may have produced different results. (The Lasker Award is a sign of "pre-Nobel recognition"; it may actually reduce the chances of becoming a Nobel Laureate if it is received when a person is young [39].) However, more precise measures of eminence than being cited in a book or winning an award are needed to identify the most outstanding individuals across all fields. Most importantly, this will require better measures of performance and accomplishment [23]. Most definitions of eminence include fame, yet some people's important achievements may be recognized only within their particular discipline—and if one's birth as a twin is also unknown then twins (like Elvis Presley) will be overlooked.

Some researchers have argued that the low occurrence of twins among elite performers makes it impossible to estimate how much genetic factors affect extraordinary levels of achievement [40]. That is because many twin pairs are needed to calculate these figures. However, as I indicated earlier, it is too early to say whether or not twins are less likely than non-twins to reach expert levels of performance. I can imagine that talented twins might collaborate in their abilities to achieve greatness because, as one paralympic athletic twin told me, prior to his injury he and his brother benefitted from having a readily available practice partner.

In fact, there are twins who create joint businesses (*Twinfully Sweet*), medical practices (*Twins Chiropractic*), and award-winning paintings (*Singh Twins*) [41]. As one of the chiropractic twins remarked, "Being twins has been one of our greatest marketing tools. People easily forget names, but they won't forget identical doctors." Some pairs become famous for their talents, such as the Olympic skiers Steve and Phil Mahre, PBS antiquarians Leigh and Leslie Keno, and British businessmen Sir David and Sir Frederick Barclay, but might not be considered eminent due to ineffective identification methods, poor definitions, and lack of knowledge about a person's twinship, as described earlier. There are other talented twins out there—like Levi-Montalcini who was overlooked among the Nobel Laureates, possibly because she was a fraternal twin and did not collaborate with her sister.

Additional notes: Some readers will be interested in further details of Levi-Montalcini's life. In 2008, she became the longest living Nobel prize winner, surpassing Tadeusz Reichstein of Switzerland who earned the distinction for hormone research leading to the isolation of cortisone and its treatment of arthritis. Levi-Montalcini passed away in 2012 at the age of 103, surpassing Reichstein by 4 years. Her twin sister, Paola, was an artist until her death in 2000 at age 91. Readers may also wish to know that at least one twin, medical geneticist Victor McKusick, won the 1997 Albert Lasker Award for Medical Science, the 2001 National Medal of Science, and the 2008 Japan Prize in Medical Genomics and Genetics [42,43]. McKusick's identical twin brother, Vincent, was Chief Justice of the Maine Supreme Judicial Court and was a possible contender for appointment as a United States Supreme Court Justice. The McKusick twins were recognized in April 2016 by the prestigious *American Philosophical Society*, of which both were members. I was privileged to deliver a lecture in their honor, one that touched on their lives and accomplishments, as well as on twin research in general.

4. *Identical twins who obtain the same test scores must have cheated.*
    Reality Check: False
    Short Answer: As I noted in this chapter's introduction, I have received a number of phone calls, letters, and (most recently) email messages from parents whose identical twins, identical triplets, and one fraternal twin pair were variously accused of cheating on in-class exams, course assignments, and standardized tests. Knowing their children well, these desperate parents hoped to clear their children of charges they felt were so unfairly brought against them.

    It is very disturbing for me to hear teachers and professors bring unsubstantiated accusations of cheating against identical twin students (mostly) who perform very similarly in the classroom [44]. By now, evidence from numerous twin studies has shown that identical twins' shared genes contribute, in part, to their closely matched academic abilities and skills. Therefore, I do *not* believe that the twins I defended were cheating—rather, their matching test scores and written essays merely reflected their similar abilities, interests, and talents.

    Cheating charges are serious and are sometimes brought before administrative school committees, and even courts of law. I have served as an expert witness for a number of such cases—when I do, I refer to the scientific evidence of twins' similar, genetically based intellectual behaviors. I argue that what would be strong evidence of cheating among nontwins is simply twins being themselves.
    More of the Story: Scores of studies show that identical twins perform alike on general intelligence tests, special mental ability batteries, information processing tasks, and scholastic achievement tests [45,46]. Identical twins

do not show perfect intellectual similarity, but they are more alike than any other pair of people. In fact, identical twins *raised apart* show greater intellectual resemblance than fraternal twins and virtual twins (near-in-age unrelated siblings) *raised together*—these observations underline the importance of genetic influence on mental ability. The conclusion from this research is that genetic factors influence general intelligence as well as specific skills. It is, therefore, not surprising that identical twins sometimes obtain exactly the same test score, make the same unusual mistake, or reach the same unexpected conclusion when writing a paper or completing a thought. Some fraternal twins do as well, but less often.

Some real life examples of twins' matched abilities illustrate my point. Identical twins Alec and Eric Bedser were famous British cricket players in the 1950s. According to their biographer Alan Hill:

They always shared their distinctions, finishing alternately first and second in the form [class] throughout their school days. The consistency of their results prompted one teacher misguidedly to accuse them of cheating in class. He sought to rectify matters by separating them. 'We still came up with the same answers, or made the same mistakes, so we proved him wrong,' say Alec and Eric. (p. 17) [47].

Whether in academia or elsewhere, twins should not be held to higher standards than nontwins. In other words, it is unlikely that two unrelated students would be charged with cheating for obtaining the exact same test score without hard evidence of "cheat sheets" or attempted communication during test sessions. Therefore, to attribute twins' identical scores to cheating *just because they are twins and perform alike* is unjustifiable. I believe that twins should feel free to study together as nontwin classmates do, but it would be prudent for them to sit apart for exams to avoid the slightest hint of collaboration. I trust that the rise in twinning rates since 1980 will enhance public awareness of twins' behaviors, especially among teachers, faculty, and administrators.

5. *Identical twins have identical brains.*
Reality Check: False
Short Answer: Identical twins think more alike than any two people—but they do *not* have identical brains. Advances in medical technologies (brain imaging) have allowed physicians to examine and compare twins' brains and they have discovered some fascinating things by doing so. Genetic factors play an important role in affecting brain volume (e.g., frontal lobe volume—areas concerned with personality, learning, and voluntary movement), regional brain areas (e.g., cortical thickness of

Wernicke's area—part of the brain concerned with language comprehension), and age-related changes in structure and volume, as shown by greater identical than fraternal twin similarity in adult pairs [48,49].

However, as with virtually all other human characteristics measured in twins, identical twins' brains are not exactly the same, either due to influences before or after birth. For example, heavier birth weight MZ twins show greater cortical surface area (the folded gray matter of the brain associated with consciousness) [50]. And evidence of about a thousand different gene mutations in brain neurons (nerve cells) make it likely that identical twins will show different mutational patterns—although how such differences might affect intellectual functioning are unknown [51]. Here again, I am amazed at how similar identical twins can be, despite the environmental forces working hard to make them different.

More of the Story: Several of my favorite studies beautifully illustrate MZ twins' brain differences. In one study, researchers performed magnetic resonance imaging (MRI—radio waves used to produce images of internal organs) on a pair of hand-discordant (left-handed vs. right-handed) identical female cotwins to see how their brains worked when they solved language and mental rotation problems. Language tasks typically engage the brain's left hemisphere, while mental rotation tasks (which involve imagining what an object looks like from a different position) typically engage the brain's right hemisphere. The twins showed a striking reversal in how their brains worked—the right-handed twin showed the typical pattern described earlier, while her left-handed twin sister processed language in her right hemisphere and mental rotation in her left hemisphere [52].

A second study by the same researchers used MRI to see which side of the brain (left or right) was favored by pairs of identical same-handed and opposite-handed twins while they solved two different language tasks. One task involved making a decision about the meaning of a word, and the other task involved coming up with a verb when given a noun. Twins in the same-handed pairs showed similar patterns of brain activity, but many twins in the opposite-handed pairs showed opposite patterns [53]. These two studies suggest that language functions have a genetic component that is disrupted among hand-discordant identical twin pairs.

Researchers studying 10 same-handed and 10 opposite-handed identical twin pairs used MRI to measure a brain structure called the planum temporale. The planum temporale is involved in speech and is usually larger on the brain's left side. The right-handers from both twin groups showed the expected size difference between the left and right sides of the planum temporale, but the left-handers showed no difference. The source of these differences is not fully known, but the time (days after fertilization) and location (place on the fertilized egg) at which zygotic division occurs to produce identical twins might explain some cotwins' differences in brain structure and functioning [54].

What do brains and legs have to do with one another? Research on British twins reported a link between brains and leg muscles. These findings went viral in 2015, perhaps because it paired two seemingly unlikely body parts in a meaningful way [55]. However, exercise helps to pump the blood that delivers nutrition to different cells of the body, including those of the brain; therefore, a link between leg power and brain power makes sense. This study used female identical and fraternal twins between 43 and 73 years of age, who completed mental ability tests at two time points, 10 years apart. It turned out that the fitter twins showed more total gray matter, larger ventricles (cavities filled with fluid that protect the brain), and brain activity at the first testing and at the follow-up. This study suggested that both cognitive aging and general brain structure could be improved by exercise, and that muscle fitness (as demonstrated by leg power) was a clue to mental performance. Staying healthy and smart can be easy, enjoyable, and, hopefully, inexpensive.

Bridging the connection between this chapter and Chapter 8, I introduce new material while continuing the themes raised here. I will focus on the great school debate: the pros and cons of placing twins in the same or separate classrooms. I will then proceed to a related subject that has some bearing on twins' school situation, namely, twins' language abilities, and how they compare with those of nontwins. I hope these discussions help the countless parents and educators who have contacted me over the years for help in these matters.

REFERENCES

[1] Encyclopaedia Britannica, Extrasensory Perception (ESP), 2016. Available from: http://www.britannica.com/topic/extrasensory-perception
[2] R.L. Mayfield, Double Takes: Twins+Triplets Working Together, Orange Coast Magazine, September 15, 2015. Available from: http://www.orangecoast.com/features/double-takes/
[3] N.L. Segal, Born Together-Reared Apart: The Landmark Minnesota Twin Study, Harvard University Press, Cambridge, MA, (2012).
[4] G.L. Playfair, Telepathy and identical twins, J. Soc. Psych. Res. 63 (No. 854) (1999) 86–98.

[5] B. Zhu, C. Chen, E.F. Loftus, C. Lin, Q. He, C. Chen, et al. Individual differences in false memory from misinformation: cognitive factors, Memory 18 (5) (2010) 543–555.

[6] T.A. Busey, G.R. Loftus, Cognitive science and the law, Trends Cognit. Sci. 11 (3) (2007) 111–117.

[7] T.D. Duane, T. Behrendt, Extrasensory electroencephalographic induction between identical twins, Science 150 (3694) (1965) 367.

[8] Letters to the Editor, Science 150(3701) (1965) 1240-1244.

[9] T.D. Duane, T. Berendt, Letter to the Editor, Science 151 (3706) (1966) 28–30.

[10] S.J. Blackmore, F. Chamberlain, ESP and thought concordance in twins: a method of comparison, J. Soc. Psych. Res. 59 (No. 831) (1993) 89–189.

[11] A. Parker, A ganzfeld study using identical twins, J. Soc. Psych. Res. 74 (2 No. 899) (2010) 118–126.

[12] A. Parker, C. Jensen, Further possible physiological connectedness between identical twins: the London study, EXPLORE J. Sci. Heal. 9 (1) (2013) 26–31.

[13] G. Brusewitz, L. Cherkas, J. Harris, A. Parker, Exceptional experiences amongst twins, J. Psych. Res. 77 (4 No. 913) (2013) 220–235.

[14] D. Francois, E. Bander, M. D'Agostino, A. Swinburne, L. Broderick, M.B. Grody, A. Salajegheh, Folie à deux in monozygotic twins with cerebral palsy, Clin. Schizophr. Relat. Psychoses (2014) 1–10.

[15] Medscape, Shared Delusional Disorder, 2014. Available from: http://emedicine.medscape.com/article/293107-overview

[16] D.H. Ropschitz, Folie à deux, Br. J. Psychiatry 103 (432) (1957) 589–596.

[17] A. Lazarus, Folie à deux: psychosis by association or genetic determinism? Compr. Psychiatry 26 (2) (1985) 129–135.

[18] R.S. Shiwach, P.B. Sobin, Monozygotic twins, folie à deux and heritability: a case report and critical review, Med. Hypotheses 50 (5) (1998) 369–374.

[19] A. Reif, B. Pfuhlmann, Folie à deux versus genetically driven delusional disorder: case reports and nosological considerations, Compr. Psychiatry 45 (2) (2004) 155–160.

[20] M. Voracek, T. Haubner, Twin-singleton differences in intelligence: a meta-analysis 1, Psychol. Rep. 102 (3) (2008) 951–962.

[21] N.C. Myrianthopoulos, P.L. Nichols, S.H. Broman, Intellectual development of twins—comparison with singletons, Acta Genet. Med. Gemellol. 25 (1) (1976) 376–380.

[22] R.G. Record, T.H. McKeown, J.H. Edwards, An investigation of the difference in measured intelligence between twins and single births, Ann. Hum. Genet. 34 (1) (1970) 11–20.

[23] Myrianthopoulos et al. (1976). See reference note 15.

[24] D. Posthuma, E.J. De Geus, N. Bleichrodt, D.L. Boomsma, Twin-singleton differences in intelligence? Twin Res. 3 (2) (2000) 83–87.

[25] K. Christensen, I. Petersen, A. Skytthe, A.-M. Herskind, M. McGue, P. Bingley, Twin/singleton differences in intelligence? Comparison of academic performance of twins and singeltons in adolescence: a follow-up study, Br. Med. J. 333 (7578) (2006) 1095.

[26] D. Webbink, D. Posthuma, D.I. Boomsma, E.J.C. de geus, P. Visscher, Do twins have lower cognitive ability than singletons? Intelligence 36 (6) (2008) 539–547.

[27] K. Cherry, Environmental Influences on Prenatal Development, April 7, 2015. Available from: https://www.verywell.com/environmental-influences-on-prenatal-development-2795112

[28] R.S. Wilson, Twin growth: initial deficit, recovery and trends in concordance from birth to nine years, Ann. Hum. Biol. 6 (3) (1979) 205–220.

[29] G.A. Ronalds, B.L. De Stavola, D.A. Leon, The cognitive cost of being a twin: evidence from comparisons within families in the Aberdeen children of the 1950s cohort study, Br. Med. J. 331 (7528) (2005) 1306.

[30] I.J. Deary, A. Pattie, V. Wilson, L.J. Whalley, The cognitive cost of being a twin: two whole-population surveys, Twin Res. Hum. Genet. 8 (4) (2005) 376–383.

[31] D.K. Simonton, Scientific talent, training, and performance: intellect, personality, and genetic endowment, Rev. Gen. Psychol. 12 (1) (2008) 28–46.

[32] N.L. Segal, See: prominent twins' passing, Twin Res. Hum. Genet. 16 (3) (2013) 751–757.

[33] K.A. Ericsson, Why expert performance is special and cannot be extrapolated from studies of performance in the general population: a response to criticisms, Intelligence 45 (2014) 81–103.

[34] V. Goertzel, M.G. Goertzel, 300 Eminent Personalities: A Psychoanalysis of the Famous, Jossey-Bass, San Francisco, (1978).

[35] V. Goertzel, M.G. Goertzel (with updates by T.G. Goertzel, A.M.W. Hansen), Cradles of Eminence, second ed., Great Potential Press, Inc, Scottsdale, AZ, 2004. Note: A computer search through the text of this book found only Diego Rivera. (Ted Goertzel, personal communication, January 16, 2016)

[36] Elvis Presley, March 11, 2016. Available from: https://en.wikipedia.org/wiki/Elvis_Presley

[37] D.K. Simonton, Career landmarks in science: individual differences and interdisciplinary contrast, Dev. Psychol. 27 (1) (1991) 119–130.

[38] J.A. Martin, B.E. Hamilton, M.J. Osterman, Three Decades of Twin Births in the United States, 1980-2009, US Department of Health and Human Services, Centers for Disease Control and Prevention, National Center for Health Statistics, Hyattsville, MD, (2012).

[39] E. Tenner, The Novel Prize Has Some Competition, The Atlantic, August 2, 2012. Available from: http://www.theatlantic.com/international/archive/2012/08/the-nobel-prize-has-some-competition/260558/

[40] K.A. Ericsson, R.W. Roring, K. Nandagopal, Giftedness and evidence for reproducibly superior performance: an account based on the expert performance framework, High Abil. Stud. 18 (1) (2007) 3–56.

[41] Mayfield, The Singh Twins, 2015. Available from: http://www.singhtwins.co.uk/PRO-FILE.html

[42] Johns Hopkins: News and Publications, A. Victor, M.D. McKusick, Father of Medical Genetics, July 23, 2008 Available from: http://www.hopkinsmedicine.org/news/media/releases/victor_a_mckusick_md_father_of_medical_genetics_1921_2008

[43] S. Mistler, Vincent McKusick, Bright and Kind Former Chief Justice in Maine, Dies at 93, December 8, 2014. Available from: http://www.pressherald.com/2014/12/04/vincent-mckusick-former-maine-chief-justice-dies-at-93/

[44] N.L. Segal, Education issues, Twin Res. Hum. Genet. 8 (4) (2005) 409–414.

[45] N.L. Segal, Born together-reared apart: the landmark Minnesota twin study, Harvard University Press, Cambridge, MA, (2012).

[46] N.G. Shakeshaft, M. Trzaskowski, A. McMillan, K. Rimfeld, E. Krapohl, C.M. Haworth, et al. Strong genetic influence on a UK nationwide test of educational achievement at the end of compulsory education at age 16, Plos One 8 (12) (2013) e80341.

[47] A. Hill, The Bedsers: Twinning Triumphs, Mainstresam Publishing Company, Ltd, London, (2012).

[48] J.S. Peper, R.M. Brouwer, D.I. Boomsma, R.S. Kahn, H. Pol, E. Hilleke, Genetic influences on human brain structure: a review of brain imaging studies in twins, Hum. Brain Mapp. 28 (6) (2007) 464–473.

[49] J.N. Giedd, J.E. Schmitt, M.C. Neale, Structural brain magnetic resonance imaging of pediatric twins, Hum. Brain Mapp. 28 (6) (2007) 474–481.

[50] A. Raznahan, D. Greenstein, N.R. Lee, L.S. Clasen, J.N. Giedd, Prenatal growth in humans and postnatal brain maturation into late adolescence, Proc. Natl. Acad. Sci. 109 (28) (2012) 11366–11371.

[51] J. Keeley, R. Gutnikoff, Study Examines Scale of Gene Mutations in Human Neurons, HHMI News 1 (2015) 1–2.

[52] I.E.C. Sommer, N.F. Ramsey, A. Bouma, R.S. Kahn, Cerebral mirror-imaging in a monozygotic twin, Lancet 354 (9188) (1999) 1445–1446.

[53] I.E.C. Sommer, N.F. Ramsey, R.C.W. Mandl, R.S. Kahn, Language lateralization in monozygotic twin pairs concordant and discordant for handedness, Brain 125 (12) (2002) 2710–2718.

[54] H. Steinmetz, A. Herzog, G. Schlaug, Y. Huang, L. Jäncke, Brain (a)symmetry in mono-zygotic twins, Cereb. Cortex 5 (4) (1995) 296–300.

[55] C.J. Steves, M.M. Mehta, S.H. Jackson, T.D. Spector, Kicking back cognitive ageing: leg power predicts cognitive ageing after ten years in older female twins, Gerontology 62 (2) (2015) 138–149.

CHAPTER 8

Going to School and Speaking Out Loud

The question of whether or not to separate twins at school is clearly the most frequent question I have received from parents and educators over the years. For some families, this issue is just one of many concerns faced by parents raising twins, but for others it has escalated into a bitter battle with teachers and administrators. Most schools wish to separate twins due to fears that twins will fail to develop as individuals apart from their twinship. However, many parents of young twins prefer to keep them together, at least in the early years, especially if they get along and interact well with others—parents reason that going to school is a new experience that can be much easier and more pleasant if a familiar person (the cotwin) is there, too. It is time to bring reason, rationale, and reality to this important issue. I also discuss twins' language development and how it compares with that of nontwins (Fig. 8.1).

1. *Twins should always be placed in separate classrooms.*
   Reality Check: False
   Short Story: No one worries about identity issues if singleton children attend school with their best friends; in fact, research shows that children are livelier and more engaged in new classroom activities when a familiar peer is close by [1]. This is an important message for anyone concerned with twins' happiness and well-being. Instead, educators and administrators worry that twins will fail to develop a sense of identity and individuality if they are not separated when they first arrive at school.

   I wish to emphasize that I am unaware of set policies for deciding the school placement of *nontwin* children. I have argued many times that twins should not be held to higher standards than nontwins—all children leave their parents and familiar surroundings on the first day of kindergarten, so it is unnecessary and unfair (at best) and insensitive and cruel (at worst) to additionally require twins to separate from one another.

   My real Short Story comes at the end of this section because I'd like to first describe one of my early school experiences that illustrates the

Figure 8.1 *Twin boys enjoying a book together. (Reprinted with permission. Image source: Shutterstock.com/Sonya Etchison).*

trauma of separating from my twin. The memory remains very vivid and a little scary. In this writing I will tell it in great detail for the first time.

I was 4 years old when I first entered kindergarten. My mother walked my fraternal twin sister, Anne, and me to our new school located a block and a half from our home in North Philadelphia. Suddenly, Anne and I had to say good-bye to each other without knowing why. Anne was escorted to a large, lively classroom with a smiling, enthusiastic teacher, while I was sent to a smaller, less exciting classroom run by what appeared to me to be a scowling, intimidating "tyrant." I was terrified. I recall that someone (perhaps my teacher) sent for Anne to come to my classroom to calm me down.

The next few days were difficult and I recall sitting on my dad's knee, refusing to go to school. My dad gently lectured me (at the age of 4!) about the importance of a good education for getting ahead in a competitive world. Reluctantly I agreed to try, and over the weeks and months I adjusted. When we moved to New York City the following year, my sister and I were placed in the same kindergarten and stayed together in our first and second grade classes before we were separated again in third grade. By that time, at age 8, our different abilities, interests, and friends were obvious and separation was the right choice; consequently, the transition from shared to separate classrooms went smoothly. I am still bothered that we weren't placed together in Philadelphia after my clear display of uneasiness, because I now know from my research on this topic that other young twins are experiencing similar situations. We were kept apart because our school maintained a mandatory (and unjustified) separation policy when it came to twin children, one that was not research based and did not consider each pairs' unique circumstances.

My Short Story (Finally!): *There should be no school policies* regarding whether or not twins are placed in the same or separate classrooms. *Every twin pair has their own special needs*, not to be determined by policy. Separate classrooms may be advised for twins performing at different ability levels, copying each other's assignments, or fighting a lot when they are together. In contrast, common classrooms might be best for twins who get along well and work together cooperatively at comparable levels, while mixing well with their peers. School officials often favor separating twins because "they will not develop individual identities" (I still do not know what that means!), but that has never been proven.

There are many different ways to keep twins together while allowing them some time apart: (1) Identical twins can wear different outfits and hairstyles, and/or possibly name tags, to distinguish between them. Separating identical twins just to prevent teachers and classmates from confusing them does not justify this routine practice. (2) Closely attached cotwins can be assigned to different tables and play groups so they will mingle with other children, while still allowing them to track the whereabouts of their twin. Social closeness does not preclude the development of a sense of self. (3) Periodic parent and teacher monitoring of twins' academic and social progress can be scheduled. Based on the outcomes of such sessions, new decisions regarding twins' classroom placement can be implemented if, for example, one twin speaks for both or one twin overshadows the other twin academically.

More of the Story: In 1992, I interviewed 63 Minnesota mothers of twins, 48 of whom were aware of their children's school policies regarding twins. *None of these mothers believed that schools should maintain established practices*. This view was echoed in a 1999 National Organization of Mothers of Twins Clubs survey and guidelines for United States schools [2]. When Australian parents could choose their twins' classroom placement most kept them together in their early years, citing interference with evolving twin relations if the twins were parted [3].

Over the years, parents wishing to keep their twins together in school have felt increasingly frustrated by teachers and principals insensitive to their situation. In 1994, Oklahoma passed a resolution supporting parents' rights to affect twins' classroom placement. Ten years later, lobbying efforts by Minnesota mothers and fathers led to Governor Tim Pawlenty's signing of a bill giving parents in that state a significant voice in their twins' school placement; that event took place on May 5, 2005 [4]. As of 2016, 12 states have enacted laws, 10 states have sponsored bills, 2 states have passed resolutions allowing parental input, and 10 states are awaiting sponsorship [5,6]. However, it is unclear when these findings were last updated.

When Minnesota enacted the school legislation in 2005, the *St. Paul Pioneer Press* newspaper published an unfavorable editorial [7]. It was argued that "it is not state government's role to step in and cure every miscommunication or squabble at the local level" and that "One child's trauma should not set the course for a statewide law" (p. B12). I disagreed in writing then and do now—the bill alleviated the difficulties of countless twins and parents, and served as a model for states that followed. It still does. Countless twins and parents of twins are also helped by research on how classroom placement impacts twins' behavior and school performance.

Until recently, few studies properly evaluated the effects of same classrooms versus separate classrooms on twins' school performance and adjustment. A British study found that twins separated at the age of five showed more internalizing behaviors (behaviors directing problematic energy toward the self, such as depression and loneliness [8]) and lower reading scores 18 months after the separation, compared to twins separated later or twins who were not separated at all. Identical twins showed more of these difficulties after separation than fraternal twins [9]. An American study of 4- and 7-year-old identical twins concurred that problem behaviors were greater for separated than nonseparated twins, as rated by parents and teachers [10]. And a Dutch study found that for both identical and fraternal 7-year-old twins, classroom separation at the age of 5 was linked to more internalizing behaviors and externalizing behaviors (problem behaviors directed outside the self, such as fighting and stealing) than nonseparation, as rated by mothers and teachers. However, only the mothers' ratings suggested that internalizing problem behaviors at the age of 7 were caused by the classroom separation, rather than by preexisting behavioral difficulties noted at the age of 3 [11].

The Dutch study also found that separated and nonseparated twins did not differ in academic achievement at the age of 12 [11]. Similarly, two other studies found either no differences or slight literacy differences between separated and nonseparated sets in grades one and two [12,13]. However, a study of twins' performance in grade two found that non-separated twins did better in language and somewhat better in math than separated twins, differences that were larger between separated and nonseparated same-sex pairs. Performance in the higher grades was similar for separated and nonseparated pairs, although between grades six and eight separation for at least 3 years increased the language scores of male–female twins [14]. Unfortunately, the same-sex sets could not be organized into identical and fraternal pairs. It is, therefore, impossible to know if separation had different academic consequences for the two types of twins in this study.

In general, separating twins at school seems to have short-term, rather than long-term effects on twins' behaviors and school performance. These findings may offer some guidance when it comes to twins' school placement, but the situation and circumstances of each individual pair should carry greater weight (Fig. 8.2). Additional research on the immediate and possibly enduring emotional consequences of separating twins at school is needed.

2. *It is unwise for twins to always wear the same outfits.*
    Reality Check: False
    Short Answer: The question of whether parents should choose matching outfits for their twins—or whether twins should choose matching outfits for themselves—has probably been debated as often as the issue of placing twins in the same versus separate classrooms. This discussion is more relevant to identical than fraternal twins because fraternal twins are less likely to be confused for one another—but I will say some things that apply to fraternal twins, as well.

    There is nothing inherently wrong with parents dressing twins alike *on occasion* as long as each twin is recognized and treated as an individual. This means addressing each twin by name and allowing them to engage in activities apart from one another if they wish. As I indicated earlier, when twins go to school it is prudent to dress them differently (especially identical twins), or to style their hair differently to allow students and teachers to recognize them as individuals on opening day. Similar outfits in contrasting colors may be a convenient compromise for some twins since this acknowledges the pair, but distinguishes its members.

    Adult identical twins often pick similar outfits. This makes sense because both twins look good in certain colors and styles, and like the feel

Figure 8.2 *Boy–girl twins heading off to school. (Photo courtesy: Dr. Susan Sy).*

of particular fabrics and textures—likely due, in part, to their shared genes. In fact, a number of identical reared-apart twins wore the same shirt, eyeglasses, or jewelry when they first arrived at the University of Minnesota to participate in research. For some pairs, dressing alike also reinforces the closeness they feel in their relationship with one another. Some adult fraternal twins also enjoy dressing alike on occasion as a way of acknowledging their twinship, but fraternal twins generally prefer to wear different articles of clothing on an everyday basis.

There is no single clothing practice or policy that applies equally to every twin pair. The important goal is to achieve happiness and balance in twins' lives. Most twins, both identical and fraternal, tend to dress differently as they enter late childhood and adolescence. For those who do not, dressing alike is acceptable as long as it does not hinder individual development or become a means for getting attention. Of course, simply dressing alike would probably not impair twins' psychological growth—but it may be one sign of several that some time spent apart from their twin may be needed.

More of the Story: Research shows that twins who were dressed alike as children are *not* more similar in personality than twins who were dressed differently [15]. This important finding challenges the common mythconception that twins who are treated alike behave alike, while twins who are treated differently behave differently. It may be that twins who enjoy dressing alike encourage this practice on the part of their parents, rather than the other way around.

Over the years, a number of mothers and fathers have told me that dressing young twins alike increases their safety by helping parents identify their two children in a crowd. Providing similar outfits can also reduce jealousy or envy if certain clothing items are favored equally by both twins. This applies to both identical and fraternal pairs, although fraternal twins are more likely to show individual preferences. I can say this with confidence—when I was small, some family friends gave my twin sister and me matching skirts and blouses, both of which looked better on one of us (I cannot recall who). I felt uncomfortable wearing them because it seemed that we were trying to look like twins. Today, my sister and I would never choose similar dresses, skirts, or slacks—our bodies, personalities, and style sense are just too different!

Dressing alike can be enjoyable for some twins on some occasions—it can be an opportunity to affirm their relationship or a chance to have fun by fooling people. I have also observed that some reared-apart twins (both identical and fraternal) enjoy wearing the same t-shirts or matching jewelry, as a way of experiencing a childhood pleasure they missed and/or identifying with their newfound relationship. Many reunited twins also discovered the unique advantages of having an identical twin: (1) the possibility of seeing how you *really* look in an outfit, and (2) doubling your wardrobe by buying different items, as long as there is willingness to share.

Dressing alike does not necessarily hamper twins' individuality—but when twins' individuality *is* hampered by dressing alike, it may be time for them to go shopping on their own.

3. *Twins should always attend the same school.*
   Reality Check: False
   Short Story: The short story will follow after a brief detour into my adolescent past—and that of another pair of adolescent twins.

Sometimes twins' differing abilities, talents, or interests prompt them or their parents to seek unique opportunities offered to each cotwin by different schools. In New York City (where I grew up) there were "special schools" (e.g., the Bronx High School of Science, Brooklyn Technical High School, Music and Art, the Fashion Institute, and so on) that catered to some students' special interests in the natural sciences, engineering, applied arts, and clothing design. Admission was free, but getting into these schools was highly competitive. My twin sister was one of three sixth grade female students accepted by Hunter College High School for entry the following year. I was one of three students in my class selected to sit for the entrance exam, but I did not make the final list. I like to think that I performed poorly because of a strange incident that happened during the test.

I was seated at a long high table in a chemistry lab. During the test, I accidentally leaned into one of the gas jets, turning it on, and sending scores of nervous teachers and students into the streets for safety. Testing resumed shortly thereafter, but I was shaken. Several months later I found out that I didn't make the cut, but I wasn't upset—in fact I was happy in our local junior high school as the newly elected president of the Honor Society. I also wanted to go to a coed school, which Hunter College High was not. Anne and I both thrived academically and socially in our separate schools, so being apart was the right choice for us. I eventually attended the Bronx High School of Science, beginning in the tenth grade.

This past experience explains my interest in 17-year-old Henry and Nina Vogel, male–female twins from Los Angeles [16]. These twins attended different schools from age 12 onward, although both competed athletically (Henry in basketball and Nina in equestrian) and both were editor (Henry) and coeditor (Nina) of the student newspaper in their respective schools. Then something surprising happened—the twins' separate experiences led to the same outcome—both twins independently applied to, were accepted by, and chose to attend Dartmouth

College in Hanover, New Hampshire. I suspect that had they attended the same schools, their friendly competition over who turned out the better newspaper or who was the better athlete might have intensified, preventing them from doing their best work.

Shorter Story: I am finally ready to tackle the belief that twins should always attend the same school: False—placing twins in separate schools is good for some pairs, but not for others. When twins' interests diverge, like Anne's and mine, separate schools work well. But even when twins' interests match, like Henry and Nina's, attending different schools can be beneficial as it turned out for them. Many factors affect decisions about which school twin children will attend, such as each twin's personality and plans, their parents' finances, and available opportunities. Even transportation options must be considered since two children, not just one, must be picked up and dropped off.

Most twins attend the same schools until high school graduation and fare just fine. Furthermore, most schools today offer more enriched and diverse curricula than in the past, meeting the needs of most students. When twins wish to attend different schools, but cannot do so because good educational options are inconvenient or unavailable, then online opportunities and community college courses may satisfy their cravings for individual study and independence.

More of the Story: Unfortunately, there is literally no research on why some twins attend different elementary, junior high, or high schools, or what the pluses and minuses might be, forcing me to rely (hesitantly) on related studies and parental feedback. I did discover many websites with questions and comments from parents and psychologists mulling over this issue—strong testimony as to how important twins' shared or separate schooling really is in their lives.

With some exceptions, each twin's individual interests and talents are unlikely to emerge in the lower grades, so enrolling then in the same school makes perfect sense. However, when one or both twins show unusual ability in art, music, dance, or drama, enrolling them in extra-curricular activities is a good solution. In most cases, the different school dilemma does not come up until twins prepare for college, at which time their similar (or dissimilar) interests may affect the school(s) of their choice. Another critical factor that arises at this time is the twins' relationship with each other—for many pairs, leaving for college may mean living apart from one another for several months at a time, a prospect that can seem daunting to some.

When I researched the topic of what lies behind twins' college choices, I found that the appropriate studies are nonexistent in this area as well. In fact, some related research only uses twins to estimate how having a college degree affects future opportunities and earnings [17,18]. But I did learn several things from other sources and I have listed them next [19].

Three key issues surrounding twins' college choices are: (1) finding colleges suited to their interests and talents, (2) deciding if it is best to attend the same or separate schools, and (3) determining if applying to the same college(s) helps or hinders twins' chances for acceptance. Some of these issues also apply to younger twins considering separate public or private schools.

Substituting for research at the moment, or until the necessary research appears, is *Twiniversity*, a website covering all things twin-like, including some helpful college guidelines for parents [20]. But the big picture is murky because colleges are divided as to whether they should admit or reject both twins, and whether twins should apply at the same time or advise one to apply for early admission and the other to apply with the regular application pool. We know nothing about how often twins attend college together and then decide to separate to attend different schools—or decide to attend different colleges before reuniting at the same school later on. We also do not know how this process varies across twin types and why. Good statistics will offer clarity and guidance for twins as a whole, but final decisions will rest on many factors specific to each individual twin pair.

My take on twins' college choice parallels my take on the questions of same or separate classrooms—there should be no policy! Twins should do what feels right for them, and not feel pressured by what they feel they should do, based on the expectations of academic institutions. Even when colleges establish particular policies regarding twins, they are not always followed. I heard from a family whose identical twin sons were closely matched in their interests and abilities, and wished to attend college together. The twins applied to a local university whose policy was to accept or reject both twins—so when just one twin was accepted, the family was crestfallen. Fortunately, an appeal proved successful and the twins will enjoy their college years together.

Many options are available. Twins uncertain about going to school together or apart may decide to attend the same college, but live in different dormitories or apartments. Adjustments can always be made. Twins declaring the same major may purposefully choose different class schedules for independence; then if they realize they work better together they can coordinate their classes for the semesters that follow. Above all, twins, like all people, should first and foremost apply to schools and study subjects that keep them happy and interested—the best plan for nurturing their lives and careers.

4. *It is acceptable to assign twins to different school grades.*
Reality Check: Unlikely
Short Story: Continuing the education theme, I do not favor placing twins in separate grades. This issue has come to my attention from a number of concerned parents whose twin children (identical and fraternal) perform at different academic levels. In such cases, teachers and other school personnel often recommend allowing one twin to advance to the next grade, while retaining the second twin. However, this situation will invite unfair and unkind questions and comments from friends, neighbors, and especially the twins' playmates: "Why are you one grade behind?" "Are you the dumb twin?" "You *are* the dumb twin" or "Why are you older than everyone else—were you left back?" There is little question that this child's self-esteem will be affected, especially if he or she continues to lag a grade behind and cannot catch up. Knowing this, some parents have considered retaining both twins in the lower grade, but reluctantly because it is unfair to hold back the child who is progressing.

I believe that the best solution to this trying situation is to advance both children to the next grade, placing them in separate classes and providing tutorials and assistance to the twin in need. If this is not possible, then separate schools may be a workable option because the twins' different grades would not be front and center for all to see.
More of the Story: Again, there is a complete absence of research on the advisability and outcomes of twins' attending separate grades. I know from my conversations with parents facing this decision that most mothers and fathers favor advancing both twins to the next grade and assisting the twin who needs help. Of course, such interventions may introduce other problems, such as jealousy on the part of the more able twin over the extra parental (and academic) attention given to his or her cotwin. These problems may never arise, but it is prudent to anticipate the possibility so as to prepare for all outcomes.

Deciding on separate schools when twins show marked differences in academic ability might work for some families. In fact, regardless of twins' similarities or differences in academic performance or school readiness, it may be easier for parents interested in private schools to have their twins accepted by *different* schools, rather than the same school. I have been privy to a peculiar buzz emanating from the "parental underground"—it seems that some private schools are reluctant to accept twins because of potential reductions in donors and donations. Think about this—twins have two sets of grandparents (i.e., two potential donors), whereas two unrelated students have four sets of grandparents (i.e., four potential donors). However, not all parents have observed such practices, school administrators are unlikely to admit to it and I have not researched this possibility fully. I would like to hear from families who may have had this experience.

5. *Forty percent of all twins create a secret language during early childhood (at about 3–8 years of age).*
   Reality Check: Likely, but …
   Short Answer: In February 2011 a video of diapered 18-month-old toddler twins enchanted anyone who watched it on social media [21]. The two little boys were intensely absorbed in a verbal back and forth that was unintelligible to everyone but them. An utterance by one twin delighted his brother, eliciting hysterical laughter and another succession of sounds that produced the same excited reaction in the first twin. The significance of their exchange—meaningful communication or nonsense syllables—was widely debated in the press. Language experts who saw this video concluded that the twins were communicating by mimicking sounds they had heard in adult conversations—that is, they were not creating a secret language, but were displaying a normal phase of linguistic development. (Near-in-age nontwin siblings also show this behavior, although less frequently.) The video was a lovely illustration of how humans are born biologically prepared to talk, and will do so in a supportive language learning environment.
   Based on available studies, it is safe to say that about 40% of twin toddlers engage in some form of "twin-speak," not unlike that witnessed in the video. But that figure does not convey just how complex twins' language development turns out to be.
   More of the Story: Only in the last 15 years (probably because of increased attention to twins, due to increased twinning rates) have psychologists revealed the complexity of what has been labeled twins' "private

speech," "secret language," and "autonomous language." Autonomous language generally refers to speech that differs from the speech that it typically used in the child's environment, and which is understandable to only one or two other children acquiring language at the same time. Differences in definition, measurement methods, and the age at which twins are studied explain why the estimated frequency of their unusual verbal behaviors ranges so widely, from less than 2% to 47% [22,23].

Some popular labels for twins' unusual language patterns include "cryptophasia" (Greek for "secret" and "speech") and "idioglossia" (private form of speech invented by children who are in close social contact) [24,25]. However, these terms are rarely used by professionals in the field because there is nothing "secret" about them—in fact, twins become upset when their parents fail to understand them. Furthermore, twins do not invent a new language; they tend to produce atypical forms of the language they are exposed to.

Recently, some specific forms of twins' verbal exchange have been recognized and defined: [23] *shared verbal understanding* is a term for speech used within the pair. It is also directed to other people even though it is unintelligible to these others. Shared verbal understanding is *not* directed exclusively to the other twin and is *not* abnormal in form (i.e., it does not show word repetitions or omissions). According to one study, about 50% of twins engage in shared verbal understanding at the age of 20 months, compared with about 20% at the age of 3 years. It is typical to see a decline in twins' reliance on shared verbal understanding as their social circles start to extend beyond the home and family.

In contrast, *private language*, also unintelligible to others, is speech used *exclusively* within the twin pair. Private language has been observed among only 11.8% of 20-month-old twins and 6.6% of 3-year olds, much lower than the rates of shared verbal understanding. Both types of communication typically decrease over time and are replaced by normal language skills. The smaller number of twins (mostly male) at risk for language problems by the age of 6 are those who used private language at the age of 3 *and* did not develop normal language skills along with their private speech.

Most studies of both twins and nontwins report that males are more likely to experience speech and language problems. This finding has been partly linked to sex differences in brain development—specific areas of the brain are dedicated to language functions, but they develop sooner in females and are distributed more widely throughout the brain.

Therefore, females are generally better able to process language than males [26,27].

Some researchers have recognized yet another form of twin-to-twin communication known as *restricted language*. This type of speech refers to ordinary language dedicated to intimate communication between partners who share beliefs and expectations that come from a shared life history, and who use the same abbreviated expressions [28]. For example, as a young child I could not tolerate fried eggs that were not completely dry—if I detected one bit of moisture around them I would yell, "gush gush!" and my mother would return them to the frying pan. In fact, my twin sister and I still use that term when eggs are not prepared to our liking. I believe this third category is helpful because understanding that some parts of twins' speech may take this form prevents it from seeming atypical or abnormal. And as I suggested with my egg example, restricted language is qualitatively not that different from the private or made-up words, phrases, and jokes shared by good friends and family members. Of course, identical twins may come by these expressions more easily than nontwin companions because they understand the world in the same way and spend a lot of time together. Unfortunately, the different studies did not always address twin-type differences (e.g., identical vs. fraternal) in their analyses of twin-to-twin communication.

Organizing twins' speech into specific forms and studying these forms systematically has brought needed clarity to the onset and nature of twins' verbal behaviors. However, the nonverbal counterparts of shared understanding and private language have been overlooked. A look, a glance, or a gesture often conveys more information than an extended verbal conversation. *Mind reading*—the process of associating someone's facial expressions and body movements (as well as utterances) with his or her mental or emotional states—is a unique human skill that is of great interest to psychologists and philosophers [29]. (I find the term for this behavior—mind reading—unfortunate, as it implies a form of telepathic communication, always a controversial topic.) It is likely that identical twins are good "mind readers" because subtle visual or postural changes detected between them probably develop early and persist. However, overreliance on these nonverbal signals (as well as on shared understanding and private language) could hamper twins' language development, leading to their well-known language delays—the topic to which I will turn next.

6. *Twins show language delays, relative to singletons.*

   Reality Check: True

   Short Answer: Most studies find that 3–8-year-old twins' language development is delayed, relative to that of singletons. Again, this does not mean that all twins lag behind all nontwins, but rather that twins, as a group, reach their linguistic milestones at later ages. In the absence of childhood disabilities (e.g., hearing problems or visual difficulties), research holds the unique social-interactional patterns of the twin–parent triad mostly responsible for twins' language delays [30]. Compared to ordinary parents–child dyads, parent–twin triads include more interruptions, less individually directed speech, and greater parental control when twins are 20 and 36 months old. These features are even found in the speech styles of mothers talking to their 4-month-old twins [31]. One study of infant multiples found that mothers directed more positive attention, as well as vocalization, to the healthier cotwin [32].

   I was interested to learn that several recent reports have challenged these claims with evidence that twins' language production "outstripped" that of singletons [33–35]. These studies noted that membership in a multiparty social arrangement facilitates taking turns, monitoring interactions, mobilizing responses, and timing replies. I believe it is important to look closely at these studies that may show how some parents encourage such behaviors, thereby offsetting typical twin-associated language problems. But I also believe that the language deficit observed among many twins is a real phenomenon that must be addressed.

   More of the Story: The significant role that the twin relationship plays in twins' language learning environment is both theoretically and clinically important. Twin toddlers develop close social ties, perhaps earlier than nontwins, partly due to their physical proximity and shared time. However, the various studies often failed to draw the crucial distinction between twin types, either MZ or DZ—I would expect a higher proportion of identical than fraternal twins to show language difficulties, due to their generally closer social relationship and matched verbal abilities.

   Surprisingly, twin research shows no link between twins' linguistic delays and adversities in their prenatal environments or their mothers' obstetrical complications [33,36]. It makes intuitive sense that twins' prematurity and/or risky deliveries might be largely responsible for their difficulties with language and speech. Perhaps these factors apply in some individual cases, but the data are the data! Knowing that the parent–twin triad may depress twins' language development for the reasons cited earlier, further examining mother–twin verbal interaction patterns where cotwin advantages are present is worth doing.

One such study gathered 20 hours of mother–twin interaction in the home over a 5-year period, beginning when the twins (fraternal boys) were 16 months old; however, the verbal exchanges that were analyzed took place when the twins were 4. While the twins worked with kitchen utensils and playdough, their mother adjusted her gaze and body posture to respond individually to each twin whose focus on the activity differed. She sometimes posed follow-up questions and often said "we" to include both children in the interaction. According to the investigator who conducted this study, the twin situation *improves* twin children's turn-taking abilities, interactional monitoring, and response ability to get another person to respond: "… although twins are initially linguistically delayed, they are not socially delayed from an interactional perspective (p. 96)" [35]. This case report and two modest-sized twin studies showing *language benefits* from twins' triadic situation are encouraging [34,35], but require replication with larger twin samples, organized by twin type. Until results from such efforts are available, the conclusion that twins generally perform below nontwins on verbal exchanges and language tasks will remain. I suspect that new findings will offer ways to reduce the disparity between twins and nontwins in speech and language skills.

One of the few studies to consider twin type in relation to children's language proficiencies is an old favorite of mine. I like this study, conducted in 1966 at the University of Chicago (where I received my PhD) [37] because it investigated many aspects of twinship (e.g., mental abilities, personality, twin relationship) *and* did so across the different twin types (identical males and females, fraternal males and females, and opposite-sex). In the area of language, the researcher, Dr. Helen Koch, compared the speech sounds (phonetics), word structure (morphology), and word arrangement (syntax) of 5- and 6-year-old children's speech.

Koch found that the fraternal females from same-sex and opposite-sex pairs outperformed the identical and fraternal male twins on these three measures, as judged by teacher ratings, Dr. Koch's ratings, and a standard verbal ability test. The fraternal females also outperformed their singleton counterparts in articulation (expressing thoughts or feelings). Interestingly, the female twins were socially closer to their cotwins than the male twins (based on interviews with the children that asked about the quality of their relationship, how much time they spent together, and what they liked about being a twin), but this did not appear to hamper their language learning. Even the identical female twins whose teacher ratings and word counts were below those of the fraternal females were judged to be highly people-involved; thus, some twins may be linguistically, but not socially delayed [35], consistent with the case report I reviewed previously.

Koch's study also revealed that the fraternal male twins from opposite-sex pairs spoke as well as the male nontwins who were examined. Perhaps exposure to their linguistically proficient twin sisters made a difference even though these twins were not as socially close to one another as the identical females.

Families raising two near-in-age children show different communicative features than families with twins [30,38]. Maternal responsiveness, maternal involvement, and the range of individual experiences are higher in families with two singletons than in families with twins—all three measures have been associated with non-twin siblings' more favorable language outcomes. It is easier for parents to focus their attention on single children than on twins whose more chaotic circumstances require greater control.

Chapter 9 explores biological variations from a twin study perspective, bringing in a lot of material on the neglected twins—the male–female pairs who are endlessly fascinating and who are gaining celebrity in various research circles. But first I will define some commonly used terms that are often misused. I will then examine factors affecting sexual orientation, the behavioral characteristics of male–female twins, as well as twin studies of autistic tendencies and other behaviors.

REFERENCES

[1] J.C. Schwarz, Effects of peer familiarity on the behavior of preschoolers in a novel situation, J. Pers. Soc. Psychol. 24 (2) (1972) 276.
[2] R. Moskwinski, School placement of multiples, Twin Res. 2 (3) (1999) 239.
[3] L. Jones, K. De Gioia, The same or separate? An exploration of teachers' perceptions of the classroom assignment of twins in prior to school and kindergarten to Year Two school settings, J. Early Child. Res. 8 (3) (2010) 239–253.
[4] N.L. Segal, Education issues, Twin Res. Hum. Genet. 8 (4) (2005) 409–414.
[5] Available from: http://www.twinslaw.com/Welcome_to_Twinslaw.com_Where_the_twin_bond_is_celebrated_and_protected_under_law%21.html.
[6] N.L. Segal, Same or separate classrooms: a twin bill, Twin Res. Hum. Genet. 9 (3) (2006) 473–478.
[7] St. Paul Pioneer Press, Micromanaging Multiples, April 21, 2005, p. B-12.

[8] R. Fraser-Thill, Internalizing Behaviors Definition. About Parenting, 2016. Available from: http://tweenparenting.about.com/od/behaviordiscipline/a/Internalizing-Behaviors.htm

[9] L.A. Tully, T.E. Moffitt, A. Caspi, A. Taylor, H. Kiernan, P. Andreou, What effect does classroom separation have on twins' behavior, progress at school, and reading abilities?, Twin Res. 7 (2) (2004) 115–124.

[10] L.F. DiLalla, P.Y. Mullineaux, The effect of classroom environment on problem behaviors: a twin study, J. Sch. Psychol. 46 (2) (2008) 107–128.

[11] M. Van Leeuwen, S.M. Van Den Berg, T.C. van Beijsterveldt, D.I. Boomsma, Effects of twin separation in primary school, Twin Res. Hum. Genet. 8 (4) (2005) 384–391.

[12] W.L. Coventry, B. Byrne, M. Coleman, R.K. Olson, R. Corley, E. Willcutt, S. Samuelsson, Does classroom separation affect twins' reading ability in the early years of school?, Twin Res. Hum. Genet. 12 (5) (2009) 455–461.

[13] B. Byrne, W.L. Coventry, R.K. Olson, S.J. Wadsworth, S. Samuelsson, S.A. Petrill, et al. "Teacher effects" in early literacy development: evidence from a study of twins, J. Educ. Psychol. 102 (1) (2010) 32–42.

[14] D. Webbink, D. Hay, P.M. Visscher, Does sharing the same class in school improve cognitive abilities of twins?, Twin Res. Hum. Genet. 10 (4) (2007) 573–580.

[15] J.C. Loehlin, R.C. Nichols, Heredity, Environment, and Personality: A Study of 850 Sets of Twins, University of Texas Press, Austin, TX, (1976).

[16] E. Sondheimer, Twins' Separate Paths Lead to the Same College, Los Angeles Times, December 25, 2015, p. D3.

[17] E. Eide, D.J. Brewer, R.G. Ehrenberg, Does it pay to attend an elite private college? Evidence on the effects of undergraduate college quality on graduate school attendance, Econ. Educ. Rev. 17 (4) (1998) 371–376.

[18] J.R. Behrman, M.R. Rosenzweig, P. Taubman, College choice and wages: Estimates using data on female twins, Rev. Econ. Stat. 78 (4) (1996) 672–685.

[19] N.L. Segal, College-age twins: university admissions policies, Twin Res. Hum. Genet. 17 (6) (2014) 594–598.

[20] Twiniversity. Available from: http://twiniversity.com/?s=college

[21] Winnepeg Free Press, Viral Video of Babbling Twin Babies Has Experts Talking, April 4, 2011. Available from: http://www.winnipegfreepress.com/arts-and-life/life/viral-video-of-babbling-twin-babies-has-experts-talking-119167464.html

[22] P. Bakker, Autonomous languages of twins, Acta Genet. Med. Gemellol. 36 (1987) 233–238.

[23] K. Thorpe, R. Greenwood, A. Eivers, M. Rutter, Prevalence and developmental course of 'secret language', Int. J. Lang. Commun. Disord. 36 (1) (2001) 43–62.

[24] J.-K. Jordan, 1 Language That Only 2 People Speak: The Secret Language of Twins, 2016. Available from: https://www.babbel.com/en/magazine/twins-secret-languages.

[25] Idioglossia, 2016. Available from: http://www.dictionary.com/browse/idioglossia

[26] L.E. Berk, Child Development, ninth ed., Pearson, Boston, MA, (2013).

[27] H.D. Nelson, P. Nygren, M. Walker, R. Panoscha, Screening for speech and language delay in preschool children: systematic evidence review for the US Preventive Services Task Force, Pediatrics 117 (2) (2006) e298–e319.

[28] K. Mogford, Language development in twins, in: D. Bishop, K. Mogford (Eds.), Language Development in Exceptional Circumstances, Churchill Livingstone, Edinburgh, 1993, pp. 80–95.

[29] C.M. Heyes, C.D. Frith, The cultural evolution of mind reading, Science 344 (6190) (2014) 1243091.

[30] K. Thorpe, Twin children's language development, Early Hum. Dev. 82 (6) (2006) 387–395.

[31] S. Butler, C. McMahon, J.A. Ungerer, Maternal speech style with prelinguistic twin infants, Infant Child Dev. 12 (2) (2003) 129–143.

[32] J. Mann, Nurturance or negligence: maternal psychology and behavioral preference among preterm twins, in: J. Barkow, L. Cosmides, J. Tooby (Eds.), The Adaptd Mind: Evolutionary Psychology and the Evolution of Culture, Oxford University Press, New York, NY, 1992, pp. 367–390.

[33] M.E. Barton, R. Strosberg, Conversational patterns of two-year-old twins in mother–twin–twin triads, J. Child Lang. 24 (1) (1997) 257–269.

[34] H. Tremblay-Leveau, S. Leclerc, J. Nadel, Linguistic skills of 16- and 23-month-old twins and singletons in a triadic context, First Lang. 19 (56) (1999) 233–254.

[35] J. Rendle-Short, L. Skelt, N. Bramley, Speaking to twin children: evidence against the "impoverishment" thesis, Res. Lang. Soc. Interact. 48 (1) (2015) 79–99.

[36] M. Rutter, K. Thorpe, R. Greenwood, K. Northstone, J. Golding, Twins as a natural experiment to study the causes of mild language delay: I: Design; twin–singleton differences in language, and obstetric risks, J. Child Psychol. Psychiatry 44 (3) (2003) 326–341.

[37] H.L. Koch, Twins and Twin Relations, University of Chicago Press, Chicago, (1966).

[38] K. Thorpe, M. Rutter, R. Greenwood, Twins as a natural experiment to study the causes of mild language delay: II: Family interaction risk factors, J. Child Psychol. Psychiatry 44 (3) (2003) 342–355.

CHAPTER 9

Human Behavioral Variations: Sex and Sex Differences

Male–female twin pairs pose a wonderful natural experiment for studying sex-related differences in behavioral development. But first I want to talk about some problems in the way that scientific findings are presented to professional colleagues and to the public.

Every field has its own special jargon that facilitates communication among the members of that discipline. However, these communicative shortcuts may be misused and misunderstood when adopted by individuals outside the field. I was inspired to include this section because of a 2015 paper, "Fifty Psychological and Psychiatry Terms to Avoid" [1]. I will then delve into the fascinating findings and fables surrounding male–female twin pairs, as well as medical conditions that, contrary to some reports, are not more frequent among twins than nontwins.

1. *A number of terms and expressions used in twin research are misused and misunderstood.*

   Reality Check: True

   Short Answer: I am variously frustrated/upset/perplexed by certain words, concepts, and expressions that are improperly used in both the scientific and popular literature on twins (as well as in books and articles describing genetic and environmental influences on behavior, based on family and adoption studies). This is a good point in my book to identify some of these troublemakers and replace the confusion with clarity. Knowing what these terms mean, and do not mean, will be helpful for understanding the material that is to come. I will only examine the few that I find most relevant: "a gene for," "fraternal twins," "concordant versus discordant, and "heritability."

   More of the Story: The expression *"a gene for"* (as a gene for mood disorder) is misleading because most complex traits, such as intelligence level, extraverted personality, and depressed mood, are influenced by many genes in combination, each having a small effect on the behavior. In this sense, these traits (which are influenced by many genes) differ from those medical conditions linked to a single gene(s), such as cystic fibrosis, Huntington's disease, and Duchenne muscular dystrophy.

Twin Mythconceptions
http://dx.doi.org/10.1016/B978-0-12-803994-6.00009-3

183

The way that genes are expressed is a matter of probability, not certainty—having a particular set of genes predisposes a person to show a certain level of ability or type of temperament, but nongenetic factors (e.g., social experiences, epigenetic events) can affect how the genes actually get expressed. A person born with a tendency to be extraverted will be somewhat less so, if social conventions discourage such behavior. Even traits strongly influenced by genes may never appear—an allergic reaction to penicillin has a genetic basis, but if you never receive the vaccine you will never show the response.

* Same-sex fraternal twins? Males or females? The *Merriam-Webster Dictionary's* simple definitions of *fraternal* are "of or relating to brothers," "made up of members who share an interest or purpose," and "friendly or brotherly." The full definition also includes "derived from two ova: dizygotic or fraternal twins" [2]. Many people, including me, have wondered why the term *sororal* (think of sorority) is never used to denote fraternal female twins. It would be more accurate and less cumbersome to have this term available; as things stand, researchers, relatives, and twins must specify the sex of the pair, alongside the twin type, for example, fraternal males or fraternal females. I wondered if languages that use gendered terms have separate labels for the different types of twins. It turns out that Spanish (as spoken in Colombia, South America where I have most recently conducted twin research, and elsewhere in the Spanish-speaking world) has convenient designations for the different types of twins: *gemelos* (identical males); *gemelas* (identical females); *mellizos* (fraternal same-sex males); *mellizas* (fraternal same-sex females), and *mellizos* (the masculine form is used for male-female twins); however, one might say *mellizos: un niño y una niña*—one boy and one girl—to indicate an opposite-sex twin pair. French and Italian also use gendered nouns, but do not have such distinctive labels for twins.

Separate terms for identical male and identical female twin pairs in English would be helpful, as in Spanish. Perhaps this has never come up because identical is a gender-neutral term, whereas fraternal is not. It is also the case that a simple term for opposite-sex twins has never been found—even the Spanish term (actually a phrase) is long and awkward. Most researchers, parents, and twins refer to this twin type as male–female, boy–girl, or opposite-sex. I did a synonym search for a better expression, but I could not find one. Suggestions are welcome—tracking down the presence or absence of specific twin-type terms across languages and cultures may be one of my personal future projects....

* Concordant for eye color? Discordant for depression? The term *concordant* is the label generally reserved for twin pairs in which both cotwins show the same trait or are affected by the same medical condition. If both twins in a pair have blue eyes or are diagnosed with diabetes, they are concordant for both of these traits. However, twins do not have to be perfectly matched in order to be concordant—twins can be concordant for a disorder, but differ with respect to the specific signs and severity they display. Recall from Chapter 2 that the famous identical Genain Quadruplet sisters, born in 1930, all showed signs of schizophrenia, but their symptom profiles and degree of illness varied [3].

The term *discordant* indicates twin pairs that include one affected twin and one unaffected twin, either with regard to having a certain trait or condition and/or having different symptoms and severity. Earlier, I described a pair of twins in which one twin had Klippel–Trenaunay syndrome and the other twin did not—these twins were discordant for this disorder. I have also mentioned hand-discordant twin pairs, in which one twin is right-handed and the other twin is left-handed. These twins are discordant for hand preference; however, two right-handed or two left-handed twins could be concordant for hand preference, but differ (be discordant) in the *strength* of their hand preference—just like the Genain Quadruplets were concordant for schizophrenia, but discordant for symptoms and symptom severity.

* Another misused term in twin research is *heritability*, the proportion of variation in a particular trait that is explained by genetic differences among the people in that population at a particular point in time. To say that intelligence has a heritability of about 70% or that personality has a heritability of about 50% is correct, but does not convey the complete story. I will try to do that here:

If everyone from a particular population completed a personality questionnaire, there would be variation in the scores—some people would score low in extraversion, some would score high, and others would score somewhere in the middle. Twin studies can estimate what percentage of the score differences among the people who took the questionnaire are due to the genetic and environmental differences among them. But even if the heritability for extraversion turned out to be 50% (which it is! [4]), this does *not* eliminate the impact of the environment on personality, which is responsible for the other 50% of the variation in the scores. Furthermore, the environment may have an especially strong effect *in individual cases*—if a potentially extraverted child was severely punished, even beaten, for speaking or laughing, this youngster might learn to avoid others or remain solitary because of an environmental effect, that is, his or her upbringing. This would be an example of an extreme environment overwhelming the genes. Percentages of genetic and environmental effects apply to populations, not to individual people.

Heritability is not a rigidly fixed figure, but can change depending on the population, time of measurement, measuring instrument, and age of the people being measured. Interestingly, five major studies of reared-apart identical twins show that the heritability of general intelligence is .73—even though these studies occurred in different years and different places, used different populations of different ages, and administered different ability tests [5]. Agreement among the results increases confidence in that figure, although the percentage could change some day. Note that the genetic influence on intelligence among 7-year-old twins from low socioeconomic status families is near zero (another possible example of extreme environments overwhelming genes), while the shared environment (such as home facilities and/or educational opportunities) accounts for 60% of the variation in measured mental ability and individual experiences account for about 40% [6,7]. Just the reverse was found using twins from affluent families, and these results were repeated in a subsequent study of infants and toddlers [8]. Of course, it was not possible to determine which aspect of the shared social environment might be associated with intellectual decline. In addition, as the investigators noted, socioeconomic status may not be strictly an environmental measure, but could partly reflect genetic factors.

Family environments reflect actual genetic influences to some extent, so separating the two is challenging. People who love to read will have many books on their shelves, and people with an artistic bent may surround themselves with paintings and sculptures. The items in our current home did not appear by magic—they were chosen by us and reflect our genetically influenced interests and abilities. Of course, many items in our childhood environments were placed there by our parents. As a 10-year-old, I was thrilled when my athletically minded father installed a chinning bar at the doorway to my bedroom—I would swing on it each time I entered or exited the room. But my fraternal twin sister Anne, while good at many sports, showed no interest in this apparatus. Indeed, I would have a chinning bar in my home today if the ceilings were sufficiently high. Twin research shows that the kinds of physical activities we like and are good at have a partial genetic basis [9].

2. *A heritability estimate of 50% for personality traits means that half of a person's extraversion is due to genetic factors and the other half is due to environmental factors.*
   Reality Check: False
   Short Story: The genetic and environmental factors that shape the personality of a single person work together and *cannot* be separated. It is not possible to "dissect" the personality of a single person, and attribute 50% to the genes and 50% to the environment. As I indicated earlier, heritability (the estimate of genetic influence) refers to a *population as a whole*. In other words, it tells us how much the differences from person to person in a population are associated with the genetic differences among them.
   More of the Story: What is true about the heritability of personality is true for all human traits—nearly every twin study shows some degree of genetic influence on just about every measured trait. These traits include (but are not limited to) social beliefs, political attitudes, religiosity, and well-being [4]. Very few twin studies have revealed a lack of genetic influence, although an analysis of love styles (how quickly or slowly one falls in love) is a good example [10]. Using John A. Lee's six love styles, twins' self-descriptions leading to their categorization as *Eros* (falls in love at first sight), *Ludos* (prefers momentary fun), *Storge* (falls in love slowly), *Pragma* (is practical and realistic), *Mania* (has low self-esteem and a need to be loved), or *Agape* (is willing to sacrifice anything for the partner) did not show significant genetic influence [11]. This result is somewhat surprising, but agrees with the finding that the shared family environment influences the personality trait of sociability [12]. It may also be partly due to the fact that one's love style is affected by the partner's behaviors. It is also surprising that further twin research on this topic has not appeared since the publication of the original report in 1994.
   Most behavioral traits show heritabilities of about 50%, but some traits, such as the mid-frequency of alpha activity (brainwave indicating degree of relaxed brain activity) [13–17] show 80%, and intrinsic job satisfaction (aspects of a job that reflect personal gratification, such as challenge and achievement) show 32%. These values were based on participants in the Minnesota Study of Twins Reared Apart, who represent

a range of ages, occupations, and job complexity, and were replicated using twins reared together.

Somewhat paradoxically, some highly genetically influenced human traits have heritabilities equal to zero, such as having a nose or having two eyes—that is because heritability expresses variation and (barring developmental errors) having a nose and two eyes is part of the basic human plan that we all share. However, heritability would *not* be zero when it comes to nose shape or eye color, characteristics that do differ from person to person.

Estimates of genetic influence on behavior have been misinterpreted in ways that researchers probably never anticipated. Consider the next mythconception that concerns homosexuality.

3. *If one identical twin has a homosexual orientation then his or her cotwin must have one, too.*
    Reality Check: False
    Short Story: If one identical twin is homosexual, then his or her cotwin has a higher probability of being, or becoming, homosexual relative to a fraternal twin or nontwin relative. However, the chance is far less than 100%. Based on twin studies published between 1991 and 2012, the probability of an identical twin being homosexual if he or she had a cotwin that was, ranges from .18 to .65. In contrast, the same probability for a fraternal twin ranges from .00 to .29. The higher probability values for identical than fraternal twins demonstrate genetic influence on sexual orientation, but also show that environmental components (both before and after birth) play a role.

    The earliest published twin study of sexual orientation, reported in 1952, found 100% concordance for homosexuality among male identical twins. However, I omitted it from the probability ranges I reported in the previous paragraph because it has never been replicated. The reason that the investigator, Dr. Franz Kallmann, found complete resemblance among his twin pairs reflects the methods he used to find the twins [18]. In the section that follows, I will discuss this issue, which also explains why the probabilities vary so much from study to study.
    More of the Story: An insightful section on twin studies can be found in a 2016 overview of findings and controversies concerning the origins of sexual orientation [19]. A critical distinction is made between studies that used targeted sampling and those that used probability (registry) sampling. Targeted sampling refers to the identification of participants

because they are homosexual, typically accomplished by newsletter mailings, magazine advertising, or similar means. Franz Kallmann who conducted the 1952 study, referenced earlier, located his twin subjects in gay bars. His technique most likely introduced bias into the results because (1) concordant pairs are more likely to be found congregating in gay bars than discordant pairs, and (2) concordant pairs are more likely to consent to research participation than discordant pairs. (Homosexual twins with heterosexual cotwins may decline participation to avert any suspicion that the cotwin is gay or to avoid within-pair stress over this difference.) Such studies will, consequently, yield inflated estimates of heritability because the participating identical pairs would tend to be concordant.

Such biases are generally avoided with the use of twin registry data. That is because the members of twin registries (especially those that draw upon populations rather than volunteers) are enrolled without reference to the behavior of interest. Comparing findings from studies that assembled their samples according to these different methods is informative.

The median correlations across studies that used targeted sampling yielded correlations of .52 (MZ) and .17 (DZ). In contrast, the median correlations across studies that used registry data were .25 (MZ) and .13 (DZ). It is clear that heritability is less when calculated from the registry data—the correlations are lower, as are the differences between the MZ and DZ twin pairs.

The authors noted that calculating the degree of genetic and environmental influence separately for males and females was precluded by the availability of too few registry samples. However, available estimates for male sexual orientation have ranged from 100% in 1952 [20] to 39% in 2010 [21,22]. Estimates of heritability (genetic influence) on female sexual orientation have ranged from 8% in 2000 to 32% in 2015 [21–23]. A consistent trend has been that genetic factors are more influential in male than female sexual orientation. The wide ranges reflect the different methods of participant identification. However, one set of findings, based on an anonymous survey completed by Australian twin registry volunteers, found that genetic influence on sexual orientation was twice as high for females (50–60%) than for males (30%) [24]. Given the growing number of twin registries worldwide, such as in Brazil, future analyses should resolve these conflicting findings [25,26].

In summary, sexual orientation has a genetic basis, but it has nongenetic components, as well. Some nongenetic influences may be prenatal, such as maternal stress, hormonal exposure, and developmental disruption [27,28], although findings vary across studies. It is also known that male homosexuals tend to have a greater number of older brothers than heterosexual men, heterosexual women, and homosexual women [29].These effects are distinct from social environmental influences (e.g., seduction by an older same-sex individual or rearing by homosexual parents), wrongly identified for triggering homosexual tendencies in the absence of definitive evidence [19]. Finally, a limitation of the extant twin studies is that sexual orientation was assessed by self-report which may produce some false reports or denials.The authors raised the possibility that identical twin discordance may be less than the research suggests if more valid methods, such as penis plethysmograph-measured arousal (PPG) in response to male and female erotic stimuli become available for identical male twins.

The 2016 review referenced above is introduced by thoughtful commentary from Dr. Ritch Savin-Williams (2016), Professor of Human Development at Cornell University (and a former fellow graduate student of mine at the University of Chicago).

4. *Half of all twins are gay.*
Reality Check: False
Short Answer: I raised this issue earlier, but I feel compelled to repeat it because it is so important for twins, families, and everyone else to understand where it came from and why it is *not* true.

In 1991, a Northwestern University twin study reported that if one member of an identical twin pair was homosexual then the chances of homosexuality were 52% for male cotwins and 48% for female cotwins [30]. Findings from this study appeared in newspapers nationwide [31,32], prompting one multiple birth mother to ask me, "Is it true that half of all twins are gay?" My answer was/is that twins are *not* more likely to be homosexual than anyone else in the population. However, because sexual orientation is partly genetically influenced, an identical twin has a higher chance of being gay if his or her cotwin is gay. The chance (as reported in the 1991 study) was also higher for a fraternal twin whose cotwin was homosexual (22% for males and 16% for females) than for someone in the general population. But it was less than for identical twins because fraternal twins have fewer common genes.

More of the Story:The prevalence (percentage of a population with a certain trait) of homosexuality varies with respect to geographical region, date of assessment, and measured component of sexual orientation

[21,33]. Population surveys indicate that 3–20% of males and 2–9% of females will engage in homosexual behavior at some time during their life. No one knows for certain, but it is unlikely that homosexuality is higher among twins than nontwins. In a large, 2010 population-based study from Sweden the percentage of twins reporting any lifetime same-sex partner was within the range reported for nontwins: 5.6% for male twins and 7.8% for female twins. However, the average number of same-sex sexual partners at the time of the study was higher for males (12.86) than for females (3.53) [21]. During 2011–13, the median number of same-sex partners among United States adults aged 25–44 years was 6.6 for males and 4.3 for females [34].

New avenues for twin research relating to sexual preference have opened up, some involving female twins. The relationships among female sexual orientation, sex typicality, and mating success have been explained by the finding that the same genes affect these various measures [23]. Furthermore, female homosexual identical twins from discordant (1 gay, 1 straight) pairs show a lower fingerprint ridge count (total number of ridges across all 10 fingers) than their heterosexual twin sisters. These twins also show a lower ratio between their second and fourth fingers (2D:4D ratio) than their heterosexual cotwins. It should be noted that a low 2D:4D ratio has been linked to higher levels of the male hormone androgen. Both females and males have circulating estrogen and androgen, but in different proportions—females have more estrogen and males have more androgen.

In contrast, identical female twins concordant for sexual orientation do not differ in these measures. These findings suggest that conditions in the womb may be implicated in some aspect of sexual development among cotwins who differ, possibly in their degree of exposure to androgen. A curious wrinkle is that discordant male identical twins did not differ in the 2D:4D ratio, suggesting that prenatal influences on sexual orientation in males and females are not the same [35–47].

Studies of gene expression (epigenetic analyses) using male twins may explain why genetically identical twins do not show complete concordance for homosexuality. The suggestion by a University of California-Santa Barbara researcher that epigenetic factors may affect sexual orientation prompted UCLA investigators to look more closely at this issue. The epigenetic profiles of 37 identical male twin pairs discordant for sexual orientation included 5 places or regions in the human genome where the epigenetic information (markers) was associated with being heterosexual or homosexual. The twins were then divided into two groups and the relationships between these markers and the twins' sexual orientation was examined in one group—then they tried to see if this relationship was also found in the second group. It turned out that the same relationship was found in nearly 70% of the second group. This is exciting work, raising key questions as to why identical twins' epigenetic markers differ and why they affect sexual orientation. Such efforts can bring needed clarity to the currently competing theories of sexual orientation that variously emphasize genetic influence and socialization. Hopefully, epigenetic research on sexual orientation will include female twins, as well.

5. *The behavioral and physical traits of female twins in male–female pairs are affected by prenatal exposure to male hormones.*
   Reality Check: Possible
   Short Answer: People love to talk about sex differences in behavior, so it might seem curious that male–female twin pairs have been relatively neglected by people studying twins. But I understand why these twins have not been popular research participants in some studies. Mostly, researchers worried that the cotwin sex difference would sway the results. That is because the difference between opposite-sex twins might be greater than the difference between same-sex twins in some traits. For example, females tend to outperform males on some verbal tasks like vocabulary. Thus, the vocabulary difference between male–female twins might be greater than the difference between same-sex fraternal twins. This is important because the greater the difference between fraternal cotwins, relative to identical cotwins, the greater the degree of genetic influence. This problem can be overcome by comparing identical twins with same-sex fraternal twins only. It is also possible to include male–female twins in a study and then compare their degree of resemblance with that of same-sex twins—if there is no difference then the two twin groups can be combined.

   Think about being surrounded by hundreds of male–female pairs—it would be impossible to know that these partners were twins, because visually, they are indistinguishable from friends, near-in-age siblings, significant others, and married couples. However, thanks to the renewed interest in biological and psychological influences on the behavioral and physical differences between males and females, opposite-sex twins have attracted lots of research attention in the last 20 years. And the dramatic

Figure 9.1 *Boy–girl twins at play. (Photo courtesy: Dr. Susan Sy).*

rise in twinning rates has increased scientific and societal interest in twins more generally.

An issue that I want to address is if, and how much, females are affected by male hormones when they share a womb with a twin brother. This notion comes from the nonhuman animal literature showing that female mice, rats, and gerbils turn out to be more aggressive in life if situated between two males in the uterus—however, these effects are not seen in female rodents located near other females. It is also known that female cattle gestated with a male twin are infertile as a result of exposure to their wombmate's hormones. The prenatal circumstances of human and nonhuman mammals differ, yet the nonhuman findings form the basis of the *Twin Testosterone Transfer Hypothesis (TTTH),* which is gaining attention (Fig. 9.1).

More of the Story: The TTTH proposes that females with twin brothers will show some masculinization of their behavioral and physical traits (e.g., increased aggressivity and/or reduced fertility), due to prenatal exposure to testosterone [38]. Twin studies report mixed evidence regarding the TTTH—the choice of toys (dolls and doll houses) and interests in stereotypical feminine activities (reading love stories and poetry) of female twins with twin brothers *do not* differ from those of female twins with twin sisters [39–41]. Male–female twins' scores on four questions concerning gender identity (e.g., I feel discomfort with my own gender) did not differ from those of male and female twins from same-sex pairs [42]. However, increased sensation-seeking tendencies, better spatial ability skills, more masculine attitudes, smaller vocabularies, and slightly more rule breaking among female twins with twin brothers versus female twins with twin sisters has been observed [43].

Female twins with twin brothers tend to have larger teeth (like males) and a larger brain volume than female twins with twin sisters. These twins also show a different "craniofacial signature," or series of facial measures—the distance between the inside corners of the eye sockets and the distance between the left-third-molar and chin are larger in females from opposite-sex pairs than in those from same-sex pairs [44–47]. Females with male cotwins also show half as many spontaneous otoacoustic emissions (SPOEs—sounds caused by the motion of the sensory cell hairs of the inner ear in response to sounds [48]) as those with female cotwins, more typical of males [49,50]. Some studies, but not all, have reported delayed menarche (onset of menstruation) among female twins with twin brothers, consistent with the TTTH [51,52], although the degree of difference is small.

Of course, not all female twins from male–female pairs show these effects. Moreover, some of these female twins' behaviors could be explained by their social experiences—females growing up with a male cotwin might model their brother's sensation-seeking behaviors, either through observation or encouragement. Male twins who enjoy rock climbing, skydiving, or hang gliding might inspire their twin sisters to join them. Of course, females are also involved in high-risk sports, but there are more male enthusiasts [53,54]. Later in this section, see my thought experiment that shows how this issue may be resolved.

The exposure of female cattle twins to male hormones in the uterus causes infertility among these female cattle, a phenomenon known as the freemartin effect [55]. This finding, and increased evidence that hormones affect human behavioral and physical traits, has directed research attention toward female twins from opposite-sex twin pairs. The TTTH, as mentioned previously, has been tested by numerous studies—many conducted since 2010—comparing a wide range of behavioral and physical traits between females from same-sex and opposite-sex twin pairs [38]. Scientific support for the TTTH is generally more consistent for physical measures (e.g., SPOEs, referenced earlier) than for behavioral traits (e.g., disordered eating and left-handedness) [56–58]. That is partly because physical traits can be measured more objectively and reliably than behavioral traits. It is also harder to explain masculinization of female twins' physical traits by social experience with males. In fact, some behavioral differences in traits related to attention deficit hyperactivity disorder (ADHD) and autism (e.g., limited concentration; sudden change in mood or feelings), which in childhood occur more often in males [59,60], are *lower* in females with twin brothers than those with twin sisters [61].

The cognitive trait of spatial ability as assessed by mental rotation tasks (e.g., imagining what an object would look like if seen from another angle) is of great interest to researchers because males typically outperform females in this area. However, in studies, females with twin brothers consistently outperformed females with twin sisters, as predicted by the TTTH [62–64]. In contrast with spatial ability, a study from Denmark found that adolescent female twins from opposite-sex pairs scored significantly *below* same-sex twins and nontwin females in mathematics; however, mathematical skills (e.g., computation or calculation, in which females typically excel) are different from the visual and spatial skills required for mental rotation. Differences between the two female twin groups for ability in Danish and in English were not found [65].

Females with twin brothers do not differ in height, weight, waist circumference, or other body size measures from females with twin sisters [38,66]. However, as indicated earlier, the teeth and brains of female twins in male–female pairs show some degree of masculinization [38], while findings regarding age at menarche are mixed. Infertility does not appear to differ between females from same-sex and opposite-sex twin pairs, with one exception: a 25% reduction in having children *was* found among female twins from opposite-sex pairs in a preindustrialized Finnish society, supporting the TTTH [67]. It may be that prenatal hormonal effects on fertility are masked in modern twin samples because the latest medical interventions and reproductive technologies override those effects. I would like to see an independent replication of this study in a population similar to the preindustrial society studied in Finland [68]. Exactly how the TTTH produces its effects on females from opposite-sex cotwins is uncertain. Except for estriol (E3), which is a form of estrogen, the levels of androgen and other hormones do not appear to differ between female twin fetuses from opposite-sex or same-sex pairs. However, blood samples used in this study did not come from the fetuses themselves, but from the mother at mid-pregnancy and from umbilical cords at delivery—thus, this evidence is indirect. The passage of fetal hormones across the fetal membranes and placenta that can penetrate fetal skin is possible in early pregnancy (8–24 weeks). Therefore, future studies in this area should target this particular window of time [38]. Fetal skin becomes less permeable later on, although hormones may still be transferred by fetal membranes and by mother–fetus circulation [69].

About 20 years ago, I did a thought experiment and came up with a study design that could test the TTTH [55]. The study would include one twin group (male–female twins reared apart) and one virtual twins group (male–female virtual "twins" reared together who are biologically unrelated). Reared-apart twins share their prenatal environment, but not their rearing environment; therefore, the effects of intrauterine hormonal exposure on behavior could be observed. Virtual twins share their rearing environment, but not their prenatal environment; therefore, the effects of shared socialization on behavior could be seen. The TTTH would be supported if the female reared-apart twins showed more frequent or higher levels of male-typical behaviors (e.g., aggression or spatial skill) than the female virtual twins. Some investigators have overlooked such designs, reasoning that assembling these groups would be "notoriously difficult" [38]. I know it would *not* be difficult because I continue to find them. Some day I will do the study that I thought about…

6. *Feminization of some behavioral and physical traits of male twins with twin sisters occurs.*
    Reality Check: Possible
    Short Answer: How sharing the womb or growing up with a twin sister affects the development of a twin brother has not been studied very much (relative to how sharing a womb or growing up with a twin brother affects the development of a twin sister). The few studies that have been done show a general lack of behavioral differences between males with twin sisters and males with twin brothers, but there are a few.

    Male twins from same-sex and opposite-sex pairs show *no differ-ence* in math and physics performance, mental rotation skill, frequency of left-handedness, and preference for masculine or feminine-type toys [41,58,70]. In contrast, males with twin sisters *do* differ from males with twin brothers as shown by their increased rule breaking, bigger vocabularies, and more disordered eating; the last two differences suggest a feminizing effect [38,52,56]. There is also some evidence that males with twin sisters show fewer problem behaviors related to communication and social behavior than males with twin brothers [71].

More of the Story: A few studies have looked at how having a twin sister affects male behavioral and physical development. The University of Chicago study of 5- and 6-year-olds (again, one of my favorites) found slightly lowered activity levels, greater obedience, and reduced confidence among boys with twin sisters, compared to boys with twin brothers. There was also some indication that these boys enjoyed their sister's guidance and protection, even while feeling threatened by their social maturity [72].

An adolescent twin study found that males with twin sisters are twice as likely to report same-sex attraction (different from same-sex experience) than males with twin brothers [73]. This finding was explained by the absence of strong gender socialization that might come from having male siblings as social models. In contrast, the study of Finnish twins growing up in preindustrial times (see earlier) found that males with twin sisters were as likely to marry as were males with twin brothers, and that having a twin sister did not affect the likelihood of becoming a father [67].

Worrying is more frequent among older male twins (mean age 41.2 years) with twin sisters than younger male twins (mean age 23.2 years) with twin sisters [52]. This could reflect the greater number of complex decisions related to marriage and work, faced by all older males. However, the added stresses experienced by some male twins could be exacerbated by their twin sisters' concern and protection (a legacy of their childhood years). And some male twins may miss the advice and assistance of their sisters who might be living far away, causing them to worry even more.

Explaining why males from opposite-sex and same-sex twin pairs might differ in some ways is a challenge for those who study them. The TTTH cannot explain the possible effects of sisters' prenatal hormones on their twin brothers—because male and female fetuses have *similar* levels of the female hormone estrogen [74]. Therefore, any feminization of male twins with twin sisters is more likely to reflect socialization effects than hormonal effects. Of course, it is also possible that some feminization effects reflect very subtle hormonal influences.

The study of relationships between hormones and behavior is a lively field and opposite-sex twin pairs are playing critical roles in this quest. Opposite-sex twins are no longer the forgotten twin pairs of days past when research focused on identical and same-sex sets. Refining the methods for exploring hormone–behavior relationships, and identifying the critical time periods for doing so, are key goals for future research.

Like all twins, males with twin sisters are a diverse group of people. Some young male twins will enjoy their sister's "maternal" attitude toward them when they are children, while others may resist it. Not all adolescent males with twin sisters experience same-sex attraction, and not all older males with twin sisters are worriers. It is important to remember that twins are individuals, as well as part of a pair and a community of multiples.

7. *Twins are more likely to have autism than nontwins.*
Reality Check: Unlikely
Short Answer: I am now sure how this myth got started, but I think it might have been partly through word of mouth among a particular social set. A wealthy acquaintance of mine conceived fraternal twins by intracytoplasmic sperm injection (ICSI), one of whom was considered mildly autistic, and several of her friends had a similar experience. If many of these families sought assistance from the same medical facility in their area, this could give the impression that young twins show higher than expected rates of autism.

Autism is a neurodevelopmental condition that is marked by impaired social interactions and restricted repetitive behavioral patterns [75]. Twins *are not* more likely to be autistic than nontwins, according to a 2011 study that reviewed three decades of research on this topic. Three large population-based studies from the United States, Sweden, and Western Australia, did not find differences in the frequency of autism between twins and nontwins [76]. However, autism does have a genetic basis, so that if an identical twin is affected, then his or her cotwin is more likely than a fraternal twin or someone randomly chosen from the population at large to be affected, as well.

More of the Story: Debates surrounding the question of whether or not twins are more likely to have autism than nontwins has been ongoing since 2001. Contrary to my reality check of unlikely, several studies have reported an excess of affected twins relative to nontwins [77,78]. The reason for the conflicting findings is that these studies specifically identified (targeted) pairs of affected siblings, which does not allow the risks for twins and nontwins to be properly tested—to do that, population-based studies that do not select affected twins are required [79]. It is also possible that twin pairs with two autistic cotwins are very likely to come to medical and research attention, falsely inflating the frequency among twins; twin pairs with only one autistic cotwin may be more likely to escape notice.

Twin studies have demonstrated high heritability for autism, but the values are very inconsistent. Using strict diagnostic criteria (just a few selected symptoms), the median concordance (twin similarity) values are 76% for identical twins and 0% for fraternal twins. When the diagnostic criteria are broadened to include more signs and symptoms of autistic behavior, these values increase to 88% for identical twins and 31% for fraternal twins [76]. Note, however, that identical twins do not show complete concordance for autism, even with the use of broadened criteria, thereby implicating environmental factors occurring before or after birth. A study of Swedish twins found that affected cotwins in autism-discordant twin pairs, both MZ and DZ, had a lower than average birth weight. However, the role of birth weight in the onset of autism is unclear [80]. It is unlikely that birth weight alone causes autistic symptoms; instead, birth weight may be a proxy for delayed physical growth that could trigger autism in young children predisposed to that condition.

8. *Twins are at lower risk for suicide than nontwins.*
   Reality Check: Possible
   Short Story: Twins are about 25% *less* likely to commit suicide than nontwins according to a Danish study that compared suicide rates in these two populations [81]. This finding was true for both males and females, and for both identical and fraternal twins. Reduced suicide among twins was also observed when the twins were divided into six different groups based on their time of birth, each spanning 10 years (1870–79, 1880–89…ending in 1920–30). The researchers suggested that twins' unusually close relationship, which offers companionship and support, lowers the chances of suicide, presumably by means of emotional support in times of need. Of course, this study (the only one of its kind) requires replication in other European countries and around the world.
   More of the Story: In related work, researchers in the United States examined suicide attempts among adolescent female twins [82]. At least one suicide attempt was reported by 4.2% (143/3401) of the twin participants. This figure is below the 10.9% for nontwin females reported by the 1999 National Youth Risk Behavior Survey, consistent with twins' lower suicide rate reported above. If the findings and conclusions are confirmed by future studies, then psychotherapists and bereavement counselors might focus even more intensely on encouraging people

to provide emotional and educational assistance and support to family members at suicide risk.

I became keenly aware of the unique aspects of losing a twin in 1983 when I was a postdoctoral fellow at the University of Minnesota. Since then, I have studied the behavioral and emotional consequences of twin loss [83]. I began this project in response to requests for information and assistance from bereaved twins and their families. I have now received completed inventories from over 750 "twinless twins." Among the many issues this project was designed to address, are two key questions: (1) Is grief severity greater among identical twins who generally express closer social relationships than fraternal twins? (2) Is twin loss more devastating than the loss of other relatives who passed away during the surviving twins' lifetime? As part of a comprehensive questionnaire, I ask the twins to rate their grief intensity for their deceased cotwin on a scale of 1–7 [1 = No Grief to 7 = Total Devastation (Suicide Point)], as experienced 1–2 months after the loss. I also asked them to rate the intensity of their grief for the loss of any other relatives, friends, or acquaintances that occurred within their lifetime.

The answer to the first question is yes—grief appears to be slightly, but consistently higher among the surviving identical twins than fraternal twins. The answer to the second question is also yes—grief is rated as *more intense for a deceased twin than for any other deceased relative or friend*, with some exceptions. In particular, I found that grief experienced following the loss of a spouse is nearly the same as the grief experienced for the loss of a twin. However, only a very small number of twinless twins in my study also lost spouses (fortunately), so this finding is not yet conclusive. In addition, very few twins lost children so this particular comparison could not be made—also fortunately.

This is an opportunity to set aside the mythconception that when a twin dies, the other twin immediately feels this loss. Such an event would require a demonstrated telepathic or extrasensory connection between the twins, which has not been definitively demonstrated as I described in an earlier chapter. I have heard of twins who were very accurate in knowing the time of their cotwin's death—but constant concern about a twin brother or twin sister does not translate into actually feeling the loss as it happened, even when the timing of the concern on the part of the surviving twin and the loss of the other twin coincide.

The bases of suicidal behavior have also been of interest and importance to psychologists, psychiatrists and families. Suicidal behaviors may represent a genetic susceptibility that can be triggered by extreme stress.

The loss of a twin is clearly an extremely stressful event, but is unlikely to lead to suicide by the surviving co-twin in the absence of an inherited predisposition. In particular, I have shown that surviving identical twins whose cotwins' deaths were due to *nonsuicidal* causes (e.g., accidents or illnesses) are unlikely to engage in suicidal attempts. Suicidal ideation was indicated by a slightly higher percentage of identical twins (28%) than fraternal twins (24%), but the difference was not statistically meaningful. These findings, and findings from other twin studies, implicate genetic factors in suicide and suicidal behavior [84–86].

9. *Identical twins tend to die at the same time.*
Reality Check: Possible—Unlikely
Short Story: The simultaneous loss of newborn twins from sudden infant death syndrome (SIDS) breaks the hearts of mothers and fathers. SIDS is the unexplained death of infants prior to the 1st year of life, an event that usually occurs when the infant is asleep; however, 90% of SIDS cases occur within infants' first 6 months of life [87]. These deaths baffle both parents and professionals because most SIDS infants generally appear normal and healthy. At the other end of the age spectrum are elderly twins who pass away on the same day from the same condition. The deaths of 92-year-old identical twin Franciscan friars, Julian and Adrian Rister, are noteworthy in this respect—both twins died from heart failure on June 1, 2011 within 15 hours of each other [88].

These stories of infant and elderly twins (mostly identical) attract public attention because their simultaneous deaths seem to defy the odds. Unfortunately, such events feed the notion that twins are destined to die at the same time. This is simply not so, but it is possible in some cases—factors surrounding the cause and time of twins' deaths are far more complex than the media stories suggest.
More of the Story: The term SIDS has been renamed as Sudden Unexplained/Unexpected Infant Death (SUID) to include accidental deaths (e.g., suffocation), sudden natural deaths (cardiac disorders), and homicides (random killings). About 4000 sudden infant deaths occur each year in the United States, half of which are classified as SIDS cases [89]. Published reports of the simultaneous SIDS deaths of infant twins have appeared. To the extent that twins share developmental deficits that might predispose them to SIDS, their simultaneous deaths are understandable [90]. It is not possible to predict which infants will succumb to SIDS, although risk factors, such as prematurity and limp muscle tone have been identified. It is suspected that when such infants experience

breathing problems during sleep they are unable to recover [91]. However, reevaluation of some cases suggests that some twins' simultaneous deaths, allegedly due to SIDS, were instead caused by injuries or environmental hazards [92,93].

As I explained in Chapter 6, genetic influence on the life span appears highest at older ages. The reason for this is uncertain, but could be due to the expression of specific genes later in life. The important point, however, is that even identical twins are *not* programmed to die at the same time. A study of Danish twins born between 1870 and 1880 estimated the heritability of the life span to be modest, at .33 [94]. The average age difference at death was 14.1 years for the identical twins and 18.5 for the fraternal twins, a difference that was significant and consistent with modest genetic influence. However, only 5.0% of the identical twins and 5.5% of the fraternal twins passed away within 1 year of each other, a likely reflection of nongenetic factors. The majority of Finnish twin pairs born before 1958 (with both alive in 1974 and both deceased by 2013) differed in age at death by an average of 24.88 years, or less. The differences were 23.74 years, or less, for identical twins and 25.79, or less, for fraternal twins (J. Kaprio, The figures reported represent the cumulative ages in the 95th percentiles, Personal communication, July 29, 2016.).

Nongenetic factors associated with differences in twins' dates of death include accidents, infections, medical malpractice, and terrorist attacks. The horrific assault on the World Trade Tower, Pentagon, and United Flight 93 on 9/11 deprived approximately 40 individuals of their twin brother or twin sister. Countless children, parents, and spouses lost mothers and fathers, sons and daughters, and husbands and wives who were twins [95].

The surviving twins in my twin loss study further challenge the mythconception that twins die at the same time. These twin participants had lost their cotwins 6.6 years, on average, before taking part in the study, an interval that did not differ between identical (6.69 years) and fraternal twins (6.49 years). Furthermore, the time that had elapsed since individual twins had lost their cotwins varied widely—in some cases cotwins had died as long as 54 years before the twins completed my twin loss surveys.

Losing a twin is a devastating emotional event that is not well understood, except by the surviving twins who experience it. The same can be said for parents who lose a twin child—I have an ongoing study of such families and I am grateful that there are only a few participants because this event is so tragic for everyone involved. I believe that the best therapy for these twins, mothers, and fathers is to be in touch with other twin survivors and their families. I applaud the efforts of local, national, and international organizations that work hard to make this possible [96].

More could be said about twins' lives and minds because a lot is still unknown. However, other misconstrued areas of twinship deserve attention, such as: Are there good and evil twins? Are spouses attracted to their partner's cotwin? Are twins more likely to be abused than nontwins? I will consider these issues and more in Chapter 10.

REFERENCES

[1] S.O. Lilienfeld, K.C. Sauvigné, S.J. Lynn, R.L. Cautin, R.D. Latzman, I.D. Waldman, Fifty psychological and psychiatric terms to avoid: a list of inaccurate, misleading, misused, ambiguous, and logically confused words and phrases, Front. Psychol. 6 (2015) 1100.

[2] Merriam-Webster Dictionary, Fraternal, 2015. Available from: http://www.merriam-webster.com/dictionary/fraternal

[3] D. Rosenthal, The Genain Quadruplets, Basic Books, New York, (1963).

[4] N. Segal, Born Together-Reared Apart: The Landmark Minnesota Twin Study, Harvard University Press, Cambridge, MA, (2012).

[5] N. Segal (2012). The mean ages of the twins in four of the studies ranged from 26.1 to 51.4 years, while the twins in the fifth study were drawn from a sample of twins with a mean age of 65.6 years, Cambridge, MA.

[6] E. Turkheimer, A. Haley, M. Waldron, B. D'Onofrio, I.I. Gottesman, Socioeconomic status modifies heritability of IQ in young children, Psychol. Sci. 14 (6) (2003) 623–628.

[7] E. Turkheimer, E.E. Horn, Interactions between socioeconomic status and components of variation in cognitive ability, Behavior Genetics of Cognition Across the Lifespan, Springer, New York, (2014) pp.41-68.

[8] E.M. Tucker-Drob, M. Rhemtulla, K.P. Harden, E. Turkheimer, D. Fask, Emergence of a gene × socioeconomic status interaction on infant mental ability between 10 months and 2 years, Psychol. Sci. 22 (1) (2011) 125–133.

[9] N.L. Segal, A tale of two sisters, Psychol. Today 88 (2015) 68–75.

[10] N.G. Waller, P.R. Shaver, The importance of nongenetic influences on romantic love styles: a twin-family study, Psychol. Sci. 5 (5) (1994) 268–274.

[11] Chart of the Six Love Styles, Psychology Charts. Available from: http://www.psychologycharts.com/six-love-styles.html

[12] A. Tellegen, D.T. Lykken, T.J. Bouchard, K.J. Wilcox, N.L. Segal, S. Rich, Personality similarity in twins reared apart and together, J. Pers. Soc. Psychol. 54 (6) (1988) 1031.

[13] R.D. Arvey, T.J. Bouchard Jr., N.L. Segal, L.M. Abraham, Job satisfaction: environmental and genetic components, J. Appl. Psychol. 74 (2) (1989) 187–192.

[14] T.J. Bouchard Jr., D.T. Lykken, M. McGue, N.L. Segal, A. Tellegen, Sources of human psychological differences: the Minnesota Study of Twins Reared Apart, Science 250 (4978) (1990) 223–228.

[15] L.M. Keller, R.D. Arvey, T.J. Bouchard Jr., N.L. Segal, Work values: genetic and environmental influences, J. Appl. Psychol. 77 (1) (1992) 79–88.

[16] R.D. Arvey, B. McCall, T.J. Bouchard Jr., P. Taubman, M.A. Cavanaugh, Genetic influence on job satisfaction and work values, Pers. Individ. Dif. 17 (1) (1994) 21–33.

[17] Alpha Brain Waves: Definition, Functions, and Benefits. Available from: http://www.brainwavesblog.com/alpha-brain-waves/.

[18] F.J. Kallmann, Comparative twin study on the genetic aspects of male homosexuality, J. Nerv. Ment. Dis. 115 (4) (1952) 283–298.

[19] J.M. Bailey, P.L. Vasey, L.M. Diamond, S.M. Breedlove, E. Vilain, M. Epprecht, Sexual orientation, controversy and science, Psychol. Sci. Public Interest 17 (2) (2016) 45–101.

[20] F.J. Kallmann, Twin and sibship study of overt male homosexuality, Am. J. Hum. Genet. 4 (2) (1952) 136.

[21] N. Långström, Q. Rahman, E. Carlström, P. Lichtenstein, Genetic and environmental effects on same-sex sexual behavior: a population study of twins in Sweden, Arch. Sex. Behav. 39 (1) (2010) 75–80.

[22] J.M. Bailey, M.P. Dunne, N.G. Martin, Genetic and environmental influences on sexual orientation and its correlates in an Australian twin sample, J. Pers. Soc. Psychol. 78 (3) (2000) 524.

[23] A. Burri, T. Spector, Q. Rahman, Common genetic factors among sexual orientation, gender nonconformity, and number of sex partners in female twins: implications for the evolution of homosexuality, J. Sex. Med. 12 (4) (2015) 1004–1011.

[24] K.M. Kirk, J.M. Bailey, M.P. Dunne, N.G. Martin, Measurement models for sexual orientation in a community twin sample, Behav. Genet. 30 (4) (2000) 345–356.

[25] Y.-M. Hur, J.M. Craig, Twin registries worldwide: an important resource for scientific research, Twin Res. Hum. Genet. 16 (1) (2013) 1–12.

[26] N.L. Segal, Brazilian Twin Registry: a bright future for twin studies, Twin Res. Hum. Genet. 19 (3) (2016) 292–296.

[27] L. Ellis, S. Cole-Harding, The effects of prenatal stress, and of prenatal alcohol and nicotine exposure, on human sexual orientation, Physiol. Behav. 74 (1) (2001) 213–226.

[28] Q. Rahman, G.D. Wilson, Sexual orientation and the 2nd to 4th finger length ratio: evidence for organising effects of sex hormones or developmental instability?, Psychoneuroendocrinology 28 (3) (2003) 288–303.

[29] A.F. Bogaert, M. Skorska, Sexual orientation, fraternal birth order, and the maternal immune hypothesis: a review, Front. Neuroendocrinol. 32 (2) (2011) 247–254.

[30] J.M. Bailey, R.C. Pillard, A genetic study of male sexual orientation, Arch. Gen. Psychiatry 48 (12) (1991) 1089–1096.

[31] T.H. Maugh, Survey of Identical Twins Links Biological Factors With Being Gay, Los Angeles Times, December 15, 1991.

[32] B.C. Coleman, Study of Twins Suggests Basis of Homosexuality Might Be Genetic, Orange County Register, December 15, 1991, p. A7.

[33] R.C. Savin-Williams, Who's gay? Does it matter?, Current Directions in Psychological Science 15 (10) (2006) 40–44.

[34] National Survey of Family Growth, 2015. Available from: http://www.cdc.gov/nchs/nsfg/key_statistics/n.htm

[35] L.S. Hall, Dermatoglyphic analysis of total finger ridge count in female monozygotic twins discordant for sexual orientation, J. Sex Res. 37 (4) (2000) 315–320.

[36] L.S. Hall, C.T. Love, Finger-length ratios in female monozygotic twins discordant for sexual orientation, Arch. Sex. Behav. 32 (1) (2003) 23–28.

[37] K. Hiraishi, S. Sasaki, C. Shikishima, J. Ando, The second to fourth digit ratio (2D: 4D) in a Japanese twin sample: heritability, prenatal hormone transfer, and association with sexual orientation, Arch. Sex. Behav. 41 (3) (2012) 711–724 Note: Hirasoshi et al (2012) did not find differences between females or males from same-sex and opposite-sex twin pair, but the opposite-sex sample sizes were very small.

[38] A.L. Tapp, M.T. Maybery, A.J. Whitehouse, Evaluating the twin testosterone transfer hypothesis: a review of the empirical evidence, Horm. Behav. 60 (5) (2011) 713–722.

[39] B.A. Henderson, S.A. Berenbaum, Sex-typed play in opposite-sex twins, Dev. Psychobiol. 31 (2) (1997) 115–123.

[40] R.J. Rose, J. Kaprio, T. Winter, D.M. Dick, R.J. Viken, L. Pulkkinen, M. Koskenvuo, Femininity and fertility in sisters with twin brothers: prenatal androgenization? Cross-sex socialization?, Psychol. Sci. 13 (3) (2002) 263–267.

[41] C.S. Rodgers, B.I. Fagot, A. Winebarger, Gender-typed toy play in dizygotic twin pairs: a test of hormone transfer theory, Sex Roles 39 (3–4) (1998) 173–184.

[42] S. Sasaki, K. Ozaki, S. Yamagata, et al. Genetic and environmental influences on traits of gender identity disorder: a study of Japanese twins across developmental stages, Arch. Sex. Behav. 45 (2016) 1681–1695.

[43] B. Luke, M. Hediger, S.J. Min, M.B. Brown, R.B. Misiunas, V.H. Gonzalez-Quintero, et al. Gender mix in twins and fetal growth, length of gestation and adult cancer risk, Paediatr. Perinat. Epidemiol. 19 (s1) (2005) 41–47 The University of Chicago study referenced above found better language skills among twins form male-female pairs than same-sex pair, but they did not examine vocabulary specifically.

[44] K. Marečková, M.M. Chakravarty, C. Lawrence, G. Leonard, D. Perusse, M. Perron, et al. Identifying craniofacial features associated with prenatal exposure to androgens and testing their relationship with brain development, Brain Struct. Funct. 220 (6) (2015) 3233–3244.

[45] D.C. Ribeiro, A.H. Brook, T.E. Hughes, W.J. Sampson, G.C. Townsend, Intrauterine hormone effects on tooth dimensions, J. Dent. Res. 92 (5) (2013) 425–431.

[46] P.J. Dempsey, G.C. Townsend, Genetic and environmental contributions to variation in human tooth size, Heredity 86 (6) (2001) 685–693.

[47] P.J. Dempsey, G.C. Townsend, L.C. Richards, Increased tooth crown size in females with twin brothers: evidence for hormonal diffusion between human twins in utero, Am. J. Hum. Biol. 11 (5) (1999) 577–586.

[48] D. Kemp, Otoacoustic emissions, their origin in cochlear function, and use, Br. Med. Bull. 63 (1) (2002) 223–241.

[49] D. McFadden, A masculinizing effect on the auditory systems of human females having male co-twins, Proc. Natl. Acad. Sci. 90 (24) (1993) 11900–11904.

[50] D. McFadden, Masculinization effects in the auditory system, Arch. Sex. Behav. 31 (1) (2002) 99–111.

[51] J. Kaprio, A. Rimpelä, T. Winter, R.J. Viken, M. Rimpelä, R.J. Rose, Common genetic influences on BMI and age at menarche, Hum. Biol. 67 (5) (1995) 739–753.

[52] J.C. Loehlin, N.G. Martin, A comparison of adult female twins from opposite-sex and same-sex pairs on variables related to reproduction, Behav. Genet. 28 (1) (1998) 21–27.

[53] S.J. Jack, K.R. Ronan, Sensation seeking among high-and low-risk sports participants, Pers. Individ. Dif. 25 (6) (1998) 1063–1083.

[54] C.R. Harris, M. Jenkins, D. Glaser, Gender differences in risk assessment: why do women take fewer risks than men? Judgm, Decis. Mak. 1 (1) (2006) 48–63.

[55] N.L. Segal, Entwined Lives: Twins and What They Tell Us About Human Behavior, Plume, New York, (2000).

[56] K.M. Culbert, S.M. Breedlove, C.L. Sisk, P.K. Keel, M.C. Neale, S.M. Boker, et al. Age differences in prenatal testosterone's protective effects on disordered eating symptoms: developmental windows of expression? Behav, Neurosci. 129 (1) (2015) 18–36.

[57] E. Vuoksimaa, C.P. Eriksson, L. Pulkkinen, R.J. Rose, J. Kaprio, Decreased prevalence of left-handedness among females with male co-twins: evidence suggesting prenatal testosterone transfer in humans?, Psychoneuroendocrinology 35 (10) (2010) 1462–1472.

[58] S. Ooki, An overview of human handedness in twins, Front. Psychol. 5 (2014) 10. doi: 10.3389/fpsyg.2014.00010

[59] Science News, Study Uncovers Why Autism is More Common in Males, February 27, 2014. Available from: https://www.sciencedaily.com/releases/2014/02/140227125236.htm

[60] J. Collingwood, ADHD and Gender, 2016. Available from: http://psychcentral.com/lib/adhd-and-gender/.

[61] J. Attermann, C. Obel, N. Bilenberg, C.M. Nordenbæk, A. Skytthe, J. Olsen, Traits of ADHD and autism in girls with a twin brother: a Mendelian randomization study, Eur. Child Adolesc. Psychiatry 21 (9) (2012) 503–509.

[62] E. Vuoksimaa, J. Kaprio, W.S. Kremen, L. Hokkanen, R.J. Viken, A. Tuulio-Henriksson, R.J. Rose, Having a male co-twin masculinizes mental rotation performance in females, Psychol. Sci. 21 (8) (2010) 1069–1071.

[63] S. Cole-Harding, A.L. Morstad, J.R. Wilson, Spatial ability in members of opposite-sex twin pairs, Behav. Genet. 18 (6) (1988) 710.

[64] M. Heil, M. Kavšek, B. Rolke, C. Beste, P. Jansen, Mental rotation in female fraternal twins: evidence for intra-uterine hormone transfer? Biol, Psychol. 86 (1) (2011) 90–93.

[65] L. Ahrenfeldt, I. Petersen, W. Johnson, K. Christensen, Academic performance of opposite-sex and same-sex twins in adolescence: a Danish national cohort study, Horm. Behav. 69 (March) (2015) 123–131.

[66] P. Korsoff, L.H. Bogl, P. Korhonen, A.J. Kangas, P. Soininen, M. Ala-Korpela, R.J. Rose, R. Kaaja, J. Kaprio, A comparison of anthropometric, metabolic, and reproductive characteristics of young adult women from opposite-sex and same-sex twin pairs, Assessing Prenatal and Neonatal Gonadal Steroid Exposure for Studies of Human Development: Methodological and Theoretical Challenges 28 (2015) 36.

[67] V. Lummaa, J.E. Pettay, A.F. Russell, Male twins reduce fitness of female co-twins in humans, Proc. Natl. Acad. Sci. 104 (26) (2007) 10915–10920.

[68] L.J. Ahrenfeldt, A. Skytthe, S. Möller, K. Czene, H.O. Adami, L.A. Mucci, et al. Risk of sex-specific cancers in opposite-sex and same-sex twins in Denmark and Sweden, Cancer Epidemiol. Biomark. Prev. 24 (10) (2015) 1622–1628.

[69] C.C. Cohen-Bendahan, C. van de Beek, S.A. Berenbaum, Prenatal sex hormone effects on child and adult sex-typed behavior: methods and findings, Neurosci. Biobehav. Rev. 29 (2) (2005) 353–384.

[70] A. Ho, R.D. Todd, J.N. Constantino, Brief report: autistic traits in twins vs. non-twins—a preliminary study, J. Autism Dev. Disord. 35 (1) (2005) 129–133.

[71] A. Ho, R.D. Todd, J.N. Constantino, Brief report: autistic traits in twins vs. non-twins—a preliminary study, J. Autism Dev. Disord. 35 (1) (2005) 129–133.

[72] H.L. Koch, Twins and Twin Relations, University of Chicago Press, Chicago, IL, (1966).

[73] P.S. Bearman, H. Brückner, Opposite-sex twins and adolescent same-sex attraction1, Am. J. Soc. 107 (5) (2002) 1179–1205.

[74] F.S. Vom Saal, Sexual differentiation in litter-bearing mammals: influence of sex of adjacent fetuses in utero, J. Anim. Sci. 67 (7) (1989) 1824–1840.

[75] Autism Speaks, What is Autism: DSM-V Diagnostic Criteria, 2016. Available from: https://www.autismspeaks.org/what-autism/diagnosis/dsm-5-diagnostic-criteria

[76] A. Ronald, R.A. Hoekstra, Autism spectrum disorders and autistic traits: a decade of new twin studies, Am. J. Med. Genet. Part B 156 (3) (2011) 255–274.

[77] D.A. Greenberg, S.E. Hodge, J. Sowinski, D. Nicoll, Excess of twins among affected sibling pairs with autism: implications for the etiology of autism, Am. J. Hum. Genet. 69 (5) (2001) 1062–1067.

[78] C. Betancur, M. Leboyer, C. Gillberg, Increased rate of twins among affected sibling pairs with autism, Am. J. Hum. Genet. 70 (5) (2002) 1381.

[79] P.M. Visscher, Increased rate of twins among affected sib pairs, Am. J. Hum. Genet. 71 (4) (2002) 995.

[80] M. Losh, D. Esserman, H. Anckarsäter, P.F. Sullivan, P. Lichtenstein, Lower birth weight indicates higher risk of autistic traits in discordant twin pairs, Psychol. Med. 42 (5) (2012) 1091–1102.

[81] C. Tomassini, K. Juel, N.V. Holm, A. Skytthe, K. Christensen, Risk of suicide in twins: 51 year follow up study, Br. Med. J. 327 (7411) (2003) 373–374.

[82] A.L. Glowinski, K.K. Bucholz, E.C. Nelson, Q. Fu, P.A. Madden, W. Reich, A.C. Heath, Suicide attempts in an adolescent female twin sample, J. Am. Acad. Child Adolesc. Psychiatry 40 (11) (2001) 1300–1307.

[83] N.L. Segal, Twin, adoption and family methods as approaches to the evolution of individual differences, in: D.M. Buss, P. Hawley (Eds.), The Evolution of Personality and Individual Differences, Oxford University Press, Oxford, 2011, pp. 303–307.

[84] A. Roy, N.L. Segal, M. Sarchiapone, Attempted suicide among living co-twins of twin suicide victims, Am. J. Psychiatry 152 (7) (1995) 1075–1076.

[85] N.L. Segal, A. Roy, Suicidal attempts and ideation in twins whose co-twins' deaths were non-suicides: replication and elaboration, Pers. Individ. Dif. 31 (3) (2001) 445–452.

[86] N.L. Segal, Suicidal ideation and suicide attempts in surviving MZ and DZ co-twins, Suicide Life-Threat. Behav. 39 (6) (2009) 569–575.

[87] P.L. Carolan, Sudden Infant Death Syndrome (SIDS), 2016. Available from: http://www.medicinenet.com/sids/article.htm

[88] L. Warren, 92-Year-Old Twin Friars Who Died the Same Day Lived Lives of Service, June 8, 2011. Available from: http://www.christianpost.com/news/50973/#JH0mVsvjVpSTf70f.99

[89] American SIDS Institute, What is SIDS/SUIFD?, 2016. Available from: http://sids.org/what-is-sidssuid/

[90] Y. Balci, M. Tok, B.K. Kocaturk, Ç. Yenilmez, C. Yorulmaz, Simultaneous sudden infant death syndrome, J. Forensic Legal Med. 14 (2) (2007) 87–91.

[91] L.E. Berk, Child Development, ninth ed, Pearson, Upper Saddle River, NJ, (2013).

[92] M. Bass, The fallacy of the simultaneous sudden infant death syndrome in twins, Am. J. Forensic Med. Pathol. 10 (3) (1989) 200–205.

[93] V. Ramos, A.F. Hernández, E. Villanueva, Simultaneous death of twins: an environmental hazard or SIDS?, Am. J. Forensic Med. Pathol. 18 (1) (1997) 75–78.

[94] M. McGue, J.W. Vaupel, N. Holm, B. Harvald, Longevity is moderately heritable in a sample of Danish twins born 1870–1880, J. Gerontol. 48 (6) (1993) B237–B244.

[95] N.L. Segal, Indivisible by Two: Lives of Extraordinary Twins, Harvard University Press, Cambridge, MA, (2005).

[96] Twinless Twins Support Group assists surviving twins. Available from: http://www.twinlesstwins.org; the Center for Loss in Multiple Birth (CLIMB) is available to parents who have lost twins during pregnancy, infancy and early childhood. Available from: http://www.climb-support.org/index.html?bothorall

CHAPTER 10

Good Twin–Evil Twin and Other Family Ties

On January 1, 2016, I saw the movie *Legend*, the 2015 biopic about London's 1960s identical twin gangsters, Reginald (Reggie) and Ronald (Ronnie) Kray. Born in 1933, the twins went from leading teenage gangs to owning and operating lavish West End nightclubs, while engaging in unspeakable violence that combined drugs, gambling, and murder. Witnesses to their crimes did not betray them for fear of their lives and their families' lives. But Scotland Yard eventually caught up with the Krays and both twins were given life sentences for their accumulated crimes. Reggie spent nearly 30 years behind bars until his early release at the age of 66, followed by his death from cancer 8 weeks later. Ronnie spent his last days at the Broadmoor Mental Hospital until his death by heart attack at the age of 61. The twins are buried next to each other at the Chingford Mount Cemetery, in Waltham Forest, London [1–3].

The film *Legend* reminded me of a question I often hear when people meet twins for the first time. Partly in gest, but somewhat seriously, people want to know, "Who is the good twin and who is the evil twin?," implying that every pair comes with one of each. In this chapter, I argue that the question of good twin–evil twin is one that should not be asked. I will also look into the belief that after delivery, new mothers of twins are more likely to become depressed than new mothers of singletons. These topics, in addition to a number of other twin-related issues, are important and timely because of their impact on individual and family well-being (Fig. 10.1).

1. *There is a* good *twin and an* evil *twin in every pair.*
   Reality Check: False
   Short Story: Conversations about good twins and evil twins set up false, and somewhat different dichotomies between cotwins depending on whether twins are identical or fraternal. Identical twins are more likely than fraternal twins to fill just slightly different within-pair roles, such as good and "more good" twin, or evil and "more evil" twin. That is because most identical twins' personality and temperamental differences are a matter of *degree*, not substance or quality. However, people tend to

Twin Mythconceptions
http://dx.doi.org/10.1016/B978-0-12-803994-6.00010-X

Figure 10.1 *We won't know till they're older which one is the evil twin. (Reprinted with permission from Condé Nast, the Cartoon Bank).*

exaggerate twins' minor differences by "assigning" each twin a different label to help distinguish between them. Identical twins are also convenient literary devices that allow writers to explore the duality of good and evil, wealth and poverty, and honor and shame. Fictional works, however, are allowed poetic license so the novel, play, or poem can deviate from reality within believable bounds—but, sadly, the misguided notion that opposing themes are embodied separately in each twin has become a common belief.

In contrast with identical twins, fraternal twins of both the same and opposite sex are more likely to express entirely opposite and/or different behavioral traits from their cotwin, partly because each has inherited different sets of genes. Family and friends, therefore, have less need to "assign" different roles to fraternal twins because they display their different tastes and temperaments naturally, making it easy to keep their individuality (e.g., extravert vs. introvert, or intellectual vs. athlete) in mind.

My twin sister Anne and I were, and are, typical fraternal twins, easily assuming personas that are distinct from one another. We are still like most fraternal pairs, with differences characterizing many aspects of our lives. I wear eye-catching outfits, while Anne dresses conservatively. I enjoy swing dancing as one of my favorite recreational activities, while Anne goes to the theater. I have lived in cities across the entire United States, whereas Anne has remained on the East coast. And we are both "good" and both "evil" in our own ways.

More of the Story: The crime-concordant Kray twins raise the question of how much genetic factors affect delinquent behavior. The Krays also raise the opposing question of what factors underlie empathy and kindness.

The diagnosis of antisocial personality disorder (APD) is given to individuals aged 18 and older who violate the rights of others (e.g., stealing or performing violent acts) without feeling remorse. These individuals are characterized by callous unemotional traits that show high degrees of genetic influence [4]. Children formerly diagnosed with APD now received diagnoses of oppositional defiant disorder (ODD), a change made in 2013 with the publication of the fifth edition of the *Diagnostic Statistical Manual*. The studies reviewed next were conducted prior to that change.

Twin studies have found both genetic and environmental influences on APD, but the impact of these influences is different if children are emotional or nonemotional. When children show little emotionality, APD is mostly a product of genetic factors [5,6]. In contrast, when children show some emotionality, then APD is affected partly by genes and partly by the environment the child shares with his or her twin, such as socioeconomic status and the peer group. Of course, not all APD-diagnosed children become hard-core criminals—tracking these children as they develop may identify those at greatest risk. Interestingly, a study of antisocial behaviors in twin children, between the ages of 5 and 10, found that collective efficacy (the level of social cohesion among neighbors and their willingness to intervene for the common good) reduces antisocial behavior in kids from economically deprived areas, but not from affluent ones [5].

In contrast to APD for which genetic findings are clear, twin research has generally failed to find genetic effects on juvenile delinquency, except for a 1983 study of self-reported delinquent acts [7]. But the two traits that actually underlie delinquency in youth are of greater interest. A 2010 twin study found genetic influence on *low self-control* and *contact with delinquent peers*, factors that predict delinquent behavior among adolescents, but are often thought to be socially induced [8]. Little self-control, combined with attraction to wayward friends is a great recipe for disruptive behavior. These findings encourage new directions (e.g., greater attention to biological processes; increased collaboration across medical and psychological disciplines) for future research on delinquent teens. In this study, parental influence had little sway over their twins' behavioral outcomes, which is important to know if effective behavioral interventions are to be found.

I love the title of psychologist Steven Pinker's 2011 book, *The Better Angels of Our Nature*. This phrase has an intriguing history. It begins with an early draft of Lincoln's 1861 inaugural address, edited by William Seward, Lincoln's Secretary of State who was an avid reader of Charles Dickens. Seward added the words "better angel" to Lincoln's text, similar to Dickens's "our better angels" from his novel *Barnaby Rudge*. Lincoln then transformed the phrase to read as it appears in Pinker's title [9].

The idea that people are born with a sense of right and wrong (good vs. evil) is captured in a series of simple, but elegant studies of 4- and 5-month-old infants. These videotaped sessions, conducted by Yale University researchers Paul Bloom and Karen Wynn, were aired on CBS's program *Sixty Minutes* [10]. I never tire of watching these tiny people showing us what they "know" about human behavior just by being themselves. In one scenario, the babies observed a puppet help another puppet in distress, then saw a third puppet fail to offer assistance. Presented with the helpful and hurtful puppets, more than three-quarters of the babies reached for the helpful one when given a choice. But there are person to person differences in altruism and empathy—after all, not all the babies chose the nice puppet. And all of us know people who are mean, selfish, and unable to empathize or show remorse. Think about the Krays—two evil twins—and their companions.

Twin studies show that genetic factors also influence prosocial traits like empathy, on the order of 25–35% at ages 14 and 20 months, 19–44% at age 3.5 years, and 50% in adulthood [11–13]. The increase in genetic influence over time most likely reflects each person's growing freedom

to act in ways that are compatible with their inclinations as family influences wane. Increasing genetic influence across the life span character-
izes other behaviors, such as general intelligence and religiosity.

Prosocial behavior has several dimensions. When it is broken down
into more specific parts, it turns out that empathic concern for another
and sharing with others are characteristics affected mostly by genes (76
and 67%, respectively) [14]. In contrast kindness is less affected by genetic factors than the other prosocial traits (47%) and is more affected by
the environment shared between the twins. The reason for these findings is unclear, but I suspect that kindness is a more complex prosocial
behavior than the others—kindness combines inner feelings, observable
behavior, knowledge of what action eases the pain of another, and the
ability to deliver that action.

Even though parents, families, friends, and society help shape children's social rules and practices, genetic influence on these behaviors
increases with age. (Recall the changing percentages mentioned previously.) Most children acquire social behaviors deemed appropriate for
civilized human society, but not all do. Increasing evidence shows that
specific genes may lead to brain impairments that predispose individuals
to APD as adults and delinquent behavior (ODD) when young, especially when surroundings are violent and unpredictable [15]. Lacking
remorse for their actions, such people may view the world in ways that
are hard for most of us to comprehend.

Why unfavorable conditions like APD and ODD remain in the human behavioral repertoire is a matter of some speculation. One answer
is that behaviors that were adaptive in early human history are no longer
adaptive today because societies change faster than genes. For example,
threats to our social status do not jeopardize our survival as in the past,
but can still trigger rage and violence. Road rage (e.g., attacking another
driver) is a good example of a response that is often out of proportion to
its cause (losing your parking spot because someone sneaks in ahead, as
if to imply, "I am more important than you!"). All of us, not just people
with behavioral disorders, may sometimes show these behaviors. Perhaps
that is because social status strongly affected our ancestors' resource access, mate selection, and social respect, tendencies that linger today. Of
course, not everyone is equally prone to violent outbursts. Most importantly, genetic influences on rage and violence do not condone these
behaviors, nor mean we should tolerate them; the best solution is to help
people manage their out-of-control flare-ups [16]. Fortunately, when

introduced to identical twins, we do not need to worry over which twin is the evil one since they probably share any evil tendencies to similar degrees.

2. *Twins are more likely to divorce than nontwins.*
   Reality Check: Unlikely
   Short Story: "I tell him/her things I would never share with my spouse."

   I have heard this quiet confession from a number of identical twins, perhaps explaining the belief that twins experience more marital discord and divorce than nontwins. In other words, it is assumed that a nontwin spouse would be less attuned to the moods of his or her twin spouse than the spouse's cotwin. It is also assumed that nontwin husbands and wives resent their spouses' need for "twin time," setting the stage for marital friction. However, some research shows *exactly the opposite*—divorce rates among Danish twins are actually *lower* than those of singletons. But there is an exceptional finding that challenges this conclusion: British female twins were more likely to have married and then divorced than singleton women at ages 23, 33, and 46 years. I attempt to reconcile these findings here.

   More of the Story: One of the best recent studies I could find, conducted in 2011, obtained data from the Danish Twin Registry that links to Statistics Denmark. This study showed that twins in Denmark are less likely to divorce than nontwins, but also found that twins' marriage rates are *lower* than those of nontwins [17]. I concur with the authors' interpretation of these results: Twins have more experience being in a close relationship than most people, so may be better positioned to cooperate and compromise. Twins may also have less need for a marriage partner because of their lifelong support system, that is, their cotwin, explaining their lower rates of marriage.

   In contrast, female twins (15%) in Great Britain were more likely to have married and divorced than their singleton counterparts (10%) at the age of 33 [18]. I believe the difference between these two studies reflects the younger age of the British twins (all born the same week in 1958), for whom divorce was less stigmatized and easier to obtain, compared with the Danish twins (born in 1940–68). In addition, the British study conducted periodic interviews with participants and lost a number of twins over the years. Finally, female twins are more likely to participate in research than male twins [19], possibly tilting the British findings toward greater female twin than nontwin divorce.

In related work, researchers at the University of Minnesota found greater resemblance in divorce frequency between identical twins than fraternal twins, demonstrating genetic influence on this critical decision [20]. This does not mean that twins are more likely to divorce than nontwins—it means that the cotwins of divorced identical twins have a higher chance of divorcing at some time, relative to the cotwins of divorced fraternal twins. Of course, genes coding specifically for divorce do not exist—instead, it seems that certain genetically influenced personality traits put people at increased or decreased risk for marital struggles. Anyone (twins and nontwins) able to exercise constraint (self-control) are less likely to divorce, whereas people with positive emotionality (extraversion) and negative emotionality (neuroticism) are more likely to divorce. The Minnesota study estimated that 30% of the inherited divorce risk among women was due to genetic factors affecting personality (of one spouse), while the risk was 42% among men.

A subsequent study by a different research team also found that both marriage and divorce were genetically influenced [21]. The researchers speculated that traits shared by spouses (e.g., religious background) might protect against divorce, whereas traits they did not share (e.g., alcoholism) might precipitate separation.

In addition to genetic findings, the Minnesota study also found that the percentage of divorced twins in Minnesota (18%) did not differ from the percentage of divorced nontwins (18.4%). This result provides independent confirmation of the Danish study's findings that twins are not more likely to divorce than nontwins. I believe that when twins divorce, their lawyers and marriage counselors take note because twins attract attention—this might give the impression that twins are especially likely to experience marital difficulties, thereby perpetuating the myth. I have heard therapists comment on the "high rate of divorced twins" they see in their practice, but statistics tell more of the story.

3. *Parents of twins are more likely to divorce than parents of nontwins.*
Reality Check: Likely
Short Story: Twins are "double blessings" to some couples, but these blessings pose "double difficulties" for others. Parents of twins are more likely to divorce than parents of nontwins, according to studies conducted in the United States (Harvard University) and Great Britain (University of Birmingham) [18,22]. However, in these studies the increased risk for divorce was only *slightly* higher than it was for parents of singletons. Note that the multiple birth parents in the

United States study most certainly conceived their twins naturally—these couples divorced in the early 1980s, *before* assisted reproductive technologies were widely available. (IVF was introduced into the United States in 1983.) Clearly, these findings do *not* apply to couples with assisted conceptions. In contrast, the British study included parents born in 1958, so some women, but not all, could have had their twins by IVF or other assisted means. (The first IVF infant was born in the United Kingdom in 1978).

In related research conducted in Denmark, marital stress (i.e., disruption of the marital relationship due to children's demands and/or persisting thoughts of divorce) was found to be higher among couples who conceived twins (either naturally or by assisted means), relative to singletons conceived by assisted means [23]. Interestingly, fewer couples who conceived twins (7.3%) by assisted reproduction separated or divorced 4 years after the delivery, relative to couples who conceived twins naturally (13.3%). The desire for children that compels people toward assisted conception, plus the emotional and financial investment of creating them in this way, probably combined to keep these couples together.

Financial stress has been commonly cited for creating marital problems, mostly associated with the extra expenses of caring for multiple birth children. Emotional stress comes in the form of feeling overwhelmed by caring for two newborns simultaneously, coping with some twins' early health problems and trying to give each twin equal attention. I urge all new multiple birth mothers and fathers to seek the support of parents of twins organizations. These groups offer clothing and equipment exchanges, helpful reading material, and other resources to offset the financial and emotional costs posed by efforts involved in raising multiple birth babies.

More of the Story: The rise in multiple births has changed many facets of society, including the number of couples who are at risk for divorce. The 1980 United States Census data from the Harvard University study revealed that when a couple's first birth is twins, the risk for divorce is somewhat higher than when the first birth is a singleton (13.7% vs. 12.7%) [22]. However, the degree of risk does not apply equally to everyone—it is especially high for mothers who have not completed college, mothers whose twins are older than 8 years of age, and mothers with one or more twin daughters. There is nothing magical about the age of 8—the study suggested that parents might postpone divorce until their children are older so as not to harm them as much emotionally. The research also suggested that daughters pose greater financial burdens for parents than sons. Divorce risk was also greater when families in the study had three older children before the birth of the twins, compared with families whose twins arrived earlier in the birth order. Many mothers with twins, followed by a nontwin, have told me that raising a singleton is much easier than raising twins—so when the reverse happens the stresses of raising young twins *and* older children understandably threaten a marriage.

Divorce among multiple birth versus single birth parents is also more common in the United Kingdom, according to a 2010 report, but the difference is slight. Parents of twins and triplets were more likely to be married (65%) than parents of nontwins (63%) when their multiples were born. However, parents of twins and triplets (18%) were also more likely than parents of nontwins to divorce or separate (15%) [18]. Financial pressure was the most commonly cited source of marital conflict—multiple birth families were twice as likely to be delinquent in paying bills and to deplete their savings. In fact, 62% of these couples experienced greater financial difficulties after the birth of their babies, compared with 41% of the nontwin couples.

The University of Birmingham report called for creative solutions to problems posed by rearing multiples, such as generous maternity leaves (as in France and Spain), extended paternity leave (as in France), and child benefit payments (as in the Czech Republic and Bulgaria). These benefits are not extended to mothers in the United States, possibly because assistance is offered by the many local, state, and national mothers of twins clubs (now called *Multiples of America*), but also because of limited maternity leave practices, in general. However, some colleges in the United States offer two-for-one scholarships to twins and some companies provide discounted clothing for young multiples [24,25]. But more can be done by government agencies, private and non-profit organizations, and concerned individuals. I would like to propose that some medical services (especially DNA testing for twin type), travel packages, and tickets to recreational events be tailored to twins and their families. I would also encourage nations around the world to join ICOMBO, the *International Council of Multiple Birth Organizations* whose dual mission is to promote awareness of the needs of twins, triplets, and more, and fulfill those needs [26]. Its members take part in each biennial meeting of the *International Society of Twin Studies*, facilitating communication and cooperation between the researchers who study twins and the families who raise them.

4. *New mothers of multiples experience greater depression than new mothers of singletons.*
   Reality Check: True
   Short Story: Several years ago, I was speaking at a parents' of twins club meeting when a distraught young mother entered the room holding 3-week-old twins, one in each arm. She was instantly welcomed by the more experienced moms who helped with the immediate care of the babies during the meeting and provided her with advice for the days to come. Had she not sought the assistance of older and wiser multiple birth mothers, she may not have fared well emotionally.

   Perhaps not surprisingly, depression among new mothers of twins exceeds that of new mothers of nontwins. Not all new multiple birth mothers are prone to depression, but for those who are, it is important to know why it can happen and how to handle if it does.
   More of the Story: The frequency of depression among multiple birth mothers varies across studies, but occurs among up to one-third of women expecting twins [27,28]. It is especially disturbing that depression can linger after the twins are born. Of course, not all multiple birth mothers will become depressed, and those who do are unlikely to experience a severe psychosis (i.e., mental illness that interferes with the capacity to meet the demands of everyday life). However, if left untreated, depression may last 6 months or more, increasing the risks for alcoholism, smoking, and poor health. But when treated, depressive symptoms tend to resolve in 1 or 2 months [29].

   It has been estimated that 50–70% of multiple birth mothers undergo "transient depression" (i.e., teariness, irritability) and that 10–15% undergo "classic postpartum depression" (i.e., anger, fatigue, change in appetite). Hormonal changes might, in fact, affect the mood of some mothers [30,31], although the biggest problem in some cases is simply lack of sleep.

   In a nationally representative United States sample, self-reported moderate or severe depressive symptoms were higher among mothers with 9-month-old twins (19%) than mothers with 9-month-old nontwins (16%). However, when background factors, such as socioeconomic status were considered, the mothers of twins were over 40% more likely to experience depressive symptoms than the mothers of singletons.

Unfortunately, only about one-fourth of the multiple birth mothers sought professional assistance [32].

Similar results emerged—even sooner—when both mothers and fathers of twins and nontwins were interviewed at the end of the second trimester and when the twins were 2 months old: depressive symptoms were higher among the multiple birth couples. Prematurity and parity (number of pregnancies) did not affect mothers' responses, but prematurity negatively impacted social functioning among fathers of naturally conceived twins [33]. Findings for mothers are mixed—one study found that mothers conceiving twins naturally or by ART did not differ in mental health [34], while another found that IVF mothers were at greater risk [35].

This story continues. A British study showed that mothers of twins' increased depression can persist up to the time that the twins turn 5. Understandably, mothers who had lost one twin were even more likely than mothers of singletons to experience depression. And while both mothers of twins and mothers of singletons with closely spaced children were at risk for depression, the mothers of twins were at greater risk [36].

Concern over caring for two infants at the same time, especially if twins have physical and/or behavioral problems, are main sources of maternal depression. Twins born very early (before 32 weeks gestation) pose a greater parenting challenge than very early born singletons. This can come across as reduced responsivity to 3-month-old twin infants by their mothers in daily interactions and in teaching tasks, compared to mothers of age-matched singletons [37]. Again, I believe that the best solution is joining a mothers of twins club. Most maternity hospitals offer lists with locations and contacts for local twins clubs and support groups for mothers who have lost a twin at any time from the pregnancy to childhood, such as *CLIMB* (Center for Loss in Multiple Birth) whose members understand this devastating event without explanation.

Oddly, some people (including hospital staff) have told some bereaved mothers: "At least you still have one!" after the recent loss of a newborn twin. However, research shows that couples losing a twin are just as devastated as those losing a singleton, although mothers in both groups express more grief reactions than fathers [38]. The surviving twin does not compensate for the loss of the other; in fact, the survivor becomes the constant reminder of the deceased twin, deepening the loss even more.

5. *Twins are more likely to be abused as children than nontwins.*
    Reality Check: True

    Short Story: A growing number of studies find that young twins are more likely to suffer abuse and maltreatment than nontwins. This is a particularly distressing problem because twinning rates are rising in most developed nations, meaning that more twins may be subject to abuse than in the past. More than one in five infertile couples undergoing assisted reproduction hope for twins, but some of these prospective mothers and fathers underestimate the emotional and financial pressures associated with raising them [34,39,40]. Certainly, not all multiple birth parents are at risk for abusing their children; instead, a subset of multiple birth parents are more likely to abuse their children than singleton parents *if they have limited resources and very short tempers.*

    It is uncertain if parents conceiving twins by natural or assisted means, and whose circumstances place them at risk for child maltreatment, are equally likely to abuse their children. Parenting stress related to competence and health is reportedly higher among new mothers of twins conceived by ART, rather than by natural means [41]. However, higher levels of maternal warmth, parental interaction, and mothers' emotional involvement with ART children have been found, relative to children conceived naturally [42]. It may be that the first few years of raising twins, especially preemies, are the most challenging—there is comfort in that thought.

    More of the Story: Studies documenting the stress and strain of raising multiple birth babies and young children are plentiful. These studies have focused on the negative effects of parents coping with limited assistance from family and friends, financial difficulties, medical expenses, and premature twins' physical complications. Fewer studies address the consequent maltreatment of twins in some families under such pressures, but those that do provide a consistent picture: twins are more likely than nontwins to suffer abuse and neglect. These studies identified the abused twins in national databases, hospital records, and countrywide surveys.

    In my 2000 book, *Entwined Lives*, I reviewed this literature, citing studies published in 1985 and 1990 that followed this trend [43]. An especially informative study from Japan found that 10% of 231 child abuse cases included multiples, and that it was more often the case that one twin, rather than both twins, was abused. The affected twins' maltreatment was associated with his or her unfavorable behavioral traits, such as being less active and less lovable than the cotwin, and/or physical problems, such as having a congenital disease or a birth weight below 2500 g (5.5 lbs). Unfortunately, studies conducted as recently as 2013 still report more frequent abuse among twins than nontwins. However, some new findings may help alleviate the situation by alerting parents and professionals to the risk factors involved.

Based on national data, the risk of death from maltreatment appears highest for male twins, twins born to African-American mothers, mothers who smoke and mothers under the age of 25. Even among healthy full-term infants, twins are at higher risk for mortality than nontwins. There is also the disturbing possibility that some abused twins are overlooked in these studies due to missing or inaccurate data, suggesting that twins may be maltreated at even higher rates [44].

Research on 19 twin pairs evaluated from 2006 to 2009 found that both twins were abused in 10 pairs and only 1 twin was abused in 9 pairs, consistent with the earlier Japanese study and a 1985 Australian study [45]. Why some twins were abused while their cotwins were not was unclear, but (as indicated earlier) parents' perceptions of one twin as less attractive or less healthy than the cotwin could be the reason. Most of the alleged perpetrators (mothers and fathers) lived with their twin children [46].

A nationwide survey in Japan, covering cases reported between 2003 and 2011, also found that twins are at higher risk for abuse than singletons [47,48]. This difference was explained by the stress of caring for two children and possible parental comparisons between the twins. However, in contrast with the earlier Japanese study, in most cases both twins were abused—here, the abusive behavior was attributed to caregiver characteristics, possibly being a teenage parent or lacking sufficient child support. When only one cotwin was abused, the possibility of unfavorable child characteristics was raised as a possible explanation, but was not investigated.

I see two key goals that could be met by collaboration between twin researchers and social workers. The first goal is to focus like a laser beam on factors predisposing parents and caregivers toward abusing twins. Providing families with assistance and resources even before twins are born, and maintaining it during the twins' early years seems essential. As I have mentioned, mothers of twins clubs are good support systems in this regard. Interestingly, the widespread availability of these groups may discourage governments from offering financial assistance to families in need.

The second goal is to identify twin pairs in which one twin is abused and the other is not, and then determine the reasons behind the difference. In Chapter 8, I noted that healthier cotwins are spoken to more often than their less healthy cotwins who are probably discharged from the hospital at a later date. Perhaps the second twin to arrive home is perceived as an "intruder," either consciously or unconsciously, thereby upsetting an established family routine. This scenario might segue into an abusive situation if assistance, resources, and educational materials are unavailable.

Most people, enchanted as they are at the sight of two charming infants being wheeled through a shopping mall or playing in the park, are probably unaware of the stress twins pose for some families. My hope is that by writing this book I will help increase awareness of this public health problem. I also hope to inspire people to take action by supporting families with twins, and to follow-up on evidence that abuse of any infant, twin or nontwin, is taking place.

6. *When identical twins marry identical twins, the various partners are socially interchangeable.*

Reality Check: False

Short Story: I once thought (foolishly!) that in quaternary marriages (marriages of twins in one identical pair to twins in another identical pair) the question of which twin married which twin didn't matter. After all, the faces, figures, and temperaments would be closely matched because the genes are the same. I was wrong. As I explained in my 2007 book *Indivisible by Two*, I learned this lesson in 2004 during a visit with identical married couples Craig and Diane, and Mark and Darlene in their adjacent homes outside Houston, Texas [49,50]. Slight differences in each twin's physical features and personality traits were critical factors when it came to social attraction and mate choice. It is also perfectly possible for someone to be attracted to one identical twin and not to the other for the same subtle reasons. The nature of twins' marriages, whether to twins or to nontwins, ranks among the most fascinating of twin-related topics (Fig. 10.2).

More of the Story: When identical twins marry nontwins, or when nontwins marry identical twins, we can learn a great deal about mate selection. My standard reference has been a seminal paper by two of my Minnesota colleagues who mailed a Choice Questionnaire to members of the Minnesota Twin Registry. Twins were asked to rate the similarity of their clothing and household furnishings, and their like or dislike of

Figure 10.2 *I don't like the look of yours... (Reprinted with permission. Image source: Cartoonstock.com).*

their cotwin's occupation, vacations, and choice of spouse (as recalled when the cotwin decided to marry). The confidentiality of the responses was emphasized to encourage honest responding. A key finding was that only 13% of identical twins' nontwin husbands and 7% of identical twins' nontwin wives "could have fallen for their spouse-to-be's identical twin" [51]. These percentages seem low because identical twins typically share their friends, interests, occupations, and more [52]. My colleagues concluded that romantic infatuation is the key to mate choice, and that who we fall for is decided in unpredictable ways. However, they did not dismiss the possibility that some unknown, yet to be discovered rule or law affects who we love and marry.

I thought about this a lot in 2010 when I learned about the romantic liaison between Marc Glasby and identical twin Dorothy Loader [53]. Dorothy and her twin sister Belle were born in Malaysia, but were adopted separately because their parents could not afford to raise two premature infants. Belle was adopted by an Anglo-Dutch family that eventually left Malaysia for Singapore, while Dorothy was adopted by a Chinese mother and British father and raised in Malaysia. The twins were reunited in Perth, Australia in 2008, when they turned 50.

Marc was married to Belle Glasby, Dorothy's identical twin sister, whom Dorothy met for the first time at their 2008 reunion. Marc's attraction to his wife's twin sister Dorothy was immediate, overwhelming, and mutual—and even though this is just one case it challenges the Minnesota findings. However, the Minnesota research was based on twins raised together, whereas Dorothy and Belle had been raised apart. Perhaps the twins' rearing situations changed the significant other dynamics as well.

No one has investigated the nature of cross-twin spousal attraction in reared-apart twins, so the single example provided by Marc and Dorothy must be viewed cautiously. Their experience may not be characteristic of separated twins in general, especially because Dorothy was in a troubled marriage when she and her twin first met. However, the immediate attraction Marc felt for his wife's identical twin, and her reciprocation of his feelings, justifies examining and reconciling their responses with the available research. I'll begin with a description of the incest taboo.

The incest taboo, or Westermarck effect, describes the lack of sexual attraction that develops from the experience of growing up with opposite-sex family members (e.g., fathers and daughters, mothers and sons, brothers and sisters) [54]. The lack of attraction is not taught, but evolves naturally and is believed to provide the psychological basis for choosing mates who differ genetically from the self. In this sense, the incest taboo is adaptive because close relatives have a greater chance than unrelated partners of conceiving a child with a genetic defect. That is because close relatives are likely to carry copies of the same detrimental recessive genes, so a child these relatives might create would have a 25% chance of expressing a disorder, such as Tay–Sachs disease or sickle cell anemia. Consider that future spouses of reared-together twins usually spend time with their fiancée's cotwin in a nonromantic context—this raises the possibility that a kind of "incest taboo" between the future spouse and future in-law evolves, blocking the development of potential attraction between them. In other words, once a twin is committed to a certain partner, both the fiancée and the cotwin "back off."

However, the social circumstances would differ for the spouses of reared-apart twins who lack opportunities to interact with their significant other's twin brother or twin sister. Perhaps when a spouse meets this brother-in-law or sister-in-law for the first time (and this person is identical to his or her husband or wife) it rekindles the feelings of attraction that were present at the start of their relationship. Perhaps this is what happened to Marc Glasby (mentioned previously). It is also conceivable that a kind of "backing off" could occur by both the twin and nontwin spouse to avoid conflict. Of course, my ideas about this are speculative at present because little is known about reared-apart twin spousal relations, but I believe these alternatives would be worth testing.

The bases of mate attraction and selection could also be explored by identifying the pairs of reared-apart opposite-sex twins who have fallen in love and married *without knowing they were twins*. Marital partners show varying degrees of resemblance in height, weight, intelligence, values, and especially religiosity, so male–female cotwins could be attracted to one another partly due to their similarities in these traits and others [55,56]. The few individuals who have unknowingly dated or married their cotwin recalled unusually strong attraction to one another.

Identical twins, both reared together and apart, show similarities across a wide range of behavioral domains. Therefore, the Minnesota finding that most identical twins lack interest in their cotwins' spouse seems surprising. I suspect that the right experiments have not yet been conducted, except for one very modest "experiment" that has escaped public attention. In 2003, I participated in a television program *Britain's Most Identical: The Identity Test*, produced by the British Broadcasting Company (BBC), in London. The members of four sets of identical twins were in separate rooms and introduced to one member of several other sets of identical twin pairs in succession. This series was designed to determine if identical twins are attracted to the same person as a potential dating partner. It turned out that most of the twins preferred members from the same pair, suggesting that twins are often attracted to the same person or type of person in dating situations. This outcome, combined with Dorothy having met her twin sister's spouse for the first time, makes her attraction to Marc more comprehensible.

It would be informative to repeat the BBC's experiment with larger twin samples and under more controlled conditions. Extending this line of research to reared-apart twins and their spouses would also tell us more about whom we are attracted to and why. Distinguishing between "liking" and "feeling attracted to" the spouse's cotwin would be a key element of such a study.

In this chapter and elsewhere in this book I have shown that when two sets of identical twins marry, the biological and social relationships among the spouses, parents, aunts, uncles, cousins, and children are dramatically altered. However, there are other twin-like pairings that have emerged since the introduction of in vitro fertilization in 1978, and the new family structures that have evolved serendipitously by divorce and remarriage. These exotic pairs have huge research potential, as well as human interest. In addition, discussions following the birth of the cloned Scottish sheep Dolly, in 1996, sparked considerable speculation about what the revised family relationships would look like, and what they would mean for parent–child and husband–wife relationships and well-being. Twin studies can shine a lot of light on these issues and showing how they do that is my next task.

REFERENCES

[1] A. Barra, The Twin Gangsters Who Rules London, November 22, 2015. Available from: http://www.thedailybeast.com/articles/2015/11/22/the-identical-twin-gangsters-who-terrorized-london.html

[2] The Daily Beast, Find a Grave: Chingford Molunt Cemetery. Available from: http://www.findagrave.com/php/famous.php?page=cem&FScemeteryid=658396

[3] J. Glatt, St. Martin's Press, New York, NY, 1999.

[4] D. Porter, 2016. Available from: http://www.theravive.com/therapedia/Antisocial-Personality-Disorder-DSM--5-301.7-(F60.2).

[5] C.L. Odgers, T.E. Moffitt, L.M. Tach, R.J. Sampson, A. Taylor, C.L. Matthews, A. Caspi, The protective effects of neighborhood collective efficacy on British children growing up in deprivation: a developmental analysis, Dev. Psychol. 45 (4) (2009) 942.

[6] E. Viding, R.J.R. Blair, T.E. Moffitt, R. Plomin, Evidence for substantial genetic risk for psychopathy in 7-year-olds, J. Child Psychol. Psychiatry 46 (6) (2005) 592–597.

[7] D.C. Rowe, Biometrical genetic models of self-reported delinquent behavior: a twin study, Behav. Genet. 13 (5) (1983) 473–489.

[8] K.M. Beaver, J.E. Shutt, B.B. Boutwell, M. Ratchford, K. Roberts, J.C. Barnes, Genetic and environmental influences on levels of self-control and delinquent peer affiliation, Crim. Justice Behav. 36 (1) (2010) 41–60.

[9] G. Griessman, A Quotation You Can Use in Writing: Charles Dickens and Abraham Lincoln, 2012. Available from: http://www.whatyousay.com/a-quotation-you-can-use-in-writing-charles-dickens-and-abraham-lincoln/

[10] Sixty Minutes, CBS, Born Good? Babies Help Unlock the Origins of Morality, November 18, 2012. Available from: https://www.youtube.com/watch?v=FRvVFW85IcU

[11] J.P. Rushton, D.W. Fulker, M.C. Neale, D.K. Nias, H.J. Eysenck, Altruism and aggression: the heritability of individual differences, J. Pers. Soc. Psychol. 50 (6) (1986) 1192–1198.

[12] A. Knafo, C. Zahn-Waxler, M. Davidov, C. Van Hulle, J.L. Robinson, S.H. Rhee, Empathy in early childhood, Ann. NY Acad. Sci. 1167 (1) (2009) 103–114.

[13] C. Zahn-Waxler, J.L. Robinson, R.N. Emde, The development of empathy in twins, Dev. Psychol. 28 (6) (1992) 1038–1047.

[14] A. Knafo-Noam, F. Uzefovsky, S. Israel, M. Davidov, C. Zahn-Waxler, The prosocial personality and its facets: genetic and environmental architecture of mother-reported behavior of 7-year-old twins, Front. Psychol. 6 (2015) 112.

[15] A. Raine, From genes to brain to antisocial behavior, Curr. Dir. Psychol. Sci. 17 (5) (2008) 323–328.

[16] P. Wallisch, Unleashing the beast within, Science 351 (6270) (2016) 232.

[17] I. Petersen, T. Martinussen, M. McGue, P. Bingley, K. Christensen, Lower marriage and divorce rates among twins than among singletons in Danish birth cohorts 1940-1964, Twin Res. Hum. Genet. 14 (2) (2011) 150–157.

[18] S. McKay, The Effects of Twins and Multiple Births on Families and Their Living Standards, Twins & Multiple Births Association (TAMBA), London, United Kingdom, (2010).

[19] D.T. Lykken, A. Tellegen, R. DeRubeis, Volunteer bias in twin research: the rule of two-thirds, Soc. Biol. 25 (1) (1978) 1–9.

[20] V. Jockin, M. McGue, D.T. Lykken, Personality and divorce: a genetic analysis, J. Pers. Soc. Psychol. 71 (2) (1996) 288–299.

[21] B.A. Jerskey, M.S. Panizzon, K.C. Jacobson, M.C. Neale, M.D. Grant, M. Schultz, et al. Marriage and divorce: a genetic perspective, Pers. Individ. Dif. 49 (5) (2010) 473–478.

[22] A.B. Jena, D.P. Goldman, G. Joyce, Association between the birth of twins and parental divorce, Obstet. Gynecol. 117 (4) (2011) 892.

[23] A. Pinborg, A. Loft, L. Schmidt, A.N. Andersen, Morbidity in a Danish National cohort of 472 IVF/ICSI twins, 1132 non-IVF/ICSI twins and 634 IVF/ICSI singletons: health-related and social implications for the children and their families, Hum. Reprod. 18 (6) (2003) 1234–1243.

[24] N.L. Segal, C.A. Mulligan, Twins reunited: scientific and personal perspectives/twin research studies: multiple birth effects on IQ and body size, Life style, muscles, and metabolism; Monochorionic-dizygotic twins with blood chimerism; Amniocentesis for twins/twins in the media: identical doctors; Freedom fighter for twins; Twin scholarships; Auguste and Jean-Felix Piccard; Twins born apart, Twin Res. Hum. Genet. 17 (2) (2014) 134–139.

[25] Twin Pregnancy and Beyond, Discounts for Twins, 2016. Available from: http://www.twin-pregnancy-and-beyond.com/discounts-for-twins.html

[26] ICOMBO. Available from: http://icombo.org

[27] G.R. Benute, D.C. Nozzella, C. Prohaska, A. Liao, M. de Lucia, M. Zugaib, Twin pregnancies: evaluation of major depression, stress, and social support, Twin Res. Hum. Genet. 16 (2) (2013) 629–633.

[28] P. Belluck, Panel Calls for Depression Screenings During and After Pregnancy, New York Times, January 27, 2016, p. A-1.

[29] Columbia Psychiatry. Available from: http://asp.cumc.columbia.edu/psych/asktheexperts/ask_the_experts_inquiry.asp?SI=90

[30] C.L. Agnew, A.H. Klein, J.A. Ganon, Twins: Pregnancy, Birth and the First Year of Life, William Morrow, New York, NY, (2007).

[31] A. Tylee, P. Gandhi, The importance of somatic symptoms in depression in primary care, Prim. Care Companion J. Clin. Psychiatry 7 (4) (2005) 167–176.

[32] Y. Choi, D. Bishai, C. Minokvitz, Multiple births are a risk factor for postpartum maternal depressive symptoms, Pediatrics 123 (4) (2009) 1147–1154.

[33] S. Vilska, L. Unkila-Kailo, R.-L. Punamaki, P. Poikkeus, L. Repokari, J. Sinkkonen, A. Tiitinen, M. Tulppala, Mental health of mothers and fathers of twins conceived via assisted reproduction treatment: a 1-year prospective study, Hum. Reprod. 24 (2) (2009) 367–377.

[34] C. Glazebrook, C. Sheard, S. Cox, M. Oates, G. Ndukwe, Parenting stress in first-time mothers of twins and triplets conceived after in vitro fertilization, Fertil. Steril. 81 (3) (2004) 505–511.

[35] H. Colpin, A. De Munter, K. Nys, L. Vandemeulebroecke, Parenting stress and psychosocial well-being among parents with twins conceived naturally or by reproductive technology, Hum. Reprod. 14 (12) (1999) 3133–3137.

[36] K. Thorpe, J. Golding, I. MacGillivray, R. Greenwood, Comparison of prevalence of depression in mothers of twins and mothers of singletons, Br. Med. J. 302 (6781) (1991) 875–878.

[37] C. Beer, C. Israel, S. Johnson, N. Marlow, A. Whitelaw, C. Glazebrook, Twin birth: an additional risk factor for poorer quality maternal interactions with very preterm infants?, Early Hum. Dev. 89 (8) (2013) 555–559.

[38] M. Cuisinier, M.D. Kleine, L. Kollee, G. Bethlehem, C.D. Graauw, Grief following the loss of a newborn twin compared to a singleton, Acta Paediatr. 85 (3) (1996) 339–343.

[39] G.L. Ryan, S.H. Zhang, A. Dokras, C.H. Syrop, B.J. Van Voorhis, The desire of infertile patients for multiple births, Fertil. Steril. 81 (3) (2004) 500–504.

[40] M. D'Alton, Infertility and the desire for multiple births, Fertil. Steril. 81 (3) (2004) 523–525.

[41] L.A. Tully, T.E. Moffitt, A. Caspi, Maternal adjustment, parenting and child behaviour in families of school-aged twins conceived after IVF and ovulation induction, J. Child Psychol. Psychiatry 44 (3) (2003) 316–325.

[42] S. Golombok, R. Cook, A. Bish, C. Murray, Families created by the new reproductive technologies: quality of parenting and social emotional development of the children, Child Dev. 66 (2) (1995) 285–298.

[43] N.L. Segal, Entwined Lives: Twins and What They Tell Us About Human Behavior, Plume, New York, NY, (2000).

[44] B. Luke, M.B. Brown, Maternal risk factors for potential maltreatment deaths among healthy singleton and twin infants, Twin Res. Hum. Genet. 10 (5) (2007) 778–785.

[45] M.H.B. Nelson, C.A. Martin, Increased child abuse in twins, Child Abuse Negl. 9 (4) (1985) 501–505.

[46] C.A. Lang, M.J. Cox, G. Flores, Maltreatment in multiple-birth children, Child Abuse Negl. 37 (12) (2013) 1109–1113.

[47] S. Ooki, Fatal child maltreatment associated with multiple births in Japan: nationwide data between July 2003 and March 2011, Environ. Health Prev. Med. 18 (5) (2013) 416–421.

[48] S. Ooki, Characteristics of fatal child maltreatment associated with multiple births in Japan, Twin Res. Hum. Genet. 16 (3) (2013) 743–750.

[49] N.L. Segal, Indivisible by Two: Lives of Extraordinary Twins, Harvard University Press, Cambridge, MA, (2007).

[50] C.C. Taylor, Marriages of twins to twins, Acta Genet. Med. Gemellol. 20 (1) (1971) 96–113.

[51] D.T. Lykken, A. Tellegen, Is human mating adventitious or the result of lawful choice? A twin study of mate selection, J. Pers. Soc. Psychol. 65 (1) (1993) 56–68.

[52] J.P. Rushton, T.A. Bons, Mate choice and friendship in twins: evidence for genetic similarity, Psychol. Sci. 16 (7) (2005) 555–559.

[53] N.L. Segal, Reunited twins: spouse relations, Twin Res. Hum. Genet. 14 (3) (2011) 290–294.

[54] D. De Smet, L. Van Speybroeck, J. Verplaetse, The Westermarck effect revisited: a psycho-physiological study of sibling incest aversion in young female adults, Evol. Hum. Behav. 35 (1) (2014) 34–42.

[55] R. Plomin, J.C. DeFries, V.S. Knopik, J.M. Neiderhiser, Behavior Genetics, sixth ed., Worth Publishers, New York, NY, (2013).

[56] D. Watson, E.C. Klohnen, A. Casillas, E. Nus Simms, J. Haig, D.S. Berry, Match makers and deal breakers: analyses of assortative mating in newlywed couples, J. Pers. 72 (5) (2004) 1029–1068.

CHAPTER 11

Twins, Clones, and Other Extraordinary Pairs

In Chapter 1 and elsewhere in this book I described the two types of twins, identical and fraternal, as well as the various forms each twin type can take. I also explained that there are a growing number of curious "twin-like" pairs that replicate some of twinship's defining features, such as matched age and matched appearance, but are *not* twins. I enjoy studying these exotic pairs because they give us another way of addressing the origins and development of human behavior. I believe we will see more of these twin "copycats" because of advances in fertility treatment and changes in traditional family structures. Couples may have children from embryos they created at the same time, but implanted and delivered years apart. The second marriages of husband and wife can mean raising his and her near-in-age children under the same roof. The lack of appropriate labels for these exceptional sibships feeds mythconceptions surrounding these siblings' relationship to one another and how similar or different their parents can expect them to become.

In this chapter I will examine beliefs about twins and clones, siblings created by in vitro fertilization (IVF), the unusual genetic relationship between children born to identical twins, the basis of personality similarity between twins, and twins' and siblings' social relationships. I will begin with a notion involving genetically identical twins and human clones, immediately followed by its counterpart (Fig. 11.1).

1. *Identical twins are clones.*

   Reality Check: True

   Short Answer: Clones are, by definition, genetically identical organisms, DNA sequences or cells [1]. MZ (identical) twins are clones because they are genetically identical beings, produced asexually when a single fertilized egg divides. However, as I explained earlier, it is possible that identical twins do not share *exactly* the same DNA because of mutations in specific genes or errors in cell duplication. But for all practical purposes identical twins qualify as clones. In fact, most identical twins realize this and some confess that they enjoy "cloning around."

   More of the Story: Cloning can occur naturally or artificially [1]. An example of natural cloning would be reproduction in plants, such as when

Twin Mythconceptions
http://dx.doi.org/10.1016/B978-0-12-803994-6.00011-1

Figure 11.1 *The controversies surrounding human reproductive cloning generated some humorous—but fictitious—portrayals of its consequences.* However, like identical twins, clones and their donors would never be exactly the same. *(Reprinted with permission. Image source: Cartoonstock.com).*

a water hyacinth produces multiple genetically identical copies by a process called apomixis (the replacement of sexual reproduction with asexual reproduction) [2]. In contrast, artificial cloning is the creation of an organism that is genetically identical to another organism by manipulating reproduction in the laboratory. The best recent example of artificial cloning is the birth of Dolly, the world's most famous lamb.

You may recall the 1996 cloning of Dolly by Professor Ian Wilmut of Edinburgh, Scotland, an achievement that stunned the worlds of science and society. People wanted to know how Dolly was conceived (explained later in the chapter), how difficult it was to accomplish (it took 277 tries), and what this development might mean for human families (a topic that is still contentiously debated). This cloning event was achieved through a process that involves taking a cell nucleus from an adult donor and inserting it into an unfertilized egg that has had its own nucleus removed. (The nucleus of a cell contains the chromosome pairs or DNA of the organism.) In scientific terms, this process is called somatic cell nuclear transfer. After the transfer, scientists apply an electric current to the unfertilized egg to "jumpstart" the egg cell toward its development into a blastocyst (hollow cell structure giving rise to the embryo). At this point the egg is ready for implantation in the uterus.

Dolly was created from a mammary gland cell taken from an adult sheep. In fact, Dolly is the namesake of the well-known American country music singer and songwriter, Dolly Parton. According to Dr. Wilmut, "Dolly is derived from a mammary gland cell and we couldn't think of a more impressive pair of glands than Dolly Parton's." [3]

2. *Clones are twins.*
Reality Check: False
Short Answer: Identical twins are clones, but clones are *not* identical twins: clones are not twins because they do not meet the specific criteria that define identical twins, and that distinguish them from nontwins. Beginning in 1997 after Dolly's birth, I have refined my ideas on the defining features of identical twins and have listed them as follows [4–6]. For the most part, these criteria qualify a pair of individuals as a pair of twins, with some exceptions that follow this list:

* Simultaneous conception. Identical twins form at the same time following the division of a single fertilized egg.

* Shared parents. Identical twins are conceived by the same mother and father.

* Shared intrauterine environments. Identical twins develop in the shared womb of the mother who conceived them.

* Same birth place and rearing home. Identical twins are born and raised at the same time and place.

There are several naturally occurring exceptions to these four criteria, but they do *not* diminish the importance of the four characteristics that collectively separate identical twins from nontwins.
More of the Story: When the cloning of Dolly the sheep was announced in 1997 both scientists and lay persons used the terms "twins" and "clones" interchangeably in the ethics and safety discussions that followed. Clones

were also called "delayed genetic twins" and "belated genetic twin-sisters." [7] The editor of the law and science journal *Jurimetrics* asked me to consider my views on human reproductive cloning from the perspective of a twin researcher. I published a paper in that journal in which I objected to the terms that I listed earlier, because they did not consider the specific features that to me identify identical twins [4]. In particular, I described how ignoring twins' unique defining features explains the inappropriate interchangeability between the words "twins" and "clones."

This casual usage disturbed me back in 1997 and it disturbs me now. In the event that human reproductive cloning is approved and practiced, donor parents would acquire misconceptions and false expectations regarding their children's development were they to believe that clones are twins. Just like it would be wrong to consider virtual twins (same-age unrelated individuals reared together) as twins—because they are not—it would be unfair to consider clones as twins. The term "twins" connotes concepts of physical resemblance, synchronized development, and social closeness, which is not the same for donor–clone and identical twin pairs. Dolly's birth was, for me, a catalyst for developing the identical twin criteria I listed earlier.

At the same time, there are naturally occurring exceptions to each of these four conditions:

- Exception to simultaneous conception. Identical triplets result when a single fertilized egg (zygote) divides to produce two zygotes (let's say zygote A and zygote B), followed by division of one of the other zygotes (let's say B) to yield zygotes B and C. This means that zygotes A and C would be produced at slightly different times. This is a minor point, but it is a departure from strict simultaneous conception.

- Exception to shared parents. When it comes to human reproductive cloning (cloning of an individual from a donor's cell), there is a distinction between (1) sharing your parents in a technical sense, as when the same mother and father physically conceive both children, and (2) sharing your parents in a biological sense, as when two people have the same genetic relationship with each of their biological parents, which is 50%. I know this sounds complex, but it is really straightforward.

Identical twins share their parents in a technical sense because they were conceived by the same mother and the same father. Identical twins also share their parents in a biological sense because they were physically created by the same mother and father, and were gestated by that mother. However, a donor and his or her cloned child would share their parents *only* in a biological sense, *not* in a technical sense. Their biological connection comes from the fact that (1) the donor's parents (who are the cloned child's grandparents) conceived the donor, and (2) the donor and his or her cloned child have identical genes. Therefore, the clone and the donor each share 50% of their genes with each of the donor's parents. However, donors and clones do not share their parents in a technical sense. That is because the donor's mother (the cloned child's grandmother) gestated the donor, but not the clone. And the donor's father (the cloned child's grandfather) did not physically create his grandchild, even though he is the "genetic parent" of that child—thus, the donor and clone do *not* share their parents in a technical sense.

Another interesting wrinkle to this story distinguishes between different types of donor parents, and it concerns mitochondrial DNA (mtDNA). mtDNA, found outside the cell nucleus, is comprised of 37 genes that are responsible for converting energy from food into a form that can be used by the cells. A unique feature of mtDNA is that it is transmitted intact from a mother to each of her children [8]. If a female donor gestated a child conceived from one of her own cells that was inserted into one of her own eggs, she and her child would share their mtDNA, as do ordinary biological mothers and their children. However, a female donor with impaired or aging eggs might be impregnated with an egg donated by a different female, after the egg was enucleated (had its nucleus removed) and replaced with the donor's cell. These donor mothers would *not* share their mtDNA with their cloned child, a circumstance that could cause differences between them in brain, heart, respiratory functioning, and disease [9].

Of course, males do not gestate their own children. Therefore, a male wishing to clone a child would have one of his cells inserted into the enucleated egg of a woman who would carry the child for him—or the child could be carried by a different female surrogate, involving three people in the process. Either way, this donor father would not share his mtDNA with his child—unless the egg donor was his sister—but ordinary fathers never do.

* Exception to shared intrauterine environments. Most identical (and fraternal) twins share their intrauterine environment until the time of birth. However, sometimes one twin is ready to be born before the other, and arrives days, weeks, or even months before his or her cotwin, due to their mother's premature labor or other unpredictable events. As such, these twins would not share the womb for the full duration of the pregnancy, but their different delivery times would have occurred

naturally so would not detract from their status as twins. Several examples of twins born at different times were described in an earlier chapter.

- Exception to birth at the same time and rearing in the same place. As I discussed in Chapter 5, twins do not always share their date of birth—one pair of twins was born 87 days apart. And some twins are delivered in different countries, such as fraternal twins Dylan and Hannah, born in England and Scotland, respectively, and Heidi and Jo, born in Wales and England.

There are also twins who are reared apart from birth by adoption, and some who are accidentally switched at birth and so grow up apart. Some of these twins are even raised in different countries and cultures. However, these exceptional events do not diminish the multiple birth status of the twins involved because they belong to the same generation and are exposed to many similar (albeit, some dissimilar) societal and historical changes. And, of course, reared-apart twins are conceived at the same time, have the same parents, and inhabited the same womb.

The debate over twins and clones is likely to continue and, no doubt, some readers will think of further additions or exceptions to my twinning criteria. In fact, another exceptional type of twin should be acknowledged—twins whose cotwins pass away at any time before, during, or after birth. I have known twins who mourned the loss of a cotwin due to miscarriage. And Elvis Presley was also deeply affected by his twin brother, Jesse, who died at birth [10]. These twins have been recognized as "twinless twins" by a national organization established to meet their unique needs [11]. I believe that twinless twins meet the criteria I have listed earlier, although early loss would preclude rearing at the same time and place.

3. *Identical cotwins are more alike than a donor parent and his or her cloned child would be.*
   Reality Check: Possible—probably depends on the trait
   Short Answer: At the present time, we do not know if identical twins would be more alike than donor parents and their cloned children because we do not have the data. Human reproductive cloning has never been done, so it is impossible to conduct the studies that would give us the final answer. It is possible, however, to speculate on this question, based on what we know from available research and observations.

   Twin studies have shown that attitudes and interests are partly influenced by genetic factors [12,13], and we know that both identical twins and donor–clone pairs share 100% of their genes. However, identical cotwins may be more alike than donor–clone pairs in their attitudes toward premarital sex or their interest in extreme sports. That is because identical twins, unlike donor–clone pairs, are born at the same time and become part of the same generation, subjecting them to the same technological developments, societal standards, and fashion trends. As an example, older generations of adults, having grown up prior to modern technological advances, may hesitate to use computers and cell phones. However, most people under 25, born into a wired world, embrace these devices enthusiastically.

In contrast, the birth weights of clones and their donors might be more alike than those of identical twins because birth weight has a partial genetic basis [14], *and* because each would have been gestated individually without competing for prenatal space and nutrition (unless the donor was also a twin). Of course, clone–donor similarity in birth weight would also depend on the prenatal environments of the mothers who gestated them—if one mother smoked cigarettes or experienced high levels of stress during the pregnancy the birth weight of her newborn would be reduced [15,16].

More of the Story: When the birth of Dolly the lamb became widely known in 1997, I was troubled by the conflicting and sometimes incorrect statements made in response to her birth, issued in a report by the National Bioethics Advisory Commission (NBAC). First, the committee members emphasized the "distinct" personality differences between identical twins. At the same time (in other parts of the report), they claimed just the opposite, namely that identical twins' physical identity causes others to see them as identical people, due to the intertwining of body and behavior. In other words, the committee members worried that people who look alike are perceived as being alike, making it impossible to distinguish between them. Viewers' impressions were, therefore, expected to diminish the psychological well-being of donors and their cloned children should human reproductive cloning become a reality.

I disagreed with both statements when they were made and still do. First, research shows that identical twins match considerably across personality traits, although they are not exactly the same. That is, identical twins as a whole are unlikely to show "distinct" personality differences— one twin is unlikely to be warm and kind, while the other is cold and calculating. Second, there is no proven connection between appearance and personality—heavy people are not necessarily jolly, and blondes do not always have more fun—instead, personality originates partly in our genes and partly in the unique experiences we have in life. As such, donors and clones *are* likely to resemble one another in personality—but whether or not their degree of personality similarity is less than or greater than that of ordinary identical twins is unknown and could vary from trait to trait.

It is conceivable that donors and their clones might be more alike than identical twins on some personality measures, despite their age and generational differences. Both donors and clones and identical twins have the same genes, predisposing them to behave in certain classes of ways. However, donors and their cloned children would not interact as peers, possibly allowing their genetic potential to be expressed *more fully and more similarly*. Regardless, I believe it is unlikely that other people would see or consider the donor and cloned child as "identical people," because their age difference would preclude such a response—all of us look different today than we did as small children.

Interestingly, identical twins, who interact often and as peers, tend to assume somewhat different social roles in relation to one another— one twin may be somewhat more outgoing than the other when they are together, a difference that would decrease when they are apart. The British twin researcher James Shields found that reared-apart identical twins were more alike in extraversion and neuroticism than reared-to-gether identical twins. Some, but not all past studies found that identical twins living apart were more alike in extraversion than identical twins living together, explaining this by the suppressive effect one twin has on the other. Current twin studies have not concurred, possibly due to the use of different personality inventories. This phenomenon, which is widely observed anecdotally, warrants further analysis [17–20].

A related concern, raised by critics of cloning, is that the individuality of the cloned child would be substantially diminished by sharing 100% of his or her genes with a parent. That is the topic to which I turn next.

4. *Human reproductive cloning would detract from individuality and would irrevocably harm family relationships.*
   Reality Check: False
   Short Answer: The birth of Dolly was exciting for many people, but worrisome to even more. Fears surrounding the consequences of possible human reproductive cloning were voiced by scientists, ethicists, lawyers, and members of the concerned public—if it was possible to clone a sheep, then why not a human being? However, the fears were mostly in the form of emotionally driven speculation, rather than well-reasoned inquiry based on relevant research.

   With the goal of examining the cloning controversy both systematically and scientifically, I looked to psychological twin studies. Based on findings that identical twins are not at increased risk for difficulties linked to their matched appearance and behaviors, shared a more intimate relationship with one another than any other set of people, and genuinely enjoyed being twins, I concluded that concerns over identity, individuality, and family relationships were overstated and without merit [4–6]. Additionally, I examined the life stories provided by unusually similar parent–child pairs and found that the members relish their physical and behavioral likeness. (Scientific studies of such pairings are unavailable.)

It also occurred to me that donor parent–cloned child relations might be quite favorable because of likely similarities in their mental abilities, personality traits, and information-processing strategies. These similarities might lay the basis for greater mutual understanding than that found between ordinary parent–child pairs—especially during adolescence. I also indicated that eliminating or weakening these fears as I did through my research did not necessarily justify the practice of human cloning.

More of the Story: Research shows that identical twins maintain closer social relationships with each other throughout life relative to fraternal twins, but without forfeiting their individuality and identity [21]. In fact, most identical twins claim that they have two identities—the one they share with their twin and the one they enjoy as an individual. Like most teenagers, some identical twin adolescents question their relationships with their family members, wondering if they are too closely attached to their parents or to their twin, but most emerge from these challenges without psychological scars. Furthermore, most research shows that twins are *not* more likely than nontwins to suffer from behavioral problems [22–25]—those who do may experience difficulties related to issues of separation and individuation, more so for identical than fraternal twins. These twins may seek psychological assistance, either on their own or as a pair (Dr. E. Pearlman, Personal communication, April 18, 2016; Dr. J. Friedman, Personal communication, April 18, 2016).

It is reasonable to conclude that if most identical twins do *not* tend to experience identity crises to a greater degree than nontwins, it is unlikely that donor parent–cloned child pairs would suffer such difficulties because they differ in age and, therefore, generation. In fact, every year in the United States and elsewhere, hundreds, if not thousands of twin pairs (mostly identical) gather at festivals and other organized get-togethers to celebrate being a twin. These commemorative events recognize twinship as a happy and fulfilling circumstance of life, not as a frustrating and demoralizing situation they want to escape.

The idea that interpersonal family relationships could be damaged by human reproductive cloning has been voiced [6]. More specifically, it has been suggested that donor parents would entertain unfair expectations for their cloned children, based on their own abilities and life experiences. However, careful consideration indicates that this fear is also groundless. Most biological, adoptive, and foster parents expect and hope that their children set personal goals and strive to achieve them—oftentimes, these goals are an extension of the met or missed goals of the parent. Ordinary parents might also pressure their children to continue the family business or abandon their acting career for one that would guarantee a steady income, something not all children desire. In contrast, it is possible that donor parents, given their own life experiences, might be especially adept at recognizing and guiding their children toward satisfying goals and dreams.

Even though donor parents and cloned children would belong to different generations, they would resemble one another physically, and their resemblance would probably increase as the cloned child approached the donor parent's age. As I indicated earlier, I have reviewed the comments from some ordinary biological parent–child pairs whose appearance is quite similar, and found that these individuals enjoyed their similarities and their relationship with each other [21]. At the same time it is possible that a father might find it disquieting to raise a cloned daughter who was the genetic replica of his partner—and a woman might find it unsettling to raise a cloned son who was the genetic replica of hers. Same-sex couples might face similar concerns. I believe, once again, that we need to identify and explore the living examples that illustrate this situation, such as children who look very much like one parent and not the other, and siblings born at different times who look and act remarkably alike. I have never encountered such a study, but believe that one would be worth doing because it would furnish crucial information for informed assessment and decision making on the subject of human reproductive cloning.

Studies aside, history also teaches important lessons. When IVF was first performed in the United Kingdom in 1978 and introduced shortly thereafter in the United States, there was concern over the implications of this procedure for the quality of family relations. However, over time and due to widespread familiarity with the process (and the resultant children!), these concerns have disappeared and countless otherwise infertile families are enjoying the pleasures of raising a family. Human reproductive cloning could conceivably follow a similar route. I want to reiterate that dismissing possible concerns about human cloning does not justify its practice—we are far from examining the full range of cloning's biological and behavioral consequences.

One last word—it is ironic and somewhat amusing that cloning critics have never objected to the fact that IVF and other assisted reproductive methods are responsible for a kind of cloning. Recall that in IVF, laboratory manipulation of the fertilized egg has been linked to division of the fertilized egg, producing identical twins. And identical twins *are* clones by definition.

5. *A baby born from a frozen embryo implanted in his mother's womb is the fraternal twin of an existing 2-year-old child, who was conceived by IVF at the same time. Reality Check*: False

Short Answer: One evening in the mid-1980s I was invited to speak at a mothers of twins club get-together. It was the day that the *Minneapolis Star Tribune* carried a story about siblings *conceived at the same time* by IVF, but born years apart—one of the embryos had been frozen and stored for later implantation. When one of the mothers in the group asked me if these children were, in fact, twins I replied *no*. Everyone nodded their heads in agreement.

IVF has introduced new kinship categories that are challenging to name, but it is wrong to include them in existing categories by default. The term "twin" carries connotations of similarity and social connectedness that do not apply to IVF siblings born years apart. A future challenge for behavioral and medical researchers is to create appropriate labels for these novel brothers and sisters.

During a May 2016 visiting lectureship in Europe, I was fascinated to meet Maja and Linea, the parents of 3-year-old Cornelia and 18-month-old Herman and Hubert. Maja conceived and carried Cornelia and Hubert, while Linea conceived and carried Herman, using the same sperm donor. Thus, Cornelia and Hubert are full siblings, while Cornelia and Herman, and Herman and Hubert are half-siblings through the father. An added twist to this family is that Herman and Hubert were born 2 months apart making them twin-like, but not twins. Maja explained that she has joined an online group for mothers of twins because she will be confronting the same issues as the other members, such as school separation and clothing choices. It turns out that several mothers have not welcomed her on the grounds that Herman and Hubert are not strictly twins. I believe that Maja is justified in joining this group because her children are genetically related and closely matched in age and, as such, will present her with many of the same "twin-like" questions and dilemmas faced by the group's members. The fact that twins can be born 2 months apart provides another bit of supportive evidence—but Maja's children and and other children like hers should *not* be referred to as twins. Ideally, local and online clubs and organizations devoted exclusively to families with unusual, closely spaced siblings will become available. *More of the Story*: Some couples create multiple embryos through assisted reproduction, but implant just one, or a few, at a given time, before freezing the others for later implantation. Older and younger siblings can, therefore, be conceived at the same time, but the two children *do not* fulfill the twinship criteria of being born on the same day (or even the same year), or of developing under the same intrauterine conditions. (Twin deliveries can be separated by as much as 87 days, as I discussed earlier, but the birth of nontwin siblings would greatly exceed this interval.) Like ordinary fraternal twins, these siblings (conceived at the same time, but born at different times) would share 50% of their genes, on average—however, labeling them as "twins" would acknowledge a level of psychological similarity and social relatedness that is unwarranted. Such labeling would also be likely to invite unfair behavioral and physical comparisons by others. Moreover, these two siblings would enter the family at very different times, when family dynamics, living conditions, and/or financial circumstances would not be the same for each child as they would be for twins. Twins can, of course, come home from the hospital at different times due to newborn health differences, but their arrivals would not be years apart.

6. *Embryos created by the same donor couple and implanted into different women at the same time would be twins.*
   Reality Check: False
   Short Answer: I am intrigued by the process of simultaneously implanting two embryos into a woman's womb, known as double embryo transfer. It is an assisted reproductive technique aimed at producing fraternal twins.

   My interest in this procedure stems from an unusual and unplanned "experiment" that came to my attention in late 2014. I was contacted by one of a group of three women living in different countries (the United States, Canada, and Australia) who underwent double embryo transfer at the same time, at the same clinic, with all six embryos having been created by the same couple. The three mothers became friends, no doubt because they share something of great importance—each mother is raising the "siblings" of the other two families' children. I am tracking the developmental progress of these children who belong to three different, but related twin pairs. I have labeled the individual twins US-1 and US-2; CAN-1 and CAN-2; and AUS-1 and AUS-2.

Members of the different pairs (e.g., US-2 and AUS-1) replay many features of reared-apart fraternal twins, such as sharing their biological parents and their time of conception. And the largest birth date difference between any two children is just under 6 weeks, which is *less* than the interval between the births of some naturally conceived twin pairs. Of course, the pairs of children from the different families, such as US-2 and AUS-1 or CAN-1 and US-1, did not experience the same intrauterine environment so to call them twins or even full siblings would *not* be technically correct—full siblings do not share the same womb at the same time which is why I placed the term "siblings" in quotation marks earlier.

More of the Story: Psychological science makes the greatest gains by comparing pairs of people who vary in their genetic backgrounds and in their environmental surroundings. The genetic relatedness of the six children I am studying (50% shared genes, on average) is the same. However, each pair is being raised in a different country and culture, allowing for many behavioral and physical comparisons between them. When the children turned 1.5 years of age (which they did within 2–6 weeks of each other), I used the Infant Behavior Questionnaire to gather data on their behaviors related to affect, emotionality, and regulation [26]. Six months later, when the three twin pairs celebrated their second birthday I gathered comparable information, as well as information on when they had reached certain developmental milestones, such as sitting alone and speaking their first word.

On some measures, some children are more similar to a child in a different pair than to their own cotwin, as I expected [27]. After all, the six children are full biological brothers and sisters, and siblings vary in how alike and how different they can be. As I continue to track the development of these children as they age, it will be possible to compare more complex behaviors, such as motor skills between twins and language development across pairs. This unplanned accidental "experiment" can offer unique insights into what makes us who we are, and should generate new ideas for testing with larger samples.

The success of double embryo transfer can vary widely, from 12% to 55% [28]. Several factors improve the success of double embryo transfer if performed on day 3 after embryo formation. They include younger maternal age (35 years or less); higher bodyweight (greater than 132.28 lbs or 60 kg); better embryo quality (more than 14 blastomeres or cells produced after the fertilized egg divides); and lack of irregular embryonic features (absence of uneven cell division and atypical shape) [29]. Some researchers have even developed more formal models to predict the outcomes (successful or unsuccessful) from double embryo transfer [28,30]. These models additionally consider factors such as prior full-term births and previous fertility treatments.

Since twins are high-risk pregnancies to begin with, and because assisted reproductive methods are improving steadily, current trends favor the successful implantation of single embryos. However, some couples, especially those who are childless, understandably seek twins in the interest of having a larger family more quickly and providing each child with a sibling—while witnessing the fascinating unfolding of development in two age-matched individuals. I am enjoying this process along with the families I am studying, although I am seeing it from the sidelines as a spectator.

The three sets of parents from the United States, Australia, and Canada plan to meet at Disneyland in Anaheim California in 2017 when the children turn 4 years old. I will be there.

In Chapter 12, I will continue the discussion of unusual family relationships generated by twins when they do what everyone else does—get married. I will present research showing what these families can tell us about relations among twins, spouses, and in-laws. I will also focus on a new twin-like couple I find utterly fascinating—*unrelated look-alikes*. I will explain the importance of using these doppelgängers to address some criticisms that have been raised in conjunction with twin studies.

REFERENCES

[1] Biology Online, Cloning, 2012. Available from: http://www.biology-online.org/dictionary/Cloning
[2] Biology Online, Apomixis, 2009. Available from: http://www.biology-online.org/dictionary/Apomixis
[3] BBC News, 1997: Dolly the Sheep is Cloned, February 22, 1997. Available from: http://news.bbc.co.uk/onthisday/hi/dates/stories/february/22/newsid_4245000/4245877.stm

[4] N.L. Segal, Behavioral aspects of intergenerational cloning: what twins tell us, Jurimetrics 38 (1) (1997) 57–67.

[5] N.L. Segal, Human cloning: a twin-research perspective, Hastings Law J. 53 (5) (2002) 1073–1084.

[6] N.L. Segal, Psychological features of human reproductive cloning: a twin-based perspective, Psychiatric Times XXIII (December) (2006) 22.

[7] W. Szybalski, Human clone or a delayed twin?, Medycyna Wieku Rozwojowego 5 (1) (2001) 39–43 A. McCarthy, Cloning, Linacre/CTS Explanations Series, 2003.

[8] Genetics Home Reference, Mitochondrial DNA, 2016. Available from: https://ghr. nlm.nih.gov/mitochondrial-dna

[9] United Mitochondrial Disease Foundation, What is Mitochondrial Disease?, 2016. Available from: http://www.umdf.org/site/c.8qKOJ0MvF7LUG/b.7934627/k.3711/ What_is_Mitochondrial_Disease.htm

[10] L. Geller, The Mystery of Jesse Garon, February 4, 2011. Available from: http://www. elvispresleybiography.net/elvis-presley-hairstylist-larry-geller-blog/?p=60

[11] Twinless Twins Support Group. Available from: http://www.twinlesstwins.org

[12] K. McCourt, T.J. Bouchard, D.T. Lykken, A. Tellegen, M. Keyes, Authoritarianism revisited: genetic and environmental influences examined in twins reared apart and together, Pers. Individ. Dif. 27 (5) (1999) 985–1014.

[13] J.H. Fowler, C.T. Dawes, Two genes predict voter turnout, J. Polit. 70 (3) (2008) 579–594.

[14] A. Lunde, K.K. Melve, H.K. Gjessing, R. Skjærven, L.M. Irgens, Genetic and environmental influences on birth weight, birth length, head circumference, and gestational age by use of population-based parent-offspring data, Am. J. Epidemiol. 165 (7) (2007) 734–741.

[15] P.H.C. Rondo, R.F. Ferreira, F. Nogueira, M.C.N. Ribeiro, H. Lobert, R. Artes, Maternal psychological stress and distress as predictors of low birth weight, prematurity and intrauterine growth retardation, Eur. J. Clin. Nutr. 57 (2) (2003) 266–272.

[16] The Health Consequences of Smoking: A Report of the Surgeon General, US Department of Health and Human Services, Centers for Disease Control and Prevention, National Center for Chronic Disease Prevention and Health Promotion, Office on Smoking and Health, Atlanta, GA, 2004, 62.

[17] J. Shields, Monozygotic Twins Brought Up Apart and Brought Up Together, Oxford University Press, Oxford, UK, (1962).

[18] G. Claridge, S. Canter, W.I. Hume, Personality Differences and Biological Variations: A Study of Twins (Monographs in Experimental Psychology), Pergamon Press, Oxford, UK, (1974).

[19] G.J.S. Wilde, Inheritance of personality traits, Acta Psychologia 22 (1) (1964) 37–51 note: Wilde found that identical twins living apart were more like than identical twins living together in psychosomatic complaints, but not in extraversion.

[20] N.L. Segal, Born Together-Reared Apart: The Landmark Minnesota Twin Study, Harvard University Press, Cambridge, MA, (2012) and references therein.

[21] N.L. Segal, Entwined Lives: Twins and What They Tell Us About Human Behavior, Plume, New York, (2000).

[22] E.J. Oord, H.M. Koot, D.I. Boomsma, F.C. Verhulst, J.F. Orlebeke, A twin-singleton comparison of problem behaviour in 2-3-year-olds, J. Child Psychol. Psychiatry 36 (3) (1995) 449–458.

[23] F. Levy, M. McLaughlin, C. Wood, D. Hay, I. Waldman, Twin-sibling differences in parental reports of ADHD, speech, reading and behaviour problems, J. Child Psychol. Psychiatry 37 (5) (1996) 569–578.

[24] S.C. Robbers, M. Bartels, F.V. Van Oort, C.T. van Beijsterveldt, J. Van der Ende, F.C. Verhulst, et al. A twin-singleton comparison of developmental trajectories of externalizing and internalizing problems in 6-to 12-year-old children, Twin Res. Hum. Genet. 13 (1) (2010) 79–87.

[25] C. Tomassini, K. Juel, N.V. Holm, A. Skytthe, K. Christensen, Risk of suicide in twins: 51 year follow up study, Br. Med. J. 327 (7411) (2003) 373–374.

[26] S.P. Putnam, A.L. Helbig, M.A. Gartstein, M.K. Rothbart, E. Leerkes, Development and assessment of short and very short forms of the Infant Behavior Questionnaire–Revised, J. Pers. Assess. 96 (4) (2014) 445–458.

[27] N.L. Segal, A.C. Killian, DZA Twins Conceived via Identical Double Embryo Donors: Behavioral Features of Three Infant Pairs Raised in Different Countries, Behavior Genetics Association, San Diego, CA, June 17-20, 2015.

[28] B.M. Lannon, B. Choi, M.R. Hacker, L.E. Dodge, B.A. Malizia, C.B. Barrett, et al. Predicting personalized multiple birth risks after in vitro fertilization–double embryo transfer, Fertil. Steril. 98 (1) (2012) 69–76.

[29] M.S. Kim, J.H. Kim, B.C. Jee, C.S. Suh, S.H. Kim, Factors affecting occurrence of twin pregnancy after double embryo transfer on day 3, J. Obstet. Gynaecol. Res. 41 (8) (2015) 1223–1228.

[30] B. Luke, M.B. Brown, E. Wantman, J.E. Stern, V.L. Baker, E. Widra, et al. A prediction model for live birth and multiple births within the first three cycles of assisted reproductive technology, Fertil. Steril. 102 (3) (2014) 744–752.

CHAPTER 12

Twin Spouses and Unrelated Look-Alikes: New Views

When identical twins marry non-twin sisters (or non-twin brothers) their children become unusual close cousins and atypical "part-siblings." I will talk about these, as well as findings related to the unique types of relatives that emerge when twins have children, that offer insights into the roots of social affiliation and social closeness. The curious twin–like pairs composed of two unrelated look-alikes add another interesting twist to what we know about the origins of personality development and self-esteem. I will also delve more deeply into the nature and quality of twin pair relationships, both inside and outside the womb.

1. *When identical twins marry non-twin sisters (or non-twin brothers) their children become unusual first cousins and atypical half-siblings.*
   Reality Check: True
   Short Answer: In Chapter 2 I reviewed the Children-of-Twins research design, created naturally when identical twins marry unrelated partners and both twins raise children. Recall that the two sets of children in such a case are legal first cousins, but they are also genetically equivalent to half-siblings (sharing 25% of their genes, on average) because they each have one genetically identical parent. I also described the rare situation in which identical twins marry identical twins, producing children who are genetically equivalent to full siblings (sharing 50% of their genes, on average). However, if identical twin brothers were to marry nontwin sisters then their children's average biological relatedness would fall between 25% and 50%—not quite full siblings, but closer than cousins and half-sibs.
   More of the Story: Chang and Eng Bunker are among the most famous conjoined twins, as I discussed in Chapter 1. They are known for many things. In 1843, these identical twin brothers married nontwin sisters, Adelaide and Sarah Yates, settled in Mount Airy, North Carolina and raised 22 children between them—Chang and Adelaide had 10 children and Eng and Sarah had 12. The two families maintained separate households, and to keep things fair they alternately spent 3-day periods in each home. According to Chang and Eng, the sisters' parents' main

objection to their marriage was the twins' Asian origin, not the fact that they were conjoined [1–3].

The genetic relatedness of these twins' children to one another is curious to consider. The fathers are identical twins, related by 100%, so the chance that children conceived by each twin share their paternal genes is 50%. The mothers are full siblings, related by 50%, so the chance that children conceived by the two sisters share their maternal genes is 25% (half of 50%). Averaging these figures yields 37.5%, the average genetic relatedness of children born to identical twins who marry full siblings.

The Bunker twins left hundreds of descendants that convene every year in Mount Airy for a family reunion. Several sets of twins (none conjoined) have been born in later generations of that family, such as fraternal twins Chang Bunker and Eng Bunker (Eng's great-grandsons), who attended the 25th annual reunion of the Bunker twins' descendants, held in 2014 at the First Baptist Church. This event included approximately 200 descendants of the original conjoined twins.

2. *Identical twins generally have closer social relationships with one another than fraternal twins.*

Reality Check: True

Short Story: Research shows that identical twins, on average, are socially closer and more emotionally involved with each other than fraternal twins. But like many other features of twinship that I have examined in this book, there is plenty of variation and overlap—some identical twins are not very close to one another and some fraternal twins are exceptionally close. I believe that the bases of these relationship differences come from identical twins' perceptions of their similar abilities, interests, and ways of looking at the world, all of which are genetically influenced at some level. In contrast, many fraternal twins lack the similarities in intellect, personality, and interests that draw and keep identical twins so closely together.

Since about 2013, I have been corresponding with Miriam Cohen, a 25-year-old identical female twin from a religious Jewish community on the East Coast of the United States. Miriam's description of her relationship with her sister Devorah Cooper beautifully captures the essence and subtleties of identical twinship:

"The love that a twin has for a [co-twin] sister is parallel to the love a mother has for her child! When I found my husband and got married a half of me wasn't complete because my twin didn't find hers...Becoming pregnant was the next step and there was always a small doubt:

"what if it doesn't happen?" So when both of us married and became pregnant it was magical and breathtaking. Thank G-d that she became pregnant a month after me, or my happiness wouldn't have been complete!" Miriam (left) and Devorah are the identical twins pictured on the cover of this book.

Reflections from a male fraternal twin reveal a different side to twinship. "While it was great in childhood, and I love my brother, I've always resented comparisons: "Who's smarter? Who's faster? Who's better looking? Who has more luck with women? It irritates me when people ask me those kinds of things. Many people seem to be really insensitive to that kind of stuff. Or maybe I'm just too sensitive. Consequently, I usually don't discuss being a twin with people I'm not close to."

Both of these comments could apply to identical *and* fraternal twins, underlining the social-interactional overlap between the two types. However, in both my research experience and personal contacts with twins and their families the different comments presented earlier better characterize identical pairs and fraternal pairs, respectively.

More of the Story: There is a large body of research showing that identical twins are socially closer in many ways than fraternal twins [4–6]. This is true regardless of the age, sex, and rearing status (together vs. apart) of the twins, as well as the varied theoretical orientations (e.g., psychodynamic, social-genetic) and methods (questionnaires, observation) particular to each study. And as I showed earlier, the loss of a twin is somewhat more devastating for identical twins, mirroring the research on social relations. Thus, these findings are very robust.

Contrary to the kinds of relations that typify the different pairs, I occasionally encounter identical and fraternal cotwins who claim to dislike—even loathe—each other. My first real experience with such twins occurred in the mid-1990s when I was invited as a guest on the *Oprah Winfrey Show.* The program was to be about twin relationships and I was intrigued. But witnessing the set-up piece from the green room just minutes before my airtime, I was horrified by what I saw: several sets of identical and fraternal twins described cruel and insensitive behavior toward one another—one identical female twin had actually pushed her sister out of their car while her sister was pregnant. Worried that the parents and twins who tuned into the show would get a distorted view of twinship, I informed viewers that these scenarios were rare exceptions, and hardly typical of how the vast majority of twins act toward one another.

At the same time, twin-to-twin relations are complex and what twins sometimes say about each other is not always what they mean. Harsh words toward his identical twin were voiced by a gentleman at one of my book signings, so it surprised me when he purchased two copies of my book—one for him and one for his twin brother. I was also fascinated by the relationship maintained by reared-apart identical twins Jack (raised Jewish in Trinidad) and Oskar (raised Catholic in Nazi Germany). Despite their very different historical and political opinions and outlooks, these twins stayed in close contact, even while they argued. These incidents highlight the intense attachment and devotion that twins feel toward one another, even if they do not always get along.

Two of my colleagues are clinical psychologists as well as identical twins, so they are uniquely suited to guiding twins through their tense times with each other. It is often easier to abandon a difficult relationship, but psychologically that does not seem to be a viable option when you are a twin—twins cannot divorce!

3. *Unrelated look-alikes (doppelgängers) are as similar in personality and self-esteem as identical twins.*
   Reality Check: False
   Short Answer: There is an unusual group of individuals whose faces and forms are nearly identical, giving them the appearance of identical twins—only they are *not* genetically related. These curious look-alikes have been beautifully photographed by French Canadian photographer François Brunelle for his project ironically titled, "I'm Not a Look-Alike!" The members of these pairs are usually identified when someone who knows Person A comes across Person B who looks a lot like Person A. I had this amazing experience at the University of Minnesota when I encountered a young woman in a supermarket who closely resembled a young woman I already knew. My colleague, Professor Bouchard and I asked the two women to complete part of the same test battery we gave to our reared-apart twins, but we could conclude little from just one case. We had no idea that there were a number of unrelated look-alikes out there.

   Brunelle maintains a website for describing his project and recruiting new look-alikes for his photo gallery [7]. One of my students discovered this site while surfing the Internet and forwarded the link to me. I immediately wanted to study these pairs to address a serious challenge raised in opposition to twin studies—namely that identical twins are alike in personality because people treat them alike, due to their matched physical appearance. However, I reasoned that if personality is shaped mostly by how one is treated then unrelated look-likes should be as similar in personality and self-esteem as identical twins reared apart.

The answer is that unrelated look-alikes are very *dissimilar* in both personality and self-esteem. If people treat identical twins alike (and they do) it is because identical twins' matched behaviors evoke or encourage similar responses from others. As my late colleague David C. Rowe reminded us, "Personality and temperament reside in the brain, not in a face" (p. 48) [8]. Of course, some look-alikes will resemble one another in personality, interests, or values—I have worked with unrelated look-alikes who share vocational and leisure-time interests. However, the bottom line comes from the degree of similarity across many look-alike pairs, not just a few—*there is no meaningful connection between how much people resemble one another in appearance and how much they resemble one another in behavior* (Fig. 12.1).

More of the Story: Scientific collaborations are often formed in whimsical and unpredictable ways. I presented findings from my first unrelated look-alike project, in 2012, at the 14th International Congress of Twin Studies, in Florence, Italy. I showed the audience the data demonstrating that the pairs I studied showed no personality similarity at all. When the session ended Dr. Ulrich Ettinger from Bonn, Germany approached me to say that he had tested the *same* group of participants when he was in Canada, expecting them to be similar in personality—but when he discovered that they were not, he no longer pursued the project. I was instantly intrigued because his findings matched mine, so I asked him to send me his data, which he did. Our joint efforts resulted in a second paper involving personality similarity in unrelated look-alikes using the same participant pairs, but comparing their scores on two different personality questionnaires—his and mine [9]. This second paper replicated the results from the first study, lending confidence to the findings.

In my initial study conducted solo, 23 look-alike pairs completed the Questionnaire de Personnalité au Travail (PfPI or Personality for Professionals Inventory) and the Rosenberg Self-Esteem Inventory. The second study combined these data and Ettinger's personality data from the French version of the 60-item Neuroticism–Extraversion–Openness (NEO) Inventory. Both personality questionnaires yield scores across the

Figure 12.1 *Bizarro's bizarre perspective on the origin of unrelated look-alikes.* *(Reprinted with permission from Dan Piraro. Image source: Bizarro.com).*

Big Five personality traits of openness, conscientiousness, extraversion, agreeableness, and neuroticism.

The average correlations across the five personality traits were −.05 in the first study and −.03 in the second study. In contrast, the mean correlations for identical and fraternal twins raised apart and together are .53 and .15, respectively; even fraternal twins who do not look physically alike show some degree of personality similarity. The correlation for the unrelated look-alikes in self-esteem was −.03, in contrast with correlations of .30–.35 for reared-together identical twins and .11–.16

for reared-together fraternal twins. This pattern of findings supports the view that *identical twins' resemblance in personality and self-esteem comes from their shared genes, not from their similar treatment by others.*

It is worth restating this conclusion using different words: to the extent that identical twins are treated alike (and they are), their similar treatment comes from the fact that they elicit similar responses from others, based on their behaviors. Behavioral geneticists call this process *active* or *evocative gene–environment correlation,* the idea that we respond to people based on our perceptions of their moods, actions, and talents. When parents encourage shy children to be more socially active, restrain rambunctious children from speaking out of turn, or offer swimming lessons to children who love the water they are personifying active gene–environment correlation.

Together, these studies generate several important implications for families with identical and fraternal twins. If parents actively encourage their twin children to wear the same clothing, have the same friends, or join the same activities, this does *not* make the twins more alike in most personality traits than twins whose parents offer them different opportunities. If parents treat twins alike it is partly out of their desire for fairness, but partly because twins (mostly identical) evoke similar treatment from their parents. Studies show that even when parents misjudge their twins' twin type—that is, parents think that their identical twins are really fraternal, and vice versa—their ratings of their twins' personality traits tend to agree with the children's *actual* twin type [10].

I often tell mothers and fathers, "You do not bring up your children—your children bring you up." Parents know that how they respond to and raise their obedient son does not work as well with their rebellious daughter. Either knowingly or not, parents adjust their rearing practices in accordance with each child's individual temperament and talents.

4. *Just like reared-apart identical twins, doppelgängers form close social relationships with one another once they meet.*
   Reality Check: False
   Short Answer: Very few of the unrelated look-alikes I have studied were socially attracted to one another or developed a close relationship. It seems that doppelgängers lack the "social glue" (i.e., the behavioral similarities and the perception of these similarities) needed to form and maintain close social relations with one another. Just looking like someone else does not mean that you behave alike, nor does it mean that you will become socially close.

*More of the Story:*The unrelated look-alikes photographed by Brunelle give us the unique opportunity to explore a fascinating question: Do these unusual pairs form close social relations with one another, like their genetically related parallels, that is, reared-apart and reunited identical twins?

In order to help us answer this question, I had the look-alike pairs complete a questionnaire regarding their initial and current feelings of social closeness and familiarity—the same form was completed by the reunited twins in my earlier study [9]. It turned out that only 17% of the look-alikes felt, or anticipated, feeling "very close" to one another when they first met. Even more revealing, this percentage increased only slightly, to 21%, when they described their current relationship—while the greatest increase occurred in the "not close" category. In contrast, over 70% of the identical reared-apart twins felt, or anticipated, feeling close to one another upon meeting, a percentage that increased to 80% for their current relationship [4]. I concluded that each identical cotwins' perception of their similarities explained the different results.

Despite what the data revealed, I believe that other explanations warrant consideration. It could be argued that twins' knowledge and confirmation of their twinship (e.g., through birth records or DNA testing) was an important factor in shaping the findings—that is, perhaps *knowing* someone is your twin could conceivably trigger feelings of closeness and familiarity. However, I do not agree with this view. First, the reunited fraternal twins were also aware of their twinship, yet fewer felt as socially bonded as the identical twins, probably because most fraternal twins are less alike behaviorally. Second, there are examples of twins and siblings who have been strongly attracted to one another without knowing they were related.

A pair of 20-year-old identical reared-apart Canadian twins, George and Brent, fell easily into a close friendship for a full year before considering the possibility that they were twins—they had thought all along that they were exceptional look-alikes. And before knowing they were related, 5-year-old reared-apart identical female twins from England became close school friends, despite their families' efforts to keep them apart; both sets of parents knew that their daughters were twins. I will say more about these young girls in the final chapter.

Separated siblings and half-siblings do not look as alike as identical twins, but some who met each other at work formed close relations before knowing that they were biologically related. Furthermore, as described earlier, strong social attraction between reared-apart opposite-sex twins has led to marriages between several such sets without their knowledge of being twins. In addition, my research on switched-at-birth twins who grew up in the wrong family shows that they are generally loyal toward the unrelated siblings with whom they were raised (their alleged fraternal twin), but lack the close understanding and compatibility that they quickly develop with their newly found identical twin. These examples suggest, but do not prove, that the mutual perception of similarities in intelligence, personality, and/or interests provides a basis for social attraction between people. The challenge is to find additional ways to confirm this conclusion; therefore, I am continuing my studies of unrelated look-alikes with the aim of doing so.

5. *Identical twins reared apart are as similar in personality as identical twins raised together.*
Reality Check: True
Short Story: Dr. Thomas J. Bouchard, Jr., Director of the Minnesota Study of Twins Reared Apart, used to say it is counterintuitive, but true, that identical twins reared apart are as alike in personality as identical twins reared together. Logic tells us that people living in the same home should resemble one another more than people living in separate homes, but an abundance of twin data tells a different tale: the reason why some family members share personality traits is because they share genes, *not* because they share environments. It is also true that some family members, despite years of living together, differ considerably in emotionality, extraversion, and/or traditionalism because while they share genes, they do not share genes associated with those traits. This is a great example of how twin research findings offer insight into nontwins' behaviors, telling us why we resemble some family members, even those we have never met, but not others.
More of the Story: One of the most provocative findings to have emerged from the Minnesota Study of Twins Reared Apart was that identical reared-apart twins are as similar as identical reared-together twins across 11 personality traits, as measured by the Multidimensional Personality Questionnaire [11]. The median correlations were .49 and .52 for the identical reared-apart and reared-together twins, respectively. These findings demonstrate that personality similarity is based on shared genes, not shared environments.

These results were largely misconstrued by the public and by some colleagues who believed that our findings dismissed the influence of the social environment, parenting practices, and other experiential influences on personality development. However, we noted that the influence of the environment was evident in the size of the 11 correlations for the reared-apart identical twins, which were mostly about .50—this meant that half of the personality differences (variation) from person to person were explained by the environmental differences among them. But for the majority of traits we measured, such as well-being and traditionalism, it was mostly unique individual experiences (nonshared environmental factors) that mattered, possibly taking a class or living abroad. Thus, the environment helps shape personality, but not by making relatives who live together more alike—the events we experience individually tend to make us different from our family members, while the genes that we share tend to make us alike.

An exception in our results was that the personality trait of sociability *did* show evidence of shared environmental influence. This means that growing up with family members *does* increase similarity in some social behaviors. Showing high levels of affiliation toward a relative by acknowledging his or her birthday or anniversary would usually be responded to in kind, with high levels of affiliative behavior. Conversely, overlooking a family member's birthday or other important dates would probably be matched by comparable neglect. This mirroring of actions and inactions illustrates the shared environment or shared family effect on behavior.

Parents can sway children's behaviors in one direction or another, but they can rarely change their child's basic personality traits. Most mothers and fathers know this, especially parents of fraternal twins and virtual twins, who constantly witness the simultaneously different expression of personality traits in their two same-aged children.

6. *Identical twin aunts and uncles are more involved with their nieces and nephews (i.e., their cotwins' children) than fraternal twin aunts and uncles.*
   Reality Check: True
   Short Answer: As I've indicated throughout this book, identical twin aunts and uncles are the "genetic mothers and fathers" of their cotwin's children. In contrast, fraternal twin aunts and uncles enjoy the usual biological aunt/uncle–niece/nephew relationships with their cotwin's sons and daughters. It is, therefore, not surprising to find that identical twin aunts and uncles scored higher than fraternal twins aunts and uncles on a questionnaire designed to assess the twins' social closeness toward their nieces and nephews. Sample questions were, "This child thinks of him/herself as

one of my children," and "I generally think of this child as my own," to which the twins answered either true, somewhat true, or untrue.

I could not help but think of my own twin situation as I reviewed the results from this study. My fraternal twin sister Anne has a son whom I love very much, but I would never consider him to be my own child. I was also reminded of my conversation with an identical twin whose sister passed away, leaving several young children behind. The surviving twin was adamant about gaining custody of these children, feeling that she had greater claim to them than the children's father. I never learned the outcome of this case, but it made a deep impression on me, causing me to think carefully about the driving force behind this twin's behavior that I discuss in more detail later in this chapter.

More of the Story: Evolutionary psychology, a relatively recent discipline, formalized in the late 1970s and early 1980s, goes beyond the "what" of behavior to address the "why." This discipline is dedicated to finding the psychological mechanisms that evolved to meet the environmental challenges and demands that confronted our ancestors. An evolutionary perspective helps us understand why reputation matters, why children are important, and why males and females respond differently to partner infidelity. Evolutionary psychology also provides insights into altruism and why the desire to help others evolved.

A longstanding dilemma for evolutionary researchers has been accounting for altruistic behavior, because acting altruistically involves some cost to the self while benefitting another. In 1964, the evolutionary biologist William D. Hamilton resolved this impasse by proposing that we are predisposed to be more altruistic toward close kin (i.e., individuals likely to carry common genes) than distant kin (individuals likely to share relatively fewer common genes)—this would be an indirect means by which one's genes are transmitted to future generations. Hamilton also came up with the concept of *inclusive fitness,* defined as an individual's reproductive success (transmitting copies of one's genes to future generations by having children), plus the reproductive success of relatives other than children (the transmission of copies of one's genes by close relatives who share some of these genes). Of course, people would not consciously calculate their degree of genetic relatedness toward a potential recipient before performing a kind deed—but perhaps perceptions of similarity trigger emotions giving rise to a range of helping behaviors that are more or less likely, depending on the relatedness and circumstances of the recipient.

I have always believed that identical and fraternal twins are ideal subjects for testing evolutionary-based hypotheses related to affiliation and cooperation. That is because the two twin types differ in their degrees of genetic relatedness, but their same age and social background hold many complicating factors constant. I, therefore, launched the "Twins Who Are Parents Study" to compare the social relatedness of identical and fraternal twin aunts and uncles toward their nieces and nephews [12–14]. Every participant completed a Closeness Questionnaire, specially designed for this study. The two main findings from this ongoing study are that (1) identical twins express greater overall closeness toward their cotwin's children than fraternal twins, and (2) regardless of twin type, twins with female cotwins express greater closeness toward their cotwins' children than do twins with male cotwins.

Identical twin aunts and uncles are as closely related to their nieces and nephews as the twin mother or father who conceived these children. It may be that these identical twins perceive similarities between themselves and these children, giving rise to the greater social closeness they express, relative to the fraternal twin aunts and uncles. (This is similar to the process that may underlie the close social relations between identical twins that I described earlier.)

The greater closeness indicated for the children of twin sisters than twin brothers is consistent with predictions from *paternity uncertainty*. In other words, males can never be sure that a child born to their partner is truly theirs because of concealed ovulation (there are no clear signs to indicate when a woman is ovulating), internal fertilization (human eggs are fertilized inside the body so it is unclear if and when fertilization occurs), and continuous female receptivity (human females can engage in sexual activity at any time in the menstrual cycle). In contrast, there is certainty that a child born to a sister is a true genetic relative—if a woman bears a child, of course it is *hers*—possibly enhancing feelings of social connectedness toward that child on the part of aunts and uncles.

I was surprised that the frequency of gift giving and the cost of gifts presented to nieces and nephews did not differ between identical and fraternal twin aunts and uncles. Perhaps such behaviors are guided by societal expectations, limiting gift giving to birthdays and holidays. However (regardless of their own sex), twins with female cotwins gave more gifts to their nieces and nephews than did twins with male cotwins, consistent with expectations from paternity uncertainty.

The data from this study have been analyzed 3 times as the sample size increased, yet the results did not change. Were I to replicate this study I would question the children about their social relationships with their identical or fraternal twin parent and twin aunt or uncle. I might ask a niece if she feels as close to her aunt as she does to her mother (her aunt's identical twin), or ask a nephew to compare his degree of physical resemblance to his uncle and to his father (his uncle's identical twin). This information would provide another approach to the class of questions concerning genetic influences on social relatedness. Such a study would further illustrate the many ways twin methods can be used in psychological research, and offer another example of how informative twins can be just by acting naturally.

7. *The enduring social bond between twins is shaped by their interactions in the womb.*

Reality Check: Unlikely

Short Answer: I was fascinated the first time I sat through a short film featuring pairs of fetal twins who seemed happily at play. It was the mid-1990s and I was at a meeting of the *International Society for Twin Studies*. One fetal twin initiated a movement, such as kicking the leg of the cotwin and causing the cotwin to move. Since then, I have seen more of these cinematic wonders made by Dr. Alessandra Piontelli from Italy and Dr. Birgit Arabin from the Netherlands. The different twins variously hug, kiss, and even take swings at each other.

It is tempting to believe that twins' prenatal interactions lay the basis for the social relationship they will later display as children and as adults. A mothers of twins club bulletin noted that twins "start *deliberately* (my emphasis) interacting at 14 weeks" [15]. And according to some members of the media, "There's been a long-held belief that twins have a special bond. And it looks like it *starts* (my emphasis) when they're in the womb together" [16]. Finally, a study of the effects of cobedding on preterm twins' stress (following heel lance to obtain blood for phenylketonuria testing) asserted that cobedding twins allows "recognition of familiar auditory and olfactory stimuli and a *continuation* (my emphasis) of the twin relationship that began in utero" (p. 598) [17].

These statements fuel a mythconception that is unlikely, but is also difficult to disprove conclusively. Twins *do* interact with one another in the womb, but there is no hard evidence that their physical interactions *before* birth lay the basis for the social interactions they experience *after* birth. At the start of their prenatal encounters, identical twins are more behaviorally alike than male–female twins, but this difference disappears during prenatal life [18]. I believe that if twins' prenatal behaviors were tied in a meaningful way to their later social relationship, then interactional differences between identical and fraternal twins should be observed in the womb—and they are not. Scores of studies tell us that identical twins share a closer social bond than fraternal twins—I would, therefore, argue that the social bond between twins develops *after* birth, as the similar tendencies and temperaments of identical twins draw them more closely together than fraternal twins (see number 2).

It is also important to consider the distinction between *interaction* and *social interaction*. Interaction can occur without awareness of others and actions can occur without intent (e.g., intrauterine kicking and punching). In contrast, social interaction requires awareness of others and actions can be expressed with intent (e.g., young infants' social smiles and cries for attention). It is possible that some of what transpires between twins in the womb affects their relationship after birth— perhaps the odor or sound of a newborn twin, familiar from prenatal days, begins or continues their earliest interactions as some researchers have alleged. And perhaps prenatal experiences facilitate relations between reared-apart twins when they are reunited as adults. I believe that both possibilities are very unlikely, but we simply do not know.

More of the Story: As I indicated earlier, twins interact physically with one another before they are born—in fact, fetal movements are detected at about the 7th gestational week. At this time, most twins are too far apart in the womb to touch and most are separated by their amniotic membranes. But by weeks 11–13 most twins engage in physical contact with one another and react to that contact from the cotwin—Dr. Piontelli calls this "intrapair stimulation" (p. 35)—and by week 15 such behavior occurs constantly [18]. Twins move their arms and legs, touch their heads and limbs and hang on to their umbilical cords.

Prenatal twins' interactive behaviors do not appear to be expressed with any intention or awareness of the other. Low oxygen tension in fetal blood, as well as pregnanolone and prostaglandin D2 that are provided by the placenta, keep the fetus sedated [19]. If prenatal cotwins' interactive activities influence the nature of their postnatal relationship, then identical twins should show more sustained coordinated behaviors in the womb than fraternal twins, but that is not the case. Research conducted in 2012 found no evidence that fetal dichorionic twins' body movements and rest–sleep cycles are coordinated, challenging some previous reports. It seems, instead, that any synchronized behaviors displayed by twins are infrequent, brief, and unintentional [20].

I am, however, curious about some parents' observations of their young single surviving twin children who variously crave physical contact, show unusual interest in twins, and/or talk about twins often. Consider this comment sent to me by a surviving triplet:

"I forget how old I was when my mom told me, but when I was a young girl, she told me that I was a triplet and my triplet brother and sister were miscarried. In my crib, I would sleep with my head in the corner. As a young adult, I am very cuddly and if there's a sleepover where lots of people have to share one mattress, I'm very content being the one squished in the middle. I wonder if this could have something to do with being the Baby B in a set of triplets."

The triplet quoted above made a convenient connection between sharing prenatal quarters with two others and currently feeling comfortable in small spaces. However, a causal relationship cannot be assumed, especially since most miscarriages occur before the 12th week of pregnancy, limiting shared intrauterine time [21]. Dr. Piontelli suggests that the tactile sensations twins experience in the womb might be recalled at some level. That may be possible, but has not been demonstrated conclusively and so cannot be linked in a meaningful way to being born a twin or triplet.

8. *Twins growing up apart sense the absence of their cotwin.*
   Reality Check: False
   Short Answer: There is no evidence that twins separated at birth and raised in different homes are aware of being a twin. During my 9-year association with the Minnesota Study of Twins Raised Apart and beyond, I have met people who (as adults) were shocked to discover that they had a twin brother or sister. Many of them had been adopted and learned the news from adoption agencies while searching for their biological family members or from other sources.

   My latest example of discovering one's twinship later in life concerns fraternal twins, Ann Hunt and Elizabeth (Liz) Hamel, born in England in 1936 [22]. Separated at 5 months of age, Ann was given up for adoption, while Liz was raised by the twins' single biological mother; Liz and her mother moved to the United States when Liz was in her 20s. Ann never knew she had a twin, while Liz (who learned this from her mother) believed that finding her sister in another country would be too difficult. But when Ann's daughter Samantha conducted a search for her mother's biological relatives she discovered that her mother had a twin sister living in Oregon and tracked her down. The twins' reunion at 78 years of age, witnessed by their children, my research team, and the BBC, occurred on my campus in Fullerton, California, in May 2014. The event was thrilling, moving, and unforgettable. Ann and Liz are now featured in the *Guinness World Records* book as the world's longest separated pair of twins [23].

A sad ending to this story is that Liz passed away the following November, just 6 months after meeting her twin. But Ann is so grateful for the brief time they enjoyed together, as are their children who discovered new aunts, uncles, nieces, nephews, and cousins. When Ann turned 80, her beautifully decorated cake read, "Happy 80th Birthday, Ann & Liz."

More of the Story: We know that twins growing up together respond to one another as social beings quite early in infancy, possibly before nontwin infants for whom exchange of smiles and evaluation of peer behaviors have been observed at 6 months [24,25]. Pediatrician, T. Berry Brazelton, offered this description: "As early as three and four months of age, when one [twin] baby was out of the room the other seemed disoriented and looked around as if watching and waiting... when they were propped up facing each other, they played and cooed for long periods. At times, the pleasure they gave each other seemed more important than anything the parents could offer..." (p. 84) [26]. No doubt, twins' physical proximity enhances their mutual responsivity, behavior that could conceivably evolve between some unrelated near-in-age infants.

Twins raised apart, even after spending their first 2–3 years together, would not recall such early interactions with one another. In June 2010 I met Tairi, an identical twin from Puerto Rico who was inadvertently switched at birth, but returned to her biological family at 18 months when the exchange was discovered. Not surprisingly, Tairi has no recollection of her first home or her first "twin"—memories are typically not recalled until children reach their 3rd birthday [27].

This discussion made me wonder—when do twins become aware that they are part of a multiple birth set? We do not know exactly when the concepts of twins and twinning are acquired, but we do know that they have to be taught. I can recall my mother explaining the "twin facts of life" to me when I was about 4 years old...And in my opinion, twins reared apart are our best test of that question. The reared-apart twins I have studied, such as Roger and Tony, Debbie and Sharon, and Samantha and Anaïs, despite having shared a womb, did *not* know that they were twins until they learned this from a relative, gained access to their medical records, or underwent DNA testing after being mistaken for someone else. There is no evidence of intrauterine knowledge of twinship. True, some adopted away twins have told me that once they met their cotwin they felt that a missing piece in their lives had finally been filled. I believe them. But many adopted individuals experience such feelings of "inner emptiness," even those from loving homes— and many people, not just reared-apart twins or adoptees, await the person, place, or event that will make their lives complete [28].

Some beliefs about twins, namely, those concerning the effects of prenatal environments on their evolving twin relations, cannot be fully examined because the technology needed to do so is unavailable. Perhaps one day we will have better methods for monitoring twins' interactions in the womb, revealing findings that will surprise and excite us.

In the final chapter, I will address some unresolved issues in twin research, such as which investigator conducted the first twin study and the risk of breast cancer among mothers of twins and twins. I will also take a look at twin research today and offer an opinion about where it should be headed tomorrow. For example, research on twins with special needs is a growing area, given the dramatic increases in twinning rates, but there are misunder-standings about how disabled twins affect the family, especially the mentally and physically able cotwin.

Trends are also toward the increased use of twins in epigenetic, molecular, and genomic studies, but there are limits to what these studies can reveal, and these limits are important to understand. I will talk about that. The role that the classic identical–fraternal twin comparison will play in future twin research has come into question. However, knowing which behavioral and medical traits are interesting and important for genetic stud-ies are decided largely from studying twins up close and listening to their life stories in person. That is also where the fun is. That is why I am con-vinced that the simple and elegant identical–fraternal twin comparison will never lose its allure. I will talk about that, too.

REFERENCES

[1] Available from: http://www.journalnow.com/gallery/news/th-bunker-family-reunion/collection_3181b062-153f-11e4-84c5-001a4bcf6878.html?mode=nogs.
[2] N.L. Segal, Entwined Lives: Twins and What They Tell Us About Human Behavior, Plume, New York, NY, (2000).
[3] A.D. Dreger, One of Us: Conjoined Twins and the Future of Normal, Harvard University Press, Cambridge, (2004).

[4] N.L. Segal, S.L. Hershberger, S. Arad, Meeting one's twin: perceived social closeness and familiarity, Evol. Psychol. 1 (1) (2003) 70–95.

[5] N.L. Segal, Twins: the finest natural experiment, Pers. Individ. Dif. 49 (4) (2010) 317–323.

[6] N.L. Segal, Twin, adoption and family methods as approaches to the evolution of individual differences, in: D.M. Buss, P. HawleyBuss (Eds.), The evolution of personality and individual differences, Oxford University Press, Oxford, 2011, pp. 303–307.

[7] I'm Not a Look-Alike! Available from: http://www.francoisbrunelle.com/web/francois_brunelleindex.html. Other websites also purport to unite look-alikes. Available from: https://www.dramafever.com/news/doppelgnger-wesbite-will-help-you-find-your-look-a-like-anywhere-in-the-world/.

[8] D.C. Rowe, The Limits of Family Influences: Genes, Experience, and Behavior, Guilford Press, New York, (1994).

[9] N.L. Segal, Personality similarity in unrelated look-alike pairs: addressing a twin study challenge, Pers. Individ. Dif. 54 (1) (2013) 23–28.

[10] N.L. Segal, I.I. Gottesman, N.G. Martin, E. Turkheimer, M. Gatz, The value of twin studies: a response to Slate Magazine, August 2011.

[11] A. Tellegen, D.T. Lykken, T.J. Bouchard Jr., K.J. Wilcox, N.L. Segal, S. Rich, Personality similarity in twins reared apart and together, J. Pers. Soc. Psychol. 54 (6) (1988) 1031–1039.

[12] N.L. Segal, J.P. Seghers, W.D. Marelich, M. Mechanic, R. Castillo, Social closeness of monozygotic and dizygotic twin parents toward their nieces and nephews, Eur. J. Pers. 21 (4) (2007) 487–506.

[13] N.L. Segal, W.D. Marelich, Social closeness and gift giving by MZ and DZ twin parents toward nieces and nephews: an update, Pers. Individ. Dif. 50 (1) (2011) 101–105.

[14] N.L. Segal, S. Mollova, W.D. Marelich, K. Preston, K, Does relatedness affect social closeness toward nieces and nephews?, Society for Personality and Social Psychology: Evolutionary Psychology Pre-Conference, Long Beach, CA, February 26, 2015.

[15] York White Rose, Interesting Facts About Twins, 2014.

[16] H. Scribner, Desert New/Twins Interact With One Another As Early as 14 Weeks in the Womb. Available from: http://newsok.com/twins-interact-with-each-other-as-early-as-14-weeks-in-the-womb/article/5459428.

[17] M.L. Campbell-Yeo, C.C. Johnston, K.S. Joseph, et al. Co-bedding between preterm twins attenuates stress response after heel lance, Clin. J. Pain 30 (7) (2014) 598–604.

[18] A. Piontelli, Twins: From Fetus to Child, Routledge, London, (2002).

[19] H. Lagercrantz, J.-P. Changeux, The emergence of human consciousness: from fetal to neonatal life, Pediatr. Res. 65 (3) (2009) 255–260.

[20] E.J.H. Mulder, J.B. Derks, M.W.M. de Laat, G.H.A. Visser, Fetal behavior in normal dichorionic twin pregnancy, Early Hum. Dev. 88 (3) (2012) 129–134.

[21] Miscarriage. Mayo Clinic. Available from http://www.mayoclinic.org/diseases-conditions/pregnancy-loss-miscarriage/symptoms-causes/dxc-20213666.

[22] N.L. Segal, F.A. Cortez, L. Zettel-Watson, B.J. Cherry, M. Mechanic, J.E. Munson, J.M.A. Velázquez, B. Reed, Genetic and experiential influences on behavior: twins reunited at seventy-eight years, Pers. Individ. Dif. 73 (January) (2015) 110–117.

[23] Guinness World Records 2016, Humans: Twins, 2015, Guinness World Records Limited, London, UK, pp. 62–63.

[24] G.W. Ladd, Children's peer relations and social competence: a century of progress, Yale University Press, New Haven, CT, (2005).

[25] J.K. Hamlin, K. Wynn, P. Bloom, Social evaluation by preverbal infants, Nature 450 (7169) (2007) 557–560.

[26] T.B. Brazelton, It's twins, Redbook Magazine 80 (1980) 83–84.

[27] L.E. Berk, Child Development, nineth ed, Pearson, Upper Saddle River, NJ, (2013).

[28] J.P. Triseliotus, In Search of Origins, Kegan Paul, London, (1973).

CHAPTER 13

Of Two Minds: Old Questions and Fresh Answers

Advances in data collection and data analysis since the 1980s have elevated twin research to celebrity status within many behavioral, medical, and social science fields. This final chapter is an exploration of how twin research evolved: where it has been, where it is going, and where I would like to see it go. Along the way I will touch upon some twin-related questions and controversies that persist because of challenges from new findings, as well as from old findings that have been overlooked.

LOOKING BACK

Early twin studies offered readers a more detailed description of twins' lives than the studies conducted today, particularly the ways in which specific environmental events could craft behavioral and physical differences between two genetically identical people. The three early volumes on reared-apart twins appended each twin pair's rich life history material to the quantitative findings [1,2]. We learn that twins Helen and Gladys showed the largest difference in measured intelligence of the 19 pairs studied by Newman, Freeman, and Holzinger in 1937. These twins also had the largest difference in their educational background—Helen completed high school and college, whereas Gladys did not advance beyond the third grade. Twins Polly and Megan studied by James Shields in 1962 were both obsessional in their behavior, but Megan was more so, possibly due to her more obsessional father and husband. And twins Dorthe and Petrine described by Juel-Nielsen in 1965 recognized important social and economic differences in their childhood homes, but claimed to be more like each other in personality than the unrelated siblings with whom they were raised. Both twins were described as extroverted, emotional, and energetic, but there were differences between them. Petrine, raised as an only child by a wealthy family, spoke more elegantly and cultivated her words more carefully than Dorthe, raised with four older siblings by a poor family. Interestingly, however, Dorthe was "more apt to finery" and appeared "more ladylike" than her twin sister (p. 247). The twins did not show marked differences in general intellectual ability despite

Twin Mythconceptions
http://dx.doi.org/10.1016/B978-0-12-803994-6.00013-5

their different rearing environments. Both twins were in school from ages 7 to 14, but Petrine attended a private school, while Dorthe attended a public school.

I treasure the twin studies published during the early 1900s through the 1970s, especially the landmark books I consider to be classics, and which had such significant impact on ongoing twin research at the time. (My top 10 twin volumes are listed in Appendix 4, reproduced from a 2015 article I authored on this topic for the journal *Twin Research and Human Genetics*. [3]) Researchers in those days were less limited by participant privacy issues, allowing them to publish twins' life history material and photographs along with the scientific findings, although the twins' names were disguised. Some instances of highly unethical practices regarding research participant safety and welfare, the greater ease of personal information acquisition, and the increased trend toward filing lawsuits when participant safety and confidentiality are compromised have made current investigators exceedingly cautious over the material they include in their scientific papers [4]. In addition, competition for publication has reduced the page limits of manuscripts accepted by many scientific journals, such that quantitative findings have gained priority over qualitative descriptions.

Photographs of the twins were a fascinating and informative addition to these older texts, offering readers a glimpse of how much shared genes shape the physical appearance of MZ twins at just about any age. These pictures made the data visually alive by showing the same two receding hairlines, or the same hand and leg positions. Unfortunately, this material is rarely published today, given the constraints on investigators imposed by institutional review boards worried about confidentiality breaches and days in court. I appreciate and support the need to protect research participants, but twins are unique people—they recognize their value to science and many want to share their experiences, not just their data. Of course, obtaining twins' permission to publish their personal stories is mandatory.

I learned a lot about twins from the classic books that I studied as a student. Today, I keep these books in special places in both my office and home. When I reread certain sections I am impressed still by the investigators' keen scientific insights that remain relevant today. In his 1962 study of British reared-apart twins, Dr. James Shields discussed the unusual situation of his youngest subjects, 8-year-old Jessie and Winifred [5]. These identical twin girls lived apart, but in the same town. After meeting at the age of 2 they were strongly attracted to one another, and eventually ended up in the same school at the age of 5. Their teacher claimed that despite not knowing they were twins, "they were never apart, wanted to sit at the same desk and progressed at the same rate" p. 191 [5].

Soon after that the young girls discovered for themselves that they were twins. But it was not to be. Jessie's mother discouraged the twins from meeting and purposely enrolled her daughter in a different school; regardless, the girls continued to meet in a park after school hours. (When they turned 8 they attended the same school again, for administrative reasons.) These observations of the twins' close social connections led Shields to wonder if there was a biological basis for the strong attraction he observed between many of the identical cotwins that he studied. In support of this idea, he referenced research showing that separated cattle twins pick each other out from among their nonrelatives, and end up grazing together in farm fields. Such instances of social attraction in the nonhuman animal literature do not end with cows. Another example is a ewe's (mother lamb's) preference for a baby lamb taken from her at birth, compared with an unrelated lamb and, even further, zebra fishes' recognition of siblings with whom they were not raised [6,7].

Close genetic relatives are more likely to share genes coding for body odor than distant relatives. Studies show that nonhuman kin recognition happens when an animal detects familiar body odors in an unfamiliar animal. This recognition may explain why genetic relatives are more likely to associate with one another and to be closer together physically that nonrelatives. Human kin recognition is also affected by such cues, but these indicators are less accurate for humans and work alongside culturally based ways of identifying relatives, such as verbal labels (e.g., classification of individuals as one's cousin or great grandfather) and court rulings (e.g., assignment of legal parenthood to adoptive mothers and fathers) [8]. Furthermore, in the present period of DNA testing, laboratory analyses can alter one's sense of relatedness to a person, such as a father discovering that his alleged son was conceived by another male. Nevertheless, Shields's twin story and the following examples of evolving relationships between reared-apart relatives— *who did not know they were related*—support theories that acknowledge genetic influence on human social attraction.

SWITCHED AT BIRTH AND REARED APART

In Chapter 12 I referred to switched-at-birth identical male twins, Brent and George, from Canada. These 20-year-old twins met each other when George's friend Sasha introduced him to a look-alike (Brent) she had discovered at the University of Ottawa. Based on my interviews with the twins and with the members of Brent's family, I learned that George and his duplicate became instant friends, enjoying their striking similarities in appearance, taste in old movies, passion for board games, and mastery of sports statistics. They believed that these parallels in their lives were coincidental, a view that would eventually change. As the months passed, George and Brent began sharing stories from their childhood years, and learned that as newborns they had been in the same temporary foster care facility at the same time. The possibility that they could be identical twins began to dawn on them and was eventually confirmed by their matching DNA [9].

A classic work on twins is Amram Scheinfeld's 1967 book *Twins and Supertwins,* a volume that includes some material that is rarely found elsewhere. When I was a graduate student, Scheinfeld's volume alerted me to the first known case of switched-at-birth twins, born in 1941, in Fribourg, Switzerland. This extraordinary case involved the inadvertent exchange of a newborn twin (named Ernstli by the nontwin family who raised him) and singleton (named Paul by the twins' family who raised him). The switch was discovered when the twins were 6 and all three boys (Paul, Ernstli, and Philippe—the twin raised by the right family) ended up at the same school. The unmistakable physical resemblance between the two boys raised by different families (Philippe and Ernstli) shocked their parents and led to a series of medical tests (briefly discussed in Chapter 5) to determine if the look-alikes were truly twins—they were. The two switched boys (Ernstli and Paul) were returned to their biological families just days before they turned 7 as decided by the local judge, a traumatic event from which their families never recovered.

In 2013 I visited Fribourg, a large medieval town having a population of around 33,000, and was able to see the hospital where the twins were born [10]. This case sparked my interest in finding other switched-at-birth twin pairs (of which there are 9 recorded cases worldwide), given the implications for mother–infant identification, hospital management of newborns, legal decisions regarding switched children, parent–child attachment, and nature–nurture questions [11]. The most recent case, discovered in 2014, involves two pairs of identical twins from Bogotá, Colombia, that I described in Chapter 2.

Earlier, I also mentioned several sets of reared-apart opposite-sex twins who, unaware that they were twins, fell in love, married, and raised families. These opposite-sex twins described very strong attraction and love for one another, and some even continued their relationship after learning the truth. I have also learned about pairs of siblings and half-siblings who were friends before learning they were genetically related [12]. The genetic underpinnings of social attraction between people constitutes a key area of study, known as kinship genetics, for evolutionary psychologists today.

WORTH A SECOND LOOK

A look back at historical developments in twin research highlights issues that were effectively resolved years ago, but have stimulated fresh discussion in light of new findings and challenges. John Loehlin and Robert Nichols's 1976 investigation, *Heredity, Environment, and Personality: A Study of 850 Sets of Twins* (see Chapter 8), showed that identical twins who were treated alike, dressed alike, played together, spent considerable time together, had the same teacher, and slept in the same room were *not* more similar in personality and ability than twins who were raised differently. Other studies have confirmed this 40-year-old finding, namely, that treating twins alike does not make them alike in ability, personality, or other areas, but twin study critics turn a blind eye. Clinging to environmentalist perspectives (the *nurture* part of the nature–nurture equation), these critics fail (even refuse) to acknowledge significant genetic effects on behavior, despite the consistent evidence from twin studies [13,14].

Debates are evolving in other areas of twin research. I will introduce the next one by paraphrasing a famous line from the 1950s television show *To Tell the Truth:* "Will the real inventor of the twin method please stand up?" Anyone who watched this program will recall that it centered around three individuals, all claiming to be the same inventor, specialist, or expert. The three individuals answered questions from a celebrity panel whose task was to separate the real luminary from the imposters. This program reminds me of the controversies over (1) who invented the classic twin method of comparing trait similarity in genetically identical twins to that of nonidentical twins to assess the degree of genetic influence on that trait, and (2) who conducted the first twin study. A distinction between the inventor of the method and the first person to use it is generally not made, but these two roles deserve separate treatment. At the center of these two controversies is the British investigator, Sir Francis Galton.

As I indicated in Chapter 2, Galton's famous 1875/1876 essays show how twins can be used to address the relative effects of nature and nurture on human traits. The question is: Did Galton really invent the classic twin method? Countless scientific articles and textbooks recognize Galton as the "Father of the Twin Method," a role that my colleagues and I never questioned, having studied Galton's signature pieces. However, a 1990 paper triggered a debate over whether or not Galton deserves this recognition. This paper came as a surprise to me and to many of my colleagues that was impossible to ignore, given the importance of maintaining an accurate historical record.

Galton's primacy was first questioned by Richard Rende and coworkers in 1990 on the grounds that Galton did not explicitly state that comparing the two types of twins (known today as MZ and DZ) offered evidence of hereditary influence [15]. According to Rende, Galton was interested in knowing how environmental influences caused some cotwins who were initially alike in appearance and behavior to become different, and caused some initially different cotwins to become alike. He explained that Galton was aware that there were two types of twins (the look-alikes and the nonlook-alikes), but thought that *all* twins were genetically identical. Given the foregoing, Rende credited both the American psychologist Curtis Merriman and the German dermatologist Hermann Siemens for their 1924 discovery of the classic twin method as we know it today.

Rende also asserted that Galton's failure to continue his twin research after 1875 showed that Galton did not realize the value of comparing the two types of twins to assess genetic influence. This is not necessarily true—people begin and end their research projects for all sorts of reasons, most likely making Rende's position on this point one of conjecture.

Not everyone agreed with Rende, and rallied in support of Galton. According to biographer Nicholas W. Gillham, whose book appeared 10 years after Rende's publication, Galton knew that there were two classes of twins, those "closely alike in boyhood and youth," and those "who were exceedingly unlike in childhood" (p. 193) [16]. Of course, the biological bases of twinning had not yet been established in Galton's time, and the words *monozygotic* and *dizygotic* did not appear until 1922 (proposed by Leslie Brainerd Arey, as indicated in Scheinfeld's list of "Trailblazers"). Still, as many researchers do today, Galton gathered information about the twins' behavioral traits, physical features, health histories, and life events by sending "circulars of inquiry" to twins and the relatives of twins. Gillham argued that, "Galton was building a qualitative case for nature's importance in determining human behavior as psychologists have often done since, though they also use quantitative tools such as the IQ tests that were unavailable to Galton (p. 194)" [16].

In 2003, 2 years after Gillham's book appeared, another Galton biographer, Michael Bulmer, disputed Gillham's conclusion that Galton was the inventor of the classic twin method. Bulmer wrote, "Galton thought that the zygote [fertilized egg] contains a large number of hereditary elements, which collectively form the 'stirp' [17]. According to Galton, all twins and nontwin siblings had identical stirps, and only those pairs exposed to the same prenatal developmental events went on to become what we now know to be identical or MZ twins. In other words, only some of the many hereditary elements composing the stirp developed into the cells of the adult, while the rest remained latent. Genetic differences between twins and siblings, despite their identical stirps, were due to differences in the cells derived from them. Bulmer continued, "Thus, Galton did not use the classical twin method of comparing the behavioral and physical similarities of identical and fraternal twins because he did not know that dizygotic twins only share half their genes while monozygotic twins are genetically identical" (p. 66) [18].

The debate about Galton's role in the history of twin research was continued by biologist and statistician Oliver Mayo who claimed that, "The origins of this [twin] method are frequently and correctly traced to Galton (1875)" p. 237 [19]. Mayo acknowledged that limited knowledge about twinning prevented Galton from making the biological distinction between the two types of twins, but that Galton "was very close."

To round out the debate over luminaries and imposters, in 2005 researchers seized the twin study crown from Merriman and Siemens by crediting the German ophthalmologist Walter Jablonski with conducting the first classical twin study. Jablonski's 1922 research, comparing the visual similarities of 40 identical and 12 fraternal twin pairs, places him 2 years ahead of Merriman and Siemens who published their studies in 1924 [20]. Jablonski showed that total refraction (failure of the eye to properly bend incoming light, leading to blurriness) and total astigmatism (blurred or distorted vision due to the shape of the cornea, or front layer of the eye) were more alike in identical than fraternal twins, demonstrating genetic influence on these conditions. Jablonski's study clearly predates those of both Merriman and Siemens, but whether Jablonski or Galton deserve credit for conducting the first classical twin study can still be questioned.

As I followed this debate it occurred to me that Galton may truly have done the first classical twin study, *but did not know it.* It is possible to invent something for one purpose that actually serves a different function. In 1924, the Kimberly–Clark Company marketed cellucotton (originally used in gas masks during World War I) as facial tissues for make-up removal [21]. Women loved them, but complained to the company that their spouses and children used them for nose wiping. When the company determined that 60% of the people used the tissues for this other purpose, they were remarketed as disposable handkerchiefs and sales doubled. The facial tissues were performing like handkerchiefs, only the manufacturers didn't know it. Even if Galton used twins to find environmental reasons for their differences and could not have known the biological distinction between the two types, he did compare look-alike (presumably identical) and nonlook-alike (presumably fraternal) twins, and concluded that, "nature prevails enormously over nurture (p. 404) [22]." His conclusion came from observing that some twins with very different experiences were very much alike. I believe Galton was conducting a classic twin study all along.

Of course, as I explained in Chapter 1 and elsewhere, cotwins' physical similarity is not a precise way of establishing twin type unless it is assessed through standard physical resemblance questionnaires developed for this purpose. Items concern twins' similarity in physical features, such as height and weight, and degree of confusion (e.g., frequently, occasionally, or never) by parents, teacher, and friends. Recall that just one question—were you and your twin as alike as two peas in a pod?—correctly classified 98% of the twin pairs in a Swedish study. The first twin-typing questionnaire was not developed until 1961, but Galton may have applied something similar in his own way, via his inquiries.

I know that the dialog about Sir Francis Galton will continue because it questions his role as a prominent individual whose contributions to twin research are at the very heart of our field. The future course of twin research will not be changed by this discussion—but challenges to long-held beliefs can be unsettling as well as enlightening for those who hold them, experiences to which both readers of this book and I can attest.

MIRROR-MIRROR

While studying twins Galton encountered examples of what might be misconstrued by some as twin telepathy—the mental communication of knowledge, thoughts, and feelings from one twin to another. Galton described a twin who correctly claimed that his brother was experiencing severe eye inflammation at the same time as he, as well as twins who gave each other identical gifts of glassware. I reviewed the findings on "twin-tuition" in an earlier chapter and concluded that the scientific evidence does not support such communication between cotwins. Still, I wonder if there could be a specific biological basis (linked to identical twins' shared genes) that explains the exceptional experiences some twins report. I think about mirror neurons.

Mirror neurons were discovered accidentally in 1996, in an animal laboratory in Parma, Italy [23]. When a monkey watched a lab assistant eat an ice cream cone, the scene activated areas of the monkey's brain that would resonate as if the monkey were doing the eating. This unexpected finding led to the discovery of mirror neurons, the nerve cells involved in our ability to respond to the actions and circumstances of others as if we were performing or experiencing them ourselves. Such abilities are crucial to a highly social species, such as humans—if we see a person laughing with delight or crying out in pain, we respond empathically because our brains simulate that experience, making it our own. Mirror neurons are located in the parts of our brain concerned with certain memory functions (medial temporal cortex) and emotional responses to events (medial frontal cortex) [24,25].

Of course, not everyone is equally adept at "reading" other people's emotions (let alone their own)—there are individual differences in the degree to which people experience empathy as I indicated in Chapter 10, and twin studies show that these differences are partly based on genetic factors. But there has never been a twin study of mirror neuron activation.

Mirror neurons work best in face-to-face interactions; therefore, the actions and experiences of one twin could be observed by his or her cotwin, while researchers monitor the brain activity of both. If identical twins show more synchronized patterns of mirror neuron activation than fraternal twins, this might partly explain the unusual behaviors of identical twins that are often chalked up to telepathy, such as finishing each other's sentences or sensing each other's feelings without conversation. (Not just twins, but some married couples, friends, and coworkers display these behaviors because of their long history of shared experiences, easily spreading the myth that telepathy is responsible.) I once proposed a twin study of mirror neuron activation to a brain researcher, but he appeared only mildly interested—our mirror neurons apparently misfired, but I still believe such a study is worth doing. Adding reared-apart twins as participants would further reveal how much shared genes affect neuronal harmony.

TWO TO ONE?

Our understanding of why some twins are raised by two different families has evolved over the years. In fact, when I tell people that I study reared-apart twins, many are surprised to hear that twins are still being separated. They are, but some reasons for their separation have changed. In the early 1900s, most twins were separated because their families could not afford to raise two children, their parents were physically and/or emotionally unable to care for them or their mother wished to avoid the stigma of bearing children out of wedlock.

Single parenthood is no longer a source of disgrace in many social circles and, in fact, some women and men choose to conceive and/or raise children on their own. But even today families lacking financial and/or emotional resources may decide to relinquish one or both twins, albeit often unhappily. Mothers and couples giving up both twins for adoption usually do so in their children's best interests and in response to the issues I've described, but there are no guarantees that the two children will stay together. Adoption workers are growing more sensitive to the social benefits gained by placing twins and siblings together (e.g., familiar companionship; continuing family tie). Currently, however, there are no rules or regulations in the United States mandating twins' or siblings' common placement, although there are government issued placement guidelines and visitation regulations [26]. I am unaware of formal rules or regulations having been implemented elsewhere.

Some infertile couples seek assisted reproduction without fully understanding that this may create two babies when only one is wanted—or they believe that implanting two embryos boosts the odds that just one will survive. Some couples may keep one twin and put the other twin up for adoption, although other couples in this predicament have chosen fetal reduction—reducing a pregnancy from twins to a singleton by intentional termination. Reasons for doing so variously include parents being of an older age (making them feel less able to cope with the demands of raising two crying infants who they fear will grow up into two sassy teenagers), concern that children from a previous marriage might feel neglected, anticipation of future career goals, and uncertainty about their financial security. Since the advent of assisted reproduction, physicians have reduced the high-risk quadruplet and triplet pregnancies to two in the hope of a successful outcome. However, many doctors are uneasy about reducing twins to one, even though twin births do pose greater risks than singleton births. Some doctors have refused to perform this procedure altogether. Doctors who have agreed to do it may advise their patients to hide their decision from family members and friends to avoid disapproval and blame [27].

The problems posed by higher-order multiple pregnancies have led some governments to take measures to reduce these risks. Federal regulations have been issued in England and Italy that limit the number of embryos to be implanted [28,29]. Such legislation has been introduced in several

US states, but has failed to pass. Some fertility specialists have argued that such regulations would limit the pregnancy chances of women who need more than two embryos to become pregnant, such as women older than 40. (A 2012 survey showed, however, that implanting three embryos rather than two did *not* result in more live births, but did lead to more unfavorable perinatal outcomes. Of course, decisions regarding embryo transfer are best made on a case-by-case basis [30]). There is fear, too, that regulations might be used in a discriminatory fashion against ethnic minorities and same-sex couples. And according to the *Assisted Reproductive Technology Surveillance and Research Team*, legislation restricting the number of transferred embryos is unlikely to be successful in the United States, given the uniqueness and complexity of its healthcare system [31].

In place of inflexible rules, recent *guidelines* have been developed by the *American Society for Reproductive Medicine* for women with a good pregnancy prognosis [32]. It is advised that, at most, two embryos should be implanted in women under the age of 37; and at most, three embryos in women between the ages of 38 and 40. Guidelines for patients with less certain reproductive histories suggest, at most, five embryos for women of ages 41–42; and one additional embryo for women in any of the above age categories who experienced two previously unsuccessful pregnancy attempts. Reproductive technology has improved considerably over the years, with the result that successful pregnancies are now more likely with just one embryo, but some unplanned twins will still be born—and some will be separated.

LOST AND FOUND

Until 2001, I was certain that I had discovered all the different reasons that would cause twins to be separated at birth. Then, I unexpectedly discovered a brand new source of reared-apart twins. I received an email message from a mother searching for information about how to raise *one* twin child adopted from China, who claimed (correctly) that no such literature existed [9].

Beginning in 1979, China limited urban couples to one child and rural couples to two as a way of curbing population growth. The Chinese people also maintain a traditional preference for male children in order to continue their family lineage, especially in rural areas. These two practices led to the sterilization of countless numbers of women and the abandonment of thousands of baby girls outside police stations and in market squares—among them twins [33]. Most of these twins were placed in orphanages prior to their adoption, but even then not all twins ended up together with their sister.

I have tracked down close to 20 pairs (both identical and fraternal) for an ongoing study of these twins' behavioral traits, physical features, and social adjustment. I did this with the help of referrals from families already in the study, news reports, and a website established for adopted twins and siblings from China. (The website that I used—sisterfar.com—is no longer active. There is, however, a larger organization known as *Families With Children From China* that includes local chapters in 47 states, several European nations, Canada, and Australia; fwcc.org). My study is unique in that the twins' development is recorded prospectively—as it happens—whereas the previous reared-apart twin studies included mostly adults whose life events and medical history information were gathered retrospectively—after the fact—without the benefits of ongoing observations from parents and teachers.

In my first analysis of the twins' reunions, based on their mothers' reports, I found that separated twins who met one another after 18 months of age were very strongly attracted to one another, more so than twins meeting before 18 months of age who were less socially and cognitively advanced [34]. As I gather additional cases I hope to compare the quality of social relationships between the identical and fraternal reared-apart Chinese twins, just as I did for the twins I studied in Minnesota. I applaud the twins' parents for bringing their families together as often as possible so the children feel more like twins than distant cousins. As a companion project, I am also studying Chinese twins who were fortunate enough to have been adopted together. I also applaud these adoptive families for their willingness to take in *two* children who, by virtue of being born together belong together.

Women who adopt twins become part of a unique class of mothers. While they encounter many of the joys and difficulties of natural parenting, they do not experience the physiological challenges of a multiple pregnancy, or its less well-touted advantages, which I explore later in the chapter.

MULTIPLE BIRTH MOTHERS AND FEMALE TWIN DAUGHTERS

My own mother was a worrier and she worried a lot about getting breast cancer. I was never sure why. Breast cancer did not run in her family and her yearly mammograms revealed nothing remarkable except for a small benign cyst when she was about 40. My mother lived until her late 80s, succumbing not to cancer, but to pulmonary fibrosis, a likely legacy of her childhood pneumonia.

When I wrote my first book, *Entwined Lives,* in the late 1990s, I came across two studies showing that my mother's cancer fears were largely unfounded [35]. These studies reported that bearing twins actually protected women aged 55 and younger *against* breast cancer [36,37]. This protective effect was explained by the higher levels of hormones to which women carrying multiples are exposed, relative to women carrying a singleton. One such hormone is alpha-feto protein, a fetal substance found in the mother's bloodstream and in amniotic fluid that can help identify some congenital defects [38]. One set of researchers puzzled over the additional finding that this barrier to breast cancer was *lost* if a woman experienced a subsequent singleton pregnancy. These two studies were conducted in 1989 and 1997, so for the sake of this book, I reviewed the more recent literature to see if this finding might have changed or been further confirmed.

A 2010 review of 18 studies found that breast cancer risk was 10–30% *lower* for mothers of multiples than mothers of singletons, but the results were inconsistent across the different studies [39]. Eight studies showed a link between having a multiple pregnancy and a reduced breast cancer risk, but the remaining studies did not. A 2007 study (surprisingly omitted from the 2010 review) also found a lower frequency of breast cancer in mothers of twins. This effect was particularly strong among women who had delivered their twins before the age of 30, and had had three or more pregnancies and had delivered their twins last [40]. In addition, the 2010 review described another likely benefit from a multiple pregnancy, namely, a 20–23% reduction in preeclampsia and/or gestational hypertension (both of which are forms of high blood pressure during pregnancy).

I regret that the disadvantages of having twins, such as preterm births, increased frequency of congenital anomalies among the infants, and financial pressures on the families have been emphasized to the near-exclusion of twinship's advantages, both physiological and social. Many formerly childless couples celebrate their "instant family" created from just one pregnancy. Parents of twins also enjoy seeing the companionship develop between their two children who serve as occasional "baby-sitters" for each other, freeing their parents from becoming full-time twin entertainers.

The health benefits to mothers of twins appear likely—they are not a myth, although they will not apply equally to every woman who bears twins. Still, I wish my mother (who had delivered my sister and me at the age of 32 as her first and only pregnancy) were around so I could ease her breast cancer concerns—somewhat.

This discussion of breast cancer reminds me of a 2000 study showing that postmenopausal fraternal female twins are at increased risk for this disease, relative to identical female twins, female twins with twin brothers, and female nontwins [41]. The explanation was that fraternal females are exposed to higher levels of prenatal hormones, such as estrogen and gonadotropin, because of their two separate placentae (or one large fused placenta), whereas two-thirds of identical twins have one shared placenta so experience lower hormone exposure. A problem with this study was that the pairs were classified as identical or fraternal simply by asking them what kind of twin they were, a procedure likely to introduce misclassification errors—identical twins are more likely to believe they are fraternal twins than fraternal twins are to believe they are identical. If the fraternal female twin sample included a high percentage of identical twins, then maybe fraternal females are *not* especially predisposed toward breast cancer.

As a member of a female fraternal pair, this report was not welcome news, but it was important to make this news known. I summarized this study in my regular column in the journal *Twin Research and Human Genetics* [42]. In the hope that this finding might be just a mythconception, I looked at more recent studies in this area.

A 2007 review of eight studies confirmed the earlier research in that six studies showed an increased breast cancer risk among fraternal same-sex female twins, while one study found no twin-type difference and one study found a lower risk among the fraternal twins [43]. It was surprising (and disappointing) to find so few recent studies in an area of such importance to the health of female multiples. However, I did discover two studies suggesting a *higher* breast cancer risk for female twins with twin brothers [44,45]. The dual explanation was that (1) male fetuses are exposed to higher levels of maternal hormones than female fetuses, so maternal hormones are increased for females from male–female pairs, and (2) in opposite-sex twin pairs the prenatal presence of a female prolongs the pregnancy for the male and increases the birth weight of the female, and higher birth weight in female cotwins with twin brothers is a key risk factor for breast cancer. I concur with the investigators that these explanations may account for the finding of increased breast cancer risk in female twins from opposite-sex twin pairs. However, some investigations have found no difference in early breast cancer risk between females from same-sex and opposite-sex twin pairs, so additional research is required.

The increased frequency of breast cancer in female twins is not a myth as I had hoped. Overall, the research indicates an elevated breast cancer risk for females from same-sex fraternal pairs, and possibly opposite-sex pairs.

The rate of fraternal twin births is rising, making it essential that researchers closely examine the origins, treatment, and prevention of breast cancer in female twins. The current goals of researchers in breast cancer studies are to find major genes associated with cancer, and more importantly to identify "common variants"—the many genes with small effects on breast cancer that are starting to have some clinical significance (J.R. Cerhan, Personal communication, April 3, 2016). It is also important for twins to inform their physicians of their multiple birth status and their cotwin's health history to improve the diagnosis, prediction, and prevention of this condition. Being born a twin, triplet, or more has never been included in medical history forms that individuals complete prior to examinations [46].

SPECIAL TWINS—SPECIAL NEEDS

There are other pressing concerns when it comes to twins. Rising twinning rates have also had the unfortunate effect of increasing the number of twins with developmental difficulties like learning delays and cerebral palsy that require professional intervention, such as remedial reading and physical therapy. The nature of twins' special needs (SN) is well documented in the scientific literature, but the efficacy of information distribution and resource delivery to parents is not. A former student of mine, Dr. Vanessa Costello-Harris, and I surveyed 30 women regarding their experiences raising 1 or 2 SN twins [47]. We learned that most families had received their children's diagnoses of autism, attention deficit disorder, or other behavioral conditions in a timely manner, but the few who did not understandably experienced considerable stress and concern. Some parents were not told about the specific symptoms their children might display, and how these children might differ from their unaffected cotwin: "I was never told that they would NOT cry when hungry or that being lethargic was normal," one parent claimed. However, the biggest complaint centered on learning what services were available and how to get them—nearly half of the mothers interviewed needed extra help in communicating with their child and would have appreciated additional nurse home visits. One mother recalled that she was never told what resources were available, but was only asked, "What do you want?" Such a situation with unclear choices prevents informed decision-making.

I would like to see greater attention and services directed toward helping families manage their SN twins. Informal meetings between parents with similarly affected children can be informative and supportive for mothers and fathers. I would also like to see greater assistance given to the unaffected cotwins who are often overlooked, and may be required to forfeit play dates and other fulfilling events because their SN cotwin requires unscheduled or immediate care.

Some healthy cotwins may feel jealous or resentful over the parental and professional attention lavished (necessarily) on their SN cotwin. I served as an expert witness on a case involving an identical twin toddler whose amputated leg resulted from medical malpractice. Feeling neglected, his able-bodied twin brother asked to have physical therapy sessions, as well! This request made a deep impression on me, underlining the importance of giving time and attention to these healthy twins.

In our current age of molecular genetic advances, many researchers and parents are hopeful that the genes linked to developmental difficulties can be identified. When that happens, it is likely that diagnoses can be made earlier, allowing corrective measures to be applied more expeditiously, thereby easing the suffering of everyone involved.

GENE HUNT

Identifying trait-relevant genes is a common goal, but a rare achievement. Finding the genes responsible for complex human traits, such as intelligence, personality, autism, height, and weight has been more arduous than anticipated [48]. Molecular genetic research shows that most human behaviors are influenced by many genes, each with a very small effect on a given behavior, rather than by one major gene that is chiefly responsible for that trait. Studies show that the genetic influence on height within a population is about 90%, but that about 50 genetic variants affecting height together explain less than 5% of the variation from person to person [49]. This has come to be known as the "missing heritability" problem—the inability of trait-relevant genes to account for the degree of genetic influence. However, a 2015 study (using simulated data) revised this figure upward—all 17 million genetic variants accounted for 56% of the variance. It was suggested that height heritability has been overestimated by previous studies and most likely lies between 60% and 70%. It was further suggested that the missing heritability might be small (Fig. 13.1) [50].

The slight associations found between genes and intelligence, or genes and personality, are hard to replicate by other researchers in studies of their own. Some of the difficulty in doing so comes from the small number of participants and various unknown factors at play. However, a recent genome-wide association study (GWAS) independently replicated a 2013 finding that linked three DNA sequences to educational attainment

Figure 13.1 Like many scientific advances DNA analysis enters the popular culture. *(Reprinted by permission. Image source: Cartoonstock.com).*

(highest level of school completed), using large twin and nontwin samples that only included people of European descent [51]. These DNA sequences had small effects on educational progress, but the replication is encouraging.

Molecular genetics has changed the nature of research on the origins of human traits. This has occurred partly because genetic influence on most studied human characteristics has been established. In addition, technological advances have enabled researchers to probe the entire complement of human genes, looking for associations between genes and a wide variety of behavioral and physical traits. However, I believe that this current trend does *not* threaten the future of the classical twin study because the MZ–DZ (identical–fraternal) comparison remains the simplest and the most exciting way to witness genetic effects first hand. Twin studies can, for example, forecast the amount of genetic influence that could be explained by newly discovered genetic variants [52]. Identical twins who differ in a behavior or disease offer opportunities to study the biological bases of these differences (possibly by epigenetic studies that examine gene expression) in two individuals with matching genes. Fraternal twins are better than full siblings for exploring associations between DNA markers and traits of interest (linkage studies) because fraternal twins are the same age and less likely to pose nonpaternity concerns—although recall that we do not know how often fraternal twins have different fathers.

I still marvel that the complex path from genes to behavior, with all its myriad potential prenatal and postnatal detours, can produce the highly matched intellectual, personality, and physical traits that set identical twins apart from all other biological and adoptive sibling and parent–child pairs. And I am in awe of the fact that fraternal twins (like myself), despite inhabiting "close quarters" from birth, so naturally and effortlessly traverse such different developmental routes. I see these trends repeated in my laboratory all the time—they enlighten twins, parents, teachers, and friends, while guiding the researchers searching for the genes that explain them.

Everyone knows at least one pair of twins. Everyone has his or her own theories, perspectives, and beliefs about human behavior, based on what is seen in the crib, observed in the classroom, or viewed from afar. It is easy to confuse myth for maxim, or fiction for fact, but doing so does not help the many twins and families who are eager for answers to questions about identical and fraternal twins' behaviors and development. Myths, while seemingly truthful and often entertaining, also mislead members of the general public who are fascinated with twins and want to learn how scientific findings from twin studies can enrich their understanding of their own lives and the lives of people that they know.

I have written this book to dispel, at least in part, the many mythconceptions that surround twins, their origins, their behaviors, and so many aspects of the lives they lead. In the years to come, new evidence will be discovered and new questions will be raised. And without a doubt, new fictional accounts will emerge and be told and retold, entering both public and professional arenas as *truth*. When that happens, I'll write my next book.

REFERENCES

[1] H.N. Newman, F.N. Freeman, K.J. Holzinger, Twins: A Study of Heredity and Environment, University of Chicago Press, Chicago, (1937).
[2] N. Juel-Nielsen, Individual and environment: Monozygotic twins reared apart, International Universities Press, New York, (1965).
[3] N.L. Segal, Twin classics: research that always inspires, Twin Res. Hum. Genet. 18 (4) (2015) 478–484.
[4] S.N. Hesse-Biber, P. Leavy, The ethics of social research, in: The Practice of Qualitative Research, Sage, Thousand Oaks, CA, pp. 59–89, 2010 (Chapter 4). Available from: http://www.sagepub.com/sites/default/files/upm-binaries/34088_Chapter4.pdf

[5] J. Shields, Monozygotic Twins: Brought Up Apart and Brought Up Together, Oxford University Press, London, UK, (1962).

[6] R.H. Porter, F. Lévy, P. Poindron, M. Litterio, B. Schaal, C. Beyer, Individual olfactory signatures as major determinants of early maternal discrimination in sheep, Dev. Psychobiol. 24 (3) (1991) 151–158.

[7] G. Gerlach, A. Hodgins-Davis, C. Avolio, C.C. Schunter, Kin recognition in zebrafish: a 24-hour window for olfactory imprinting, Proc. R. Soc. Lond. B 275 (1647) (2008) 2165–2170.

[8] J.H. Park, M. Schaller, M. Van Vugt, Psychology of human kin recognition: heuristic cues, erroneous inferences, and their implications, Rev. Gen. Psychol. 12 (3) (2008) 215.

[9] N.L. Segal, Indivisible by Two: Lives of Extraordinary Twins, Harvard University Press, Cambridge, MA, (2005).

[10] Population of Fribourg, Switzerland. Available from: http://population.mongabay.com/population/switzerland/2660718/fribourg

[11] N.L. Segal, Someone Else's Twin: The True Story of Babies Switched at Birth, Prometheus, Amherst, NY, (2011).

[12] N.L. Segal, J.L. Graham, U. Ettinger, Unrelated look-alikes: a replicated study of personality similarity and new qualitative findings on social relatedness, Pers. Individ. Dif. 55 (2) (2013) 169–176.

[13] B. Palmer, Double insanity: twin studies are pretty much useless, Slate Magazine, August 24, 2011. Available from: http://www.slate.com/articles/life/twins/2011/08/double_inanity.html

[14] N.L. Segal, Born together-reared apart: the landmark Minnesota Twin Study, Harvard University Press, Cambridge, MA, (2012) for discussion of this issue.

[15] R.D. Rende, R. Plomin, S.G. Vandenberg, Who discovered the twin method?, Behav. Genet. 20 (2) (1990) 277–285.

[16] N.W. Gillham, A Life of Sir Francis Galton: From African Exploration to the Birth of Eugenics, Oxford University Press, Oxford, UK, (2001).

[17] M. Bulmer, Francis Galton: Pioneer of Heredity and Biometry, Johns Hopkins University Press, Baltimore, MD, (2003).

[18] M. Bulmer, Commentary: Francis Galton and the twin method, Int. J. Epidemiol. 41 (4) (2012) 911–913.

[19] O. Mayo, Early research on human genetics using the twin method: who really invented the method?, Twin Res. Hum. Genet. 12 (3) (2009) 237–245.

[20] S.H.M. Liew, H. Elsner, T.D. Spector, C.J. Hammond, The first 'classical' twin study? Analysis of refractive error using monozygotic and dizygotic twins published in 1922, Twin Res. Hum. Genet. 8 (3) (2005) 198–200.

[21] B. Krols, Accidental Inventions: The Chance Discoveries That Changed our Lives, Insight Editions, Tectum Publishers, NV, San Rafael, CA, (2009).

[22] F. Galton, The history of twins as a criterion of the relative powers of nature and nurture, J. Anthropol. Inst. 5 (1975) 391–406.

[23] S. Blakeslee, Cells that read minds, New York Times, F1, 4, January 10, 2006.

[24] D.R. Euston, A.J. Gruber, B.L. McNaughton, The role of medial prefrontal cortex in memory and decision making, Neuron 76 (6) (2012) 1057–1070.

[25] A.R. Preston, J.D. Gabrieli, Different functions for different medial temporal lobe structures?, Learn. Mem. 9 (5) (2002) 215–217.

[26] Child Welfare Information Gateway, Sibling Issues in Foster Care and Adoption, 2013. Available from: https://www.childwelfare.gov/pubPDFs/siblingissues.pdf

[27] R. Padawer, The two-minus-one pregnancy, New York Times Magazine, MM22, August 14, 2011.

[28] R. Rao, How (not) to regulate ARTs: lessons from octomom, Albany Law J. Sci. Technol. 21 (2011) 313.

[29] J. Cafferty, Should Government Limit Embryo Implants?, March 4, 2009. Available from: http://caffertyfile.blogs.cnn.com/2009/03/04/should-government-limit-embryo-implants/.

[30] D.A. Lawlor, S.M. Nelson, Effect of age on decisions about the numbers of embryos to transfer in assisted conception: a prospective study, Lancet 379 (9815) (2012) 521–527.

[31] D.M. Kissin, S.L. Boulet, D.J. Jamieson, Fertility treatments in the United States, Obstet. Gynecol. 128 (2) (2016) 387–390.

[32] American Society for Reproductive Medicine, Society for Assisted Reproductive Technology Criteria for number of embryos to transfer: a committee opinion, Fertil. Steril. 99 (1) (2013) 44–46.

[33] China's preference for male children is less widespread today than it was thirty years ago, but some women who recall the discrimination they suffered due to being female partly explains male favoritism in that nation. "Preference of a son—A tendency preserved mainly by women?" Thinking Chinese. Available from: http://thinkingchinese.com/preference-of-a-son-a-tendency-preserved-mainly-by-women

[34] N.L. Segal, J.H. Stohs, K. Evans, Chinese twin children reared apart and reunited: first prospective study of co-twin reunions, Adopt. Q. 14 (1) (2011) 61–78.

[35] N.L. Segal, Entwined Lives: Twins and What They Tell Us About Human Behavior, Plume, New York, NY, 2000.

[36] H.I. Jacobson, W.D. Thompson, D.T. Janerich, Multiple births and maternal risk of breast cancer, Am. J. Epidemiol. 129 (5) (1989) 865–873.

[37] M.F. Murphy, M.J. Broeders, L.M. Carpenter, J. Gunnarskog, D.A. Leon, Breast cancer risk in mothers of twins, Br. J. Cancer 75 (7) (1997) 1066–1068.

[38] Alpha-feto protein, Oxford Dictionary, Oxford University Press, 2016.

[39] S. Nechuta, N. Paneth, E.M. Velie, Pregnancy characteristics and maternal breast cancer risk: a review of the epidemiologic literature, Cancer Causes Control 21 (7) (2010) 967–989.

[40] J. Ji, A. Fôrsti, J. Sundquist, K. Hemminki, Risks of breast, endometrial, and ovarian cancers after twin births, Endocr. Relat. Cancer 14 (s3) (2007) 703–711.

[41] J.R. Cerhan, L.H. Kushi, J.E. Olson, S.S. Rich, W. Zheng, A.R. Folsom, T.A. Sellers, Twinship and risk of postmenopausal breast cancer, J. Natl. Cancer Inst. 92 (3) (2000) 261–265.

[42] N.L. Segal, New breast cancer research: Mothers and Twins, Twin Res. 3 (2) (2000) 118–122.

[43] R. Troisi, N. Potischman, R.N. Hoover, Exploring the underlying hormonal mechanisms of prenatal risk factors for breast cancer: a review and commentary, Cancer Epidemiol. Biomark. Prev. 16 (9) (2007) 1700–1712.

[44] M. Kaijser, P. Lichtenstein, F. Granath, G. Erlandsson, S. Cnattingius, A. Ekbom, In utero exposures and breast cancer: a study of opposite-sexed twins, J. Natl. Cancer Inst. 93 (1) (2001) 60–62.

[45] B. Luke, M. Hediger, S.J. Min, M.B. Brown, R.B. Misiunas, V.H. Gonzalez-Quintero, et al. Gender mix in twins and fetal growth, length of gestation and adult cancer risk, Paediatr. Perinat. Epidemiol. 19 (s1) (2005) 41–47.

[46] N.L. Segal, A pair of meetings: Twins (UCLA Center for Society and Genetics) and the 13th International Society for Twin Studies Congress (ISTS, Seoul, South Korea), Twin Res. Hum. Genet. 13 (5) (2010) 508–513.

[47] V.A. Harris-Costello, N.L. Segal, The unmet needs of twins with special needs: diagnostic challenges and service recommendations, Community Practitioner 88 (2) (2015) 30–33.

[48] C.F. Chabris, J.J. Lee, D.J. Benjamin, J.P. Beauchamp, E.L. Glaeser, G. Borst, et al., Why it is hard to find genes associated with social science traits: theoretical and empirical considerations, Am. J. Public Health 103 (S1) (2013) S152–S166.

[49] J. Yang, B. Benyamin, B.P. McEvoy, S. Gordon, A.K. Henders, D.R. Nyholt, et al., Common SNPs explain a large proportion of the heritability for human height, Nat. Genet. 42 (7) (2010) 565–569.

[50] J.Yang, A. Bakshi, Z. Zhu, G. Hemani, A.A.Vinkhuyzen, S.H. Lee, et al., Genetic variance estimation with imputed variants finds negligible missing heritability for human height and body mass index, Nat. Genet. 47 (10) (2015) 1114–1120.

[51] C.A. Rietveld, D. Conley, N. Eriksson, T. Esko, S.E. Medland, A.A.Vinkhuyzen, et al., Replicability and robustness of genome-wide-association studies for behavioral traits, Psychol. Sci. 25 (11) (2014) 1975–1986.

[52] J.Van Dongen, P.E. Slagboom, H.H. Draisma, N.G. Martin, D.I. Boomsma, The continuing value of twin studies in the omics era, Nat. Rev. Genet. 13 (9) (2012) 640–653.

What About Hellin's Law? And Does Weinberg Rule?

- The *Hellin-Zeleny law* (1895) is a simple and accurate formula for determining the frequencies of identical twins, triplets, and quadruplets.
  Reality Check: Possibly
  Short Answer: The *Hellin-Zeleny law* is based on an overall twinning rate of 1/89 births [1,2]. If identical twins represent about one-third of twin births, then identical twins should occur in about 1/267 births (1/89 × 1/3).
  More of the Story: (1) The expected rate of identical triplets is calculated by multiplying 1/267 × 1/267 (the chance that the fertilized egg would split again). (2) The expected rate of identical quadruplets is then calculated by multiplying 1/267 × 1/267 × 1/267. Of course, these numbers are estimates because many factors, including improved medical management of multiple birth pregnancies and the increased use of assisted reproductive technologies have elevated the identical twinning rate in western nations. Statistical adjustments to the basic formula have been suggested based on Swedish data, with the caveat that they are used for descriptive purposes only [3].

  How do we know that identical twins occur in one-third of twin births? See Weinberg's Differential Rule immediately below for an answer.

- The Weinberg differential rule (WDR) for estimating the frequencies of identical and fraternal twins (in western populations) provides valid results.
  Reality Check: Likely
  Short Answer: The natural twinning rate for opposite-sex twins is 1/3, meaning that one out of every three twin pairs will be male–female. That is all the math you need to know in order to understand WDR.

  According to WDR (1901,1902), the overall fraternal twinning rate (same-sex and opposite-sex pairs combined) is equal to twice the rate of opposite-sex twin deliveries (1/3 × 2 or 2/3). The identical twinning rate then becomes the difference between the overall fraternal twinning (2/3) rate and 1 (1 − 2/3 = 1/3) [4,5]. Therefore, one-third of naturally conceived twins are identical, one third are fraternal same-sex, and one-third are fraternal opposite-sex.

Twin Mythconceptions
http://dx.doi.org/10.1016/B978-0-12-803994-6.00014-7

More of the Story: Two fundamental assumptions of WDR are (1) the probability of a male birth is equal to the probability of a female birth, and (2) the sex of the two cotwins in DZ twin pairs are independent (i.e., whether or not the first twin is a male or a female will not affect the sex of the second twin). The validity of WDR has been debated over the years, but has never been completely confirmed or refuted. (Recall that the current newborn male–female ratio departs slightly from 50:50, as discussed in Chapter 1.) It appears, though, that the WDR formula can be applied reliably to large sample sizes. Finnish researchers, who developed alternative statistical methods for estimating population-based twinning frequencies, found that WDR remains robust. They suggested that WDR be applied together with some new mathematical formulas that they developed to arrive at a more accurate estimate of the different types of twins [6]. Furthermore, a United States study using 21 data sources found that WDR and a method known as Maximum Likelihood Estimation, yielded very similar estimates of the frequency of the different twin types. However, the ways in which twins are identified for research can affect these estimates [7].

REFERENCES

[1] Mosby's Medical Dictionary, ninth ed., Elsevier, 2009. Available from: http://medical-dictionary.thefreedictionary.com/Hellin's+law.
[2] A. Scheinfeld, Twins and Supertwins, J.B. Lippincott, New York, NY, 1967.
[3] J. Fellman, A.W. Eriksson, Statistical analyses of Hellin's law, Twin Res. Hum. Genet. 12 (2) (2009) 191–200.
[4] W. Weinberg, Beiträge zur physiologie und pathologie der mehrlingsgeburten beim menschen, Archiv für die gesamte Physiologie des Menschen und der Tiere 88 (6–8) (1901) 346–430.
[5] W. Weinberg, Probleme der mehrlingsgeburtenstatistik, Z. Geburtsch. Gynäk. 47 (1902) 12–22.
[6] J. Fellman, A.W. Eriksson, Weinberg's differential rule reconsidered, Hum. Biol. 78 (3) (2006) 253–275.
[7] J. Hardin, S. Selvin, S.L. Carmichael, G.M. Shaw, The estimated probability of dizygotic twins: a comparison of two methods, Twin. Res. Hum. Genet. 12 (1) (2009) 79–85.

APPENDIX 2

Right-Handed or Left-Handed?

Answer: Right Always—Right Mostly—Equally—Left Mostly—Left Always

Imagine yourself performing the activity described before answering each question:

1. write
2. hold a nail while hammering
3. throw a ball
4. hold a bottle while removing the top
5. draw
6. hold a potato while peeling it
7. hold a pitcher while pouring
8. hold a scissors while cutting
9. hold a knife while cutting food
10. hold a needle while threading
11. hold a drinking glass while drinking
12. hold a toothbrush while brushing your teeth
13. hold a dish when wiping
14. hold a tennis racket whole playing

Items 1, 3, 5, 7, 8, 9, 11, 12 and 14 are scored as: Right Always (1), Right Mostly (2), Equally (3), Left Mostly (4) and Left Always (5). Items 2, 4, 6, 10 and 13 are scored in reverse. Most right-handers score between 14–30; most left-handers score between 41–70; a small percentage of right and left-handers score between 31–40. A very small percentage of left-handers in the original study scored between 21–30. When the majority of subjects were asked if they were right-handed or left-handed, the self-classified right-handers scored between 14–44, and the self-classified left-handers scored between 23–70.

Adapted from: H.F. Crovitz, K. Zener, A group-test for assessing hand- and eye-dominance, Am. J. Psychol. 75(2) (1962) 271–276.

Twin Mythconceptions
http://dx.doi.org/10.1016/B978-0-12-803994-6.00015-9

APPENDIX 3

Polar Body Twins: A Primer

Polar bodies are cells that result from meiosis, the process by which females' primitive egg cells (oocytes) develop into mature eggs (ova) [1]. The early phases of meiosis begin while the female is still in the womb, then they stop before restarting at puberty. Meiosis also refers to the development of mature sperm cells in the male.

During meiosis the primitive egg divides twice on the way to becoming a mature egg (ovum). First, the 23 chromosome pairs (or 46 individual chromosomes) in the oocyte duplicate and align. Then, the first meiotic division yields a primary oocyte and a polar body, each with 23 chromosome pairs or 46 chromosomes. The second meiotic division produces 4 products: an ovum and 3 polar bodies, all with 23 chromosomes, 1 from each of the 23 pairs. (One polar body forms following division of the secondary oocyte, and the other two form following division of the first polar body.) Fertilization of the mature egg by a sperm restores the normal human chromosome complement to 23 pairs. The three polar bodies, all smaller than the egg, are typically not fertilized and usually disintegrate—sometimes only two are seen. But that does not always happen—conception can work in whimsical ways, occasionally creating polar body twins [2].

Polar body twins could come about in one of three ways. It will help to refer to the diagram in Fig. A3.1 (that shows the primitive egg or oocyte developing into a mature ovum) and Fig. A3.2 (that illustrates chromosomal crossing over, the process that would give rise to the different types of polar body twins).

1. There are several phases that a primary oocyte goes through en route to becoming a mature ovum. At the first stage, the primary oocyte usually divides unequally, producing a secondary oocyte and a smaller first polar body. In more unusual cases, the primary oocyte might divide equally, yielding two secondary oocytes that could eventually become two separate ova. If this happens (and assuming no exchange of genes between the pairs of chromosomes) then the eggs would be no more alike than those chosen randomly from two different women. That is because the chromosomes ending up in one egg would be from the woman's mother and the chromosomes ending up in the other egg would be from the woman's father. (Every person inherits 1 chromosome in each of

Twin Mythconceptions
http://dx.doi.org/10.1016/B978-0-12-803994-6.00016-0

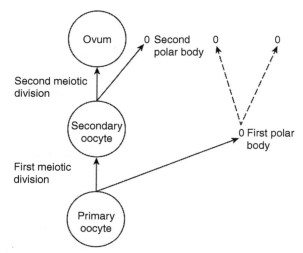

Figure A3.1 *Meiosis, the process by which an immature egg (oocyte) develops into a mature egg (ovum).* Note the different stages at which polar bodies are produced. *(Reprinted with permission from Oxford University Press. Source: M.G. Bulmer, The Biology of Twinning in Man, Clarendon Press, Oxford, 1970).*

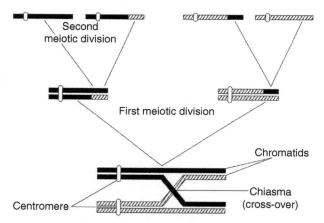

Figure A3.2 *The exchange of chromosomal material during meiosis, resulting in the different possible types of polar body twins.* The *centromere* is the structure that holds the two chromatids together. A *chromatid* is one of the two identical chromosomal strands that comprise the chromosome and which separate during cell division. The *chiasma* is the point at which the chromatids may exchange genetic material. *(Reprinted with permission from Oxford University Press. Source: M.G. Bulmer, The Biology of Twinning in Man, Clarendon Press, Oxford, 1970).* The figures are from Chapter 1, page 10, Fig. 1.1: Diagram of the maturation of the ovum, and page 11, Fig. 1.2: The behaviour of a pair of homologous chromosomes during meiosis. The paternal chromosome is dark, the maternal chromosome light.

their 23 pairs from their mother and 1 from their father.) However, some crossing over of chromosomes is likely, so the two ova would be more alike than two ova from different women, but less alike than two independent ova from the same woman. These polar body twins are called *primary oocytary.*

2. The secondary oocyte might divide equally, creating two ova. Assuming no crossing over, the two ova would be genetically identical. However, because crossing over is likely, these ova will not be genetically identical, but will be more alike than two independent ova from the same woman. These polar body twins are called *secondary oocytary.*

3. The mature egg (ovum) may divide prior to fertilization producing two eggs (parthenogenetic activation, as it is known, followed by cleavage or division of the egg [3]). If both eggs were fertilized, then the twins would be genetically identical on their mother's side, but share only half their genes, on average, from their father's side. These polar body twins are called *uniovular dispermatic.* These twins would be the "third" type of twin that everyone talks about—more alike than DZ twins, but less alike than MZ twins.

Were one to rank MZ, DZ, and polar twins in increasing order of average genetic similarity, the order would be primary oocytary (least similar), DZ, secondary oocytary, uniovular dispermatic, and MZ (most similar). The primary oocytary polar body twins would be *less* alike than typical DZ twins, so the "third twin type" *does not* always fall between MZ and twin pairs when it comes to similarity. Again, some of these twin types are theoretically possible, but have not been identified in the scientific literature. Interestingly, a study of the maternal and paternal genetic contributions to a pair of monochorionic DZ twins was consistent with their being more alike genetically than ordinary DZ twins, but less alike than MZ twins [3,4]. They sound like uniovular dispermatic twins to me.

REFERENCES

[1] M.G. Bulmer, Biology of Twinning in Man, Clarendon Press, Oxford, (1970).
[2] F.R. Bieber, W.E. Nance, C.C. Morton, J.A. Brown, F.O. Redwine, R.L. Jordan, T. Mohanakumar, Genetic studies of an acardiac monster: evidence of polar body twinning in man, Science 213 (4509) (1981) 775–777.
[3] G. Machin, Non-identical monozygotic twins, intermediate twin types, zygosity testing, and the non-random nature of monozygotic twinning: a review, Am. J. Med. Genet. C 151 (2) (2009) 110–127.
[4] V.L. Souter, R.P. Kapur, D.R. Nyholt, K. Skogerboe, D. Myerson, C.C. Ton, et al., A report of dizygous monochorionic twins, N. Engl. J. Med. 349 (2) (2003) 154–158.

Nancy L. Segal's Ten Classic Books on Twins

- H.N. Newman, F.N. Freeman, K.J. Holzinger, Twins: a study of heredity and environment, University of Chicago Press, Chicago, 1937.

- D. Burlingham, Twins: a study of three pairs of identical twins with 30 charts, Imago Publishing Co. Ltd, London, 1952.

- J. Shields, Monozygotic twins: brought up apart and brought up together, Oxford University Press, London, 1962.

- D. Rosenthal, The Genain quadruplets: a case study and theoretical analysis of heredity and environment in schizophrenia, Basic Books, Inc, New York, 1963.

- N. Juel-Nielsen, Individual and environment: monozygotic twins reared apart, International Universities Press, New York, 1965/1980.

- H.L. Koch, Twins and twin relations, University of Chicago Press, Chicago, 1966.

- A. Scheinfeld, Twins and supertwins, J.B. Lippincott, Williams & Wilkins, New York, 1967.

- M.G. Bulmer, The biology of twinning in man, Oxford University Press, Oxford, 1970.

- I.I. Gottesman, J. Shields, Schizophrenia and genetics: a twin study vantage point, Academic Press, New York, 1972.

- J.C. Loehlin, R.C. Nichols, Heredity, environment, and personality: a study of 850 sets of twins, University of Texas Press, Austin, TX, 1976.

Adapted from: N.L. Segal, Twin classics: research that always inspires, Twin Res. Hum. Genet. 18 (4) (2015) 478–484.

Twin Mythconceptions
http://dx.doi.org/10.1016/B978-0-12-803994-6.00017-2

APPENDIX 5

Glossary of Terms and Abbreviations

Terms

Allele Each of two or more forms of a gene found at the same place on a chromosome.

Amnion Inner membrane that develops at 7-9 days into the pregnancy. It encloses the zygote in amniotic fluid, maintaining constant temperature and providing protective cushioning.

Androgen A hormone that governs sexual development in males. Present in females, but in lower amounts.

Antisocial personality disorder (APD) Diagnosis given to individuals aged 18 and older who violate the rights of others without feeling remorse.

Assisted reproductive technology (ART) Methods to help women become pregnant, such as in vitro fertilization (IVF).

Blastocyst A hollow structure containing the inner cell mass or cells that give rise to the embryo.

Buccal cells Cells obtained by gently rubbing the inner cheek, often used for zygosity diagnosis.

Chimerism The presence of two or more cell lines in an individual that originated from different sources.

Chorion Outer membrane surrounding the zygote (fertilized egg, en route to becoming an embryo) that forms by the end of the second week of pregnancy. Continuous with the placenta.

Chorionic villi Small projections from the placenta that attach to the uterine wall that assist with nutrient and gas exchange between mother and fetus.

Classic twin method Comparison of trait similarity between identical and fraternal twins to estimate genetic influence on that trait.

Clones Genetically identical organisms.

Concordance Resemblance between twins for having a particular trait or disease.

Congenital anomaly A physical condition, defect, or malformation present at birth.

Conjoined twins Twins who are born physically connected to one another.

Copy number variation (CNV) Duplications of long sections of DNA that differ between most people and that might explain some differences between identical twins; however, CNVs in identical twins are rare.

Cotwin One member of a twin pair.

Cotwin control Comparison of trait similarity between identical cotwins who have received different treatments or training, to separate the effects of learning and maturation.

Dermatoglyphics The study of the lines and patterns of the skin appearing on the fingertips, palms, and soles.

Diamniotic twins Twins with two separate amnions.

Dichorionic twins Twins with two separate chorions.

Discordance Lack of resemblance between twins for having a particular trait or disease.

Twin Mythconceptions
http://dx.doi.org/10.1016/B978-0-12-803994-6.00018-4

Dizygotic (DZ) twins Twins who share 50% of their genes, on average; commonly called fraternal.

Dominant trait A trait that is carried on a given (dominant gene) that is expressed regardless of the gene with which it is paired.

Embryo The developing organism from about week 2 to week 8 during pregnancy, after a series of cell divisions in the zygote.

Epigenetics Subfield of genetics concerned with nongenetic factors that cause changes in gene expression, but do not cause changes in the DNA sequence.

Equal environments assumption (EEA) The assumption that environmental influences on traits of interest are the same for identical and fraternal twins; fundamental basis of twin methodology.

Estrogen A hormone affecting menstruation and the development of female secondary sexual characteristics. Present in males, but in lower amounts.

Fetus The developing organism from the eighth prenatal week until the end of pregnancy.

Fingerprint ridgecount The number of lines or ridges across the 10 fingertips.

Fission theory The idea that conjoined twins result from incomplete separation of a single fertilized egg.

Follicle-stimulating hormone (FSH) A hormone regulating ovulation and the development of egg cells in females.

Freemartin effect The sterilization of female cattle due to prenatal exposure to male hormones.

Fusion theory The idea that conjoined twins result from the coming together of two separate zygotes or embryos.

Gender identity A person's sense of being male or female despite their anatomy.

Gene A hereditary unit, or stretch of DNA, located on a specific place on a specific chromosome. Most genes code for proteins.

Genome-wide association study (GWAS) An examination of many common genetic variants across individuals to see if any variant is associated with a particular trait.

Genome-wide complex trait analysis (GCTA) A statistical method for estimating the genetic component of a trait that quantifies the total contribution of a particular subset of genetic variants to a trait's heritability.

Heritability The extent to which genetic differences among people within a population explain differences in measured traits.

ICSI Intracytoplasmic sperm injection, or injection of a single sperm directly into an egg, to assist conception.

Implantation Attachment of a fertilized egg to the uterine lining; may occur naturally or by assisted means.

Imprinting The differential expression of a gene in a child depending upon whether the gene was transmitted to the child by the mother or the father.

Inner cell mass Cells that give rise to the embryo.

In vitro fertilization (IVF) The fertilization and implantation of one or more embryos.

Lyonization Early inactivation of one X chromosome in all female cells; also called X-inactivation.

Mirror-image trait Traits showing reversals in identical twins, such as handedness and hair whorl.

Mirror neurons Nerve cells involved in our ability to respond to the actions and circumstances of others as if we were performing or experiencing them ourselves.

Monoamniotic twins Twins with a single or shared amnion.

Monochorionic twins Twins with a single or shared chorion.

Monozygotic (MZ) twins Twins who share virtually 100% of their genes; commonly called identical.

Mosaicism The presence of two or more cell lines in an individual that resulted from a chromosomal error or mutation.

Mutation A change in a gene, not necessarily for better or worse.

Nondisjunction Failure of chromosomes to line up properly as the primitive egg cell and sperm cells mature.

Oppositional defiant disorder (ODD) Formerly antisocial personality disorder.

Paradominant inheritance Sudden expression of a gene linked to an illness that did not appear in a family for many years.

Placenta Temporary structure allowing the transmission of oxygen and nutrients from the mother to fetus, as well as the release of carbon dioxide and waste materials from the fetus.

Polar body One of three products produced as the immature egg undergoes divisions toward becoming a mature egg.

Polar body twinning Twins formed by the fertilization of the mature egg and a polar body.

Recessive trait A trait requiring two copies of a given (recessive) gene in order to be expressed.

Recombination Exchange of genetic material between chromosomes.

Sexual orientation The sex to which an individual is attracted; the preferred sex for a sexual partner.

Short tandem repeat marker (STR) Uniquely repeating patterns in specified DNA regions.

Sonographic scanning Diagnostic imaging technique for viewing internal organs and other body structures.

Superfecundation Twins resulting from the fertilization of two simultaneously released eggs by two sperm in coital acts, occurring several days apart. Some cases have involved different fathers.

Superfetation Twins resulting from the fertilization of two eggs, released and fertilized several weeks apart. Different fathers could be involved.

Transgenderism Identification with the sex that is opposite to one's anatomical sex.

Transsexualism Identification with the sex that is opposite to one's anatomical sex, with hormonal and surgical measures taken to conform to that sex.

Twin testosterone transfer hypothesis (TTTH) The idea that females with twin brothers will show some masculinization of their behavioral and physical traits due to prenatal exposure to testosterone.

Twin-to-twin transfusion syndrome (TTTS) Shared, but unequal prenatal blood circulation between single chorion twins; poses serious physical risks to both fetuses.

Vanishing twin syndrome (VTS) The disappearance of a twin fetus, often due to resorption by the mother.

XX Female sex chromosome composition.

XY Male sex chromosome composition.

Zona pellucida The thick layer or "shell" surrounding the ovum prior to implantation.

Zygosity diagnosis Scientific determination of whether twins are identical or fraternal.

Zygote The single cell formed by the union of the egg and sperm.

Abbreviations

APD   Antisocial personality disorder
ART   Assisted reproductive technology
CNV   Copy number variation
DZ   Dizygotic
EEA   Equal environments assumption
ESP   Extrasensory perception
FSH   Follicle-stimulating hormone
GCTA Genome-wide complex trait analysis
GWAS Genome-wide association study
ICSI Intracytoplasmic sperm injection
IVF   In vitro fertilization
MRI   Magnetic resonance imaging
MZ   Monozygotic
ODD   Oppositional defiant disorder
SN   Special needs
STR   Short tandem repeat marker
TTTH Twin testosterone transfer hypothesis
TTTS Twin-to-twin transfusion syndrome
U-LA Unrelated look-alike
VTS   Vanishing twin syndrome

INDEX

83674867R00184

Made in the USA
Lexington, KY
14 March 2018